THE SEXUAL PARADOX

Men, Women, and the Real Gender Gap

SUSAN PINKER

SCRIBNER

NEW YORK   LONDON   TORONTO   SYDNEY

SCRIBNER
A Division of Simon & Schuster, Inc.
1230 Avenue of the Americas
New York, NY 10020

First Scribner hardcover edition March 2008

SCRIBNER and design are trademarks of
Macmillan Library Reference USA, Inc., used under license
by Simon & Schuster, the publisher of this work.

For information about special discounts for bulk purchases,
please contact Simon & Schuster Special Sales:
1-800-456-6798 or business@simonandschuster.com

Designed by Kyoko Watanabe
Text set in Sabon

Manufactured in the United States of America

1   3   5   7   9   10   8   6   4   2

Library of Congress Cataloging-in-Publication Data

Pinker, Susan, date.
The sexual paradox : men, women, and the real gender gap / by Susan Pinker.
p.   cm.
1. Sexual division of labor. 2. Sex differences. 3. Sex role. I. Title.

HD6060.6.P56 2008
306.3'615—dc22   2007039250

ISBN-13: 978-0-7432-8470-7
ISBN-10: 0-7432-8470-4

To Martin

I am two with nature.

—WOODY ALLEN

CONTENTS

THE
SEXUAL
PARADOX

Introduction

Female Puppets and Eunuchs

Why can't a woman be more like a man?

The question seemed innocent enough in 1964. As sung by Henry Higgins, the lovesick Victorian professor in *My Fair Lady,* social class was changeable—just a matter of tweaking accent and costume—but the gender divide was completely inscrutable. Four decades later the question is still being asked, but with a different twist. Now it usually means "*Shouldn't* a woman be more like a man?" The frustration is still there, now torqued with unfulfilled expectations.

Like Higgins, most of us don't realize that we think of male as the standard, and of female as a version of this base model—with just a few optional features added on. We have come to expect that there should be no real differences between the sexes. But the science that's emerging upends the notion that male and female are interchangeable, symmetrical, or the same. To put this book's question plainly, with what we know about the psychology, neuroscience, and economics of people's choices and behavior—fields that have exploded with amazing findings in the last ten years alone—how reasonable is it to expect that a woman be more like a man? And how likely is it for a man to be like a woman? This time, it's more about describing what is, than why can't, or shouldn't, because the expectation that male is the starting point seems to have led us astray.

The assumption that female is just a slightly different shade of male was perfectly captured by the predicament the *Sesame Street* team found itself in when trying to invent a cast of characters for its popular preschool television show. In 2006 *The New York Times* reported how *Sesame Street*'s producers had long been stymied in creating a female lead puppet out of the anxiety that any girl-like features would play into stereotypes. "If Cookie Monster was a female character, she'd be accused of being anorexic or bulimic," said the show's executive producer. Others on the team agreed that if Elmo were female she'd be seen as ditzy. Especially after the indignant reaction to the *Muppet Show*'s Miss Piggy, it just seemed safest to reflect the common assumption that male was the default setting for both sexes. Male puppets—whether flightless birds, hairy monsters, or earnest little boys—were not *really* male, but generically human. But any female puppets would be viewed as deviant, or as having girl-specific traits. As a result, it took thirty-seven years after Big Bird, Cookie Monster, and Elmo were created for the show's producers to come up with Abby Cadabby, a high-spirited puppet with magical powers and a feminine aesthetic. Her distinctly female persona was a sign that people were beginning to relax about gender, but it still made the news.[1]

I had little idea of how touchy it was when I proposed to combine two areas of personal and professional interest—extreme or distinctive male traits and women's occupational choices—in a book about men, women, and work. The plan was to profile several unusual men at least twenty years after they'd had problems as children to see what had become of them. Their stories would contrast with those of gifted women with every chance of success. The human stories were compelling, but then so was the science underlying their experiences. Trying to make sense of their stories was how I entered the politically charged world of sex differences, where, as it turned out, almost everyone I would encounter had already taken sides. Along the way, I discovered that sex differences not only colored my work, but had likely affected my own choices. As in Higgins' song, I started to wonder about myself, my female colleagues and other women I knew, "Why do they do everything their mothers do? Why don't they grow up like their fathers instead?"

I'd had every opportunity. In 1973, at the age of sixteen, I worked for my father. In those years he was a garment manufacturer's agent and for two summer months we companionably drove around rural Québec in his wood-paneled station wagon, the back loaded with a dozen navy sample bags filled with women's uniforms and sleepwear, each bag the size of a fridge and weighing about seventy-five pounds. With new respect I discovered the labor that financed our suburban, middle-class life. His years on the road eventually put three kids through college, my mother through graduate school, and would underwrite his own transition to a successful law career. The work was often lonely and physically exhausting, and like many work landscapes at the time, it was 99 percent male.

By then I was sure that a women could and would do any job a man could. In *The Second Sex,* Simone de Beauvoir had laid it all out: biology was not destiny. "One is not born, but rather becomes a woman." There was no such thing as a maternal instinct—humans were not like animals with observable, fixed habits, like rutting deer or baboons who flashed their pink behinds. We were above all that. As humans, we were "forever in a state of change, forever becoming," an existentialist take that certainly matched my sixteen-year-old world-view. So women could be defined by their current situation and their possibilities, but that was it. If there was a healthy demand for nurses' smocks and peignoir sets, it was because society defined women as caregivers and sex objects. But soon all this would change. Of course, I knew nothing about the gulf between this feminist classic and the particulars of the writer's own life, how de Beauvoir allowed herself to be treated by Sartre, not as an equal, but more as an enabler and procurer of pretty young women, some of them as young as I was at the time.[2] But that wouldn't have mattered. What happened in the forties and fifties was history. This was now.

Coming of age at the cusp of second-wave feminism, my expectations diverged sharply from those of previous generations. Unlike the women who matured during the Depression, I counted on an education and a career, not just a job. And like my friends, I didn't think getting married and pregnant was a sufficient future plan. It was precisely the one that had trapped our mothers. In 1963 Betty Friedan had shredded the idyll of postwar domesticity in *The Feminine Mystique,* portraying suburban housewives as burdened by endless chores, whiny children, and an unnamed, enveloping anomie. These were the original desperate housewives, and Friedan's strident demand that women reject that scenario was not just hot air. "We swallowed it whole," recalled my mother, who had married at nineteen and then spent the next eighteen years at home "wiping the same stretch of counter over and over." (According to the sociologist Juliet Schor, a middle-class mother of three did an average of fifty-three hours of housework a week in 1973.)[3] Galvanized by Friedan, Gloria Steinem, and others, that 1973 summer, my mother started a graduate degree. All her friends were doing the same, returning to jobs they had before they married, or seeking professional training that would allow them to work for pay.

There were other signs of a major societal attitude shift.[4] The birth-control pill had been legal since 1969 in Canada, and some of my high school friends were already on it.[5] A robust postwar economy had launched our sense of infinite possibility, but The Pill boosted it skyward, along with the idealism and individualism of the Vietnam era. None of us expected to have our aspirations curtailed by pregnancy or marriage—or to have anyone tell us what kind of work we should or could do. *The Female Eunuch* had just been published, and I was an instant convert to Germaine Greer's lusty prose. Women were conditioned to have the characteristics of a castrate, she wrote, listing passivity, plumpness, timidity, languor, delicacy, and preciousness as the female virtues that were lauded by men, and thus obediently emulated by women. "The new assumption behind the discussion of the body is that everything that we may observe *could be otherwise,*" she wrote. Her italics captured the self-assurance of the era—and its hopefulness. Everything was mutable. If only women rejected their conditioned roles by refusing to be men's handmaids, by avoiding "menial" jobs like teaching or nursing, and by abandoning the clothes, cosmetics, and even the household appliances that enslaved them, it could be a different world. The assumption was that men had it made; *they* were the standard, the ones to be emulated. Only when women dumped their female personae and took on men's roles would they truly be equal. It was true that many women in my family and social circle were plump, but I didn't know any who were remotely passive, delicate, timid, or languorous. Still, the idea of a complete overhaul had appeal.

Feminism, along with the sixties zeitgeist, had instilled a powerful belief in the freedom of choice. Behind the cultural facade, we were equal to, if not the same as, men. And once artificial barriers came down, many women assumed we'd lead similar lives. In fact, more progress had been made in my generation than in the previous 150 years, during which American women struggled—but failed—to have the same constitutional rights as had been granted to former slaves. Having been lucky enough to have been born when I was, I benefited from the hard-won achievements of second-wave feminism. Enforced domesticity didn't come crashing in on me at the age of twenty. I simply took it for granted that my views had as much value as any man's, and that I had the same rights to education and employment, to vote, to own property, and to decide if and when I'd have children. That I took these truths to be self-evident proved how far women and society had traveled in a short time.

Still, it never occurred to me that women would choose to do *this* kind of work, the work my father did for years. Sure, his earnings amply supported a family of five. But hoisting sample bags, working alone on the road, and only rarely seeing his family and friends? I mean, how many women would really want to?[6]

What women want, and why they want it, is half of what this book is about. The other half is about men, and whether it makes sense to see males as the base model when we think about women and work. Thirty-odd years after my first summer job, I wondered whether biology is, well, if not destiny exactly, then a profound and meaningful departure point for a discussion about sex differences. Most women in the West are now in the workplace. But gifted, talented women with the most choices and freedoms don't seem to be choosing the same paths, in the same numbers, as the men around them. Even with barriers stripped away, they don't behave like male clones. So I began to wonder what would happen if all the "shoulds"—the policy and political agendas—were shifted to the side for a moment to examine the science. Would female really look like an alternative version of male? As a developmental psychologist, I could see that males were hardly a neutral, homogeneous group. Instead of being what de Beauvoir called "the absolute vertical with reference to which the oblique is defined," it was clear that boys and men demonstrate a wide range of biologically based foibles that make many unpredictable, others fragile, and still others reckless or even extreme. If anyone is oblique, it's males.

For me, the question of whether males really fit our expectation of the standard, neutral gender—what I'll call the "vanilla" gender— started in my pediatric clinic waiting room. Over twenty years of clinical practice and teaching as a child psychologist, I had seen mostly males. Boys and men with learning problems, attention problems, aggressive or antisocial boys, those with autistic features, those who didn't sleep well or make friends, or couldn't sit still, dominated my practice—and that of every other developmental psychologist I knew. Research confirmed the gender breakdown of my waiting room. Learning problems, attention deficit disorder, and autism spectrum disorders are four to ten times as common in boys; anxiety and depression twice as common in girls. From the point of view of learning and self-control, boys are simply more vulnerable. Defining their strengths and weaknesses, and teaching others how to, had been the focus of the first half of my working life. I had been at it so long that many of my first charges were now adults, and to my surprise, I began to see some of them featured as success stories in the press. One had become a designer of international renown. Another had made money as a financial analyst and was leapfrogging from one investment bank to another. A third had become an electrical engineer who had pioneered an invention. A fourth was a chef on his way up. And there were more. These apparently fragile boys had overcome their early difficulties through the support of parents and teachers, who, after all, were attentive and observant enough to seek out a psychologist, presumably only one of many steps they might have taken with that child's welfare in mind. But it occurred to me that there might also be a biological thread. In some, there seemed to be a flip side to early male vulnerability. Many of these initially fragile boys continued to have obsessive interests or an appetite for risk that set the stage for their careers. Meanwhile, many of the girls their age who were light-years ahead of them in classroom learning, language, social skills, and self-control opted for paths that would not necessarily lead them to the highest status or the most lucrative careers. They had other goals. So even if being male made childhood a bumpier road, as adults at work, the situation was reversed.

In *The Sexual Paradox* I examine the trajectories of these two extreme groups—fragile boys who later succeed, and the gifted, highly disciplined girls who eclipsed them in third grade—as a way of exploring sex differences. These apparent opposites challenge our assumptions. We expect that the fragile boys will continue to struggle. We expect that high-achieving girls will shoot right to the top. That so many in these groups violate our expectations tells us something important about sex differences. If boys and girls, are on average, biologically and developmentally distinct from the start (and I'll walk you through some of the more intriguing evidence), wouldn't these differences affect their choices later? Could men's and women's diverging developmental paths and different work priorities be linked?

The History

The idea that there are inherent differences is a sensitive issue in the present because it provided cover for abuses in the past. Until the mid-twentieth century, a rigid gender gap enforced by law and tradition was the rule. Except for a tiny elite, few women had any choices. And without choices, what they wanted was moot. They could take in boarders, washing, or piecework, but up to the Second World War, married women couldn't be hired in most states in the United States, Canada, or Britain (Australia's civil service banned married women until 1966). So single women who got hitched were duly sacked, barred from jobs in most schools and offices, precisely the places where women were most likely to find work. Factories had always employed women but usually paid them less, so unions saw them as a form of scab labor that undercut men's livelihoods. Even after the privations of the Depression and the war years, when women were aggressively recruited to factory and munitions jobs to keep the economy chugging along, having a wife who "didn't work" and earning a "family wage" were seen as a woman's privilege and a man's duty.[7] Never mind Rosie the Riveter, who flexed her biceps on recruitment posters and was "on a sharp lookout for sabotage, sitting up there on the fuselage," according to the popular song. When the war ended, there were gains for some women, especially for black women, but for most there was a regression to the status quo. Gender discrimination was rife, and with

no birth control, few formal jobs, and little access to money or property, women were often trapped by their circumstances.

Poster from World War II

Second-wave feminism changed all that, along with our expectations about what would happen next. Women became an undeniable
presence in the workplace, their numbers ballooning in a single generation—my own.[8] In 1930, 25 percent of the workforce was female. In
1950, it had risen to 29 percent, but by 1975 it had become a wave of
more than 40 percent, reaching 47 percent by 2005.[9] Women got the
vote in 1918 in Canada, 1920 in the United States, and 1928 in Britain,
but it was only in the 1970s that women began to flood educational
programs that trained them to become doctors, lawyers, and architects,
just a few of the careers formerly identified as male.[10] This generational

attitude shift was duly reflected in public policy. Through the sixties and seventies, equal-rights laws were introduced in Britain, the United States, the European Union, and Canada that made it illegal to discriminate against women or to pay them any less than men. Ironically, given its role as the tinderbox of social upheaval in the sixties, the United States was alone among Western countries in failing to marshal enough momentum to write gender equity laws into its constitution—despite thirty-five years of debate and rollicking support for the idea. Instead there were targeted statutes that made workplace discrimination and sexual harassment illegal (the 1963 Equal Pay Act and Title VII of the 1964 Civil Rights Act) and prevented publicly funded schools from offering programs on the basis of sex (Title IX, enacted in 1972). A long time coming, these statutes still created controversial fallout. While eliminating obvious injustices such as separate pay scales for men and women and infelicities like "boom-boom rooms," where male employees socialized with strippers, the laws also whitewashed any fundamental differences between the sexes, creating absurd situations where allowances for pregnancy or all-male soccer teams suddenly became discriminatory practices. Still, there was no doubt that an overwhelming social movement was afoot in the West, one aimed to redress the inequalities of the past with protective legislation and affirmative action programs designed to bump up the numbers of girls and women in schools and workplaces.

Gender equity legislation and the thinking behind second-wave feminism, so formative for the baby-boom generation, had unintended effects. Together they created the expectation that *all* differences between men and women were created by unjust practices and therefore could be erased by changing same. With new laws and policies in place and women making up almost half of the workforce, there was a leap of faith that it was only a matter of time before all occupations would be split 50–50. Equal numbers of men and women working side by side, doing exactly the same work for exactly the same number of hours and pay, seemed a logical extension of the sixties-based egalitarian ideal. So when 50–50 didn't happen in all jobs by the year 2000, there was a vast feeling of letdown. "Full equality is still a distant promise," wrote British journalist Natasha Walters in 2005, about the fact that women's salaries when averaged are 85 percent of the average male salary.[11] "What's Wrong with This Picture?" ran the headline of a 2007 article by the Feminist Research Center, which reported that "at the current rate of increase it will be 475 years, *or not until the year 2466 before women reach equality with men in the executive suite.*"[12] (At 16.4 percent of all corporate officers in Fortune 500 companies in 2005, that estimate for women isn't quite right. At current rates of increase, it would take another 40, not 475 years, to have female and male CEOs in equal numbers, according to projections by Catalyst, another women's research group.) Still, the assumption seemed to be that if the social order had *really* changed, women would be exactly like men by now. They'd make the same choices, opting in equal proportions for chief executive positions, careers in theoretical physics, or political office. Even among women who haven't chosen such fields themselves, the wider the discrepancy from 50 percent, the greater the sense of chagrin. That's because it is largely taken for granted that gender discrimination is what is behind these numbers. And though discrimination still exists—both Wall Street and Wal-Mart have faced recent class action suits by women who feel their advancement has been blocked—as I talked to high-achieving women and started to look at the data, it became clear that women's and men's interests and preferences are also skewing the picture.[13] Equal opportunity doesn't necessarily lead to equal results. In fact, women's preferences stand out in higher relief precisely because they *do* have options. By looking at what has changed dramatically in thirty-odd years, and what has changed just a little, we can get a feeling for the pursuits women choose once doors are opened to them.

One of the most remarkable transformations over this period has taken place on the university campus. In 1960, 39 percent of undergraduate students were female. Now 58 percent of American university students are; indeed, women outnumber men on college campuses throughout the developed world.[14] Their strong academic profiles and broad extracurricular interests—in everything from debating to building houses for Habitat for Humanity—have meant that high-achieving women have their pick of schools and disciplines. Professional degree programs in law, medicine, pharmacy, and biology, all fields formerly dominated by men, are now evenly divided or admit more women. Two highly competitive fields—clinical psychology and veterinary medicine—

are now between 70 and 80 percent female.[15] Clearly, girls and women are excelling in the classroom and making significant inroads outside it, so efforts to narrow the gender gap have succeeded in Western countries. Fifty-six percent of all high-paying professional jobs are now held by women, and women hold more than half of all professional and managerial positions in Canada and Britain.[16] Even at the top echelons of business, where female executives have been notoriously absent in the past, a 2006 study of 10,000 Fortune 500 companies has uncovered an interesting phenomenon. While almost half the companies have no women at the helm, the other half promote more women to executive officer positions, and they move them up faster—when they're younger and have less experience than men in comparable positions (the women are promoted after an average of 2.6 years on the job while in their forties, the men after 3.5 years and in their fifties).[17] Currently, any gender gaps in pay are narrower than they have ever been. In contrast, there are many parts of the world where girls still can't go to school; are forced into labor, prostitution, or marriage as young teenagers; and as adults can't work outside the home or vote. But in Western democracies, what's the problem? Why aren't people celebrating?

THAT WAS THEN, THIS IS NOW

The percentage of degrees granted to women in male-typical fields

		1973	2003
Veterinary medicine:	Canada	12	78
	U.S.	10	71
Pharmacy	U.S.	21	65
Law:	U.K.	...	63
	U.S.	8	49
Medicine:	Canada	17	58
	U.S.	9	45
Business	U.S.	10	50
Architecture	U.S.	13	41
Physics	U.S.	7	22
Engineering	U.S.	1	18

... means no data available

Sources on p. 329

The percentage of women working in fields formerly identified as male

		1973	2003
Orchestra musicians		10	35
Lawyers:	Canada	5*	34*
	U.S.	5	27
Physicians:	Canada	...	31
	U.S.	8	26
Federal judges:	Canada	1	26
	U.S.	...	23
Employed in science and engineering		8	26
Legislators:	Canada	7	17
	U.N. countries	...	16
	U.S.	3	14
Foresters and conservationists		4	13
Aerospace engineers		1	11
Telephone and computer line installers and repairers		1	6
Firefighters		0	3
Manufacturers' agents		<1	3
Electricians		.6	2
Plumbers and pipe-fitters		0	1

... means no data available
*Data were only available for the years 1971 and 2001.
Sources on pp. 329–30

One reason for the continued hand-wringing is that though women have flooded certain disciplines where they had been rare a few decades ago, there are still noticeable discrepancies in others. More women are studying engineering, physics, and computer science than ever before, but they are not exactly falling over themselves to enter those fields the way they have in medicine and law. Even with dozens of task forces and millions consecrated to increasing gender diversity, female enrollment in engineering in most schools hasn't budged past 20 percent. Men have entered teaching, nursing, and social work—but these, too, remain predominantly female enclaves. Even with more choices, women still cluster in certain occupations, just as men continue to hang together in others.

And a second reason why people are concerned is that when earnings are averaged by sex, men still earn more. These global figures usually blend disparate occupations, different subspecialties, and work schedules into one undifferentiated blob. In the following pages we'll see how biologically based leanings and preferences might influence the telling details for both sexes. Boys' developmental differences may shine some light on why their school performance and university attendance lag behind girls'. Meanwhile women's priorities—wide-ranging and often people-based—infuse their career choices. Despite increased opportunities and affirmative action programs, many women routinely turn their noses up at many occupations now open to them, among them computer programming, cutting down trees for pulp and paper, and politics. From their educational profiles, it's clear that when it comes to making career choices, it's not a question of "can't." Nor is it a question of "shouldn't," as most formerly male dominions have made significant investments to recruit women. Yet the question of what they should or shouldn't do still dominates the women's stories here. One of the pressures gifted, high-achieving women feel keenly is to make the same choices as men. This brings us back to men, and whether it makes sense for them to be their models.

The Extremes

"There is no female Mozart because there is no female Jack the Ripper," wrote the social critic Camille Paglia, and her quip hints at a biological truth. Compared to women, there are more men who are extreme. Even though the two sexes are well matched in most areas, including intelligence, there are fewer women than men at the extreme ends of the normal distribution. Men are simply more variable. Their "means," or the average scores for the group, are roughly the same as those of women, but their individual scores are scattered more widely. So there are more very stupid men and more very smart ones, more extremely lazy ones and more willing to kill themselves with work. There are more men with biological frailties, and more with isolated areas of brilliance, including men weighed down by other deficits, such as the very problems dogging the children in my waiting room. The bell curve simply looks different for males, with more men at the tail ends of the distribution, where their measured skills are either dismal, stellar, or a mix of the two. So even though male and female averages are the same, there are more male outliers—and more "normal" women overall.[18] Comparing men and women in the middle ranges one finds fewer sex differences, but at the extremes the picture looks—well—extreme.

Sex differences at the extremes was one of the issues that sank the former president of Harvard University, Larry Summers. This book was already under way in January 2005, when I received an e-mail from one of my literary agents. "Did you see this?" she wrote, attaching an electronic article from that morning's *New York Times*. Summers had made a speech to a science and engineering diversity conference on the origin of sex differences in high-powered university science faculties. His remarks launched more than a thousand articles in the press, sparked a year of bitter dissent at Harvard, prompted several public apologies from Summers, and ultimately a commitment of $50 million to hire and promote female and minority faculty at the university. Still, by 2006 he was forced out. What was the fuss about? Summers conjectured that there were three reasons for the paucity of women in high-level science and engineering faculty positions. The first was that these jobs are so greedy that many women avoid them. "What fraction of young women in their mid-twenties make a decision that they don't want to have a job that they think about eighty hours a week? What fraction of young men make a decision that they're unwilling to have a job that they think about eighty hours a week?" he said, adding that whether it's correct for society to ask for that commitment is a different question. His second point was about male variability. If men are more variable than women, then there will be more men at the very bottom and very top of the distribution. So in research positions in physics or engineering that compete for a tiny fraction of human talent at the very top end—where there are not only very few women, but also very few men—one might find more extreme sex differences, he said.[19] This was not a new idea and was one that at least a dozen researchers had already mapped out. One Edinburgh psychologist, Ian Deary, had even documented the phenomenon after examining the records of more than 80,000 children, nearly every child born in Scotland in 1921. At age eleven, boys' and girls' IQ scores were no different, on average, Deary's team found. But the difference in male variability was unmistakable: there were significantly more boys than girls at the low and high extremes of ability.[20]

THE IQ SCORES OF
80,000 SCOTTISH CHILDREN BORN IN 1921

The Means

Number of Scottish Children in Each IQ Score Band

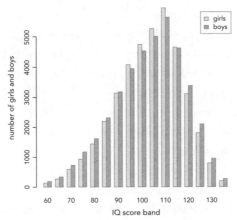

The IQ scores of almost all Scottish children born in 1921 show no sex differences on average. The boys' average IQ is 103.03 and the girls' average IQ is 103.19, and there is no statistical difference between the two. There are slightly more girls than boys in the average to high-average range. Boys are overrepresented at both extremes.

The Standard Deviations

**Significance of the Difference Between the Sexes
in Each IQ Score Band**

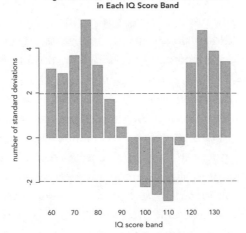

The bars represent the number of standard deviations—or how far each sex diverges from our expectation of 50–50. Positive values show a larger number of boys than girls. Negative values show a larger number of girls than boys. Despite their nearly identical averages, males show more dramatic variability that is more evident at the extremes.

Sources on p. 330

For more than a decade, other researchers—Amy Nowell, Larry Hedges, Alan Feingold, Diane Halpern, Camilla Benbow and Julian Stanley, Yu Xie, Kimberlee Shauman, the Scholastic Aptitude Testing Service, as well as my own brother Steve—had found and written about the same phenomenon, but in Summers' case it caused a furious uproar that wouldn't abate. "I felt I was going to be sick," said MIT biology professor Nancy Hopkins, who reported that Summers' comments upset her so much that "my heart was pounding and my breath was shallow." Summers went on to talk about a third factor—socialization and continuing discrimination—but few listened. His message about extremes, standard deviations, and greedy jobs had been distilled as "women are not as good as men at math and science." The electric atmosphere surrounding the discussion of sex differences became even more charged.

So the issue of biologically based sex differences was already in the spotlight when I stepped into the fray. But a chill had settled on many researchers' willingness to talk about their work. Several female scientists who are experts in the area declined to be interviewed; they didn't want to draw attention to anything that could be seen as politically incorrect, nor did they relish becoming magnets for criticism. When I asked a female social scientist why she thought highly intelligent, successful women might be making different occupational choices than men, she burst out angrily, "Not that again!" I naively asked, "Not what again?" "Not that choice thing again!" I had unwittingly touched a sore spot. Apparently in "choice feminism" women are free to choose whatever jobs appeal to them—to work part-time, full-time, or not at all—and still call themselves feminists. But this offshoot had ended up challenging the idea that any deviation from the male standard would be a retrograde step for women, as many smart and capable women were not making "male" choices. Never mind individual differences and desires. Equal opportunity for women—a principle I hold dear—was supposed to lead to a mathematically equal result. That it hasn't has sparked the incendiary Mommy Wars and a lingering feeling among scientists that the topic is taboo.

But scientists aren't the only voices in this book. Real people tell the stories of their careers and why they made their decisions. None of the profiles in this book are composites or fictionalized, although identifying details have occasionally been altered. The interviews with the men and women took on a self-reflexive quality, as all the women asked me to give them pseudonyms and the majority of the so-called fragile men insisted that I use their real names. As a result, the women whose stories are recounted here are referred to with a fictitious first name. When first and family names are used in this book, as is the case with most of the men profiled here, this is the person's real name. It was my decision to use pseudonyms for the few young men still in their early twenties, just in case they might regret being identified in a few years. Even though all the men had sensitive clinical histories, they seemed less concerned about appearing vulnerable than the women were about seeming uncommitted to their science or professional backgrounds. Although all the women spoke volubly and sensitively about their work experiences, three of the high-achieving women subsequently had second thoughts about participating—even with pseudonyms and a change of costume and hair color. None of the men had these reservations. Perhaps these men had struggled so much for their successes that they saw them as triumphs. Perhaps the freedom of women to make choices is still too recent for them to feel invincible.

"Confidence is a very fragile thing," said NFL football player Joe Montana. While it's hard to imagine a quarterback as much of an authority on fragility, the unusual men profiled in this book and the underlying data show that men are neither standard nor generic. Nor are they always the right models for women's career aspirations. After all, many men demonstrate a wide range of strengths and disabilities that skews their development as well as their fortunes. Men are more prone to developmental disabilities, to get sick, hurt, or kill others. They are also more likely to work extreme hours at extreme jobs and to die younger. *The Sexual Paradox* shows how these characteristics are at least partly linked to biology. To be seen as variations on their own theme will give a more nuanced understanding of what it means to be male. And instead of viewing women as frustrated versions of this male model, gifted women will explain why, after trying it on, that model didn't quite fit.

In reality, neither sex is a souped-up or flawed version of the other. In this book, men are not given short shrift as unfeeling, uncomplicated louts. And women are not portrayed as hapless victims prevented from achieving their goals. The stories these two groups tell and the science behind them, are the ciphers through which I examine basic sex differences. These apparent opposites—fragile men, gifted women—provide an unusual lens on the gender debate. If they are extremes on a continuum, then whatever is driving them is also true for the rest of us.

CHAPTER 1

Are Males the More Fragile Sex?

When he was a lively, quick-witted four-year-old, Cutler Dozier was profiled in *The New York Times* as one of the first of a new generation of very tiny, premature babies to survive. "We don't know what will happen when he starts school," his mother told the journalist. Her caution was well founded. Cutler had started life outside the womb at twenty-six weeks' gestation, weighing less than two and a half pounds, and for the first months of life he clung to a medical precipice. Like most very premature babies, at first he was unable to breathe on his own or even suck. He was fed through a tube threaded into his intestine and had a hole in his heart that needed immediate repair. His future was a long shot. Profiled again by the same reporter, Jane Brody, fifteen years later, Dozier had beat the odds. At nineteen he had grown into a healthy student in Asian Studies and film at the University of Minnesota, practiced martial arts, and had just won an award for his poetry.[1] Due to the care of highly trained specialists backed with state-of-the-art neonatal intensive-care units, he had not only survived, he had thrived, long before experts knew what might happen to him.

Cutler Dozier's progress merited notice not just because his was a happy story about a preemie who made it. Being male made him a particular anomaly. The preemie babies most likely to survive are girls.[2] Premature girls are 1.7 times more likely to make it than premature boys, and African American premature girls are more than twice as likely as white males to survive, according to American doctors who followed the progress of 5,076 low-birth-weight babies.[3] Like Cutler, many of these babies eventually do fine. But more than half of the preemies have attention deficit disorder or learning or behavioral disabilities, and the vast majority of the ones with these problems are boys, confirming that well before birth, males are already more vulnerable.[4] Like my waiting room denizens, many struggle with speech and language, or with learning and social skills as they grow. As if frozen at an earlier stage of development, the regions of the premature boys' brains responsible for reading, language, and the regulation of emotions are smaller than in preemie girls, and the differences in size are still visible on brain scans when the children turn eight. "When we divided the preterm group by gender we found, Bingo! The females had normal or preserved white matter volume, but the males' volumes were reduced compared to their full-term peers," said Allan Reis, the lead author of the study, describing his team's findings to a Stanford Hospital colleague. His discovery was just the latest in a long string of studies showing that preterm girls are more likely than boys to catch up to their full-term peers, in everything from height to reading. The girls, born just as early and just as small, are simply more resilient from the start.[5]

From day one, male embryos, although more numerous, are more susceptible to the effects of maternal stress. When the going gets rough, female embryos are simply more likely to make it. They're better girded to survive the uncertain first hours after conception, and they're less likely to be affected by obstetric disasters, disabilities of all kinds, and early death. Even pollution hits males harder. Demographers are finding that fewer baby boys are born downstream from heavy industry. (In an area known as "Chemical Valley" in northern Ontario, mothers in the Aamjiwnaang First Nation community give birth to twice as many girls as boys.) Sex-based culling may have an apocalyptic feel, but experts generally expect that the more fragile male embryos will be less likely to make it when environmental or social conditions are poor.

In an astonishing twenty-year study that tracked the progress of seven hundred Hawaiian children born into poverty in 1955 on the "garden island" of Kauai, American psychologists Emmy Werner and

Ruth Smith discovered that from the weeks before birth until age eighteen, the boys were dramatically more vulnerable than the girls. In this close-knit, racially diverse community, more boys than girls were affected by birth-related traumas, and more than half of these boys died in infancy, while less than a fifth of the girls did. Between birth and age two, more boys than girls had grave accidents or illnesses, and twice as many boys as girls had IQ scores below 80, or had difficulties with language, social, or motor development. The two children who died after an accident or drowning were both boys. More than 50 percent of all the boys had experienced school problems. The boys were more affected by adverse conditions—poverty, family instability, or lack of stimulation—than were the girls.[6]

From a biological perspective, being female simply offers a protective umbrella from cradle to grave. No one really knows why this is, but there are several hypotheses. Girls may be insured by having two X chromosomes, so if one is damaged or encodes deficits, girls have a spare. As many brain-related genes are located on the X, neurological traits are particularly affected. With only one X, extreme variations are more likely to show up, extremes that might have been damped down or even eliminated if a second copy of the X were in place to reduce that mutation's effects.[7] Girls are also sheltered from male hormones that slow down and skew the development of boys' brains in utero—one of this book's themes—and a reason why premature boys may already be more vulnerable than girls before they're born. Powerful chemical driver that it is, testosterone masculinizes the brain before birth and continues to rejig the system ever afterward, often with contradictory effects. Male animals are most likely to get sick and die during breeding season, when their hormone levels are highest. Testosterone exerts a similar paradoxical impact on humans. It increases aggression, risk-taking, and verve. But it is suspected to be involved in males' higher rates of just about every chronic illness, including cancer, diabetes, liver disease, heart disease, and AIDS.[8] Surges of testosterone boost strength, stamina, and to a degree, even spatial problem solving in men. But they also decrease the body's immune response. This is powerfully demonstrated by hospital survival rates. The higher their testosterone level, the less resistance men have to postsurgical infections. These infections kill 70 percent of the men who get them compared to only 26 percent of the women.[9]

So what is this biological vulnerability all about? Evolutionary history may provide the original foundation for a stronger female constitution. Women who were hardy enough to give birth to children, to feed and care for them during the long road to adulthood, were more likely to have offspring who survived. Thus the more resilient women had heirs who carried their genetic signatures. In contrast, men could procreate with impunity. Whether they survived long enough to raise offspring to maturity ultimately mattered less than whether they sired offspring in the first place. This feat cannot be taken for granted in any species in which some males mate with more than one female and others mate with none. In such high-stakes competitions, being stronger, faster, or more willing to take risks could mean the difference between reproductive success and oblivion, and if there was a cost to pay in male longevity or health in the long term, evolution would have been willing to pay it. This macho advantage of speed, strength, and fierceness can be exaggerated by females' tastes. As half of a female's reproductive fate is tied up in her sons, she may have evolved to prefer males who are stronger, faster, and who have a greater appetite for risk, since they will be more likely to father sons with those advantages.

The sex appeal of risk is not lost on thrill-seeking adolescent boys everywhere, from helmetless skateboarders in the suburbs to knife-wielding gangs in the inner city. The evidence is under our noses every time we watch young daredevils at the park or read the obituaries. The fragility of males is even more exaggerated in developing countries, where being male is the single largest risk factor for early death.[10] Take, for example, the teenage boys called train surfers in Soweto, who tempt death by practicing stunts on top of moving locomotives, limboing under bridges, hopping from car to car, and doing "the gravel"—dragging their heels along the ground while hanging from a moving train. At the funeral of one of his friends who died when he smashed into an electrified overhead pole, one member of a train-surfing gang known as the Vandals described why they take these risks. "We feel like we are in another world when doing it, in heaven or something. It's like we are floating and don't fear anything. Girls just love it and fall for us," the nineteen-year-old South African boy said. He was interviewed when the group was out train-surfing in a macabre tribute to another member of their gang who had fallen off a train a few days earlier. "Jananda forgot to go down quickly. . . . He died in front of my eyes. We just thought it would be appropriate to give our friend a fitting farewell by doing what we did with him before he died," added another boy, Julius.[11] In the grim sweepstakes of sexual selection, taking mortal risks in the here and now feels like a huge thrill.

Thus programmed to mature later, compete fiercely, and die younger, males continue to experience a precarious, truncated life span that demographers have tracked in the archaeological record as well as in modern societies over the past 250 years, and across twenty different cultures.[12] Nature still favors the reproductive oomph of testosterone over the downside of a shorter life span, one reason why the biological anthropologist Richard Bribiescas neatly summarized a man's life stages as "Stud, Dud, Thud."[13] Even now, as developments in medicine and technology extend the human life span, the gap between men's and women's mortality rates yawns wider.[14]

Men continue to take more risks, have more accidents, get sick more often, and also are less likely to pay attention to their illnesses, so they die younger (the female life expectancy is now eighty-three years, while males' is seventy-eight years). Men also drink, smoke, and use lethal weapons more than women, but use seat belts, sunscreen, and doctors less. The reality of male vulnerability struck me full force when an e-mail arrived with the subject line "Sad News." It informed me that my upcoming high school reunion would feature a memorial service for the classmates who had died. Did any of us have any photos or memorabilia? Thirteen of the seventeen classmates who had died before age fifty (some while we were still in high school), or 76 percent, were male. Thus the gender ratio was more like three male deaths for every one female, mimicking the mortality rates for fifty-year-olds in the general population in North America, where, unlike women, most men won't make it to eighty.[15]

So, who's stronger? The child psychologist's waiting room and the hospital emergency department tell the story of early male fragility. A visit to a nursing home provides the denouement; women simply outlast men.

Schoolboys

This portrait of fragility is reflected in boys' school progress. It's hard to reconcile the idea that males are more vulnerable with the common assumption that they are not only the standard, but also the more powerful sex. But the numbers are clear. History may have favored males, but biology was more stinting, and nowhere is this more evident than in the classroom. In the United States, boys are three times as likely to be placed in special education classes, twice as likely to repeat a grade, and a third more likely to drop out of high school. In Canada, boys drop out at almost twice the rate of girls and are more likely to describe school as a waste of time. They hand in less homework, are less likely to get along with teachers, and are less interested in what they are learning in class.[16] In Britain, high school girls outdo boys in every subject except science; for the past seven years girls have led boys in all their A-levels, or pre-university exams. "Right from the start of school, girls assume different attitudes toward learning, commented Diane Reay, a British sociologist of education, when asked about boys' lukewarm results. "The girls have a willingness to play by the rules of the educational game and an engagement with learning. Even if they find things tedious, they get on with it, rather than get out."[17]

Girls are less likely to second-guess the educational exercise and find it wanting, as does this tenth-grade American "behaviorally challenged student," described here by his high school teacher as he sat through his umpteenth detention: "Brandon's current problem began because Ms. Waverly, his social studies teacher, failed to answer one critical question: What was the point of the lesson she was teaching? One of the first observations I made as a teacher was that boys invariably ask this question, while girls seldom do. When a teacher assigns a paper or a project, girls will obediently flip their notebooks open and jot down the due date. Girls are calm and pleasant. They succeed through cooperation. Boys will pin you to the wall like a moth. They want a rational explanation for *everything*. If unconvinced by your reasons—or if you don't bother to offer any—they slouch contemptuously in their chairs, beat their pencils, or watch squirrels out the window."[18] A slightly more menacing account of adolescent male frustration is offered by Bill Bryson in his memoir *The Life and Times of the Thunderbolt Kid*. His chapter on school begins with this news-paper account: "In Pasadena, California, student Edward Mulrooney was arrested after he tossed a bomb at his psychology teacher's house and left a note that said: 'If you don't want your home bombed or your windows shot out, then grade fairly and put your assignments on the board—or is this asking too much?' "[19]

This is not everyone's idea of a fragile male. But the numbers tell the story of disaffection and academic underachievement on a grand scale. Girls have always done better in the classroom, a point I'll return to shortly. But since 1992 they've also beat boys with higher global scores on high school achievement tests.[20] Tests from a huge sample of fifteen-year-olds from thirty OECD countries show that girls in every one of these European countries now do vastly better than boys in reading and writing and are neck and neck with boys in math.[21] The latter parity in math is fairly recent. In the early eighties, a strong male advantage in mathematics reasoning on standardized tests was docu-mented by two American researchers at Johns Hopkins University. Camilla Persson Benbow and Julian Stanley had examined the test scores of 40,000 young high school students—half boys, half girls—who had taken the Scholastic Aptitude Test as one step in applying to a Johns Hopkins Talent Search. There was a thirty-point advantage favoring boys on mathematics reasoning in their test scores, a lead that was more exaggerated at the very topmost range, where despite having taken exactly the same math courses in high school, there were thirteen boys for every girl.[22]

That the top 1 percent of math achievers is made up of boys is one thing. As we've seen, male test scores are more spread out, reflecting wide-ranging highs and lows. And as the very bottom and the very top performers are most likely to be boys—with "more male geniuses and more male idiots," as political scientist James Wilson bluntly put it—any tests targeting the gifted will throw sex differences into high relief. But classroom performance and test scores in the general population put girls right on top. In twenty-six of the thirty OECD countries, any overall male advantage in math and science has become so slim as to be insignificant.[23] This is true in Asia, too. Among eighth graders in Japan, there's a small sex difference favoring boys (the girls' average score was 569, while the boys' was 571), while in Singapore the girls outperformed the boys, with average math scores of 611 and 601, respectively. (Both Asian countries surpassed American high school students by a good margin.)[24] Even in the United States, where boys perform somewhat better than girls on standardized math tests, girls' higher levels of literacy overshadow this male advantage by a long shot. Describing boys as "flatlining," Judith Kleinfeld, a psychology professor living in Anchorage, Alaska, described one study of 1,195 randomly selected high school students, in which a third of the girls had received mostly As on their last report card, compared to less than a fifth of the boys. The students were divided into three groups: successful students; strivers (hard workers); and alienated students, who were bitter and disillusioned. Two-thirds of the successful students were girls; 55 percent of the strivers were girls; 70 percent of the alienated were boys.[25]

Clearly, any male lead in academic performance is evaporating. While girls and women have made huge educational strides over the past thirty years, boys have run in place or lost ground. In fact, this female school advantage may be nothing new at all. Historical records show that a gender gap favoring girls has always existed in literacy levels, classroom learning, and graduation rates. Even during the latter half of the nineteenth century, boys had much greater access to education, but girls had better reading skills, according to three Harvard economists, Claudia Goldin, Lawrence Katz, and Ilyana Kuziemko. By riffling through masses of census data, they discovered that once women were given equal access to education in the 1920s, boys were less likely than girls to go to high school and 24 percent less likely to graduate. By the 1950s, girls were at the 60th percentile of their high school classes—the majority were outshining the boys. The median or average girl was 21 percentile points above the median boy in 1957. This average girl was 17 percentile points above her male counterpart in 1972 and 16 percentile points above him in 1992.[26] In other words, one hundred years before mainstream feminism and forty years after it, boys were and still are trailing behind girls in school.

When poorer academic performance spans centuries, and several countries on three continents, we're not looking at a brief cultural blip. That boys have long been behind in elementary and high school makes sense if their gaps are at least partially rooted in their biology. But are they really headed on a downward spiral? If we look at the data from the first two-thirds of the twentieth century, we would have to say no, for two reasons. First, male fragility seemed invisible when discrimination was common, when women married young and left school early to raise families. But now that women are in the race longer, the persistent gaps between males and females in development and school performance are suddenly glaring. Goldin and her team have shown that since the seventies, women have not only been delaying marriage, they have been taking just as many high school math and science courses as boys. Both factors have boosted female college enrollment dramatically.[27] So males haven't really taken a dive. It's more that the rate of change for men did not keep pace with this swift, remarkable increase in opportunity for women—one of feminism's most significant accomplishments. A second reason rests on the optimism of just such a transformation. When problems are identified—especially if they are documented scientifically and dispassionately—it's possible they can be fixed.

In the present, though, the numbers tell us that men on university campuses are outnumbered. One hundred forty women are currently awarded bachelor's degrees for every one hundred men in the United States, and the gap is expected to widen. In Canada, most campuses are 60 percent female. "It's an issue throughout the industrial world. Women are just beating the pants off guys in college," says American policy analyst Thomas Mortenson, who has tracked college admissions since the 1970s. Between 1969 and 2000, male undergraduates increased by 39 percent, whereas female undergraduates increased by 157 percent.[28] Now women have overtaken men in almost all postsecondary institutions, most dramatically in prestigious private colleges and within the black community, where there are two university-educated women for every university-educated man But it's also true among the white middle class. "There aren't many men in my Hegel class," reported my daughter at the beginning of her third year studying philosophy at McGill University. Each September the men seemed to get thinner on the ground, she said. "My classes are mostly girls, with a couple of gay guys, and if there are any boys, they're around seventeen years old. It's really slim pickings." And it was true that among her friends from preschool, all the women were in college but more than half of the men had dropped out or were struggling. Their doctor, engineer, or journalist parents worried from the sidelines as these boys drifted out of school before graduating, landing up in sales jobs, in the military, or in trade schools. Meanwhile, their sisters, subject to the same upbringing, the same neighborhoods, and the same schools, persevered.

It's not all about marks for these girls, but about engagement and big plans. The National Assessment of Educational Progress, the test of fourth- and eighth-grade American students commonly known as the nation's report card, confirms that girls are better readers and writers. They graduate from high school in higher numbers than boys, and more girls plan to go to college. And not just college, mind you, but also graduate school. The National Center for Education Statistics, another American federal research initiative, set out to monitor the long-term progress of more than 15,300 American students who were in tenth grade in 2002. When the students were asked how far they planned to go in school, 42 percent of the girls said they expected to earn a graduate or professional degree. Only 29 percent of boys said they had similar plans.[29] Girls seem happier, too. On a survey of 99,000 high school students, girls were more motivated than boys and had a stronger sense of life purpose and more self-confidence.[30]

All told, a sunny picture for girls, but not the one I had read about in the nineties when I was choosing a high school for my twelve-year-old daughter. Magazine and newspaper headlines painted girls as helpless targets of discrimination—cheated out of instruction in school, where they were apparently being left on the sidelines while teachers focused on boys. Many of these reports cited a study showing a "call-out gap"—that boys call out answers eight times more often than girls. According to the study, when boys called out, teachers listened. But when girls called out, they were reported to be ignored, or "silenced" by being told to raise their hands first before speaking. It seemed like patent neglect, or worse, overt favoritism. I was alarmed by this news, as were my friends who were mothers of adolescent girls. There was a sense of urgency as we all began scouting single-sex schools—none of which, as it happened, were in the public sector.[31] At the time we didn't know that the study had been commissioned to find evidence of discrimination, and in fact it did just that. "We wanted to put some factual data behind our belief that girls are getting shortchanged in the classroom," American Association of University Women's president,

Susan Schuster, had told *The New York Times*.[32] Indeed, the study, had we looked for it, was not easily accessible—and unlike most scientific research, it still isn't. Published research is now easy to track down, and most researchers either post links to their articles on their webpages or are happy to forward copies of their studies when asked. But my research assistant received no reply when she e-mailed a request for the call-out gap study. Instead, the lead investigator, American University education professor David Sadker, who with his late wife, Myra Sadker, wrote the book *Failing at Fairness: How Our Schools Cheat Girls,* has posted an all-purpose correction on his website: "Individual classrooms differ dramatically in the rate of the male call-out advantage. In our pilot study, we found that boys called out eight times more often than girls. In our full study, which involved more classrooms, we found a two-to-one male advantage. In the 1995 edition of *Failing at Fairness,* we describe it this way: 'Our research shows that boys call out significantly more often than girls.'"

Now, *this* was a familiar scenario. As a psychologist I often visited classrooms to observe a child who was struggling. Folded into a pint-sized chair and trying to be invisible, I often saw that more boys than girls were obstreperous—they were restless, immobilized in *their* small chairs; they dropped things, they called out to the teacher and to each other. I'd seen wise teachers who could adapt to this eager, rangy style of learning. But more frequently teachers were overwhelmed by large classes and tight schedules and reacted to this subset of needy boys with frustrated scoldings and punishments—as opposed to the solicitous, male-directed attention the research described. If anyone was favored with positive feedback, it was girls. Their behavior, on average, was more compliant and better controlled. This made it easier for them to absorb teaching that was often lecture-style. Several studies confirmed my observation that teachers reprimand and criticize boys significantly more than girls, castigating boys even when their behavior is not inappropriate.[33] So a call-out gap was plausible, although not in the magnitude reported. The vanilla gender assumption—that there *should* be no behavioral or learning differences between the sexes, and that any differences that surface automatically confer benefits on males—was far from the reality. Still, even if there is no basis to the claim that girls are silenced in school (Christina Hoff Sommers recounts a detective-style search for evidence in her book *The War Against Boys)*, a significant piece of the story is that any suspicion of differential treatment strikes a painful chord. No one wants to repeat the mistakes of the past, least of all a generation of parents and teachers who were among the first to see the gender landscape change. But in the nineties it no longer made sense to see girls as silent victims at school, and it makes even less sense now. Not only has no empirical evidence surfaced that supports such shabby treatment of girls, but if it had, it would also have to explain their stellar performance.

Leap ahead a decade from that study, and the assumption that the two sexes will behave and be treated exactly the same way has led us to another strange place: affirmative action for men. Few schools will reveal how they do it, but women's stronger academic profiles mean that if a 50–50 balance is desired on campus, then it must be engineered. And that is exactly what is taking place in many colleges. There was a suspicion that boys would start to get preference as campuses became more solidly female and, in 2005, two economics professors decided to investigate whether there was a foundation to the rumors. Sandy Baum and Eban Goodstein tracked admissions at thirteen liberal arts colleges in the United States and discovered two trends: clear evidence of a preference for admitting men in historically female colleges (where being male raised the probability of being accepted by 6 to 9 percentage points), and the bottom quarter of both applicant and acceptance pools being disproportionately male everywhere the researchers looked.[34] Here, then, was evidence of male extremes. However, this time males were shown to dominate the bottom layer, not the top.

Affirmative action for women has long been a reality in university departments such as engineering and computer science.[35] The vanilla male model—that women should want what men want and be heartily encouraged to choose it 50 percent of the time—is implicit. But even advocates for boys find that the reverse—affirmative action for men—is distasteful. When psychologist, speaker, and *Raising Cain* author Michael Thompson was asked for his reaction to Baum and Goodstein's study, he responded as a parent—that is, viscerally. "I'd be horrified if some lunkhead boy got accepted to a school instead of my very talented and prepared daughter, just because he happened to be a guy," he told *Salon* journalist Sarah Karnsiewicz.[36] The dean of admissions from the formerly all-male Kenyon College in Ohio learned just how sensitive male quotas are in March 2006 when she wrote an op-ed piece in *The New York Times* about her college's tougher admissions requirements for women who are smart, qualified, and hardworking, but part of "swollen applicant pools that are decidedly female." Two-thirds of American colleges and universities get more female than male applicants, she reported, which means that to achieve gender balance, there's a double standard about who makes the grade. Admissions officers are desperate not to reach the "tipping point," where 60 percent or more of their enrolled students are female. "We have told today's young women that the world is their oyster; the problem is, so many of them believed us that the standards for admission to today's most selective colleges are stiffer for women than men. How's that for an unintended consequence of the women's liberation movement?" Liberal arts colleges are rejecting thousands of highly qualified female candidates lest their college campuses become all-girls schools, she wrote.[37] The women were such strong applicants that without imposing quotas favoring boys, merit-based admissions would have transformed Kenyon College—all-male for 145 years—into a mostly female college in one generation.

Knuckling Down: The Self-Discipline Gap

I wondered where all the boys were one rainy June evening in 2004 at a prestigious, formerly all-male Jesuit college. Sixty-four years after former Canadian prime minister Pierre Elliot Trudeau had graduated from Collège-Jean-de-Brébeuf, 80 percent of all the academic awards went to women. As one by one, women in high heels and ponytails clattered onto the stage to collect their diplomas and awards, I thought, What happened to the boys? University of Pennsylvania psychologists Angela Lee Duckworth and Martin Seligman asked themselves the same question when their local newspaper ran a story about female valedictorians outnumbering males two to one.

Martin Seligman had long been interested in motivation—in the late sixties he had observed that animals exposed to painful situations they could not control would just lie there, inert, in most new situations. He called this learned helplessness and had spent decades trying to understand its effects on people, wanting to know who persists in difficult circumstances, who gives up, and if this can ever change.[38]

When they noticed the newspaper story, Seligman and Duckworth were exploring persistence in high school students, and had just started several studies on eighth graders that examined their self-discipline. To make sure they captured this elusive trait, they looked at it a few different ways. The students, as well as their parents and teachers, were asked hundreds of questions like these:

Do you save regularly?
Do you mostly speak before thinking things out?
Would you prefer $55 today or $75 in sixty-one days?

The students also had to rate themselves on statements such as these:

I have a hard time breaking bad habits.
I have iron self-discipline.
I have a hard time resisting things that are bad for me.

Although they didn't plan to look at gender, the sex differences that emerged were startling. "The statistics just popped out," said Duckworth. "It was just striking. Girls were always more self-disciplined on all the measures. We thought, Why are the statistics coming out this way? Maybe I compiled things wrong? That's why we did the study twice." Duckworth called it a revelation—that girls are not only more self-disciplined, but their grades were reliably higher than boys' in every subject. Even in the most advanced math class designed for the top fifth of the class, girls were significantly stronger. Once they started to talk about their findings, everyone in contact with kids—classroom teachers, school principals, SAT exam coaches—confirmed that girls just buckled down faster and applied themselves.

Duckworth and Seligman had discovered that it isn't the contentious IQ score that best predicts high school performance. It is self-discipline.[39] It should have come as no surprise that knuckling down helps girls score better grades. Yet everyone's expectation was the contrary—that women would be behind the eight ball. They seemed to be in other high-profile areas—for example, in standardized tests of math-

ematical reasoning, and the average gender gap in pay. That girls' better self-discipline and learning doesn't automatically translate into
workplace gains seems especially counterintuitive. Perhaps there are
other sex differences—in interests, priorities, and appetites for risk—
that might account for the discrepancy, I suggested to Professor Duckworth in a telephone conversation. She agreed, but mentioned something
else. Maybe self-discipline lagged in boys at first, but they caught up
later. After all, most twelve-year-old girls towered over the boys in their
classes. But by age twenty, most boys were taller. Perhaps some psychological traits took some time to appear. The boys could be slow
bloomers. It was not just that some skills and interests diverged in average boys and girls, but the rate at which they emerged might not match
up. This is what Allan Reis, the neonatologist studying preemie brain
growth, had discovered. It's also what Emmy Werner and Ruth Smith
unearthed about their vulnerable population of children in Kauai.
While boys' psychological development and physical resilience lagged
dramatically behind girls in childhood, the balance started to shift as
the group moved through adolescence. The boys in their study started
to catch up to the girls in verbal and academic performance in their
teen years, while girls started to experience more stress and mental
health problems as they entered late adolescence. And this might help
explain the paradox that girls are higher academic achievers as young-
sters, while boys overtake them in some arenas later. The observable
sex differences in discipline and achievement might be like two software programs that run at different speeds.

The Male Continuum

Why these differences might exist will be fleshed out in the coming chapters as I examine how male developmental problems might explain why
boys do more poorly in school. It's not just that learning problems,
attention deficits, social disorders, and physical aggression are biological
conditions more common in males. The preponderance of these developmental problems among males is clear, and it's common sense that
they affect how boys do in school. But the experiences of these more
unusual boys and men also tell us something important about the more
average, run-of-the-mill male. I'm suggesting that the males with these

disorders are extremes on a continuum, and that average males are more likely than females to demonstrate some of the same traits in a milder form. This doesn't mean that men and women are now switching places—that women are the standard, and that men are the misfits. In this picture, neither sex is a version of the other. Instead, the extremes within each sex illuminate the characteristics of those in the middle. So given what we know about these extremes, why would even average boys have more difficulty in school than girls? Four areas of their development give us a quick snapshot.

Movement and self-control: Attention deficit disorder, or hyperkinetic syndrome, as it is called in the United Kingdom, is at least twice as common in males as in females. Affecting the ability to marshal one's attention and rein in restlessness and impulsivity, it requires very careful diagnosis precisely *because* average, healthy boys are more restless and more impulsive than girls. (ADD is considered a disorder only when these tendencies are so extreme and pervasive that they interfere with daily life.) ADD can be seen as what happens when average sex differences in rambunctiousness and self-control—what psychologists call self-regulation—are taken to an extreme. Studies show that from a young age, boys play more high-energy, competitive games than girls, with more chasing and play-fighting and less turn-taking, waiting, and sharing. These behaviors increase when boys are in groups, as they are in school.[40] This active, restless profile affects the school progress of more average, and even gifted men. One example might be the high-tech genius Steve Jobs, the founder of Apple Computer. He dropped out of college, but sees his disenchantment with school as having taken root long before. He described the constraints of school as "pretty hard for me" because he wanted to be outdoors chasing butterflies or actively building electronic gadgets. Forced into a desk, he got kicked out of class a lot, he recalls. He said that his commencement address to Stanford's 2005 graduating class was the closest he had ever come to a university degree because "after six months I couldn't see the value in it."[41]

A things versus people point of view: The high-functioning form of autism called Asperger syndrome is ten times more common among males than females. This highly heritable disorder is characterized by opposing traits: difficulties "reading" other people, alongside an intense interest in predictable spatial, mathematical, or highly organized systems. It is hard to imagine that a person who can grasp string theory or the workings of their hard drive cannot easily decode the signs of embarrassment on someone's face. Yet reading and responding to lightning-fast signals about other people requires accessing a suite of skills that have neurodevelopmental roots. These skills include the ability to "get" the nuances of facial expressions, and the notion that other people have thoughts and feelings distinct from one's own. As a result, the deficits of autism and Asperger syndrome have been dubbed "mindblindness" because those born with the disorder seem blind to the hidden feelings and intentions of the people around them.[42] In chapter 5 we'll meet several men who have this blind spot, yet are highly gifted in areas involving math, spatial memory, or computers. Extreme men, to be sure, their profiles still illustrate a pattern that's been documented in average males; there is evidence that on average, males are more likely to master detailed spatial systems than they are to absorb social signals. Even from the first days of life, males are more likely to look at machines that move, while females prefer to look at the animation in people's faces.[43] Males are more likely to find obscure details hidden in a complex background; females are more likely to consider the surrounding context.[44] Males are better able to predict the level of water in a jar as it tilts (it remains horizontal), whereas females are more likely to focus on the context (and so expect the water level to match the angle of its container).[45] Males are better able to imagine how three-dimensional objects might look as they rotate in space, and they are also more likely to use this strategy to solve new problems.[46] Men are better at forming mental maps of a route (go north for three miles, then turn east for half a mile). Females are more likely to navigate using landmarks (drive until the red-roofed church, turn right, and continue until the river).[47] These differences tell us nothing about individuals, of course. Instead they tell us about qualities more commonly found among males, on average, that influence their interests in predictable systems, such as stars, cars, or computers.

Aggression and competition: Even though they outnumber such troubled girls three to one, there are no boys with conduct disorder in this book—the bullies, aggressors, and chronic rule-breakers who care little about how their acts affect other people. And there are no interviews with murderers, even though there are nine male killers for every female. These are male extremes, but even excluding criminals, few would really want their personal story to anchor a chapter on aggression. Even avowed competitors in legitimate forums (sports, politics, business) don't openly state that they're ruthless. Still, the numbers illustrate the competitive bent of males across the spectrum. Males are more likely than females to use aggressive means to offside their rivals, and to assert and maintain their status in a hierarchy.[48] While anger, jealousy, and verbal aggression are unisex, establishing dominance through theft, violence, and warfare have been the domain of men throughout history. For the past seven hundred years and in different societies, homicide records show that men kill other men thirty to forty times more often than women kill women. More recently, an analysis of 450 cases of shooting rampages at school or at work has found that males pulled the trigger 93 percent of the time.[49] And despite the universality of coveting other people's stuff, 94 percent of burglaries are committed by men, so there's a sex-based monopoly there, too.[50] How do we know that aggressive one-upmanship is not simply males being brought up to be brutes? Male toddlers are more aggressive than females, even before they can distinguish between the sexes and what is "right" for each one. They tell aggressive stories 87 percent of the time, while girls do 17 percent of the time. Ninety percent of children agree that parents and teachers punish more boys than girls for aggressive behavior, even if punishing aggressive boys has less impact than punishing girls. Even so, the majority of boys become less aggressive over time, not more. If aggression were a matter of being socialized to hurt others to get your way, you'd think that boys would become *more* aggressive as they get older, not less. But huge population studies by the Québec researcher Richard Tremblay show that the opposite is true: the peak of male aggression is during the preschool years, after which 96 percent of males gradually become more peaceable and cooperative as their social skills kick in and they learn greater self-control and the rules of society.[51] Early on, though, through no fault of their own, young boys are naturally less able than most girls to rein in their impulses, aggressive or otherwise. As a result, boys are more likely than girls to move around in class, be inattentive, call out impulsively, and prod others for a reaction—especially other boys—with whom they are constantly jockeying for status.

Language: There are more than four boys with language and reading problems for every girl.[52] I'm suggesting that these problems are exaggerations of brain-based sex differences in language fluency and literacy that exist in most of us. In the next chapter we'll see how language is stored and accessed somewhat differently in male and female brains. Such subtle, gender-based shifts of the neural layout influence the character and speed of children's language as they grow.[53] Girls, on average, are more fluid talkers and writers than boys. They speak earlier than boys, talk faster, use more words, generate longer sentences, and make fewer mistakes. At age two, girls have about a hundred more words in their vocabularies than boys, and as girls move through their preschool years they use more complex, varied, and spontaneous language, so it's not just a matter of volume. This edge appears as soon as spoken language does and continues throughout elementary and high school. It is reflected in girls' better reading comprehension, spelling, punctuation, and writing skills—all of which are demonstrated in stronger language and essay writing scores on achievement tests later on.[54] Girls and women are handier with reference materials, and are much quicker to generate synonyms than boys—perhaps one reason why there are so many women in publishing. The female advantage in writing is so strong that a writing subtest was added to the Preliminary Scholastic Aptitude Test (PSAT) to offset the traditional male advantage in math.[55] The female edge in verbal fluency appears so early in life and is so consistent over time and across cultures that the science of sex differences must be involved.

But how? And more to the point, how would an extreme male with dodgy language and reading skills ever manage to succeed? Some of the men with early language and reading problems have achieved success— many modestly, others brilliantly. When trying to figure out what was going on in dyslexics' brains before there were MRIs or PET scans to assist us, the British neurologist and polymath Macdonald Critchley commented that "when testing dyslexics as to their power of silent or oral reading, it is not infrequently found that the child performs no worse—sometimes even a little better—if the book is held upside down."[56] The erudite clinician was on to something decades before MRIs came on the scene. Sometimes the answer to a question is the opposite of what we expect.

CHAPTER 2

Dyslexic Boys Who Make Good

Andrew[1] looked like your standard eight-year-old boy—lopsided grin, mussed dark hair—and on the surface behaved like one, too, with a penchant for jokes about body parts. But there was nothing average about Andrew. What brought him to my clinic was that he seemed intelligent enough, but he just couldn't read with any fluency—no matter how much classroom teaching and TLC he got. After three years of education the printed word still offered him unlimited possibilities for interpretation. Looking at the first letter, he usually took a wild guess. *List* became *letter, couch* became *corn, pieces* became *pennies.* Reading was such a pain that Andrew often just looked at the pictures on the page and made up a plausible story. When I asked him what he liked best about school, he quickly replied, "Being the tallest in my class." What else? "Recess." As I considered the dozen years of school he had ahead of him, Andrew balanced on the back legs of the office chair, one hand on the corner of my desk. His feet swung freely back and forth, touched down briefly, then up they went again. I passed him a handful of paper clips while I turned to talk to his parents. He bumped his chair down and started to weave them together, humming "La Bamba."

His parents told me that it wasn't just that Andrew couldn't chop words up into sounds so he could read or spell them. At times he couldn't remember the names of some objects around the house, and he was starting to punch out boys in the school yard, too. Using the standard tools of psychological assessment, I would have to tease apart what might be interfering with his learning—hearing? inattention? family stresses?—before considering what should happen next. An assessment meant that Andrew would meet with me several times to do standardized tests of memory, problem solving, listening, language, and reading. But I already had a hunch about Andrew. His early childhood history—slow to talk, a little aggressive when he couldn't, and missing odd words when he finally did, plus the fact that his father, two uncles, and several cousins had also had language or school problems—were hints that there was a biological basis to his inability to match language sounds to inky black marks on the page. While his mother had a checkered school history, Andrew's sister and female cousins were fine students. Andrew's pattern of strengths, quirks, and handicaps was more likely to show up in the boys and men in his family. Being male had made Andrew more vulnerable.

I suspected that he had dyslexia, a language-based reading disability that runs in families. Often defined by a gap between a child's intelligence and his or her ability to learn to read, it's usually spotted once a child has been in school for a few years, and like Andrew, shows a peculiar lack of progress. But the clues exist long before that. As preschoolers, children with dyslexia are not adept at remembering nonsense words, learning ditties, or naming things fast, and often have trouble "hearing" and playing with the individual sounds that make up words, an innate ability called phonological awareness.[2] Normally preschoolers hear which parts of words sound the same and find playing with language and rhymes fun, which is why the same nonsense verses have been popular with five-year-olds for hundreds of years, though they mean little or nothing at all. The following ditty:

> *Oh, my finger, oh, my thumb,*
> *Oh, my belly, oh, my bum*

has been circulating in England since about 1910, and nursery rhymes such as "Eentsy Weentsy Spider" are highly entertaining to most small children, *especially* when repeated ad infinitum. When there are appropriate pauses, most children automatically parse the expected word, waiting to hear one with that satisfying ending. That's how they can fill in the blanks with rhyming words or ones that sound very close, a sign that their phonological awareness is developing on schedule.[3] Finding it difficult to break words into parts, dyslexic children are more likely to have trouble with this, as I rediscovered when I said farewell to Andrew that day in the office. "See you later, alligator," I said. "Good-bye, you big baboon," he responded.

Andrew did turn out to be one of about 8 percent of all males with dyslexia. For whatever reason—and as we shall see, a genetic predisposition is the most likely—the part of his brain specialized for breaking down language into its component parts had been compromised during prenatal development. Eight years later, Andrew was having problems learning to read, spell, and find his words. Even with every opportunity, including higher-than-average intelligence, caring parents, and fine teachers, he would be more at risk of leaving school earlier than girls his age. Two of every three high school dropouts are male, and many of these dropouts have learning disabilities, of which dyslexia is the most common.[4] They experience a double whammy: weaker reading and ultimately less education.

It hardly seems a recipe for career success. Given the numbers, if you were to predict the future on the basis of school achievement alone, the world would be a matriarchy. Yet some alchemy of contradictory gifts, compensatory skills, and social conditions makes it possible for some unusual men like Andrew to succeed at work. Given the right conditions and jobs, the earnings of many of these "fragile" men can eventually eclipse the salaries of the intelligent and disciplined little girls who sat beside them in third grade. A former colleague wryly observed that a boy who attended special education classes in her elementary school is now managing her company's pension fund, earning multiples of her salary, and driving a late-model European sedan. Did the financial whiz get special breaks that this female editor, a highly literate student, had no access to as a woman? Or did their biological backgrounds cause them to veer in two dramatically different directions?

For Andrew, the journey seemed toughest when he was youngest. He spent his time "listening" in a classroom or doing homework, his least favorite activities. As he got older he gradually adjusted the ratio, doing more, listening less. By the time he reached the last year of high school he had a raft of friends, played guitar, lifted weights at the gym, and had learned to drive. But he could barely get out of bed to get to class in the morning. "He struggled so much as a kid that we're really very pleased now," said his mother when I called her to follow up on him fifteen years after I last saw him. She filled me in on the missing pieces of his story. Like his middle-class friends, he had automatically migrated to college after graduating from high school, even though he knew school would be torture. It was mid-September when his older sister met a classmate on the bus who was studying to be a chef at a culinary institute. She brought the details home to Andrew. "You love to cook. Why not try this?" That's how it happened that two weeks after he had started a two-year college, Andrew had dropped out and enrolled in cooking school. One week he was struggling through *The Iliad*; the next week he was learning to julienne carrots. Suddenly the six-foot-two bodybuilder was no longer the one who could never remember how to spell the word "people." No one cared whether he read the word *shirts* as *shorts,* or snickered when he said that the guy at the club played *bangoes.* For once, he was in a place where his physical presence, his keen eye for visual detail, and his methodical approach would get some respect.

This transformation, if you can call it that, merited a visit so I could see it for myself. I arranged to meet my husband and a friend at the swanky French restaurant where Andrew now worked, and after lunch I ducked into the kitchen to check up on my former charge. I pushed open the double swinging doors, and there he was in chef's whites, his head towering above the Plexiglas partition separating his station from the steady parade of servers filing in and out, hands grabbing plates from the pass-through. Every time the doors swung shut, the scrawled orders fluttered on the rack above him. Andrew was fanning out shreds of raw red tuna into a peak, then squirting an S of pale wasabi cream from a squeeze bottle. "How ya doing?" He greeted me with a shy grin but didn't stop layering tuna and endive. As we made small talk, I took in the furious activity of a posh commercial kitchen at the end of the lunch rush and observed the adult version of the former plodding reader, literal thinker, and random speller. While the tension crackled in the tight space of the kitchen, he kept his cool. "Andrew reads a hundred orders in twenty minutes and he does it with speed and he's calm. He doesn't seem dyslexic at all," said the boss of this glittering watering hole when we chatted at the bar for a few minutes a little later. "Maybe he's learned to cope with it, but if you didn't already know, you wouldn't guess. We call him 'the professional.'"

For Andrew, cooking for a living meant that he didn't have to stay in school. And there was an unexpected ego boost: most restaurant kitchen staff come from somewhere else, he said, so compared to them, his reading and writing were excellent. I asked if his imposing physical stature earned him extra points in the kitchen, not to mention his after-hours work as a bouncer. Looking down from one foot above me, he nodded, smiling broadly. If a chef is unwilling to take the "rat tails" and the testosterone-laced put-downs of a professional kitchen, he or she won't last. "Sometimes even the guys can't take it," said Andrew of the daily mix of aggressive banter, horseplay, and character assassinations. "There's a revolving door. Whenever they bring in a new person, everyone thinks they'll be fired. Because every day you have to prove yourself." The teasing and constant yelling are "so much fun," he said. And except for the scrawled rack of orders, there's no printed text in sight. "I should be reading more recipes, but I'm not really a reader," he added.

Filling in the Biological Blanks

Just why an apparently healthy young man would find reading aversive was a mystery until fairly recently. A generation ago, there were few good lab studies, brain imaging was in its infancy—and was too invasive and expensive to use with healthy children in any case—and there was no Human Genome Project. Children like Andrew often misbehaved when the frustration mounted, or had two disorders at once—an attention deficit disorder *and* a reading disability—so there was general confusion about causes. Unrefined sugar, bad teaching, or apathy were often seen as the culprits. Closer to the mark, many believed that dyslexia was related to the brain somehow, and vaguely technical terms such as "minimal brain dysfunction" and "visuo-perceptual integration disorder" were in vogue for a while, although nobody was really sure what they meant. The waters were muddied further by teaching fads that had little science behind them. Whole-language approaches, which were popular in the seventies and eighties, didn't teach word analysis but depended on a child's intuitive ability to parse or recognize words on her own. That was exactly what dyslexic children couldn't do, so they fell further behind. For most of the twentieth century there wasn't much hard evidence that explained why a knack for deciphering written text might be present in 90 percent of humans and absent in the rest. Reading and writing are clearly learned. So why couldn't some kids just learn them?

The answer became clearer in the mid-nineties, as evidence started building for literacy's neurological and genetic roots. There is no single gene that causes dyslexia. As dyslexia can result from different permutations and combinations of language-related problems—not just phonological awareness, but compromised naming, or a sluggish memory for written symbols—it is more like a syndrome than a single phenomenon. At least eight gene variations on fragments of several chromosomes (including chromosomes 2, 6, and 15) are known to be involved in rejigging brain development. When present in various combinations, these genetic variations can interfere with the process of learning to read. Other sites on chromosomes have been identified as possibly carrying genes implicated in dyslexia, and the genome mapping is getting more refined day by day.[5]

Bolstering its biological origins, twin studies show that the likelihood of identical twins both demonstrating dyslexia ranges from 91 to 100 percent (identical twins share the same genetic signature). The chance that fraternal twins—who share roughly half the relevant genes—will both have dyslexia ranges from 45 to 52 percent.[6] Clearly, dyslexia is inherited, although environment can play a mysterious role in how it plays out in each person. And although it can be remediated with the right educational approach, it is not *caused* by bad teaching (just as bad vision can be remediated by wearing glasses, but is not caused by not having a pair handy). Nor is there any evidence that dyslexia is caused by lax parenting or a fast-food diet. It is also universal: about 10 percent of the world's population has the disorder.[7] Boys are more often affected than girls: the ratio of boys to girls is anywhere from ten to one to two to one, depending on how tightly dyslexia is defined and how seriously it disrupts day-to-day life. Severe dyslexia accompanied by multiple language problems is six times more common in males.[8]

But any sex difference is controversial. Even with the biological evidence, there was an effort in the mid-nineties to pin any boy-tilted ratio on gender bias. As with the call-out gap, the assumption seemed to be that male and female brains should be identical, or rather that girls' brains—and thus their behavior—should resemble boys' in every respect. So if more boys called out, or if 10 percent of boys had a disorder that drew a teacher's attention or a school's resources, then girls must do the same and have the same in equal proportions.[9] In her book *Overcoming Dyslexia,* pediatrics professor Sally Shaywitz identifies the problem this way: "Teachers have incorporated a norm for classroom behavior that reflects the behavior of normal girls. As a result, boys who are rambunctious—although still within the normal range for the behavior of boys—may be perceived as having a behavior problem and referred for further evaluation. Meanwhile, the well-mannered little girls who sit quietly at their seats but who, nevertheless, are failing to learn to read are often overlooked."[10] Dr. Shaywitz's studies of children in the community, who had not been singled out by their schools or clinics as having any problems, echoed the expected finding that more boys had dyslexia than girls. But she found that the differences between the sexes were less dramatic when she looked for reading problems in the community at large. Her finding of "no significant differences" contrasted dramatically with the previously large sex differences found in dyslexia, and she suggested a reason: quiet girls are slipping through the cracks.

This may be true in some cases. But it is also likely that a blanket screening for dyslexia will reveal plenty of false positives—the signs of a disorder where there really is none. Girls' academic skills tend to be underestimated by standardized tests. For example, girls' math skills can be as strong as boys' in the classroom, yet trail behind in standardized test scores. Casting the widest possible net via communitywide testing can thus be controversial: there must be enough "hits" of real cases to make up for the falsely identified ones. In the case of dyslexia, the more extreme and pervasive the disorder, the higher the likelihood that males will be affected and thus identified. Overdiagnosing a problem when there is no real-life evidence of one carries its own risks. Expensive follow-up assessments needed to confirm the diagnosis sometimes don't happen.[11] And there is no getting around dyslexia's brain-based roots. While writing this chapter I received a request to follow up on a clever but dyslexic boy I had assessed six years earlier. His father told me that he was now in a special class for children with reading problems, all fifteen of whom were boys. "The atmosphere is as chaotic as *Animal House*," the dad said, describing the scene when he'd peered in after he'd dropped his son off. It seemed likely that some of these boys had ADHD, as well as dyslexia. Boys are more likely to be doubly unlucky in having more than one developmental disorder at once. But the fundamental reasons for a higher proportion of boys with dyslexia ultimately has less to do with teachers' biases and double diagnoses than with the geography of male and female brains.

Male brains are simply less versatile when it comes to language, whether written or spoken. So if anything goes wrong, males can get stuck. It could be a clot or a bleed, or it could be the subtle miswiring of dyslexia—female brains just seem better equipped to deal with the unexpected. Much of this versatility has to do with the way the two cerebral hemispheres are organized for language storage and retrieval in men and women. MRI studies show that males have most language functions localized in the left hemisphere. Meanwhile, most females use *both* hemispheres for language.[12] One of the first of many scientific articles to demonstrate this sex difference was a 1995 MRI study in *Nature* by Sally Shaywitz and her husband, Bennett Shaywitz. Along with their Yale colleagues, the Shaywitzes showed that language tasks that are essential to reading and writing—rhyming, letter recognition, and word comprehension—are highly lateralized in the left cerebral hemisphere in males but are represented in both hemispheres in females.[13] The Shaywitzes' own findings seem to contradict the notion that the high proportion of males diagnosed with dyslexia are due to teachers' biases. But then, there has long been resistance to the idea that material, observable sex differences in the brain are meaningful, especially given that female brains have been found to be smaller and lighter.

A Canadian neuroscientist, Sandra Witelson, cleared up much of the confusion in 1995. She found that female brains might be proportionally smaller than male brains, but they are more networked for language. By literally counting neurons in very thin slices of brain tissue, Dr. Witelson and her colleagues also discovered that female brains are packed more solidly with receptors, especially in the posterior temporal cortex, a region specialized for language. This markedly higher cell density—the difference is 11 percent favoring women—might be one reason why women are equally intelligent, even with proportionally smaller brains.[14] It also might explain the general female advantage in language fluency and spelling. Here, then, was some evidence that might tell us why there is a sex difference in language skills that becomes even more acute when there is a predisposition to dyslexia. And the stage would be set for women's language skills to be better integrated with other cognitive abilities, such as memory and emotion, and more protected from any localized damage. If there were a problem in the left hemisphere, women would simply access the right hemisphere instead. Under normal circumstances sex differences would be subtle, but when things went wrong, sex differences would be extreme.

It isn't just differences between the hemispheres; there are other anatomical changes in the brain of a dyslexic child that make it distinct. While early exposure to male hormones in utero wires male and female brains slightly differently for literacy earlier in prenatal development, in the last trimester of pregnancy, several candidate genes linked to dyslexia are thought to jump-start a prenatal migration of neurons to form ectopias.[15] These are bundles of neurons that settle in the cortex where they don't belong (some scientists call them brain warts, though they don't grow).[16] And there are other visible irregularities in dyslexia. Instead of the right frontal lobe and the left occipital (back) lobes of the brain bulging out unevenly, as is the norm, in dyslexics these asymmetries are reversed, or are smaller in size.[17] Other irregularities in the cortex's creases and folds hamper the smooth transmission of neural signals related to reading in three areas: the inferior frontal gyrus (roughly behind the eyebrow), where words are broken down into sounds; the temporo-parietal region (behind the top of the ear), where more word analysis happens; and the occipito-temporal region (in the back, deep behind the earlobe), where naming and recognition of the printed word take place.[18] Navigating between these areas, it's as if the dyslexic brain's language signals traverse anatomical paths filled with potholes and hillocks, resulting in sluggish processing, miscommunication between cells, and abnormal connections. But are there convenient detours? Women's brains have more of these. With fewer other routes or neural "spare parts" to take over in a pinch, male language and reading skills are thus more vulnerable, whether to targeted brain damage or to more diffuse language disabilities such as dyslexia. British neuroscientist Uta Frith and a colleague, Faraneh Vargha-Khadem, found evidence of this when they looked at the spelling and reading of forty-five children with early localized brain damage. The boys with lesions to the left hemisphere struggled more with spelling and reading than did girls with similarly located damage. In the girls, reading and spelling were no better or no worse than in average kids, no matter which side of their brain sustained damage, because other regions of their brains could take over.[19]

Asymmetry between the cerebral hemispheres—and between males and females—is the rule for language. In this regard male and female brains are not identical.[20] Yet greater symmetry between aspects of the brain's right and left sides is a common anatomical feature of the brains of people with dyslexia. Such anatomical differences first skew the experience, then the behavior, then the diagnoses of dyslexic boys.

Male Enclaves

It's highly unlikely that Andrew knew about any of this, of course, when he decided to become a chef. But restaurant kitchens are notorious male ghettos, and after reading about the underwhelming school histories of several celebrity chefs, I began to wonder whether dropping out of school might be a prerequisite for male fame in the kitchen. The top-rated restaurants in London, Paris, Berlin, New York, and California are run by male chefs, even today. And while gender discrimination used to be standard in restaurant kitchens, especially in Europe, self-selection is more likely why women are still scarce in high-end restaurants these days. Discrimination is on its way out, but the basic environment of restaurant work never changes. It's blue-collar work that's strenuous and dirty, and the hours are punishing. Celebrity chefs notwithstanding, working in a restaurant kitchen is like working in a prison or on an oil rig—it's shift work in a macho environment.

At the outset, though, many women are interested. Half the students at the American Institute of Culinary Education and the Cordon Bleu schools are female. But disillusionment sets in quickly. Peek behind the doors of almost any restaurant kitchen any night of the week and you'll see mostly sweaty men wearing checked pants and clogs. That's because when women graduate from culinary schools, many of them discover that the hours and conditions of cooking clash with family life. When everyone else is with loved ones on evenings, weekends, or holidays, the chef is hoisting stockpots and colanders. When asked why there are so few female chefs, Missy Robbins, the executive chef at Chicago's Spiaggia, commented to a reporter, "How am I going to have kids and be at work at midnight?" Another chef said, "It's tough. I have no life. I don't date. It sucks sometimes. My life is my restaurant." "I couldn't even contemplate having a child while being a chef. It was that clear," said another female chef. "It's like being a construction worker. It's just not that friendly."[21]

Indeed, restaurant kitchens rival battle scenes as iconic male settings. Here Adam Gopnik writes about the education of three-star chef Bernard Loiseau: "He learned to cook as an intern in the kitchen of the Frères Troisgros, near Lyon, where he mastered the terrifying discipline by chopping onions and filleting fish for twelve hours a day; he even learned to kill frogs by slapping their heads casually against the kitchen table."[22] For months after reading Anthony Bourdain's candid *Kitchen Confidential,* I lost the appetite to eat food prepared in a professional kitchen, much less a desire to work in one. This is how Bourdain describes the chef and cook staff of a Provincetown restaurant where he started his career:

> They dressed like pirates: chef's coats with the arms slashed off, blue jeans, ragged and faded headbands, gore-covered aprons, gold hoop earrings, wrist cuffs, turquoise necklaces and chokers, rings of scrimshaw and ivory, tattoos. . . . They had style and swagger and they seemed afraid of nothing. They drank everything in sight, stole whatever wasn't nailed down, and screwed their way through floor staff, bar customers and casual visitors

like nothing I'd ever seen or imagined. They carried big, bad-ass knives, which they kept honed and sharpened to a razor's edge. They hurled dirty sauté pans and pots across the kitchen and into my pot sink with casual accuracy.[23]

And in *Heat*, Bill Buford's riveting account of his apprenticeship to chef Mario Batali and Batali's idol, Dario Cecchini, the reader rolls from feeling sympathy to giddy relief at not being Buford while he was learning the tricks of the trade. In a professional restaurant kitchen there's a hierarchy about space ("they bump you because they can—they're putting you in your place," Batali tells him); there are classic dominance displays about rank ("Here are the snow peas, master," but he doesn't like the look of them. "They're wrong, you arsehole. They're overcooked, you fucking moron. You've ruined them, you goddamn fucking navvy."); and there's aggression that would be called abuse anywhere else. When Buford undercooked a pork chop, Batali's response was to dismiss him from his station, publicly dress him down, then ram hot food down his throat.

He made several, topping them with gobs of white pork fat and hot chili sauce, a squishy melty concoction. Mario took a bite of one and it ran wetly down his cheek, a glistening red-hot rivulet of grease. I watched this because, again, that's what I was doing, watching. He then marched over to my corner and shoved the rest of the pizza into my mouth—quickly and with force.

"This," he said, "is the taste America is waiting for." He was inches from my face. "Don't you think this is the taste America wants?" His head was tilted back, like a boxer's, giving me his chin but protecting his nose. He had a wide, aggressive stance. The look was hard, almost sneering. He stared at me, waiting for me to agree.

"This," I said, "is what America is waiting for."[24]

Clearly there are women who can stand the heat of these kitchens for sixteen hours at a stretch, but there's a high attrition rate. For a woman to enjoy working alongside these men, she'd need the biggest balls of all—to be more foulmouthed and quick on the draw than they are. And at the end of the day, she'd have to care less about her home life than about what went on strangers' plates. Still in his twenties, this was less of a concern for Andrew—at least for the moment. Besides, what choices did he have? As he put it, "I like cooking. I wasn't happy in school." It was that simple.

Tom, Dick, Harry . . . and Wendy

Andrew's story turned out to be classic. Having dropped out of college to learn a trade, Andrew was typical of many young men with reading disabilities. In 2001 the U.S. Department of Education set out to follow about 11,000 teenagers who were receiving special education services in a prospective study called the National Longitudinal Transition Survey. This large group of thirteen- to sixteen-year-olds was being tracked as they entered adulthood, and by 2006 they'd been assessed twice. By then, the NLTS study found that three-quarters of the group had graduated from high school, and of the ones who hadn't, most were male. Only 9 percent of the group had continued on to four-year college programs and most of them were female. That seemed to be bad news for the boys. But the good news, if you can call it that, is that the learning-disabled boys were much stronger than the girls on tests of mathematics, science, and motor skills, and these skills seemed to help them go on to trades and into business. When they were last surveyed, 85 percent of them were working full-time and putting in long hours.[25]

In April 2006 I received an e-mail from Mary Wagner, the lead investigator of the study, telling me that learning-disabled boys who had left high school were twice as likely to be working full-time and were earning more per hour than the girls. Here was the paradox: the women were doing better in school, but the men were working longer hours at more highly paid jobs. Other studies that had gone back to look at how young people with learning disabilities were doing had discovered the same trend: the men were working hard at full-time jobs; the women were much more likely to be working part-time, if at all, or were home parenting children.[26] Amazingly, these men were even earning more than women without any kind of learning disability—which reminded me of my editorial colleague and the classmate managing her pension fund. His reading skills were probably still lousy, but his long hours and his drive to make money in a high-risk field were making up for it.

And there was something else. Often, those with dyslexia who managed to succeed had one all-consuming interest. Single-minded commitment is what characterized sixty successful adults with dyslexia, according to the Boston-based literacy researcher Rosalie Fink. She was interested in people with dyslexia who stuck with postsecondary education long enough to become scientists or professionals, and discovered that what characterized them was the dogged persistence to keep reading, even at a painstaking pace—and a passionate interest in a single subject. They read obsessively in that area, mastering its vocabulary so they could lean on accumulated knowledge instead of having to stop and parse each new word.[27] Happily, Fink's studies quote her dyslexic subjects talking volubly about how they educated themselves, so it wasn't just a question of combing through the data for their stories.

"It started with my interest in airplanes in grade school, that quickly converted to propellant systems in seventh and eighth grades. . . . I became fascinated with nitrogen chemistry. So the way to understand that was to start reading chemistry books. So I got organic chemistry books and read as many as I could find," said Ronald W. Davis, now a professor of biochemistry at Stanford. James Bensinger, a physicist, described his attraction to his work this way: "I knew certainly as early as fifth grade that physics was what I wanted to do. So I did a lot of reading. You know, I read magazines and books and just spent a lot of time, just reading about physics." A desire to master one area of science drove these men to read, and being extreme, they were extreme in their tastes.

The successful dyslexic women read more broadly, to experience other worlds or inhabit other minds, not to acquire a concrete fact base. Ann Brown, an educational researcher with dyslexia, described her budding literacy this way: "I remember reading many historical novels; I read those avidly, particularly about the Tudor and Stuart periods, because they were mainly love stories." Another woman described being captivated by Judy Blume novels early on. As much as

Rosalie Fink wanted to avoid gender stereotypes, there was no avoid-
ing the fact that the dyslexic men and women chose different types of
books, as do men and women in general. Eighty percent of fiction is
bought by women, probably because it allows them to try on other
people's mental states for size.[28] The dyslexic men were more extreme
than the average guy in having weaker language skills, and also were
more extreme than dyslexic women in their focus on things versus people. By focusing on a narrow field with narrow relevance they acquired
an expertise few others had.

Reading widely in one area when you're not a fluent reader is also
a sign of sheer grit. And grit, I discovered, was another characteristic
of successful men with dyslexia. Reading science fiction and Tin-Tin
adventures fired up Daniel Paley's imagination, he wrote in an e-mail,
but what really fostered his success in Silicon Valley, in his view, was
the ability to keep plodding toward a goal. Also dyslexic, Daniel's
reading was sketchy as a child, and his spelling was worse. So he
floundered, doing well when teachers evaluated him orally and doing
poorly when teachers insisted that he write timed tests. Daniel was
interested in electrical systems, and pursued an engineering degree
despite chronic reading problems and his parents' hopes that he'd find
something they thought would be easier. "Are you sure this is what
you want?" his mother remembers asking him. "He said, 'Please let
me do this.' Of my three children, he was the one who really knew
what he wanted to do. He understood best what his issues were as he
grew up and he really took charge of that. He always took charge of
himself."

This dogged persistence, along with his ability to solve spatial and
technical problems, allowed him to design digital chips "through a
large application of logic and a large application of debunking skills—
things I'm good at," he told me over the phone as he sped along a California freeway. Each time he entered a dead zone our conversation
faded away. Then my phone rang and he simply continued his sentence. Currently working on a radio frequency identification device
that will replace bar codes in big box stores, Daniel explained how his
difficulties with reading slowed him down, but paradoxically allowed
him to skirt unnecessary detail and focus on the top-down view, "like

in *Gödel, Escher, and Bach,*" he said, referring to the 1979 book by Douglas Hofstadter that drew parallels between the fields of mathematics, art, and music. Taking a bird's-eye look at a system crystallizes Daniel's strengths, apparently. Daniel's direct way of talking had him "whacking" problems and "burning" text, the metaphors he used for the slow energy required for him to read. "It's like burning with teak instead of burning with dry driftwood, which you can find anywhere on the beach," he explained, comparing his reading with how he thinks everyone else does it. "I have to expend more time and energy to get the information in." Once it's there, though, he says he can see patterns that others can't, and rarely gets sidetracked by conflict or emotions. "Once I understand a system I'm very good at manipulating it."

Unabashedly describing one's gaps and talents and matching them to a career are precisely what it takes to succeed, says researcher Paul Gerber. The dyslexic adults who make it have found a niche that fits their strengths and can pinpoint what they need to achieve, according to Gerber's studies.[29] Along with his colleague Rick Ginsberg, Gerber interviewed forty-six highly successful adults with learning disabilities, and twenty-five controls as a comparison group. The successes were not only highly goal-oriented, they were also adaptive, finding unusual solutions to their learning problems. "I interviewed a dermatologist who said there were twenty-eight medical specialties," Gerber told me. "He said the reason I'm a dermatologist is that every dermatological condition has a picture in a textbook that I can look at." Wendy Wasserstein, the Pulitzer Prize–winning playwright, spent her school days at a girls' yeshiva in Brooklyn flipping pages as quickly as possible so no one would figure out she was barely reading. But faking it was no longer required as an adult. She chose drama because she found plays easier to read than any other kind of text. "I figured out they're short, they're also printed large and there's a lot of white space on the page. And you can go to the Library of Performing Arts and read and listen to them at the same time. And later, reading the plays again, you can hear the voices of those people."[30] Along with getting a typist to correct her spelling errors, the adult Wasserstein had scoped out the liveliest written medium, one where words leaped off the page.

The Paradoxical Gift

As a playwright, Wasserstein wrote about baby-boomer women like herself not finding a straight path to fulfillment. With its detours into the comic and absurd, her work is distant from an electrical engineer's. Yet she'd agree with Daniel Paley; she also thought that "being dyslexic is a gift because you think less linearly." It's an appealing idea that people whose brains work in unconventional ways may also be equipped with unusual powers. In *The Spirit Catches You and You Fall Down,* Anne Fadiman describes how epilepsy is revered among the Hmong people of Southeast Asia. "Their seizures are thought to be evidence that they have a power to perceive things other people cannot see. . . . The fact that they have been ill themselves gives them an intuitive sympathy for the suffering of others." People with *quag dab peg,* which translates as "the spirit that catches you," are usually male and are seen as particularly fit to be spiritual leaders or healers, precisely because of their epilepsy.[31] Romantic views of brain-based disorders can have tragic consequences. Lia Lee, the young subject of Fadiman's portrait, dies due to cross-cultural confusion about whether to treat her illness, and similarly romantic views of schizophrenia have had disastrous effects. Still, people with dyslexia often mention its advantages. But is this simply putting a positive spin on an unfortunate roll of the genetic dice?

The question is whether the neuroscience that underlies dyslexia might also explain a keen grasp of numbers, or a creative and unorthodox take on the physical world. Could the genetic, hormonal, or environmental forces that foster a weak grasp of literacy be linked to other qualities? Albert Galaburda, a neurologist at Harvard Medical School, was the first to speculate that the left hemisphere deficits in dyslexia might be offset by enhanced cortical pathways in nonlanguage areas of the brain, and the American researchers Paul Gerber, Sally Shaywitz, and Maryanne Wolf agree that right-hemisphere talents in dyslexics are not just a coincidence; factors related to dyslexia might allow people to see systems or patterns where others might see an accumulation of unrelated bits and pieces.[32] Across the Atlantic, John Stein, who researches the neurobiology of dyslexia at Oxford, kicked off a lecture in 2001 by saying, "Dyslexics have different brains; so their problems

are not confined to reading, writing and spelling, but extend to incoor-
dination, left-right confusions and poor sequencing in general in both
temporal and spatial domains." That sounds pretty bad. But here's the
flip side. Stein speculated that this weak link had persisted because it
confers a "compensating advantage." He compared it to sickle-cell ane-
mia, a genetic mutation that makes red blood cells crescent-shaped and
sticky so they can't slide freely through blood vessels. Evolutionary biologists think that the disease persisted in lowland Africa because it
offered a survival advantage by protecting people against mosquito
borne malaria. Any connection between dyslexia and achievement is
more of an analogy than a straight comparison to the puzzle-perfect fit
of disease vector and host. Still, Stein suggests that "great artistic, inven-
tive, political and entrepreneurial talent may be commoner among
dyslexics than might be expected. . . . Certainly there are a great number of very famous, rich and successful people who were probably
dyslexic, such as Hans Christian Andersen, Churchill, Edison, Einstein,
Faraday, Rodin, Leonardo da Vinci to name but a few."[33]

Not everyone would agree that this cast of stars fits the dyslexia
profile. Retroactive diagnosis is always a flawed exercise. But even if
I'm skeptical about the particulars (it's hard to imagine Winston
Churchill struggling to read, or to find the right words), we've seen how
males dominate the two extreme ends of the ability spectrum. The
question is whether some males are more likely to exhibit the two
extremes at once: a disability in one area and a gift in another. Many
inventors—who usually have outstanding visual-spatial problem-
solving skills—have reported that their reading and writing skills were
compromised, and so experienced some failure at school, and Thomas
Sowell, who studied late-talking children, discovered that 72 percent
were unusually good at solving puzzles. So it seems plausible, although
the "gift" doesn't apply to just any arena. When the psychologists Ellen
Winner and Catya von Karolyi investigated whether dyslexia and
visual-spatial talents are connected, they discovered that dyslexics were
much faster and better at figuring out if complex Escher-like figures
could actually exist. They seemed to have an unusual knack for imagining how these figures would be configured in real space.[34] This might
explain Daniel Paley's intuition that he has a sixth sense for "top-
down" or bird's-eye view spatial problem solving. A suite of genes that

predisposes a person to have trouble with reading might also enhance the ability to "get" the big picture, or to see exactly what makes visual sense. The genetic or neurodevelopmental factors that cause a reading disability might also endow someone with these nonverbal gifts, according to Jeffrey Gilger, a neuroscientist at Purdue.[35]

These neurological trade-offs might explain why men like Andrew and Daniel are jinxed in the classroom but can find success at work. The most cited example of a superachiever who struck out in the classroom is Albert Einstein, notorious for being late to talk and at best, a mediocre student. There's always a danger that someone of his stature will be co-opted by an interest group anxious to identify with its adoptive mascot's promise. But in Einstein's case it's not implausible that a man whose editors and translators commented on his frequent misspellings of proper names,[36] who found memorization painful and taking tests like "walking to the guillotine,"[37] might have struggled with the rote aspects of spelling and writing—both signposts of dyslexia.

Marlin Thomas, a learning disabilities expert who pooh-poohed the idea of Einstein having learning problems, described Einstein's thinking as freely associated visual images that he struggled to communicate, as if in a tip-of-the-tongue state.[38] And Einstein described his own thoughts as images of a "visual and muscular type" in which "words do not seem to play any role."[39] We'll never know what came first, a lack of motivation in school, or a biologically based language problem that derailed Einstein in the rigid, rote-driven German educational system. "I preferred to endure all sorts of punishments rather than learn gabble by rote," was his version of events.[40] We do know that Einstein attended only the classes that interested him, and on graduating from high school failed the entrance exams to a technology institute in Zurich.[41] Ultimately, his outsized capacity for visual-spatial imagery and mathematical problem solving overshadowed any trivial gaps in spelling, speed-reading, or sociability. "I am a horse for single harness, not cut out for tandem or teamwork. I have never belonged wholeheartedly to any country or state, to my circle of friends or even to my own family. These ties have always been accompanied by a vague aloofness," he wrote, adding single-mindedness to his mix of male traits.[42]

A final aside about Einstein. Forty-four years after his death in

1955, Einstein's brain landed in Sandra Witelson's lab at McMaster University. It had been weighed, perfused with formalin, cut into 240 equal blocks, and stored for decades in a jar in someone's basement. With a bank of 99 average brains—43 male and 56 female—that she could use as comparison, Professor Witelson was well placed to see how Einstein's brain sized up. She found that Einstein's brain weighed roughly the same as the others but was 15 percent wider and had unique features. The Sylvian fissure—a deep fold that separates the frontal and parietal lobes from the temporal lobes—was shorter and tilted upward, and there was an unusual pattern of grooves in the parietal lobes, the areas specialized for mathematical and spatial reasoning. Professor Witelson thought the grooves were signs of more neural connections in the parts of the brain responsible for visual and spatial thinking, and imagining movement through space. Could extra growth and denser connections in these regions have had an impact elsewhere? Perhaps expansion of the parietal lobes impinged on the parts of the temporal lobe specialized for language (a shift of neural tissue from the temporal to the parietal areas has been thought to explain some cerebral abnormalities in dyslexics).[43] In Einstein's case, this is still conjecture. For now all we know is that the "size of a specific gyral region in the frontal operculum lobe was different in Einstein's brain from that of the control group." This anomaly may be related to biographical accounts of Einstein's atypical speech development, according to Dr. Witelson in her 1999 report on Einstein's brain.[44] It's an intriguing idea that gaps in one area can be counterbalanced by gifts in another, but for Einstein, anyway, the evidence is not yet in.

Dyslexic Girls

What about girls with reading disabilities? The research comparing dyslexic boys with girls often comes up empty because there are simply not enough girls to make strong statements.[45] But the comparatively fewer dyslexic girls who came to my office seemed very different from the boys. Not at all quiet and self-effacing as per the stereotype, they were talkative and articulate. One seven-year-old is "spritely, wide-eyed, and dramatic" in my case notes, and although her reading skills are clearly compromised, I write that "her disability is almost masked by her excellent expressive language skills." A six-year-old girl, Rebecca, is confident and outgoing, describing herself and her mood in ways that are rare among the boys. "I feel happy today, and I think I'll be good at that because I'm so good at drama!" she declares. Rebecca found it difficult to write, draw, or do any schoolwork for long.[46] Yet she was a master of engaging, socially appropriate chatter, never complaining or directly refusing any request. When I asked her to write a few sentences, she jumped up, feigning surprise. "What time is it? I think it's time for my mom to pick me up!" Perhaps it wasn't her mother knocking at the door, I suggested, but that she didn't feel like writing just then. As if disappointed for me, she looked at me apologetically and said, "Not today, but maybe another day." It wasn't the first time I'd encountered a girl with a learning problem who was aware of her own weaknesses and who seemed to want to protect herself and an adult's feelings at the same time.

This sensitivity to one's own and others' emotional states has been shown to be stronger in girls than in boys at every age and stage, an effect that is so pervasive in different environments that I have devoted an entire chapter to it. But when I caught up with these girls years later, I was still surprised to find them all in human relations jobs: as day-care educators, counselors, or as advocates for the learning-disabled. Of seven dyslexic women I've been able to track down, six had university degrees in education, psychology, or social work. Four of them worked in day-care centers. The ability to empathize and communicate with others sparked their careers. After having been invited to a lecture by the Ambassadors, an advocacy group of learning-disabled adults who gave public talks about how they succeeded, I discovered that all were female. Dyslexia might be an overwhelmingly male disorder, but when it came to educating and sharing the existential experience of a learning disability, it was women who stepped forward.

Though they outnumbered the women by at least six to one, not one of the dyslexic men I came to know as adults opted for careers in teaching; nor were any in the "helping" professions such as psychology, social work, early childhood education, or counseling. All had chosen work that created a product—food, films, investment funds, franchises—and were less focused on interactions between people as ends in themselves. I was looking for success stories, so this wasn't a random sample. But there isn't much research on the careers of successful people with dyslexia, and what there is wouldn't capture those diagnosed in adulthood—people such as Charles Schwab, of the eponymous discount stock brokerage firm. He recognized why he had always struggled with reading when his own son was diagnosed with dyslexia in 1988. Having excelled at math and sports, Schwab credits his golf game with getting him into Stanford. "The nasty little secret was that I couldn't read worth a darn," he said. "I still read very slowly to this moment." Like those profiled earlier in this chapter, Schwab felt he had a compensating gift. "Along the way, I've frustrated some of my associates because I could see the end zone of a particular thing quicker than they could, so I was moving ahead to conclusions," he told a *New York Times* reporter. "I go straight from step A to Z."[47] Other dyslexic men I tracked down as adults were also highly focused on end zones. One spent his time buying failing commercial franchises, rejuvenating them, then selling them at a profit, and was doing well despite never having completed university. Another had gone to university in England and worked as the head of his own landscape design firm, which he ran with the help of technology: voice-activated writing programs, Kurzweil software to read digitalized print aloud, a GPS system to use instead of maps, and mnemonic devices he invented to circumvent his language and memory problems. The British education system had been crucial to his success, he said. "The North American school system is so driven by the work ethic. They think that if you just do more of something, you'll get it. You don't. You just get tired. But in the United Kingdom they were much more proactive. My professors would say, 'You know you have a learning disability. Why don't you dictate your paper into a tape recorder?' But ultimately, the big difference between school and work is that at work, they don't care how you get there."

Dyslexia and Dollars

Where "there" is turns out to be a big piece of the puzzle. The men and women profiled in this chapter pursued goals consistent with their developmental profiles, and were remarkably faithful to the research that is surfacing about gender differences in dyslexic adults. The dyslexic men chose careers that took a wide detour around reading and writing. They focused instead on creating a product. The dyslexic women were far fewer in number, stayed in school longer, earned more academic and fewer vocational degrees than did the dyslexic men, and were much more likely to choose work that involved people, specifically education, psychology, social work, and counseling. They also were more likely to work part-time.[48] The career choices of dyslexic men and women thus seem to be a microcosm of the occupational choices made by the rest of us. With cognitive profiles that mimic *average* sex differences, these men, whose visual and spatial skills are vastly superior to their language skills, made choices that highlight the average tendencies of their sex. Of course, an individual is just that, and his or her choices could easily diverge from the group average. But the individual narratives and the numbers ultimately told the same story: qualitative sex differences in school performance and ultimately in career choices.

There's nothing standard about men who are more likely than women to struggle with reading. They're certainly no better or no smarter than women. The choice of things-versus-people-oriented jobs reflects their grid of strengths and weaknesses and is not a value judgment about the more worthwhile career. Still, given the same level of education, it's not hard to imagine which pays more: computer engineer or elementary school teacher; chef versus day-care worker; franchise owner or social worker. Like many women in the general population, the dyslexic women choose careers in which the experience—of interacting, teaching, advising—is an end in itself. Ultimately earning 20 percent less than men do, they also choose jobs that offer the chance of combining a career with family life. In making these decisions the women seem to be giving less weight to the market value of their choices and more to other factors, like flexibility, job satisfaction, or fun.[49]

This is exactly what three economists found when they looked at 562 college graduates in a careful cross section of American society. Women overwhelmingly chose education and liberal arts degrees, even though these choices meant that they would earn less than they would in science or business.[50] A university arts background should make you literate, and you'd think that the more literate you are, the more money you'd earn. But no. Even though girls and women—especially minority women—have higher academic ambitions, consistently do better in school, and go to university in higher numbers, as adults they choose work that often means their pockets are emptier.[51] While unfair wage disparities for the same work still exist in some places, this wage gap is about something completely different. Women who choose fields and jobs that pay less are skewing the numbers themselves, as if saying, "This is the work I want to do. This is the schedule I need. And it's worth earning a little less to get it."

Now, why on earth would they do that?

CHAPTER 3

Abandon Ship!

Successful Women Who Opt Out of Science and Engineering Careers

At the beginning of 2005, the choices of educated women became the focus of intense public scrutiny. Along with the war in Iraq, the prosecution of U.S. soldiers involved in the scandal of Abu Ghraib, the melting polar ice cap, and the mounting death toll from AIDS in Africa, the number of women in elite academic science was suddenly front-page news. A quick glance at the headlines suggested that Harvard president Larry Summers was the catalyst. He had offered some ideas about why there might be fewer women than men in high-flying academic science, math, and engineering careers. Could one reason be innate sex differences at the very extremes of performance? Or was discrimination still keeping women out? While I followed a debate that turned into a brawl, I thought about the high-achieving women in science I'd met over the years. They hardly seemed deficient at math, or in any academic area, for that matter. In fact, they seemed to have an array of options due to their native talents and their educational opportunities. Had they drifted into medicine, psychology, and teaching as consolation prizes after having been discouraged from pursuing physics or engineering careers? The answer, as it turned out, could be seen from my front porch.

* * *

When I looked out on my gentrified street, barely two blocks from the city's largest commercial thoroughfare, I saw a fairly standard urban landscape. The mailman trampled our modest flower beds as a short-cut to the sidewalk. A parade of strollers went by, pushed by babysitters from Asia and the Caribbean. There was the occasional dog walker suspended at the end of five leashes, as if holding a bouquet of horizontal balloons. Dollar stores, pawnshops, and halfway houses still lined the main streets, but this former working-class area had turned into a trendy neighborhood with handsome, aging row houses that usually took two salaries to support. Most of its residents were out of sight during the day. The only neighbors I was likely to run into on a mid-day run to the bank were the retired and the unemployed.

But in 2000, after fifteen years in this neighborhood, I noticed a new phenomenon. A growing number of well-educated, established professional women were visibly not at work. My chic, well-dressed neighbor who used to work full-time in an industrial megacomplex in the south end of the city is about to take her dog for a walk on the mountain at 10:30 A.M. on a Wednesday. She waves to me and smiles behind her sunglasses as she loads her Wheaton terrier into the hatch of her station wagon. Across the street I spot an acquaintance, usually at her full-time academic job at a university, leaving on a power walk plugged into her iPod. She swings her arms jauntily, her workout suit an ode to perfection. Behind her a housekeeper in an apron sweeps hundreds of maple seeds off her stairs and into orbit again. Meanwhile, my tennis-playing neighbor, a lawyer who lives a few doors down, has fired up her lawn mower and is pacing up and down behind it on her tiny patch of turf, turning it into tidy green corduroy. Unlike me and the rest of my female neighbors, she hasn't worked at a paying job for years. She's a stay-at-home mother.

But neither I nor the other women who have made a cameo on the street during the workday identify ourselves as homemakers per se. I've taken a leave from my job as a clinical psychologist and university lecturer to write articles and books, clinging to a working identity while I face down an infinite number of domestic interruptions. But what are these other women doing at home during the day? They have established science and academic jobs that come with all the trimmings: tenure, good salaries and benefits, even good child care. None of them has babies anymore. Some never had children. What are they doing here?

Established, and lucky enough to have choices, many of these women are making a mid-career shift. They don't see themselves as unemployed exactly, just stepping off the treadmill—often a brutally demanding one—to take stock. These are the "opt-out" women profiled by *New York Times* journalist Lisa Belkin in 2003: all ambitious, high-achieving women with advanced university degrees. They left their high-powered jobs after having discovered that they had differing notions of success than what was expected—indeed, different from what they had expected of themselves when they started out. "I don't want to be on the fast track leading to a partnership at a prestigious law firm" said one woman, who had decided to leave law to stay home with her three children. "I don't want to be famous; I don't want to conquer the world. I don't want that kind of life," said another. Belkin surmised that these women were rejecting their high-powered workplaces and not the other way around. The article provoked outrage. In the blogosphere, many female commentators ridiculed this population as either fictional, fantastically out of touch with reality, or just a few women whose views are irrelevant. Joan Walsh, writing in *Salon* the next day, proposed that "Belkin's piece is a real-time snapshot of a small cohort of privileged 30-something white women who are likely to think something entirely different in 10 years. Next Story."

But the exodus was real, and has shown itself to be real, not only in my neighborhood but in every major university, law, engineering, and accounting firm in North America and Europe. Though strong at the starting gates, many women are defecting as they advance—and it isn't only a small cohort of privileged thirty-something white moms, but women from various backgrounds and varying ages. Women are 2.8 times more likely than men to leave science and engineering careers for other occupations and 13 times more likely to exit the labor force entirely—even when marriage and small children are not relevant. And they leave these careers at every age and stage of life, whether or not they have families.[1]

I was particularly curious about the fate of women in academic science, technology, and engineering, where they have been dramatically outnumbered by men from the outset and continue to be decades after the doors were opened to them. These disciplines were male domains before feminism created opportunities for women in the seventies and are often seen as test cases for equality. Yet despite significant efforts to make engineering and computer science departments more hospitable, and even with affirmative action programs that target female students with special programs and scholarships, women's numbers have not reached a critical mass in these fields. Instead, women with a scientific bent often veer toward careers in ecology, biology, pharmacy, dentistry, psychology, or medicine. And many of the ones who embarked on physical science, technical, or engineering careers have been trickling away at a steady rate. These successful women who have invested years in their careers are ultimately opting for something else—sometimes full-time motherhood, but as we shall see, often not.

The women in this chapter have plenty of innate ability in science and math. They have already competed and excelled. The question is not whether they have the smarts or the preparation to succeed in science, but how they choose to apply their skills. As Ruth Simmons, president of Brown University and a member of the National Academy of Sciences panel asked when the panel released its 2006 diversity report, "Why aren't they electing these fields when the national need and the opportunities in the fields are so great?" Why, indeed. California economist Catherine Weinberger has shown that women with computer science or engineering degrees earn 30 to 50 percent more than the average female graduate.[2] If pay were the big motivator, you'd think the combination of opportunity and compensation would provide a double incentive for women to choose those fields and stick with them. Seeing gifted women who have left science careers as autonomous decision makers might erode a bit of the collective guilt about their absence.

Fugitives

I met Donna, the woman in the workout suit, at Starbucks a few years after she had left her tenured job in a university's computer science department.[3] She'd spent sixteen years as a professor and told me she decided to leave one day after falling asleep over a colleague's research paper. Snoozing through an academic's turgid prose is hardly breaking news, but it was an epiphany for Donna. That afternoon nap told her that her heart wasn't in her work. She was bored. University teaching had been her first full-time job and she was tired of it. "It was like marrying your high school sweetheart. I wasn't motivated anymore. I'm very much a service-oriented, down-to-earth person," she said, adding that she hoped to make a difference with real people in her next position, one where she would feel more involved with the outcome of her labors. Until this more service-oriented job surfaced, she was consulting on an ad hoc basis, exercising regularly, and getting more involved in her children's extracurricular activities.

From the outside it looked like she had had the perfect job: a tenured academic position with built-in flexibility and a month-long summer holiday, not to mention the respect of her peers, no small thing in her educated social circle. She was good at her work and said she had encountered no institutional discrimination. There were no childcare issues; her children were in school, and she had some domestic help. But despite publishing enough research to earn tenure and to comfortably sustain her position, Donna had started to doubt the value of her field and to lose interest in it. "I didn't thrive on it anymore. Besides, 90 percent of research in my field is . . ." At this she waved her hand in front of her face, as if batting away a fly.

Not only did she feel disconnected from the subject, she also felt martyred by her work. As the only woman in her department, she found that she was the one students came to for support, and was always the first picked for committees looking for gender balance. "You tend to be motherly," she said with resignation. "'Oh, you have no supervisor? I'll take you.' The men would just say, 'I'm not interested.' And then you get stuck with students nobody wanted. It was my own failing. I'd take them under my wing."

The Mentoring Trap

Several months later I came upon a paper on mentoring by an economist known for having demonstrated a link between beauty and financial success. This factoid got the avuncular Daniel Hamermesh, from the University of Texas at Austin, mentioned by Jay Leno on the

Tonight Show. But what really caught my eye was an essay Hamermesh had posted on his website: "An Old Male Economist's Advice to Young Female Economists." In it he advises women, who are likely to be one of very few female professors in their departments, not to be flattered by requests to serve on committees, not to choose "women's topics" like gender discrimination, and to avoid nurturing students, activities that they'll likely be drawn to, but which will give them few points at tenure time.[4]

"Until recently young female faculty members occupied the two offices next to mine. The constant stream of students during their office hours was striking, as was their willingness to talk with students for long periods outside regular office hours. Students don't view old guys as mother figures—even teaching huge classes, my office hours are only crowded before exams. Many students apparently believe that you are there to nurture them, but you are not their mother. Seeing them outside of a restricted set of office hours, devoting excessive amounts of time to substantive questions by one or a few students, and dealing with their personal problems all do a disservice to other students and to yourself."[5]

His advice confirmed Donna's experience that too much mentoring can add to one's woes as a mid-career female academic. But it contradicted what some women found most rewarding about teaching, as I learned at a dinner party a few weeks later. A female academic seated next to me described the heavy burden she was carrying at the end of term. She was preoccupied with counseling her students through exam jitters, financial and housing crises, all during end-of-year marking. The student-generated demands influenced her decision not to go on an early summer trip to Europe with her husband, she said, and he was planning to go ahead without her. When I questioned whether she thought her male colleagues wrapped their students in such an all-encompassing embrace, she agreed her approach was uncommon except among her female and gay colleagues. "But support and being available is what education is all about," she said, leveling her green eyes at me over the appetizers.

Female faculty becoming de facto den mothers to needy students is especially common in traditionally male disciplines such as math, technology, physics, and engineering, where there is a dearth of welcome mats for lost souls of both sexes. That makes it harder for women to resist helping students in distress. But two other factors create conflict for women who want to guard their time but who are also pioneers who want to be accepted in their fields. The first is the expectation that every committee will have at least one woman on it—which means that in some sciences, women do more committee work than men and thus have less time to do their own research. Such well-intentioned policies are intended to give women a voice, but paradoxically may be eroding their most precious resource: time.

The second conflict is the pressure to mentor. Much has been made of the paucity of mentors for women entering fields like math, physics, and technology, where a lack of female role models is almost unanimously declaimed as a deterrent to women entering these disciplines.[6] It seems plausible. If women don't see other women doing a job, they might think they can't do it, either. But commonsense ideas do not always hold up to careful scrutiny. A lack of female role models hasn't stopped women from flooding law, medicine, pharmacy, veterinary, and biology departments—all previously male-dominated disciplines that now draw an equal or greater complement of female students. And there's not much evidence that women have more difficulty than men making professional contacts. Research by the Wisconsin business professor and mentoring expert Belle Rose Ragins shows that women expect that there will be a bias against them. But in a study of 510 employees and managers, women are as likely to be mentored as men.[7] Nor is there any evidence that having a female mentor or teacher is what persuades women to choose science or math careers and to stick with them.[8] In fact, sometimes the reverse is true. Ronald Burke and Carol McKeen asked 280 female graduates early in their careers about their relationships with mentors of both sexes and found few differences. One important one was that women with female mentors felt more supported, yet also had more powerful feelings about wanting to quit.[9] Maybe the female mentors had been candid about their dissatisfaction with their careers. In Donna's case, the expectation that she would mentor students at a time when she was doubting her own career choice could have sounded the death knell for both mentor and protégé.

Successful academic women who have given all to their careers and have no lives outside of work may actually turn off their protégés by their example. Students may surmise that if this is what it takes, they don't want it. Many of the female academics I knew when I was training in the late seventies and early eighties were childless, embittered, or both. One prospective female Ph.D. supervisor grilled me about my husband's occupation and whether I was planning to have children. ("Yes" was the wrong answer.)[10] As Virginia Valian notes in *Why So Slow,* the super-achieving woman preoccupied with a tightly calibrated balancing act hardly makes academic life look attainable to mere mortals. "The notion that a successful woman can serve as a role model for others is a hoax, the outcome of which is to make many women feel inferior because they are unable to follow the model" (or unable to *be* that model, she might have added). Concrete suggestions about how to do your best work are more useful than role models, Valian writes.[11] Such pointers can come from teachers of either sex.

In Donna's case, she had been the only female faculty member in her department. Then she was gone. Those who count heads would now have one less female faculty member in science and technology, and some might infer discrimination. But Donna defected because she ultimately felt mismatched with the abstract, detached nature of her work, not because she felt mistreated. After a few years of hiatus she had found a new full-time position teaching computer applications to faculty members at a different university. Her job was to consult with researchers to help them apply the latest in computer technology to their research projects. There was no obligation to do her own research. Instead, she was interacting daily with a group of colleagues, evaluating their needs, and deploying her technology expertise.

The Power of Intrinsic Goals

Donna decided to opt for what was meaningful for her over status and money. But is this true for women in general? To begin with, intrinsic goals such as making a difference, or belonging to a community, are often *in direct opposition* to extrinsic goals like seeking financial rewards or status. Social scientist Frederick Grouzet led a cast of 10 international scientists when surveying the motivations of 1,854 students from 15 countries and different disciplines in 2006. The team found that this dichotomy was meaningful in all 15 cultures. Intrinsic and extrinsic goals often conflicted—it was unlikely that people would pursue both at once.[12] Meanwhile, several other studies have shown that women, on average, are more motivated by intrinsic rewards at work. An interest and an ability to contribute to a field, and a capacity to have an impact in the real world are more powerful drivers for women, on average, than higher salaries, job security, and benefits.[13] So women who realize they are falling asleep at their desks are more likely to scout around for a new job than to hunker down and keep their eyes on the external carrots—tenure, the corner office, the chief administrative post.

At least three large studies spanning the last three decades have demonstrated that intrinsic benefits outweigh more concrete perks for women. The most recent, the 500 Family Study published in 2005, painted a nuanced picture of modern working life at different income and education levels.[14] Through in-depth interviews, observations, time diaries, and surveys, the researchers documented nearly every intake of breath from parents and children in more than five hundred dual-career American families. It was one of the most ambitious investigations of family life ever attempted. One of their findings was that the sway of intrinsic rewards and autonomy on the job rises with a woman's level of education; women with graduate training like Donna were more likely to seek jobs that offered them a challenge. These highly educated women were also more interested in working part-time, thus fueling the opt-out phenomenon in two ways—through their search for inherent meaning at work, and via the amount of time they were willing to commit to their jobs. Both conflict with making lots of money and rising through the ranks.

Strange but True

Bearing down on whatever cross-cultural data on occupations I could find, I discovered an interesting divide. The more financial stability and legal protections offered to women, the less likely they are to choose the standard male route. If women were versions of men, you would expect exactly the opposite to be true—that with greater freedoms they would opt for men's hours and occupations in greater numbers. But when we look at what work women choose in the countries that offer them the widest array of options—Canada, the United Kingdom, Germany, Switzerland, Norway, the United States, and Japan—we find the highest rates of gender disparity.[15] The richer the country, the more likely women and men choose different types of jobs. This surprising finding applies to the fields women choose most often, and to the number of hours they choose to work. And it parallels the conflict between intrinsic and extrinsic motivations unearthed by Frederick Grouzet and his team. Suppose you had a secret benefactor who allowed you to choose the work you *really* wanted to do. Would you do what you are doing right now and put in the same hours? Would you do what puts the most food on the table? The conflict between intrinsic and extrinsic goals reflects familiar terrain: the trade-off between pursuing the biggest paycheck versus following one's star. I suspect that the freedoms offered to women in Western, industrialized countries—all countries with equal-opportunity legislation—allow them to move closer to their ideal of pursuing intrinsic rewards, perhaps at the cost of pursuing the most money and status.[16]

Early on, I referred to Catherine Weinberger's finding that women in engineering and computer science earn an average of 30 to 50 percent more than women who choose other disciplines. When extrinsic rewards are paramount, might women be more likely to choose these fields? If we look at the ratio of women taking physics, a foundation course for engineering, we can see that more women from countries with developing economies take physics as their university major. A report released by the American Institute of Physics in 2005 shows that women all over the world are far less likely than men to study physics, but that there is an economic divide. Approximately 5 percent of women choose physics as a career in Japan, Canada, or Germany, for example, but in the Philippines, Russia, and Thailand, the number of women in physics is relatively high, ranging from 30 to 35 percent.[17] Of twenty-one countries polled, those with the highest proportion of women earning physics degrees—Poland and Turkey, at 36 and 37 percent, respectively—also have the highest rates of immigration to other European Union countries and offer little fiscal support for women and families. For the most part, these are countries where both sexes are under intense financial pressures, often work at unskilled jobs, earn little, and when given half a chance immigrate to send money back to their families.[18]

Where do these immigrants go? Most often to countries like the Netherlands, Germany, and the United Kingdom (which happen to have fewer women in physics: 5, 10, and 20 percent, respectively). A sobering account of a highly educated female engineer from Bulgaria who could not find a job in her country ran in a personnel journal in 2004: "Daniela Simidchieva, a mother of three, has an IQ of almost 200, backed up with five Master's degrees. Moreover, she is recognized by the country's Mensa office as the world's cleverest woman. Daniela is qualified as an industrial engineer, an English teacher and an electrical engineer, and yet she can't get a job that commands a salary of anything more than $200 a month."[19]

The contrast between Ms. Simidchieva's situation and the elevated status of female engineers in North America reveals the cultural valence of the degree. But this doesn't tell us that women who have a panoply of occupational choices don't elect physics and engineering. There are plenty of gifted women in Western democracies who choose these disciplines and excel. It only tells us that a 50–50 gender split in these fields does not exist anywhere, and that on average, richer economies are more likely to show a bigger gap between the disciplines women and men choose. The vanilla gender assumption—that women will automatically opt for men's choices if they had their druthers—does not fit this tableau. In contrast, it is not unusual to find female engineers and computer scientists from the Philippines, China, or the former Soviet republics working as nannies, manicurists, or in entry-level jobs in Europe or North America.[20] (It would be interesting to know whether educated women from these countries have carte blanche to study what they like. Several female engineers I interviewed from Russia and China told me that their fields of study had been determined by the state, their educational institutions, or by their families.)[21] Meanwhile, in countries with the most educational options and social benefits, such as Sweden, Finland, and Germany, women opt less often for the same choices as men; thus workplace segregation becomes more exaggerated.

Policies that guarantee equal opportunity, one of the basic tenets of a democracy, do not guarantee an equal result. If they did, then progressive countries with more family-friendly policies and more opportunities for women, like Sweden and Norway, would have *less* occupational segregation than those found in still-developing countries, such as Swaziland and Sri Lanka. Instead it's the reverse: the more choice people have, the more we see sex differences in the workforce. So if women from the wealthiest countries choose different disciplines, on average, than men, does discrimination tell the whole story? It tells part of it. But there are other pieces of the puzzle, too.

When it came to circumstances, Sonia was one of the lucky ones. She'd had the opportunity to earn a Ph.D. in anything that interested her. But twelve years after her doctorate in geography she decided she didn't want to work at a university anymore. Actually, she had realized at the end of her doctoral studies that "I wasn't made for the grant-proposal writing, the competitiveness, the high pressure," but resisted saying so to her adviser, who saw her potential and was pushing her to keep going. So she completed her Ph.D. "because I was good at it," and together with her husband landed in a city with a high-profile university where she ultimately got an academic job. She was a persuasive university teacher but her heart wasn't in it. She didn't feel like competing for tenure. "Teaching adult students and managing a full academic course load and research was definitely not for me. It was too much of a high-pressure life. I wanted a life that was fairly simple," she said. So Sonia pursued a full-time position as an academic administrator, writing grants and annual reports. Yet she soon found that high-level administrative work was not the answer, either. She was forty, married with two school-age children, and had a Ph.D. in science and a new boss who was making everyone's life miserable. He was an equal-opportunity criticizer, but as she already had doubts, his bullying made her feel particularly vulnerable.

So she jumped, deciding to take a year off, a period she describes as "dancing on the head of a pin." Although many working women view a year off to ponder their vocation as a trip to Shangri-La, Sonia described it as one of the worst years of her life. Suddenly a high-powered, high-strung, high-achieving woman had no deadlines and no assignments, and wasn't expected to show up anywhere at 9 A.M. To pass the time, she volunteered in a special-education class at her children's school, and it was there that she found her vocation. Finally, she felt she was making a difference. She returned to the university where she had worked as a Ph.D.-level science professor and administrator to pursue a B.A. in education. While I was writing this book she had made the transition to elementary science specialist. Her career as a Ph.D.-trained scientist felt like a distant, other life, one where she earned more and had higher status, but that ultimately satisfied others' aspirations more than her own.

I wondered why it took twenty years for Sonia to decide that academic science was not for her. She pursued seven years of graduate education in science and then twelve years of university employment, all while doubting her interest in it. What she and Donna expressed was how difficult it is to switch directions when everyone thinks you're they're darling. Having invested so much and with parents' and teachers' hopes driving you forward, it often takes a burnout to realize your work is someone else's idea of fun. At the outset of their careers, many of these high achievers fall in step with others' expectations of them. This turns the feminist chestnut of women living out society's prescribed gender roles upside down. Instead of women being enslaved by patriarchal views of their proper domestic roles, they are now constricted by expectations of what kind of paid work is considered valuable (what stays the same, it seems, is an eagerness to please). So even if they're more interested in the humanities than they are in math and science, they dutifully follow the latter path so as not to disappoint others, as described in the following e-mail from an Ivy League law professor. The subject line read "Arm Twisting."

I graduated with a bachelor of science in molecular biophysics and biochemistry from Yale (summa cum laude) having been encouraged quite aggressively to pursue science from an early stage. This encouragement was all very positive and well-meaning, and it built on my genuine interests at the time, but the effect was that I continued far longer than I should have. Indeed, I went to Harvard Medical School in the Health Sciences and Technology program with MIT, received a research fellowship, which earned me an honors M.D. at Harvard and included time and support for more research, before I finally worked up the courage to pursue another avenue more suitable to my interests—and talents. My college roommate, a physics major with a 1600 SAT, went to graduate school in physics before dropping out and becoming a very successful architect. Yet another roommate who was a math major with an 800 math SAT score eventually went to law school. We were all very "good" girls who were eager to please everyone—except ourselves, of course. But we finally went our own way. I credit my husband in part, who said "To hell with it, do what you want." All of this is why I am very skeptical of the notion that society discourages talented women from becoming scientists. My experience, at least from the educational phase of my life, is that the very opposite is true, especially for truly talented women in the elite circles from which top scientists are drawn. Even at Yale in the early 1970s, and at Harvard Medical School and its labs in the early 1980s, I received nothing but encouragement, help, financial assistance, and praise, where praise was due. But it was, in the end, not really what I wanted to do. It may well be that there is discouragement lurking down the road—in old boys' networking or lack of flexibility for family life and the like. But those were really not the factors that were determinative for me or the women I knew.[22]

People, Words, and Ideas, Not the Decimal Places of Pi

Donna, Sonia, and my e-mail correspondent are all women who excelled at math and science but prefer work that is more service-oriented, broader in scope, and less obsessive than academic science. Where might these preferences come from? On average, women have more expansive interests, better social and communication skills than men, and are better at guessing the impact of their words and behavior on others—a portrait of women that most cognitive scientists and "difference" feminists share.[23] The mountain of evidence for a female advantage in empathy is the subject of the next chapter, whereas I touched on sex differences in verbal skills in the previous two. So we've been introduced to the idea that there's a neurological basis for an early female boost to vocabulary, verbal memory, and verbal fluency. Girls and women get this head start in interpersonal and communication skills early in life, skills they hone through play as they develop into adults, and in social contacts thereafter. One of a multitude of studies showing stronger female language abilities examined the language development of 3,000 fraternal twins comprised of one boy and one girl (they shared the same prenatal environment, roughly half their genes, and the same parents). Robert Plomin, a researcher at the Institute of Psychiatry in London, has shown that as early as age two, the girls begin to outpace the boys in vocabulary. Girls, raised in the same prenatal and postnatal environments, showed more impressive communication skills than their twin brothers from their earliest months, an advantage likely due to biological sex differences.[24]

This advantage in verbal skills and empathy might make women's career choices more eclectic. In a twenty-year follow-up study of almost 1,975 mathematically gifted adolescents, psychology researcher Camilla Persson Benbow and her colleagues at Vanderbilt University in Nashville found that the majority of the men had gone into engineering, math, and computer science, whereas most of the women had chosen medicine and other health professions.[25] The women were broader in their career choices, incorporating their science knowledge with a whole-person or community perspective. Whether they had children or not, they worked fewer hours. In a subsequent study, Persson Benbow's husband, David Lubinski, looked at this sample again and found that these women, who are brilliant at math, also have superb verbal abilities. Like my "arm-twisted" e-mail correspondent, they might just as easily have been drawn to studying English, law, or philosophy as to math and science. In contrast, there was a much bigger gap between gifted men's math abilities and their more depressed verbal skills. The gifted men's career choices were narrower.[26] This dichotomy between a steep expertise in one area, such as numbers, versus broad, more balanced gifts in math and language came to mind when I read a profile of Terence Tao, a thirty-one-year-old professor of mathematics at UCLA, who has already won a Fields Medal in mathematics as well as a MacArthur "genius" award. Professor Tao's early years were described this way by Kenneth Chang in *The New York Times*:

At age 5, he was enrolled in a public school, and his parents, administrators and teachers set up an individualized program for him. He proceeded through each subject at his own pace, quickly accelerating through several grades in math and science while remaining closer to his age group in other subjects. In English classes, for instance, he became flustered when he had to write essays. "I never really got the hang of that," he said. "These very vague, undefined questions. I always liked situations where there were very clear rules of what to do." Assigned to write a story about what was going on at home, Terry went from room to room and made detailed lists of the contents.[27]

Professor Tao started to attend math classes at a local high school when he was seven, but it seems doubtful from this account that he could have mastered advanced English at that age. Benbow and Lubinski's findings of gifted women's broader skills tell us that women with innate talent in math and science might be more likely to have verbal skills developing in tandem, and thus have a range of career options and interests. To strike a familiar chord, even gifted women at the highest level of achievement are not clones of gifted men. Their skills look different. Insisting on a 50–50 gender split in all fields could pressure talented women to take jobs they don't want, or talented men to work in areas where they have little aptitude. And what would happen in fields where women are now in the lead? Should there be an effort to reverse the trend? Women outnumber men in some sciences, earning 61 percent of undergraduate degrees in biology and a whopping 86 percent in the health professions, including medicine.[28]

That most students entering medicine are now female is often seen as a good-news, bad-news scenario. The good news is that female physicians are more likely to be patient-centered, to offer more psychological support, and to work in the community helping the poor and disenfranchised.[29] The bad news, according to many, is that most women work fewer hours than men and take time off for children—and when there are more female doctors there are fewer service hours offered to the public. (Only when men are considered the "normal" default setting could it be considered a bad thing to take time from the market economy to have children.) However, unlike female doctors who are attracted to the profession due to its intellectual challenges, its flexibility, and its humanitarian purpose, many high-achieving, science-oriented women in academic life find themselves assisting students in a context that doesn't put a premium on helping. But what would happen if these highly trained women could put their science knowledge to use in a different context?

Margaret Eisenhart, a professor of education at the University of Colorado, and Elizabeth Finkel, formerly a professor at the University of Michigan but now a high school teacher in Maine, tried to answer this question.[30] They looked at the gender gap in traditional academic science and engineering, where the proportion of women at all levels hovers between 15 and 20 percent. They then compared those traditional disciplines to four more practical science settings— a team-taught genetics course, an applied engineering internship, a conservation organization, and an environmental action group. All four had a 50–50 ratio of men to women, and Eisenhart and Finkel wanted to know why.

Eisenhart and Finkel discovered that in these applied settings women were not only better represented but also felt more satisfied with their science careers. The jobs were more hands-on and offered women the chance to feel that they were making a difference. Yet these positions also offered less pay and status than science jobs in universities or in industry. Those who worked there had the benefit of more flexible schedules, compared to the greedy demands of elite science. But that didn't mean that these women had cushy work schedules or knew less science. Many of the women put in long hours for paltry pay because they felt appreciated and involved with their work, devoted to their colleagues and a cause. It was another good-news, bad-news scenario. The good news: there are areas in science where smart, high-achieving women feel involved enough with the human or moral aspect of science to stay. The bad news: most of these were publicly funded projects with an uncertain life span that offered less pay and less power than traditional academic science. But many high-achieving women were ready to make such trade-offs if they believed they were making a difference to other people and to a project greater than themselves.

The Pressures of Academic Life

There was no lack of commitment among these female scientists, but the hours and flexibility mattered. Yet when Larry Summers mentioned eighty hours a week as the standard for success in elite academic science, this, too, was hotly disputed by academic women who asserted that they are as eager to be consumed by their work as men are. What is undisputed is that academic women face extraordinary pressures. "If you're not seen around at weekends and holidays you're seen as lazy," said a female professor in a British university. Building a portfolio and being vetted for tenure usually overlap with the birth of children and the demanding years of early childhood. At that point you're either moved up or you're out, a rigid system less likely to attract and keep women. "It shows that so long as we continue to identify the ideal academic worker as someone who works full-time, sixty-hour weeks for forty years straight—surprise!—that will be overwhelmingly be men," said Joan C. Williams, the director of WorkLife Law at American University.[31] The assumption that most women want to conform to this rigid formula is a feature of the vanilla gender myth—that women are identical to men and will opt for what men have always done. But is a system that was designed for men really the right thing for women? Only if your starting point is the interchangeability of the sexes could you consider the standard tenure clock a good way to evaluate female academics. It's not that women can't compete, but that the tenure schedule presents obvious conflicts for women in their thirties—conflicts that might not have arisen if women had been sitting at the tenure drafting table about two hundred years ago. As they were not, and as a significant faction of women is anxious to prove that there are no sex differences, those who are not willing to forgo children or to put them off for a decade can find themselves offsided by the rigid timetable. Any enterprise benefits from workers who put in sixty-hour weeks. That many female academics with young families refuse and thus trickle away should not come as a shock.

One might expect that men married to female university professors would be more likely to have egalitarian views and share child care equally, but this is another myth. Steven Rhoads, a professor of public policy at the University of Virginia, had similar assumptions. He ran a nationwide study and found that 75 percent of female faculty believed their husbands should take on equal amounts of child care, housework, and paid work. Just over half of their husbands agreed. Yet the women spent much more time with their children than their husbands did, and in universities where they were offered paid parental leave, 67 percent of the eligible women took advantage of it. Only 12 percent of male faculty took that time off, and when they did, they didn't use the time the same way.[32] "We heard stories of male academics who took paid post-birth leave in order to advance their publishing agendas," wrote Rhoads, commenting that he'd heard of one school that changed its rules as a result. Upon returning from her maternity leave, one female colleague recalled being asked by a male colleague how the leave had gone. She replied, "I used the time well." Then the man said, "So you got a lot of work done." But that's not what she meant.

If most academic mothers use a leave to spend time with their baby and more new fathers use the time to publish, then a system based on men and women being identical ends up punishing women. When these family-friendly policies are applied equally to both sexes, academic women experience more discrimination, not less. One unofficial study at an Ivy League college found that parental leave benefits available to both sexes had that paradoxical effect: no woman who had taken a family leave in the previous fifteen years had subsequently received tenure. Most if not all of the small number of men who had taken family leave did. "This was never published or even tallied up as a real study, but it became commonly cited during the tenure discussion, summarized as 'a woman takes family leave and comes back with a backlog, a man takes family leave and comes back with a book,'" a junior professor at the college wrote to me.[33] Realizing what was happening, a committee at the college tweaked the policy to allow additional leave for those who give birth (obviously, fathers wouldn't be eligible). This helped reduce the unfair advantage of so-called equal parental benefits. But even if the college had resolved the problem in a creative way, no one wanted to discuss the issue openly, allow the college to be named, or be identified in any way. The topic was taboo. This "don't look at it, don't touch it" attitude to sex differences, parenting, and productivity suggests why half of the female professors in Rhoads' survey were considering leaving their tenure-track jobs compared to a quarter of the men.[34] If no one will talk about these conflicts—not even faculty who already have jobs for life—it's unlikely that a new mother or a female professor contemplating a family will broach the issue.

The Pushme-Pullyu Effect

Not only parental leave, but marriage itself has different effects on men and women in science. Being married with children "pushes" men toward science and engineering careers, according to sociologists Yu Xie, Kimberlee Shauman, and Anne Preston, who followed scientists' careers by studying swaths of census data that spanned several decades. But it had the opposite effect on women, pulling them away. It might contribute to their happiness, but marriage and children made women more likely to veer from science and engineering toward other types of work.[35]

Married scientists also have a 10 percent higher rate of productivity than single people. This couple advantage is especially true for men, who are more likely to be married than women in science.[36] Forming one of the working world's largest Miss Lonelyhearts clubs, North American academic women who are hired within a few years of getting their doctoral degrees are 50 percent less likely to be married than male academics and 61 percent more likely to be childless; female academics have the lowest fertility rates among all professional women. Only one in three women who takes a tenure-track university job before having a child becomes a mother. This is what Mary Ann Mason, a graduate studies dean and law professor at Berkeley, and her colleague Marc Goulden discovered when they looked at what happened to 30,000 Ph.D. graduates and surveyed 4,400 University of California faculty members in 2004.[37] Perhaps female scientists don't find the time for a significant commitment outside of work during their reproductive years. This was the case for the world's oldest first-time mother, sixty-six-year-old Romanian college professor Adriana Iliescu, who had a baby girl in 2005 after nine years of fertility treatment, including donor eggs and donor sperm. "I always worked so hard in my career I had no chance to build a relationship and start a family, and after I retired I regretted it bitterly. But I never gave up hope," she told newspaper reporters.[38]

Having to make choices while the biological clock is ticking is likely why women earn 61 percent of undergraduate science degrees but only 17 percent of doctoral degrees. The ones who do choose academic science leave science careers at twice the rate of men. According to questionnaires filled out by 1,688 defectors, their reasons for leaving are dramatically different from the reasons men give. Men primarily leave science because there is more money and opportunity elsewhere. As we saw earlier in this chapter, women's reasons for leaving are as existential as they are pragmatic: they discover that they'd prefer to do work they find more engaging. Others find the time demands of a science career are incompatible with family life.[39] If there's one common element, it's that most people who leave science—women and men—don't abandon these careers because they are forced out. Most leave because they have choices, choices that permit them to have time with children, if that's their priority, or to pursue other interests. Choices also allow people to pursue more highly paid jobs in the private sector, if that's what they want. More women choose the first option and more men opt for the second.

Engineering Their Exits

A French bakery with a few small tables was where I met with Anita, an industrial engineer in her forties who left the profession several years ago. After establishing her engineering career she had decided to retrain as a teacher. Ironically, she chose to work at a math and science charter school even though she had decided to abandon a successful math and science career for a more traditional female outlet. Being a mother had nothing to do with her decision, she said. The decision was about her purpose in life.

Short and compact, with smudged glasses and wearing a bandanna to contain her Afro, Anita has been a devoted, albeit scatterbrained teacher for fourteen years. The day I visited her classroom I was surprised by the lack of decoration at year's end and the absence of basic building maintenance in this popular school; the walls were cracked, the paint peeling off in palm-sized flakes, and although it was a warm day in June, the windows were jammed shut. A torn pink bedsheet was thumbtacked over some shelves with what remained of the year's school supplies. Several leggy avocado plants adorned the windowsill; two dusty desktop computers and a wall clock showing the wrong time were the only extras. The class was empty of everything but a few students trickling in after recess. The blackboard ledge had no chalk.

But as soon as Anita entered, the atmosphere became charged. When all her students were seated in groups of four at their desks, she commanded them to pull out materials to do a review of multiplication of large decimals. Her voice booming, she read out equations and as the children scribbled them down to solve them, she circulated, eyeing their work to see who had already lost the thread. One by one she checked each student's notebook, locking her gaze on theirs to assess their understanding. While she did this I wondered why Anita had chosen to build kids' confidence instead of ventilation systems and bridge trusses. She was frank. "When I started working in engineering I said to myself, I don't like this at all. So the electrical current goes from X to Y, from here to there. Who cares? I was unhappy and didn't want to continue. I made the decision to switch as much for me as for my family. Education corresponds better to who I am, it reflects my more human side. In engineering I never felt that human relations were valued. I wouldn't have had the opportunity to help people, to form relationships with kids, and to guide them toward success. In science it's all Cartesian. But humans are not machines. They're more complicated, and that's interesting to me. I'd rather earn three or four thousand dollars less a year but feel I was open to new challenges, allowed to blossom. In high school I was pushed and encouraged to go into engineering because I was good at math and science, but if it had been my choice, I would have been a nurse. I always knew what I wanted but I was discouraged from switching out of engineering by my male teachers and by my father because teaching is less valued in society. It's great that people want more women in these disciplines but the women have to want it, too."

Even with the inevitable frustrations of teaching—lack of funding, large classes, children with behavioral problems—Anita has not regretted the switch. She had studied engineering after having been urged to pursue it. Initially she hoped to use her training to design ergonomic workplaces for the handicapped, but she had found herself working on luxury condo developments. There was a disconnect between her impulse to assist others, and work that society valued. Now her engineering background shapes her teaching, she says, and has given her the opportunity to help people, to interact with children throughout her workday.

Her skills fill an important gap, she says, as so many of her colleagues don't want to teach math. Still, in four or five years, she told me, she'd like to embark on a third career: social work.

Female university students conducting
atmospheric pressure experiments for a lab course in 1899

How Do You Know You Don't Like It
If You've Never Tried It?

Despite being a member of a visible minority and from an immigrant background, Anita was not trapped by her circumstances. She was well educated, encouraged by parents and teachers, and had a clear aptitude for math and science. Nor was lack of opportunity an impediment. But she didn't have a sustaining interest in the subject, nor did she find any way to practice meaningful science, as she defined it. Hardly a unique case, Anita's preferences are confirmed by two strands of research—one old, one new. Both show that having the opportunity and the ability to do a job doesn't mean that a person wants to do it. Interests and motivations count. Historically, interests have been measured on vocational inventories, those endless lists of questions given by guidance and career counselors that try to assess the appeal of various jobs. Indoors or outdoors? Solitary or social? Directed or autonomous? Even throughout the massive social changes of the sixties and seventies and second-wave feminism, there has been a consistent, statistical sex difference on these surveys that can be summed up bluntly as "more women are interested in working with people and living things, more men are interested in working with inanimate objects and physical processes."[40] Interest in people was one reason why the mathematically gifted women in Benbow and Lubinski's twenty-year follow-up studies chose clinical medicine more often than physics and engineering. For the gifted men it was the reverse. So we know it's not simply a question of ability; plenty of women have cognitive gifts in math and science but still choose to pursue other paths (and, of course, plenty of women gifted in math and science *do* become scientists).

What about exposure, or opportunity? One of the most common hypotheses about why there are fewer women than men in math and science careers is that women are hamstrung by a lack of math and science in high school. A 1993 article in *Science* titled "The Pipeline Is Leaking Women All the Way Along" states the theory: "By the time young women graduate high school they have taken so many fewer math and science courses that it precludes significant numbers of them from pursuing college science and engineering majors."[41] The assumption is that lack of experience early on blocks them from entering those disciplines in a university.[42] More simply, if they've never tasted eggplant, how would they know they don't like it? It's plausible, and was likely to be true in the seventies when the current generation of scientists was trained. But no longer. In 1997, when the sociologists Yu Xie and Kimberlee Shauman reviewed the histories of 57,000 students—about as many as could fit in Shea Stadium or the Roman Colosseum—it became clear that not only are girls on an equal footing in math and science course preparation in high school, they also get better grades in these courses than boys do.[43] Despite taking the same menu of advanced high school math and science courses, men and women on average still ended up veering in different directions. Researchers at the Center for Women and Work at Rutgers University wanted to know why. In 2002 they asked 1,104 people who had taken the identical advanced curriculum why they chose their college majors. A high proportion of the men said they had been turned on to science or technology careers by advanced course work. For more of the women, their other interests and the ability to combine work with family prompted their university specializations. They were good at science, enjoyed it, and had the prerequisites, but they didn't necessarily want it as a career.[44]

In the department of "woulda, shoulda, coulda," there is new evidence that it is a good idea to trust women's choices instead of pushing them to study what doesn't appeal to them. Claude Montmarquette, an economist working with colleagues from Montréal and Sweden, made a surprising discovery after analyzing the choices, profiles, and outcomes of 562 American college students who were on university campuses in May 1979. The economists used a mathematical model to predict how these students would have fared had they landed in other majors. For example, 52 percent of male business majors would successfully complete their business degrees, but had the same students, with the same academic profiles, gone into liberal arts instead, only 42 percent of them would have succeeded. The researchers discovered that male students made a decision on their college majors based on how much they expected to earn in the discipline, counterbalanced by their estimates of succeeding in it. Female students were less influenced by their expected earnings. Interestingly, both sexes were good at predicting their success rates. The women who had chosen science had an equal or even better probability of succeeding compared to students of either sex in any major. But applying mathematical models that predict future events, the women who had chosen education or liberal arts would have done poorly in science had they landed there instead.[45] The women—both those who chose science and those who didn't—knew their interests, their capabilities, their appetite for risk, where they would succeed, and exactly what they wanted.

Knowing her mind has never been a problem for Kim. She knew why she chose engineering and also why she left it. When she entered engineering in 1977, she was one of forty women of four hundred students in her program. That didn't deter her. "I'd done a lot of competitive sailing as a kid, and that was a male-dominated world, so it didn't bother me. I jumped in with full gusto. I was elected to student government. I just had a blast," she recalled. "The professors were encouraging. Ninety-nine percent of them were great."And Kim did well, placing in the top 10 percent of her graduating class. She had a strong aptitude for engineering, and parents who strongly pushed her to pursue it. So why did Kim leave the field?

I was waiting for the bomb to drop at yet another coffee bar, this time on a Friday afternoon at an outdoor, cast-iron table. Dressed in athletic wear—a sartorial theme I was getting used to in off-duty female scientists and engineers—Kim seemed delighted to be digging into apricot pie during a working afternoon, a contrast to how she usually spends her time now: helping her clients pump iron. After almost two decades of practice as a chemical engineer with an MBA, she now works as a personal trainer with a large professional clientele. It was having children and experiencing a brief brush with mortality that led her to leave the field. "I wanted to spend more time with people I love. I like how I now get to manage my time." It wasn't about discrimination or being the sole woman on her team, she insisted. "I just got tired of mixing petrochemicals and debugging software."

Of the male dominated industry, Kim said, "There's a strong boys' network in these places but I never felt there was a glass ceiling. If you were willing to work, you could move up." Even in a large petroleum plant when she found herself the only woman on the crew, she didn't feel frozen out of the action. "The guys in the plant treated me extremely well. I wore big overalls and cut my hair really short because I was sick of getting oil in it. They just treated me as one of the boys." She saw her work environments as "fiercely competitive, but great." And although she once had an unsavory experience with a manager who liked discussing projects in front of *Playboy* pinups, she didn't see this as emblematic. "When I saw that poster on the back of his door a second time, I just said, 'You have daughters, don't you? Is this how you'd like your daughters to be treated?' He was embarrassed, and that was it. I never saw those pinups again."

Kim downplayed any negative experiences, seeing them as neither iconic nor intended to exclude her. She'd filled a number of different engineering and management positions, earned an MBA, taught university courses, and after children, "flexed it all over the place," but ultimately left the discipline. "I never ran into discrimination or bad treatment in engineering." I heard a similar message from other women with successful science careers. It went something like this: there are unscrupulous people out there who behave badly. Are they targeting me as a woman? Not especially. Whether they stayed with their careers or changed their minds had more to do with internal factors than external ones.

She chose research on human brains, not physics, but having worked in experimental science for several decades, Canadian neuroscientist Sandra Witelson could offer me the long view on the research life, I thought. I was in Hamilton, a university town in the fruit belt of southern Ontario, for a conference in 2005, and came to talk to her about her work on hemispheric specialization in male and female brains, and about her research on Einstein's brain. I was also curious about her experience as one of the world's top-tier neuroscientists. We met on a rainy Friday afternoon in her office and continued chatting long after her assistant had left for the weekend. As we heard the other scientists in her office area locking their doors and saying good-bye, Dr. Witelson talked about her training in the late sixties, when women were rare in her field. With vivid, dark eyes, jet black hair, and frequently flashing a warm, expansive smile in my direction, she was firm that in forty years of science research, she had not experienced gender discrimination.

"No, I never experienced any," she said.

"You didn't?" I put down my notebook and looked at her.

"None. Either I didn't perceive it or I wasn't looking for it. Maybe if I had been trying to become dean or president of the university, if I were challenging certain power positions, I don't know. But since all I really was doing was my research and trying to do it well, which is what my chairman and my dean always wanted me to do, there was no problem."

I asked if she ever perceived that it was harder for her to do that as a woman. Was she was treated differently than the male scientists?

"How can it be harder for a woman? I mean, who is going to stop a woman from doing research? It's not logical. What chairman who has to show that his department is thriving and productive to the dean of that faculty is going to prevent a bright, competent, hardworking woman from doing what she is supposed to be doing? I can't say that every day a chairman would come up and say, 'Are you okay, Sandra? Do you need any help? Do you need any more space?' I mean, no one was actually holding my hand or trying to mentor me. But they certainly didn't thwart me, and if I wanted to put in a grant, nobody was going to refuse to sign it. And I don't think I saw discrimination against the other women, either. This is a terrific university, but I don't think this is particularly unusual."

At the risk of being tiresome, I reiterated her point. "So you think it was a level playing field?" After almost two hours of discussion, Dr. Witelson dredged up one incident from decades past that she said could have been interpreted as discriminatory. "When the university recruited me they offered to pay my moving expenses. And so we moved, and I sent in the bills, as I was supposed to. Then I got a call from the administrator saying that because I came with my husband I would have come anyway, so they didn't think they should reimburse me. That could be seen as discrimination. But I didn't perceive it that way. I just figured they were trying to get out of a deal. All I said was, 'I'm very sorry, but whether my husband came or not is irrelevant. I came. You agreed to pay.' That's all there was to it. It wasn't a big issue. It didn't make me angry. I didn't talk about it a lot. So it all depends on how a woman perceives things, and how sensitive she is."

Back in my neighborhood one evening, the subject of female physicians and discrimination came up as a bunch of mothers sat on the grass and watched their kids get red-faced as they chased a soccer ball around. Several were family physicians. Instead of opting out of their professional lives, they had organized their medical practices so they could have time for young children and other interests, and as a result were working less than a full week. I asked them the medical equivalent of the academic science-engineering question. If women outnumber men in medical school and often have better grades, why do they overwhelmingly pick specialties like pediatrics and family medicine, which pay less than ones like surgery and radiology?[46] A 2005 study by Cana-

dian radiologist Mark Baerlocher and health policy expert Allan Detsky had shown that women weren't being rejected from their first
choice of residencies. Men were, though. The odds of men being
rejected were 1.6 times higher than they were for women.[47] With more
choices than men had, why would women choose to earn less? If it
wasn't discrimination, what was it?

The female doctors talked about the rewards of following patients
for many years, and their appreciation for the intricacy of their
patients' life stories. One of them described how enamored she had
been with her surgical rotation at the beginning of her training. There
was a shortage of surgical residents, so she was allowed to do a bowel
resection by herself under the watch of a senior surgeon. It was a success, and she decided then and there that the adrenaline rush and quick
fix of surgery were for her. The next day she thought about the eight
years of surgery residency and the on-call schedule of evenings and
weekends the practice required and changed her mind. "Family medicine was a lifestyle issue," said the mother of four, crossing her ankles
in the grass as she watched her eleven-year-old play goalie. "I never had
any female mentors in family medicine or in any medical specialty—
that was irrelevant. The point is that I don't have to be on call evenings
and weekends now," she said, "and work is not the only thing I do. I
have a life."

The women's stories and the research recounted here highlight what
should be a truism: women are autonomous beings who know their
desires. One of the profound gifts of second-wave feminism was to give
women the opportunity and the right to pursue their interests and
goals. Women who have the smarts and the ambition to become scientists, university professors, or engineers are no longer stymied by the
wrong course work or by outmoded ideas about gender roles. In fact,
over the last forty years a huge number of women have gone into science, and many, such as Sandra Witelson, have made stellar contributions, especially in the biological and cognitive sciences. So there's no
evidence that women *can't* do it, or are somehow ill-equipped. Instead,
the women profiled here shine a light on something else. Especially in
the physical sciences and engineering—which, as traditionally male
fields, are seen as test cases for equality—women can now have what

men have, but many decide after trying it that they don't want it. The vanilla gender idea that given every opportunity, they *should* want it, if that's what men choose, hinges on the assumption that male is the default against which we measure everyone's wants and dreams.

But what if a significant proportion of women who have all the right ingredients for physical science or technology careers ultimately decide they have other interests and goals? They have the brainpower, they had parents and teachers who encouraged them, mentors, self-discipline, the right course work, excellent credentials, and even excellent jobs. Still, they decide they would rather do research on human questions. Or make a social impact by being teachers, law professors, or social workers. Or have more time for their children when they're small. Is this a failure of the system, or of these women? The idea that women are stymied versions of men leaves the large numbers of highly capable women who don't fit the male model cast in a familiar, infantilized role. If only they knew what they *really* wanted, they'd choose physics! Somehow, despite their achievements, they're seen as unable to decide for themselves. Somehow they're made to feel as if they're not made of the right stuff.

When gifted women decide they'd rather be doctors than physicists, teachers, not engineers, they're opting to study and spend time with people, not things. Many are demonstrating a capacity to be attuned to others. It's a proclivity that has a very long history, and as we'll soon see, one that makes women feel pretty good.

CHAPTER 4

The Empathy Advantage

No Woman Is an Island

The personal essay on the newspaper's back page was headlined "My Glass Ceiling Is Self-Imposed," and it pinged my eyes open faster than the black coffee I had just poured down my throat. A female executive on the fast track to the corner office had refused a promotion to vice president in a multinational company earning billions and felt she needed to explain why, though she was writing under a pseudonym. Methodically, systematically, she detailed how her company provided every possible perk to promote women's success, including networked home offices so they could telecommute, flex hours, no pressure to put in face time, an in-house dry cleaner and gym, an income supplement for a nanny, and on-site care for sick children. Her company was rated one of the top hundred companies for women to work for in the United States, and one of the hundred best in Europe. Still this executive had stalled her own advancement just when she was expected to rise like a helium balloon. Her promotion would have put her third from the top in a company of 12,000 employees with offices in more than 60 countries, and on the short list to become the company's CEO within a few years.

"My president here could not believe that I would turn this down. He told me, 'This is an opportunity of a lifetime,'" she said the next day when I reached her by phone. "Companies like mine work very hard to help women achieve top-level executive positions. But what if we only want to rise so high?"[1] I had tracked Elaine down after contacting one of the newspaper's editors, who forwarded my particulars along with my query about a possible interview. Elaine just might be able to fill in the blanks about why highly capable women were pulling out of the race, I thought. Hers would be only one voice; surveys would reveal the picture on a grander scale. But the motivations for such decisions would become clear. She was eager to tell me her story and we made a plan to meet.

Several months later I took an early-morning flight to a fading industrial town about an hour outside a major metropolis. Elaine told me to look for someone tall and blond behind the wheel of a big black car when I exited the terminal, but warned me not to be fooled by the glamour that implied. In fact, she was glamorous enough, with regal bearing, height, and athletic good looks. In her thirties, wearing houndstooth slacks and a black sweater, Elaine had an easygoing confidence and it soon became clear that she was hardly lacking in ambition. She had assiduously worked her way up the executive ladder, high enough to have considered buying and renovating a turreted Victorian mansion she pointed out to me on the way to lunch (in the end, she decided her tastes were simpler). But never mind that. She was a business person who got straight to the point, telling me within five minutes of my climbing into her car that aside from a job she loved, she also had two small children, a husband, and parents, all of whom were central to her happiness and to one another's. A promotion would require moving to another city, and while it would boost her status and salary, it would destabilize her family. If she enjoyed her work, was respected for it, and had a well-rounded personal life, why jinx things by climbing yet a rung higher? Still a director of her company, she didn't regret turning down the opportunity to become vice president for a minute, she said. "My husband loves his work, my children are very happy and settled, and I love my job. My long-term future is not as strong as it might have been, but I derive my happiness and sense of self-worth from much more than just my career."

Her explicit message: work is essential, but so are the needs of her family. The subtext? Saying so is somehow shameful—hence the pseudonym, both for the newspaper and for this book. It's not a wise gambit to turn down a promotion, much less ascribe one's reasons to the time warped notion that the feelings of loved ones matter to you as much as achievement at work. Over lunch, Elaine described the reactions of men in her circle. "When I said no, the president just looked at me and said, 'I think you're nuts.' My father-in-law was almost speechless—he was CEO of a company and moved his five kids all over the world. But this is not only about me. It's also about my husband and children. My seven-year-old is sensitive. Putting her in a new environment would be a risk. I might be successful, but I'll look back, and if she's screwed up, I'd never be happy or forgive myself." There was no ambivalence. Elaine was sure she had made the right decision and wanted people to know why, even if she didn't want to reveal the details. "Nobody knows that I was offered this job, and a lot of men would be very upset if they knew, as it wasn't offered to them. The company's desperate—they want women at the senior executive level." To get more gender balance at the top, she told me that offers too good to refuse were being made to other deserving women, as long as they were willing to move, and if they were successful, to move again a few years later. She had known just one who had said yes—someone without a family.

Could Elaine be representative of other highly placed women? There's plenty of evidence that many more women than men refuse promotions out of consideration for family, including women at the top of their game.[2] In 2006, when investment analyst Carolyn Buck Luce and economist Sylvia Ann Hewlett tried to get to the bottom of the "hidden brain drain" of female talent by surveying 2,443 women with graduate or professional degrees, they discovered that 1 in 3 women with MBAs chose not to work full-time—compared to 1 in 20 men with the same degree—and that 38 percent of high-achieving women had turned down a promotion or had deliberately taken a position with lower pay.[3] Instead of being forcibly barred from top positions, these women were avoiding them. When the researchers looked at women's motivations to work, they discovered that having a powerful position was the lowest-ranked career goal of highly qualified women in every sector. For 85 percent of the women, other values came first: the ability to work with people they respect, to "be themselves" at work, and to have flexible schedules. Like Elaine, and most of the women profiled here, the majority of the 2,443 women surveyed in the "brain drain" study did not feel forcibly excluded from the most lucrative positions. The conventional wisdom—that talented, capable women are routinely barred from the top ranks—did not represent the level of self-determination they expressed. In Elaine's case, the company could have sweetened the pot by paying for an MBA program for her husband, or for private education for her kids, she told me. Only if the benefits were shared among family members would she have considered the move. Yet it wasn't an economic decision or a desire to preserve her husband's job that prompted her to stay put. She was the higher earner, and could have drawn an even higher salary had she accepted to move up. It was simply that family needs carried more weight.

This chapter looks at how empathy plays a role at such pivotal moments in women's careers. Empathy is the ability to figure out what another person is thinking and feeling and to respond in kind, with appropriate feelings and actions. We'll see how women, on average, have a small but distinct empathy advantage, a phenomenon buttressed by their biology, assisted by their environment, and made plain by their career moves. Of course, averages are just that, an aggregate of millions of individuals whose identities are as easy to pick out as a single granite shard is on Mount Washington. But a panoramic view shows that reading and understanding others' emotions is spontaneous and basic for many women, as one by one they decide what jobs to do and how high they want to climb.

We started with one woman's story. But large swaths of data also show that more women than men make adjustments to their careers to care for family members, especially at life's beginning and end points. Men help their relatives more than they ever did in the past, but women are the ones who intentionally limit their careers when caregiving demands are intense. As time commitments ramp up, so do the number of women offering care. A 2005 survey of the 44.4 million adult family caregivers in the United States tells us that at the beginning of an illness, for example, when an aged parent initially needs a little help with shopping or appointments, 42 percent of it is provided by male relatives. But when someone needs to leave the office early, come in late, or take a leave of absence to assist a member of the family who is gravely ill, women do it 84 percent of the time.[4] And when it comes to helping family members with cancer, daughters and wives by far outnumber male family members.[5]

But are these real choices or just obligations? This is what several successful women told a *New York Times* reporter when asked why they gave up their high-powered jobs to look after aging parents. "Nobody asked me to do this, and it wasn't about guilt," said Mary Ellen Geist, a forty-nine-year-old news anchor who left her high-paying job in New York to move to her parents' home in Michigan to care for her seventy-eight-year-old father with Alzheimer's and to provide support to her mother. "I lived a very selfish life. I'd gotten plenty of recognition. But all I did was work, and it was getting old. I knew I could make a difference here. And it's expanded my heart and given me a chance to reclaim something I'd lost." When Rikki Grubb, a Harvard-educated lawyer, left a law partnership to look after an aging parent, many of her female colleagues expressed envy that she could leave the "gut-it-out culture" of their profession to do something meaningful.[6] Each of these women voluntarily took a hit in income and job status to provide care for a loved one.

Trying to assess such work decisions systematically, the Minnesota labor sociologist Phyllis Moen interviewed 760 people about why they chose to retire early. The majority of women said that caring for a loved one was the reason they stepped down. Most men said they had retired early because they hated their jobs or were offered a buyout.[7] Staying home with sick children? When both parents work, 59 percent of mothers say they stay home with the children when they're ill. The rest share this responsibility with their husbands, but feel torn when they aren't the ones providing the care.[8] And a hotly debated 2005 survey of current Ivy League students showed that 60 percent of the women had already decided that when they become mothers, they plan to cut back or stop working altogether.[9] The desire to care for others is there before the need is. And in a huge study of how altruism and caring for others informs teenagers' life decisions, Mihaly Csikszentmihalyi, Barbara Schneider, and David Sloan Wilson closely followed more than 1,000 adolescents from twelve locations over five years. Their survey questions included "For the job you expect to have in the future, how important is helping people?" and "How often do you spend time volunteering or performing community service outside of school?" The authors found that female students scored higher than male students in "helping" attitudes and plans.[10] For these girls and women, as for Elaine, having a choice allows them to act on their feelings of empathy.

Are they strong-armed into helping? How women get to the point where they *can* choose, answers part of that question. For women wrestling with such trade-offs, opportunities tend to materialize in their late thirties or in their forties, once they have shown their mettle. It's a classic time to weigh priorities. Many of them worked hard through their children's infancy and early childhood years and don't want to make personal sacrifices anymore. They've proven themselves, and many did so at a cost. Now they want to do what feels good, which often means continuing to work, but refusing to overdo it with a series of decisions that will keep them from their families at important junctures. From the outside looking in, this seems like a paradox. After dealing with perennial workaholism while building their careers, doing what feels good can mean having the time to consider others' needs instead of reflexively giving work first billing. It can look like self-denial, or a throwback to a time when women assumed all the caretaking. But saying no to inflated work demands to preserve a few hours with a spouse or children, or to safeguard time to take care of a sick parent can be a selfish act. Empathy for family members can trump an exclusive focus on status and money for many women, not as self-denial but as a form of self-fulfillment.

In her book *Maternal Desire*, Daphne de Marneffe, one of those Ivy League mothers who temporarily upended her career due to feelings of empathy, lyrically describes time with children as "an extraordinary pleasure." It's neither sheer obligation nor sheer drudgery—at least not all the time. And empathy does not just kick in when feeling duty-bound to step into the breach or when mulling things over at a crossroads. Even when there's no family bond and no obligation, women are more likely to roll up their sleeves when they feel others' pain. In Canada, 90 percent of volunteers working with seniors are women, as are 77 percent of all health care volunteers. And even though they earn about half of what they would elsewhere, the nonprofit workforce is three-quarters female, too.[11]

The Utopian Experiment

It's often thought that the reason why women gravitate toward people or helping jobs is that they've absorbed the message from their surroundings that they should. But in 1975, a book appeared that documented a remarkable social experiment. Two anthropologists, Lionel Tiger and Joseph Shepher, had systematically studied the lives of 34,000 people who were raised and had spent their lives on a kibbutz. Established at the turn of the twentieth century and presaging second-wave feminism, the kibbutz movement's ideology firmly opposed gender typing. Men and women were expected to do—and to want to do—any job they were given. Children lived in communal dormitories and were raised by trained child care professionals who were committed to educating boys and girls the same way. When television appeared, its use was restricted. Parents visited at mealtimes and bedtime, but food was communally prepared and clothes were laundered industrially, so there was no "second shift" of child care and chores. It was a utopian vision designed to erase any barriers of sex or class, and it was assumed that with time all sex differences would fade away. Every job would be divided 50–50.

Starting out, the two anthropologists had similar expectations, but that wasn't the scenario they observed. Nor was it the picture that emerged from their data. After four generations of trying to enforce gender-neutral family and work roles, 70 to 80 percent of the women had gravitated toward people-oriented jobs, primarily related to children and education, while the majority of men preferred work in the fields, factories, construction, or maintenance. And the longer people had lived on a kibbutz, the more polarized the sexual division of labor became. Among women who grew up there, almost none wanted to work in construction, and less than 16 percent wanted to work in agriculture or industry. Meanwhile, none of the men wanted to work with preschoolers, and less than 18 percent chose elementary school teaching. "The statistical profiles we produced unexpectedly revealed that men and women seemed to live as if in two separate communities and met mostly in their dwelling places. It is almost as if we had been studying two distinct villages. We were equally unprepared to discover, as several previous researchers had in specific kibbutzim, a strong, general, and cumulative tendency of women and men to become less, rather than more, similar in what they do and evidently want to do."[12] The female members of the collective had demanded to be near their children more often than their allotted meal and bedtime breaks. And

much like the current landscape, women and men had strong preferences about the work they preferred. They could be exhorted, cajoled,
even forced into jobs others thought they should do. But given the freedom to express what they wanted, what was expected, and what they
chose did not line up. Imposing completely gender-neutral roles on
women from the top down didn't work.

Of course, women don't have a monopoly on empathy or on people-
related jobs. Inspiring figures who sway public opinion and policy are
often male, and men are more likely to risk life and limb to help others.
But those chipping away quietly at individual suffering are often
female.[13] As an example, let's look at the elbow grease of private citizens like Marguerite Barankitse, who started off with no title, no official function, and no recognition. What drove her to adopt and raise
10,000 children orphaned by the genocide in Rwanda and Burundi?
She began with seven foster children at the start of the civil war in
1993: three Tutsis and four Hutus. Then she added twenty-five others,
whose parents had been murdered while she was forced to watch. A
year later there were 160 children in her care. By the time "Maggy's
children" numbered in the thousands, she had created an infrastructure
of family-based caregivers and dozens of small businesses to support
them, while providing training and employment for the ones who had
grown. Pointing out some of her charges to Stephanie Nolen, the *Globe
and Mail* reporter who was visiting her village, Maggy filled in some of
the details of their gruesome histories. "That one I found still tied on
his mother's back, in a pile of corpses. A grenade had blown off most
of his face. This one, his mother died of AIDS. That one, she's a child
of rape—her mother was raped by the rebels."[14] Her ability to feel
empathy and act on it in such circumstances is extraordinary. Instead
of shutting down or seeking revenge—as many men in the war zone
had done—she reached out to help others as an automatic response.

When asked why she adopted the first orphans, Ms. Barankitse
said, "There was room in my house, and that's what my mother taught
me." Like most people, she thought empathy for others' suffering and
her impulse to help were learned at home. She's partly right. Sympa-
thetic parents who express positive emotions and put a premium on
relationships transmit these values to their children, as psychologist

Marguerite Barankitse with a few of the 10,000 orphaned children
she adopted after the civil war in Rwanda and Burundi

Nancy Eisenberg has found. We don't know whether nice, empathic parents pass on genes for niceness and empathy to their children or whether children learn this by watching them. Probably both. But we do know that boys and girls absorb the message differently.

In the early nineties, Nancy Eisenberg and her colleagues did an experiment in which they showed two films to male and female college students. One, a documentary about a child with spina bifida, was meant to elicit sympathy, while the other, about a male hitchhiker picked up by a suspicious character—with evil thoughts and a knife—was anxiety-provoking, a much more distressing feeling for the observer. Eisenberg wanted to see if she could distinguish between sympathy (a feeling of identification and sorrow for someone else's suffering that makes you want to help that person) and personal distress (the desire to escape the unpleasant feelings another person's predicament evokes). Both are aspects of empathy, because feeling what the other person is experiencing is the first step in both cases. But sympathy involves concern and a desire to reduce *that* person's suffering. Distress is about putting the brakes on your own.[15]

Having measured personality traits and family background beforehand, the research team wanted to know what best predicted sympathy for the plight of the film's protagonists. Who would be most likely to identify with the person in the film and take her emotions to heart? Was it personality or someone's family background that counted? Actually, it was neither. The trait that mattered most was the sex of the observer. Of the ninety-four students, women felt the most empathy for the child. And women were also the most suggestible when reacting to the distress of another person—their palms got sweatier when seeing the male hitchhiker trapped in the car with the psychopath (sweaty hands and feet are clues that the response is automatic—proof that the women were not trying to impress people with how empathic they were). But there were individual differences. The women who reacted the most strongly to other people's emotional states grew up in families that openly expressed their emotions.[16] Dr. Eisenberg's results hint at both biological and environmental roots of empathy. (In my own case, testosterone was likely the elixir that allowed my sons to view the hostage beatings in Spike Lee's film *Inside Man* impassively. But experience prompted them to lean across their theater seats to warn me not to look.)

A few years after this evocative study, Alan Feingold at Yale discovered something similar. Still a graduate student, Feingold was looking for nothing less than traits common to all people, no matter how old they were or where they came from. He had crunched the results from 110 personality studies spanning 52 years, 7 countries, and various testing methods in a technique called meta-analysis, and his outsized idea paid off. Feingold had found sex differences that were common across the cultures he sampled. Men, on average, were more assertive than women, no matter where and when they lived, how old they were, and how much education they had. Women were more likely to be anxious, trusting of others, gregarious, and "tender-minded," which Feingold defined as nurturing—whether they were eighteen-year-olds from Poland or Canada or sixty-five-year-olds from the United States, Finland, Germany, or China. These two categories—assertiveness and tender-mindedness—cleanly divided the two sexes.[17] The cross-cultural tendency for girls and women to be moved by someone else's emotions and needs—their tender-mindedness—is likely why females have been found to provide more help and support to other people almost everywhere this has been studied.

Nancy Eisenberg and Alan Feingold had found that the ability to imagine what someone else is thinking and feeling was stronger in women. Not that every woman is more tenderhearted and less assertive than every man, of course. Just thinking of counterexamples like Catherine the Great or Margaret Thatcher is to be reminded that statistical averages include extremes on each end of the spectrum. But in general, women are better at reading other people's mental states from their facial expressions; they're quicker to identify with their emotions and to feel their pain, a finding that continues to surface, no matter how it's tested.[18]

The Empathy Rheostat

When making the link between research and everyday experience, it would be easy to think that every woman is more empathic than every man. But that would be wrong. Individuals vary, and group averages say little about any single, real person. Consider height as an example. On average, men are taller than women. But an individual women can easily be taller than an individual man. Male or female, your genetic predisposition sets the limits for your height, but your life experience—for example, your nutrition and personal health—then affects how tall you will be. Empathy is similar. Each of us has a biologically preset range of empathy that's then tweaked by experience. So it's more like a rheostat with a range of settings than an on/off switch. Unlike the yin-yang, Mars-Venus dichotomy, where gender divides us neatly into two distinct camps, when men and women's levels of empathy are measured, there's overlap between the sexes. This is what the cognitive psychologist Simon Baron-Cohen and his research team at the University of Cambridge found when they tested men and women with their Empathy Quotient, or EQ. Soft-spoken and unassuming, Professor Baron-Cohen is one of the few men actively researching sex differences, and the measured tone of his writing belies its explosive theme—that on average, men and women's distinct biologies affect the way they perceive and analyze the world. He has plenty of proof as to how, but more on that later. For now what's important is that he and his research group at Cambridge have developed an empathy test that can separate people who easily read others' emotional states from those who are relatively blind to them.

The EQ, designed to capture a stable trait in a person, can also pick up subtle differences between groups. When Professor Baron-Cohen and his team used the EQ to test the levels of empathy in 197 healthy adults, they found that, as one might predict, women scored much higher than men. They were better at identifying others' feelings and were more easily affected by them than men were.[19] There were still a lot of people—both women and men—whose levels of empathy fell somewhere in the middle. But the low end of the scale was dominated by men. The highest empathy scores were found among the women.[20]

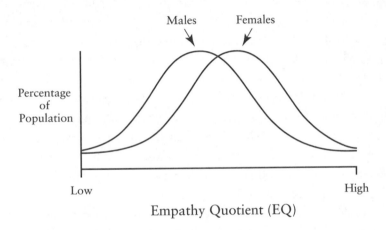

Empathy Quotient (EQ)

The EQ answered other questions, too, such as whether having empathy for others is the same as being a people-pleaser. After all, some might say that empathizing is all about guessing and giving people what they want. But the test items that measured pure empathy did not cluster together with questions that captured the desire to be liked, to be socially acceptable, and to fit in. People-pleasing and empathy are not the same thing. That's good, because as far as I can tell, being a people-pleaser comes with baggage—teacher's pet and Goody Two-shoes among the more polite epithets. So if women were found to have more of it, that might be looked at askance.

Earlier we saw that women and men don't differ on their average IQ scores. But they do on EQ. When they're asked questions such as "I find it easy to put myself in somebody else's shoes," "I can tune in to how someone else feels rapidly and intuitively," or "I can tell if someone is masking their true emotion," they differ greatly.[21] You can call this empathizing, as does Baron-Cohen; sympathy as Nancy Eisenberg describes it; or tender-mindedness, Feingold's term.[22] But whatever you call it, women are on average better at sensing others' emotional states and intentions—and sometimes feel them as deeply as their own. This cannot help but play a part in their decisions.

The Biology of Empathy: The Chicken or the Egg?

Empathy is so tightly bound to internal and environmental triggers that it's hard to pin down what comes first. We've seen plenty of evidence pointing to a female advantage in sensing others' emotions. The question is whether the basics for empathy are in place before girls and women learn about their cultural roles. There are signs of just such a biological scaffolding for later experience. Girls and women, on average, make more eye contact than men when communicating;[23] show more empathy toward friends and family;[24] and, remarkably, demonstrate signs of these skills from early infancy, well before any cultural expectations about women as nurturers can be absorbed.[25] Studies of twins show that the ability to understand social situations—which requires empathy—is largely inherited, and that there are large differences between boys and girls that are most noticeable when children are young.[26] An interest in looking at someone's face is a good clue to how empathy begins, as the cues to another person's emotions are written right there. And just a few days after birth, the majority of newborn girls show more interest in looking at a human face than at a mechanical mobile, whereas for boys it's the reverse: 43 percent of 102 male babies gazed longer at the mobile, compared to 17 percent of the girls.[27] Baby girls respond to others' distress more quickly, crying longer when another baby cries and looking sad when others are sad. As toddlers, girls are more likely to show overt signs of sympathy, such as asking "What's wrong?," attempting to comfort someone, and expressing concern with appropriate facial expressions. A small girl offering comfort to someone in distress might seem saccharine had the phenomenon not been documented repeatedly over the last thirty years.[28] Selfless acts prick our own feelings of empathy, even if we've learned to distrust such gestures as contrived, especially when they're attributed to women. But what if women's heightened sense of empathy were not viewed through an ideological lens? What if it is a naturally varying but necessary appetite, like the need for food, sleep, sex, or human contact?

When I began to research this book my grasp of hormones was rudimentary at best. They were what athletes used to bulk up. They were in birth control pills, and, to my dismay, were fed to cows to spur milk production and growth. They were in my IV line when my daughter wasn't being born fast enough, and also what my mother was taking to prevent heart attacks. Like many people, I didn't know how closely biochemical drivers like hormones are tied to psychological ones—not just moods, but subtle differences in how the architecture of the brain is laid down before birth. To understand the origins of empathy and the cascading effects of having more or less of it, hormones are key.

Hormones are the catalysts that set dynamic sex differences in motion. To begin with, a child's sex is determined at conception by whether he or she lands up with a Y chromosome. Still, female is the default setting for the human brain (not male, as it happens). All fetuses have female wiring until the eighth week of pregnancy, when the SRY gene (for sex region Y) on the Y chromosome triggers a testis determining factor. Once the tiny testes are formed, they secrete testosterone throughout the second trimester of pregnancy. This hormone then "exposes" or develops male features of the brain as it grows, much like a photographic negative gets developed by chemicals in a darkroom. Based on studies in animals—as you can't manipulate prenatal hormones in people—scientists expect that certain regions of the brain are not just transformed by hormones early on but are also endowed with androgen receptors. In that way, sex hormones don't just a have prenatal walk-on—biasing the empathy spectrum he or she inherits—but continue to play a role throughout life. Further changes are wrought by experience and by another infusion of hormones at puberty.[29]

So it's not as if a prenatal chemical stew determines one's sensitivity to others' feelings, and that life lessons and tender-loving care don't matter. A parent's level of empathy and their parenting style—say, the degree of appropriate supervision they offer, and how often they help other people—influence a child's level of empathy. But girls are more affected by early parenting style than are boys.[30] Mothers who encourage their children to talk about their feelings, who listen to them when they are upset, and who help them deal with their emotions through problem solving are more likely to have children of either sex who feel sympathy for other people's distress. But there's a sex difference. The girls are more likely to act on these feelings—by comforting a crying infant, for example.[31] So even with identical environmental input, women's biology gives them a head start, sparking the process of understanding others' emotions, then rewarding women with pleasure-inducing hormones—as well as the satisfaction of others—every time they respond. I'll get to the pleasure part in more detail shortly, but for now think of hormones and behavior in a feedback loop. The presence of certain hormones and the absence of others help prompt empathic behavior—say, picking up a fearful toddler. Comforting the child then elicits the release of hormones that make it feel deeply satisfying and thus more likely to happen again.

Even men trained to be sensitive to others' feelings say that they can't keep up with women's native empathy advantage. One male friend, a psychiatrist with ten years of professional training and thirty years of clinical experience behind him, asked me before a concert we attended what chapter I was working on. Empathy, I said. "Oh," he said, with a hint of regret. "People say I'm not very good at that." I shot him a disbelieving look, but this was no joke. This kind, insightful man was not exactly remote, but neither was he emotionally connected to others with the intensity he perceived in his wife and female colleagues. Had he known more about his prenatal environment sixty years earlier, he might have been less rueful, as that was likely when his own range of empathy had been rigged. Simon Baron-Cohen, along with his colleagues, is following the development of a group of children whose fetal testosterone was measured through amniocentesis. The researchers have discovered that prenatal testosterone is not an on/off switch, but more like a slider that works in reverse. The more testosterone a fetus has been exposed to in utero, the less eye contact he makes as a one-year-old,[32] the smaller his vocabulary as a two-year-old, the less he socializes with other children at age four, and the narrower his range of interests.[33] Now that the children in the sample are of school age, Baron-Cohen and his team have seen how the hormone is linked to their social and communication skills and their level of empathy. The more fetal testosterone (secreted in varying degrees in both sexes but in greater amounts in boys) they experienced, the lower six- to nine-year-olds' measured levels of empathy on two different tests, with girls showing stronger empathy scores than boys.[34] These biologically rigged levels of empathy seem stable as children grow. Another study, this one conducted by psychologists from Montréal, found that children who entered kindergarten with certain levels of empathy and helpfulness had similar levels when they finished school.[35] So my friend's range of empathy could have been set before he was born, before his parents could have treated him any differently than they treated his sister, and certainly long before he started his psychiatry training.

Built for Comfort, Not for Speed

If one's range of empathy is preset by sex hormones, why would many females have their dials adjusted so they feel others' emotions more acutely? From an evolutionary perspective, women are biologically primed to be expert at predicting the emotions and needs of those close to them—a talent that promoted the survival of their babies, whose needs they could "read" without language. It's no coincidence that the distance between a nursing baby's face and a mother's is perfect for eye contact. Mothers who gaze down tenderly while they nurse, imagining their baby's mood and physical comfort, hardly think of the 180 million years it took to lay down the feedback loop that binds their interests together. Infants who were born to solicitous, intuitive mothers were more likely to be fed and protected during their long apprenticeship to adulthood, while the ones born to indifferent mothers might have starved or been eaten by predators. Not only would the more empathic mothers pass on their traits to their offspring through their genes, but also through their nurturing. The feeding, nuzzling, grooming, and snuggling that mammals experience in infancy and childhood are imitated by their offspring, and amazingly, these behaviors also switch on genetic capacities that influence how the next generation will nurture their own young. So nurturing—and empathy is a prime piece of the nurturing puzzle—is not just a genetic one-way street. Not only do a mother's genes affect her offspring's in the typical way, but the mother's *style* of nurturing can alter how her offspring's genes are expressed.

I learned this from work done by the behavioral geneticist Michael Meaney. Working near me at McGill University, Professor Meaney has found that there are naturally occurring individual differences in the ways mother rats nurture their young. Their style of nurturing can actually switch on genetic functions in the pups that skew the pups' emotions and their ability to deal with stress. "Under normal circumstances, high-licking mothers are less anxious and their female offspring are less anxious," he explained to me as he drove home from work one day. Anxious mothers are less attentive—they lick and groom their pups less. But when Professor Meaney and his team matched high-licking mothers with foster pups, he found that a stress-regulating capacity in the newborns' genes was switched on by the adoptive mother's high level of nurturing. Thus modified by TLC, the gene activity allowed the pups to be less fearful. Providing all is well in the environment around them, these more relaxed pups then pass on the attentive mothering *they* received to their pups, whose brain circuits are altered in the same way—via their mother's nurturing. So it's not as if laid-back mother rats are simply grooming genetically laid-back offspring. Rather, the mother's behavior triggers a genetic reaction in her offspring that damps down the pups' stress responses.[36] The presumption is that more anxious mothers may be communicating an environmental threat to their offspring, readying them to be on heightened alert. This exquisite sensitivity in the offspring to a mother's cues may have been shaped by natural selection, said Dr. Meaney, as the offspring who respond would be more likely to survive. This clever study shows how maternal behavior, hormones, empathy, stress, and genes interact as if in a Rube Goldberg–like machine—each element affecting the other, sometimes changing it forever.

Those are rats and we're humans, you might say. Rats don't know much about the Mommy Wars—whether to consider children's needs first, or take a much-vaunted promotion. While it's hard to infer empathy in rats, there are hormonal and neural pathways that are common to all mammals. A mechanism that allows a human mother and infant to transmit their emotional states to each other would have survival benefits, and Michael Meaney's work, among others, shows that just such a system exists. The same pathways may allow Barbary macaques, monkeys found in North Africa and Gibraltar, to get similar stress-reduction benefits from grooming other monkeys. Group-living primates socialize and form alliances by grooming each other. It's long been thought that just as at the hair salon, the groomee gets the stress reduction benefits and the groomer is then owed something in return, such as thirty dollars plus a generous tip. But an interesting study by Kathryn Shutt, of Roehamptom University in London, has found that when female macaques comb through another macaque's fur, *the groomer* experiences less stress, as measured by the cortisol—a stress-related hormone—they excrete. The longer a female macaque spends grooming others, the less stressed she is. There was no relation to being primped and being less stressed. For female macaques, anyway, it is better to give than to receive.[37]

In humans, Shelley Taylor, a psychologist at UCLA, was the first to theorize that nurturing and stress reactions are tightly bound together. Having interviewed women with cancer about how they dealt with their stresses, Taylor was struck by how many of them chalked up their resilience to their social connections. The children, spouse, and friends each turned to for support helped them fight the disease, they said.[38] It dawned on her that these social networks might offer some sort of protection beyond the obvious (that's when Taylor decided it might be a good idea to have children). Could something biochemical be triggered by reaching out to others when you feel threatened?

From an evolutionary perspective, whatever prompted our female ancestors to sense their offspring's distress and tend to them solicitously might also be linked to women seeking out their friends under duress, she thought. Looking after one's own offspring when under stress is certainly a good evolutionary strategy, and the biological factors that promoted this "tending" would be selected for. But in addition to the typical fight or flight stress reaction when adrenaline and hormones put one on high alert, Taylor showed that women react to stress with a "befriend" response, instinctively reaching out to others in their inner circle. Why would befriending have any survival advantages? If women raised children cooperatively—trading child care with other women—then mutual empathy and caretaking would have protected all vulnerable young ones. Of course, this would work only if a mother's tending and befriending favors were returned. To avoid becoming a sucker who takes care of others but gets no caretaking in return, women would have to have good lie-detection and mind-reading skills—reading faces, motivations, and social contexts well enough to ensure that other women were sincere and would return the favor.

The two skills would have to work in tandem. The ability to read peoples' facial expressions *alongside* a knack for imputing their hidden thoughts and motivations would be required, as one without the other would be of limited use in the real world. People born with Williams syndrome, for example, a rare genetic disorder in which about twenty-five genes (of a total 30,000) go missing during meiosis, are interested in people and highly gregarious—they enjoy and seek out social contact and despite having lower than average intelligence, are skilled at reading facial expressions. They can process others' feelings and interests well enough to make a first stab at friendship, and their relatively advanced language skills allow them to tell compelling stories layered with emotional content. But as they're not particularly good at abstract thought and have difficulty seeing past appearances to what someone might be concealing, they miss the subtleties that allow most of us to second guess other people's intentions. So they don't know that if it's past midnight and someone says, "Please stay," she really means "Please go," or that an apparently friendly overture from a stranger might be a form of manipulation. Despite being good face readers, people with Williams syndrome are not particularly good mind readers, and thus sadly can't progress past the preliminaries of a relationship. Being endowed with one ingredient of empathy without the other is an accident of nature in this case, and a very rare one—1 in 7,500 people have the disorder. In the rest of us the two skills would have evolved together, allowing us to navigate the complex social terrain of living in groups, and in females to depend on others and trade child-minding favors when under stress.[39]

That's the hypothetical evolutionary "strategy." But the immediate behavior of tending and befriending would be driven by hormones.

Oxytocin, the hormone that greases the wheels of attachment, is the underlying driver of both tending and befriending. It is released at critical moments in women's relationships and menstrual cycles, damping down other stress responses and relaxing new mothers enough to allow them to care for and comfort their young. Secreted during childbirth, breast-feeding, nurturing, and orgasm, oxytocin engenders a unique feeling of closeness and relaxation.[40] Together with endogenous opioids released under stress, it keeps mothers going, providing sedative and analgesic effects, calming and immediately rewarding the women who instinctively reach out to others when they are in trouble.[41]

But oxytocin is not just a feel-good, nurturing drug that happens to be homegrown. It also helps people read emotions in other people's faces and increases their trust in others, according to new research. Thus it is the truest social enabler, as shown in two studies conducted at the University of Zurich. The first used a double-blind, placebo-controlled study to test whether oxytocin would improve men's ability to empathize, or more specifically, to read the emotions expressed in people's eyes. Just before a group of men took this empathy test, half of them squirted a dose of oxytocin up their nostrils. By comparing their performance on the test to the group that squirted a placebo, the researchers discovered that oxytocin had indeed boosted a facet of empathy. The hormone helped men infer subtle, difficult-to-read emotions and intentions from photographs of people's faces.[42] This is a first look at how a biological factor like oxytocin affects one aspect of empathy in men, and it will be interesting to see if future research shows that an extra shot of oxytocin boosts women's empathy, too.

A second study used the same approach to test whether oxytocin increases trust. Michael Kosfeld, Markus Heinrichs, and their colleagues predicted that oxytocin would increase trust among male investors. And they were right: in the context of an investing game, the men in the oxytocin group were more likely to trust other players, handing over twice as much cash to invest as the men in the placebo group. On the one hand, oxytocin promoted their social behaviors, but on the other, it eroded their natural defenses. One can see how being too trusting might not always work in one's favor. And while oxytocin reduced the men's suspicions in social situations, it didn't make them more relaxed or happy-go-lucky when they were alone. It's more of a social catalyst, reducing one's fear when around other people.[43]

Both studies bolster the idea that a hormone secreted in greater quantities in females—when they have babies, when they nurture them, when they cuddle or have sex with their partners, or when they reach out to others—facilitates females' capacity for empathy and their trust in others.[44] Here is evidence, then, that biochemical drivers underlie some of the most obvious behavioral differences we see between the sexes. Testosterone, secreted in greater quantities in males, may alter some neural connections related to reading others' emotional states. And oxytocin seems to do the reverse. It seems to help women guess what's going on inside the heads of other people, enabling them to trust them enough to seek them out especially when they're stressed, and to feel pleasure and relief when they do.

The desire to seek social support, especially from other women, is one of the most predictable ways men and women behave differently when under stress.[45] An animal as small as a prairie vole, a mouselike mammal that shares a lot of genes with humans, reacts to stress differently depending on whether it's male or female. When male prairie voles were forced to swim for three minutes nonstop, they reacted to this brief stress by hooking up with females. When females were stressed this way they were unwilling to pair up with males afterward, seeking out the company of other females instead.[46] And just a small sampling of the research on humans tells us that high school girls and female college students seek and receive support from other women more than male students do from anyone at all. As adults, women rely more on female friends than they do on their husbands.[47] Eighty percent of women say they share the emotional distress of their friends more often than a man does.[48] But even without research evidence, one has only to think of *Fried Green Tomatoes,* the appeal of Oprah, and the *Ya-Ya Sisterhood* to gain an appreciation for the power of female affiliation. Going it alone may be a badge of courage for men, but "we're in this together" is often the coping mantra of women.

One poignant example is Terry Fox. In 1980, the twenty-one-year-old man whose leg had been amputated after bone cancer decided to run across Canada, hobbling on a prosthesis to raise funds for cancer research. Canadians responded with a massive wave of sympathy, especially when after having run 3,339 miles, Fox had to stop after a new tumor was found. Across the country schoolchildren embarked on Terry Fox art projects and letter-writing campaigns to show their support. The Fox archives now house thousands of boys' drawings showing Terry running on a road by himself. The majority of girls drew themselves standing or running alongside Terry "each making the other feel safe, and each helping the other to complete the run," wrote Douglas Coupland in his biography of Fox.[49]

Animal Empathy

Considering the complex decisions that humans make based on guesses about others' feelings and frames of mind, it would seem as if empathy is unique to our species. It's doubtful that other animals can "read" what others are feeling the way Elaine was predicting her family's emotional needs, or the way girls imagined Terry Fox's pain on the road. But there's evidence that mammals have the rudiments of empathy. When they sense alarm in members of their group, they react with alacrity, though only survival-related feelings of panic and pain seem to be catchy (not gratitude or ecstasy, unfortunately). Biologists call this emotional contagion. This is why babies cry when they hear others cry and why mice are more sensitive to pain when they see a cage mate squirming. Simply observing another animal suffering lowers the animal's pain threshold.[50]

One spooked sheep will make the whole flock run, but animal empathy can be more nuanced than just bolting. When an albino rat sees a distressed cage mate suspended in the air by a harness, it presses a bar to lower its neighbor to the ground and then hovers close by. Rhesus monkeys, too, seem conscious of the welfare of a fellow member of their species. Given a choice between two chains, one that would give them a normal amount of food, and another that would give them twice as much—but would give another monkey an electric shock at the same time—two-thirds of the monkeys chose less food (two monkeys refused to pull either chain, literally starving themselves to avoid seeing their neighbor get a shock). The more familiar the monkeys were with the "victim," the less likely they were to tolerate him being shocked to earn a reward for themselves. In fact, when it comes to primates, familiarity breeds concern. Macaques who regularly groom each other respond more strongly to another macaque screaming in alarm if they recognize it as the cry of their grooming partner.[51] While it's hard to fathom a rat or a monkey with true empathy or a theory of mind—that is, putting itself in a fellow rat or monkey's little shoes—at its most basic level, it's not hard to see how the ability to sense the discomfort of a fellow species member might be a handy tool for survival. If you don't react fast, whatever trapped him might get you.

Animal behavior looks more like human empathy when it crosses species lines. Linking humans to other primates in *Our Inner Ape,* biologist Frans de Waal described how, in 1995, a female gorilla named Binti Jua rescued a three-year-old boy who had fallen into the gorilla exhibit at Chicago's Brookfield Zoo. She was caring for her own daughter at the time, but Binti still picked the boy up, cradled him on her lap while giving him a few reassuring pats on the back, then delivered the boy to zoo staff, prompting American politicians and community groups to wax poetic about the simian's tenderness. They saw her behavior as familiar and human, as opposed to the reverse—that our behavior might resemble hers.

Compared to a gorilla, it's easier to think of a female bonobo as our ancestor, adjusting its behavior to the needs of another creature, even one a fraction of its size. De Waal relates the story of a female bonobo named Kuni, who saw a starling hit the glass of her enclosure at the Twycross Zoo and attempted to revive it, or at least keep it from further harm. When it fell, Kuni picked up the stunned bird, gingerly set it on its feet, and when it didn't move, she threw it in the air. When the bird just fluttered a bit, Kuni then climbed to the top of the tallest tree, "wrapping her legs around the trunk so that she had both hands free to hold the bird," reports de Waal. Then unfurling its wings, Kuni launched the bird in the air again. When it landed on the edge of the moat, Kuni climbed down and guarded the starling for a long time, protecting it from the proddings of a curious juvenile bonobo until ultimately the bird flew off.[52] Now, we don't know whether Kuni imagined that the bird was a living thing with feelings separate from her own, or whether she just wanted the bird to act like a bird. It is unlikely to be empathy the way we understand it in humans, but possibly its ancestor—and a clue to how human females evolved the sophisticated apparatus that allows them to imagine someone else's inner life.

From the Outside In:
The Neuroscience of Empathy

Imagine a camera that allows you to see inside the brain of someone while they're assessing what others are thinking and feeling. With functional magnetic resonance imaging (fMRI), one can see not only the brain's geography but also how thoughts, perceptions, and motor impulses traverse its terrain. That's the medium Tania Singer and her colleagues at University College London used to get images of thin slices of the brain in real time. Assembling them into a 3-D image, a computer displayed which features of the brain were activated when a person felt pain, and which when observing someone else's pain. Singer and her team found that feeling pain and watching a loved one in pain activate some of the same neural circuits. Part of our own pain pathway is wired together with our feelings for others. Some of this route encompasses "old" parts of the brain—the brain stem and cerebellum—which control more primal functions such as heart rate, arousal, and physical coordination, and are common to all vertebrates. But some more recently evolved parts of brain anatomy are on the empathy circuit, too. The anterior insula (AI) and anterior cingulate cortex (ACC) are both involved in the way feelings affect our judgments and decision making.[53] Damage to the ACC can make people deadpan and apathetic; when this self-monitoring machinery is awry it can seem as if people don't care about making a good impression or about making mistakes. Singer and her team found that activity in these areas (the AI and the ACC) also register individual differences in empathy. Could subtle differences in the functioning of this circuit determine who cares about their impact on others and who lets the chips fall where they may? And there's another question. It's well known that women feel more physical pain than men, experiencing burns and icy water faster than men do, suffering from chronic pain conditions twice as often as men, and feeling pain more acutely when their internal estrogen is in short supply.[54] Given this shared pain network, could women's own heightened pain sensitivity spell a higher sensitivity to pain in others?

Even without this preamble, most people would predict that men would find it harder to pick up on other people's feelings. A British newspaper story headlined "What Her Think Now?" described men struggling to spot anger, fear, and disgust on women's faces, confirming the view that most men are emotionally clueless.[55] Although this may be a stereotype, it's one with data behind it. A different imaging device—positron emission tomography (PET scan)—was used by Geoffrey Hall, Sandra Witelson, and their team when they looked at sex differences in the perception of emotion. PET involves injecting radioactive isotopes into a person's bloodstream. These tracers then ride along in water or glucose molecules, which are drawn to the parts of the brain that demand the greatest blood flow. Meanwhile, stuck inside a device that looks like a giant doughnut, the test subject is shown pictures, sounds, or scenarios. Detectors buried inside the doughnut pick up the flow of isotopes, thus pointing to the parts of the brain working the hardest.

More sober in its reporting than the newspaper story, Witelson and Hall's PET scan study showed that men are slower on the uptake when it comes to processing and reacting to emotion. Different regions of the brain are recruited by women when they see emotion in others. When women looked at pictures of people's facial expressions, both cerebral hemispheres were activated and there was greater activity in the amygdala, the almond-shaped seat of emotion buried deep in the brain. In men, perception of emotion was usually localized in one hemisphere; and especially when the task became complicated by having to match someone's voice to her picture, for instance, the men's PET scans showed more activity in the right prefrontal cortex. (The cortex is the thin, pleated blanket of cells around the brain involved in learning and analysis.) Previous studies had shown that women have a thicker corpus callosum, the bundle of nerves that connects the two hemispheres, thus forming a faster superhighway for neural messages. So, similar to language, the hardware for women's processing of emotion seems to take up more space and have a more efficient transportation grid than men's. Scientists infer that this allows women to process emotion with dispatch. Hall and Witelson report that on average, men are more likely to stop and think, while women react to others' emotions more viscerally, as if to "the threat of a large animal."[56]

Turhan Canli, a young neuroscientist at the State University of New York at Stony Brook, discovered something similar. Using fMRIs to scan the brains of twenty-four people, he and his colleagues found that men and women process evocative emotional pictures via different neural networks. Larger networks in the left hemisphere of the women's brains were activated when the women first saw highly emotional images, which affected how well they remembered them three weeks later.[57] Women rated their emotional experiences as more powerful than men did, and used the left hemisphere (specifically the amygdala) to process them. In men it was the opposite: they processed strong emotional stimuli in a network involving the right amygdala. The different hemispheres recruited by men and women may also reflect how the sexes encode these memories. Given that language is lateralized on the left, and that most women also encode emotional memories in the left hemisphere, the researchers speculate that women are using some sort of internal language to process and evaluate their emotions as they experience them. In contrast, men would encode emotions in a more automatic way—in the right amygdala. In summarizing the research literature, Canli surmised that women "produce memories more quickly with greater emotional intensity, and report more vivid memories than their spouses for events related to their first date, last vacation, and a recent argument." Although this won't surprise many couples, Canli's study puts some meat on the bones of these observations by showing how women's specific neurobiological mechanisms may make them more efficient at committing their emotional experiences to memory.

Keeping emotions accessible so you can remember them, talk about them, or use them in decision making is hard if you can't identify these feelings in the first place. Raquel and Ruben Gur, two neuroscientists at the University of Pennsylvania, have used fMRIs to demonstrate that women's neural hardware makes them slightly better at distinguishing emotion than men. When volunteers were presented with pictures of actors' faces, both men and women could tell if a woman's expression was happy—the easiest emotion to identify. But when a woman's face was sad, men were correct in identifying the emotion 70 percent of the time, whereas women were correct 90 percent of the time.[58] "A woman's face had to be really sad for men to see it," Ruben Gur said. "The subtle expressions went right by them, even though their brains were working a lot harder to figure it out." The parts of women's brains used to regulate emotion were also very different from men's, according to the Gurs. Women, on average, showed more activity in the more recently evolved part of the limbic system, the cingulate gyrus (where Tania Singer found evidence of individual differences in empathic reactions to pain in others). Men, on average, had more activity in the more ancient part of the limbic system, an evolutionary relic that often prompts direct action. "This difference may explain why men are more prone to physical action, while women opt for verbal tactics," said Dr. Gur. "Beating somebody up comes from the old limbic brain. Saying 'I'm angry with you' comes from the new limbic."

How might these mechanisms relate to work? If women on average perceive, experience, and remember emotional events more intensely, and if these experiences are encoded in more areas of the brain, it makes sense that their emotional attachments will figure more strongly in their decisions. In fact, one might not only expect this of empathy but also of other emotions like resentment or righteous anger about unfair policies at work. More networked neural hardware may bring one's emotions and the needs and emotions of others within conscious reach when career decisions are made.

The Last-Straw Effect

Wired for empathy, what happens when high-powered, highly educated women work at demanding jobs that require at least sixty hours a week? Logging millions of air miles, being available 24/7, and facing unpredictable demands and tight deadlines are the mainstays of top-tier jobs. The economist, lead author of the Hidden Brain Drain study, Sylvia Ann Hewlett has found that among the highest earners, 21 percent hold these extreme, high-status jobs, and less than a fifth of them are women. When they do accept them, twice as many women as men described the negative fallout on their families, connecting their kids' behavior, school performance, television and eating habits to their own job pressures in what Hewlett calls "a veritable portrait of guilt." It's not that men's extreme jobs didn't have this impact, but that half as many men were concerned about it.[59]

In the context of extreme jobs, being aware of others' needs can ultimately be a liability if promotion is the yardstick of success. One example is Ingrid, a former senior executive in the automotive industry, who agreed to talk to me about her experience in an extreme job with the usual proviso that I give her a pseudonym. Five years before we met, her routine included flying from her North American city on the red-eye for a day of meetings in Europe, having to leave before her children went to bed and getting home after her husband or babysitter had put them to bed the next night. Sixteen-hour days were common, and the adrenaline was addictive, she said (90 percent of men and 82 percent of women say the adrenaline rush is why they do these extreme jobs). "I took a great interest in the financial aspect of the corporation, and really loved the engineering feats, the marvel of this or that new car or truck," she said. Ingrid had helped craft two mergers, dealing with possible losses of consumer and stock confidence. Through the arrival of her two children, she was the person the company called at 2:00 A.M. if there was a glitch or a public relations disaster. Accepting the 24/7 executive yoke, she had risen through the ranks.

Yet sitting on the floor of her bedroom, where we had secreted ourselves in her house to talk quietly, she seemed more the woman sharing confidences than the polished executive who took pains to project a certain image—a manly image, she said. "There weren't many women in the kind of work I was doing, and I was going to make damn sure I didn't look like one," she said. "We were the first generation of women allowed to work the crazy life of men, and we had to show them we could do it," she said. In her early fifties, Ingrid had an appealing, intelligent face with high cheekbones, green eyes, and a halo of frizzy golden hair. As one of the first women in a male industry, she said she never felt she didn't belong. But she felt an ineffable internal pressure that drove her to her limits, pushing her to put in sixty- to eighty-hour workweeks when her children were small, overshadowing her other needs. "I wanted so much to be somebody who counted," she said. With such driving ambition, why had Ingrid opted out?

Ingrid had a husband and a nanny to take over at home, and there was never any question about her competence or her commitment to her work. But her comments make it clear that her extreme job put her in conflict with her emotions. "I was a wreck. I never saw my kids. I wasn't even home to put them to bed. I never made them a meal myself," she said. Her starting assumption had been that women were versions of men, and if men could do it and were expected to, so could she. "Let's say you had a capacity for 100 percent. I thought even at 120 percent it would be a weakness. I didn't think I could ever say no. That first batch of women—we wanted so much we didn't realize that people wouldn't have thought twice if we wanted to go home occasionally. I didn't know how miserable I was." By the time a company merger and move were in the offing—with a handsome promotion to vice president offered to Ingrid—she couldn't imagine making another personal sacrifice. After watching some unsavory merger-related politicking, she realized that the corporate machine cared not a whit for her sacrifices. At that point no amount of money or stock options could hold her. She just wanted to reach out to her family and make up for lost time.

Is Empathy Dangerous?

We've seen how hormones and subtle differences in men's and women's brains point to a modest female edge in empathy. Yet greater sensitivity to other's needs may be why women generally feel more distress than men. Two sociologists, Catherine Ross and John Mirowsky, estimate that women experience distress 30 percent more often than men—and it's not just because men are more likely to keep their emotions to themselves.[60] Women really feel sadness, malaise, and anxiety more acutely and more often. When these feelings begin to dominate, women become burned out or clinically depressed, a condition that is twice as common in women as in men across all cultures and social classes.[61] Ronald Kessler, a Harvard epidemiologist who has conducted huge population studies of women and depression, attributes its prevalence in women to genetic and hormonal factors, but also to the greater emotional involvement of women in the lives of those around them. It's not that more bad things happen to women or that their lives are harder, but that their networks are wider. Women are vulnerable to negative events happening not only to themselves, but also to anyone in the circle of people they care about.[62]

That circle—who's in and who's out—is an important piece of the empathy puzzle. Female-female competition is the second pitfall for more empathic women; they may be more sensitive to covert forms of aggression. Any woman can tell you stories about female-female competition—the covert backstabbing that derails many female professionals and executives in mid-career. Most people assume that women, especially when they're underrepresented, will stick together as a sisterhood in male-dominated environments. But many behave more like lone wolves, competing viciously with other women for resources and recognition. Female colleagues sabotaging one another was such a common theme in my interviews with professional women that I began to wonder why there isn't more empirical research on the topic (most research is about chimps, children, or so-called primitive cultures). Surely if I'd experienced being frozen out by female supervisors, had received dozens of letters to my newspaper column about women treating other women shabbily, and had friends and colleagues report the same phenomenon, female exclusion should be studied more seriously.

What we do know is that women may be somewhat more empathic on average, but they are not indiscriminate in their allegiances. They compete with other women they see as threats to their reputations, jobs, spouses, or children (a subject I will explore more thoroughly in the chapter on competition). And they empathize and band together with women in their inner circle, whose hurts and disappointments they feel viscerally. When asked who benefits from their concern and comfort, women talk about their children, best friends, parents, and extended family.[63] Drawing boundaries around the community that provides support is a good evolutionary strategy, as we have seen from women's oxytocin-fueled "tending and befriending." But the same neural and hormonal circuitry is engaged when women must prioritize demands from two quarters: work and home. This is how empathy—simply a feature of human cognition—has been assigned a moral valence. It's either given the rosy hue of maternal selflessness, or seen as putting a stranglehold on women's achievement.

Politicized Empathy:
The Emotion in the Doghouse

In a political context women's increased capacity for empathy is often denigrated or denied by many writers on gender. The concern is that any sex difference, but especially one related to maternal feelings, might be used to box women in. Ironically, this neutralizing of the sexes does just that. By lumping individual women with varying degrees of empathy together, making them identical to one another and indistinguishable from men, women's options get winnowed down. The blogosphere went wild in December 2005 when Linda Hirshman, a former professor of women's studies at Brandeis, argued in an essay in *American Prospect* that educated women who want to care for their children are wasting their time on low-status, unpaid work. If they want children, they should seek out less-educated husbands to do the child care instead. "The family—with its repetitious, socially invisible, physical tasks—is a necessary part of life, but it allows fewer opportunities for full human flourishing than public spheres like the market or the government," she wrote. Hirshman blames any deviation from a 50–50 split in high-status work on women themselves and "choice feminism," which she calls a failure because many well-educated women are opting for work lives that look different from hers, or from standard male choices. But there's a piece missing from this suggestion: the desire to care for others in one's circle is not always a purely economic arrangement. Many women who reduce their working hours or who choose flexible jobs to spend time with their own families don't consider it "child care work" or themselves generic babysitters who happen to be getting a lower hourly rate than they would earn as lawyers or bond traders on Wall Street. The science showing that many women feel empathy more acutely than many men doesn't mean that they *must* or *should* make such trade-offs. It simply explains why some women might want to.

Through a political lens, women are often said to have too much or too little empathy for their own or the common good. Jane Fonda called the empathy of her early years "the disease to please," and says she has now replaced it with religious faith. Supreme Court justice Sandra Day O'Connor was criticized for not having enough of it—for ruling according to the U.S. Constitution instead of acting on "empathy to female victims of violence."[64] There is clearly a lot of ambivalence to empathy. For example, some writers assert that women learn to be empathic only because they are taught to be by parents and teachers. In an essay on gender socialization, psychologist Eva Pomerantz and two colleagues summarize this point of view: "Females are often viewed as fit for the role of caretaker, whereas males are viewed as fit for the role of breadwinner. Such beliefs about gender may cause parents to perceive their children as possessing gender-stereotypical characteristics (e.g., girls are seen as dependent and boys are seen as independent) and to hold gender-stereotypical socialization goals for their children (e.g., girls should be sensitive and boys should be assertive). This may influence parents' interactions with their children, leading them to treat girls and boys differently."[65] Others, like Carol Gilligan, use literary references and case studies to suggest that women construct their identity in terms of caring for others and affiliating with them, a heightened "moral" view that can be applied to change a more rule-driven, male-oriented system: "Sensitivity to the needs of others and the assumption of responsibility for taking care lead women to attend to voices other than their own and to include in their judgment other points of view," she wrote in her classic book *In a Different Voice*.[66] Still others assert that any sex differences in empathy are imposed by the dominant culture so that women can be exploited by men. Feminist theorist Sandra Bartky defines this terrain: "Love, affection, and the affectionate dispensing of emotional sustenance may seem to be purely private transactions that have nothing to do with the macrosocial domain of status. But this is false. . . . Insofar as women's provision of emotional sustenance is a species of compliance with the needs, wishes, and interests of men, such provision can be understood as a conferral of status."[67]

What these views have in common is that empathy—described in this chapter as a feature of human nature with genetic, neurological, and hormonal roots—is seen as imposed on women by external forces. Clearly, the history of women's oppression has left us with a jaundiced view of empathy. But as recent decades have increased opportunities for women, perhaps externally imposed gender roles are less influential than they once were, and we can look at empathy in a new light. With new information about empathy gleaned from neuroscience and neuroendocrinology, we can understand empathy more as a biological drive linked to our perception of pleasure, pain, and distress. We can gain insight into the role empathy plays in women's decision making and their ability to manage day-to-day stresses, and as one feature of women's biological makeup that might confer benefits, not just on others but on women themselves.

One of the themes of this chapter is the way empathy figures in women's tendency to seek out social connections, particularly in times of stress. Fascinating evidence is emerging that these social connections don't just make women happier. They also protect women from cognitive decline and extend their life spans. Empathy for others—including the ability and desire to connect with other people—helps preserve memory and thinking skills, and allows women to live longer. The evidence of the protective effects of empathy and social affiliation is strong. When following 1,200 people living in Stockholm, the epidemiologist Laura Fratiglioni discovered the lowest rate of dementia in people with extensive social networks. And in a long-term study of 2,761 elderly Americans, Harvard social epidemiologist Lisa Berkman and her colleague Thomas Glass found that people with social connections are less likely to die young.[68] As opposed to subjugating women, an increased capacity for empathy and social affiliation might have the opposite effect. It might confer the benefits of a better quality of life, and a longer one, too.

Society's conventions do affect us. But cultural forces alone can't confer the empathy advantage observed in girls and women from the first days of life, across different cultures, ages, and social classes. In every society, women have a stronger interest in others, show more nurturing behavior, and often value their relationships more than competition.[69] These biological differences may underlie aspects of women's occupational choices—the type of work they find appealing and how many hours they want to commit to it. Even with the dramatic changes in customs, laws, and social expectations over the past four decades, there are aspects of women's work preferences that are likely to stay the same—for example, a desire to stay in a position that accommodates family, or to find work that exploits a talent for connecting with people. Given what we know about empathy, it's implausible that it would not play a part in women's decisions. It's also implausible that business leaders such as Elaine and Ingrid would make life decisions based on the sudden revelation that it is simply their role to fall in line and please others. Blind obedience seems unlikely among this group of goal-oriented, highly successful women. Instead, at a critical juncture they tried their family members' perspectives on for size, blending multiple vantage points with their own.

Now consider what might happen when people are *lacking* in empathy. In the early nineties I knew three such boys. They had trouble understanding other people's emotions and intentions. Their ability to guess what another person might be thinking was strangely . . . missing. Never looking other people in the eye was one reason why the social scene at school was inscrutable to them. The twinkle in the eye accompanying a joke, the narrowed lips that mean anger or a fight, the raised eyebrows of sarcasm and mock surprise, these expressions were hardly glimpsed by these boys, much less understood. These extreme boys—who grew up to be extreme men—don't have to balance multiple vantage points because they are usually aware of just one: their own.

CHAPTER 5

Revenge of the Nerds

The frigid March day I met up with Bob, he opened the door to his house, looked at me without expression for a second, and said, "Oh." Then he turned around and walked inside, leaving me standing there wondering whether I should follow him and where I should hang my coat. Perhaps he thought that it wasn't that hard to find the front closet and that since I had set up the interview, I would know what should happen next. Or maybe he wasn't aware of the social rituals that usually smooth over these awkward moments. He had been reading a book when I rang the bell, and he promptly returned to the living room to continue reading. I followed and sat down on the couch facing him.

I was there to check on how Bob was faring as an adult, having known him as an adolescent who, at the time, was gifted in math and computers but fairly inept in the social sphere. He had a few friends who shared his interests in *Star Trek* and Dungeons & Dragons. But in larger groups of teenagers he stayed on the periphery, not excluded outright but not included, either. He tended to blurt out comments at all the wrong times, and his obliquely angled insights, though often thought-provoking and original, were delivered in a loud voice, otherworldly and oddly pitched. If something bothered him back then, say, if people became too noisy or rambunctious or if he was teased, this hulking teenager became as cranky as a small child and would shout out vaguely menacing remarks like "Don't provoke the bear!" or "Shut up, why don't you!" As he was over six feet tall and powerfully built, these outbursts could get him into trouble with adults. Some kids taunted him to that end, but most recognized that despite his quirks he would never hurt anybody. He was just one of those nerdy, science guys who was terrifically smart but didn't quite fit in.

Bob wasn't just brilliant at math and computer science. He also had a creative bent that allowed him to play with what-if ideas in the alternative worlds of science fiction. As if setting these talents in high relief, a basic interest in other people seemed mysteriously absent. I had come on a visit to see if Bob had been able to exploit his strengths and compensate for his weaknesses.

Only twenty-three, Bob was still a work in progress. He had set his sights on a career in computer gaming and was pursuing any avenue that brought him closer to his goal, including a degree in computer science. In the meantime, he had won a raft of math prizes and had risen in judo competitions to the level of an Olympic feeder team. According to the standard yardsticks of male achievement he was doing quite nicely, especially considering that nearly 75 percent of all American and British men have already dropped out of school at his age.[1] And although his people skills were minimal, the gap wasn't exactly engendering an excess of angst in Bob. "I don't notice other people unless they're in my line of sight," was his blunt assessment of why he was in his last semester of university and hadn't yet met a single student in his computer science program. "I sit down in the same seat every time, listen to the professor, and hardly notice that there is anyone else in my class."

This single-minded tack was antithetical to my own mental default setting, which scans any horizon for its human elements. All I remember from the one computer science course I took in university were the people in it. As my teacher droned on about Fortran programming for statistical analysis, I took in the statuesque freckled Irish beauty sitting in the front row. The teacher's fluid movements also attracted my attention as he paced like a wild cat in front of the blackboard—I had heard he was a member of a modern dance troupe in his nonteaching hours. Twenty-eight years after I took this course I can recall the faces of many of the people who took it with me—we all took turns running our computer programs and shared the frustration of having to do this over and over again when a program turned out to be missing a single comma in dozens of lines of code. One ponytailed computer hack in my class even taught me a bit of Latin he had learned in private school.

I remember something about *anguis in herba* (a snake in the grass) but nothing about Fortran.

My interest in social interaction and Bob's interest in facts, machines, and systems seemed to be at opposite ends of the people-thing spectrum. Bob was animated (and very loud) when talking about himself, and he went off on long tangents about his obscure interests, apparently unaware that I didn't understand his acronyms: CG for computer generated, RPG for role-playing games, D&D for Dungeons & Dragons. When I stopped him in the middle of one of his monologues, I discovered that he seemed to have forgotten that I was in the room. "I tend not to realize that people don't have my strengths, like when people ask me to help with something that's moron-simple, I get impatient," he said, gazing up at the ceiling, not twigging to the fact that the moron in question was me. Not realizing that other people were not there in his head with him and seeing the world from his vantage point could make him seem like "a curt individual," he admitted. His parents—one a computer scientist, the other an engineer—had been trying to help him with that, a task made all the more difficult because, in his view, they struggled with such things themselves. "They're failing to lead by example," he said.[2] Whether or not his parents had demonstrated how it's done, communicating for the sake of making a human connection seemed pointless to Bob. When the phone rang while we were talking, he picked up the handset and said flatly, "Hullo. He's not here," then hung up. I asked about the lack of chitchat with someone he obviously knew. "I really don't like the phone. I communicate with people by e-mail, but that's just for convenience. The phone irks me."

I didn't know about Asperger syndrome when I first met Bob. In that weird synchronicity of ideas, it had been defined in the 1940s by two people at the same time: the Viennese psychologist Hans Asperger, and an American psychiatrist, Leo Kanner. But few clinicians knew about the social disorder until the early 1990s, when the London neuroscientist Uta Frith translated an obscure German paper Hans Asperger wrote into English. Only then did Bob's traits, and those of two other boys in my practice start to make sense. Fluent readers and excellent thinkers, none of them would look someone in the eye, nor did they know how to take turns in a conversation, both skills that usually emerge in the first year of life. Suddenly I had a way to understand the gap between their book smarts, which were light-years ahead of their peers, and their street smarts, which trailed light-years behind.

Asperger syndrome is a high-functioning form of autism, one featuring the disorder's social disconnects without the disabling intellectual deficits that accompany its more extreme manifestations. Signs first surface when social skills *should* emerge, in toddlerhood, when children usually connect with people by making eye contact, eagerly pointing out animals and people they see, sharing toys and food, taking turns, and playing games of pretend. The gaps in social skills become increasingly noticeable as the child grows, and are often accompanied by a narrow range of interests—often obsessively pursued—and a horror of any change in routine. Yet islets of ability appear that seem to challenge the idea of a cognitive disorder. Like Bob, many people with Asperger syndrome are highly gifted in at least one area. In fact, Asperger syndrome seems defined by what it is not. Unlike more severe forms of autism that are quite often accompanied by serious handicaps, Asperger syndrome is not a lack of intelligence; there are usually no problems with hearing, vision, or with language development. And although those with the disorder can be clumsy or ill at ease in the classroom, it is not a motor problem or a learning disability. They don't have the rocking, staring, or self-stimulating behaviors that make those with more severe forms of autism seem as if they are living in a mute, incomprehensible world of their own. Often excellent readers and avid talkers, people with Asperger syndrome, at least 90 percent of whom are male, can also be gifted musicians, chess players, or mathematicians.[3]

So what is missing? Remarkably, given these complex skills, the primary gap is in perceiving and interpreting the signals that reveal what other people are thinking and feeling. Bob's checkerboard of strengths and weaknesses matched this Asperger profile. Despite ample smarts, he lacked the knack for deciphering another person's point of view.

True to the Freudian era in which Asperger syndrome emerged, at first mothers were blamed for causing it. In one of the most destructive and wrongheaded theories of twentieth-century psychology, psychologist Bruno Bettelheim and psychiatrist Leo Kanner attributed all autistic spectrum disorders to a lack of maternal warmth, to "refrigerator mothers," layering stigma and guilt on top of the superhuman hurdles already required of these parents, whose children were often unresponsive to affection or basic communication, and painfully out of sync with family life. Thankfully, the idea of parenting as the root of autistic spectrum disorders has been completely debunked. We now know it as one of the most heritable of psychological disorders, with biological roots that skew the ability to understand other people and interact with them easily. But more on genetic clues shortly.

One breakthough to understanding what was missing in autism was first revealed in a clever experiment done by Simon Baron-Cohen, Uta Frith, and Alan Leslie at the University of London in the mid-1980s. Using dolls and props, they compared three groups of children to see whether they could appreciate that others could have beliefs that were different from their own, a faculty they called a theory of mind. If they hid a marble while the child was watching, but *after* a doll had "left" the scene, would the child say that the doll "knew" what only the child had observed? Or would the child understand that the absent doll would have no way of knowing where the marble had been hidden? The psychologists discovered that normally developing preschoolers, as well as children with Down's syndrome (who have intellectual handicaps), could imagine that the doll had knowledge that was different from theirs. But though they were smarter, the children with autism could not attribute different mental states to others. Lacking "a theory of mind," they would be at a serious disadvantage in social situations, when imagining others' thoughts and feelings is critical to figuring out what will happen next.

You'd be correct in linking a theory of mind with empathy. Such social and communication skills are precisely those areas boosted by the highly networked female brain. Unlike the women we met in the previous two chapters—whose decisions were colored by their awareness of others and a mental backdrop of the "big picture"—men with Asperger syndrome seem to be the reverse: unaware of emotional cues and almost exclusively focused on fact-driven knowledge. Baron-Cohen calls it "the extreme male brain" because in later studies he demonstrated that men with Asperger syndrome are highly proficient at mastering predictable, systems-based information, a more common strength among men, yet have unusually low scores on the EQ, the empathy test he developed.

Thus people with Asperger syndrome, and others on the autistic spectrum, are driven to figure out the rules of how things work, whether they're gearboxes, RPG rules, or the migratory patterns of terns.[4] Their mastery of highly complex systems makes their blind spot for others' feelings seem all the more perplexing. How could someone be so sensitive to details in one area and so unaware of them in the social sphere?

There is more than one answer to that question, but one thing is certain. Seeing the world from a single perspective can leave a person with a literal take on the world that can seem jarring or hurtful when no malice is intended. If you can't project yourself into someone else's head, how can you predict how your comments will land? When I met up again with a likable young man I had followed in the clinic for years, his first question to me was "What happened to your Jewfro?" When I smiled he seemed confused. "Why are you laughing? You're a Jew and you had a 'fro, so what happened to it?" Although highly intelligent, he didn't understand unspoken social nuances—that honest observations about appearance and ethnicity are usually off-limits, even if they're true. In fact, finding it difficult to step outside his own experience and impute feelings or beliefs to others could make him seem callous—that he thought of people as objects. Despite an affecting tenderness of spirit and an affinity for the underdog, with little cognitive empathy Brian was perplexed as to why "sometimes I say things that come out wrong." So his reference to a former girlfriend as "right off the used-car lot" was not intended to be offensive, but simply his observation that she had once been his girlfriend but now was someone else's. When informed that people's feelings can be hurt if they're viewed as inanimate objects that are "used" like a car, he took in this information as if it were a grammatical rule. It was arbitrary, quite helpful to know, and he would try to apply it in the future. But he seemed to have little insight as to why this might be. For a short time Brian had taken English courses to pursue his interest in science fiction, yet he told me with no self-consciousness that he always writes stories in the first person, never the third, and that *Sparks Notes* (tutorial books that summarize plotlines and possible exam answers) eliminate the need to read novels. He reads books for facts and to follow a sequence of events. He doesn't read to try someone else's mental state on for size—to feel what they're feeling.

*   *   *

Despite these disconnects, Asperger syndrome has captured the public's imagination, with a spate of books and movies that turn its quirk-
iness into a metaphor for existential separateness and being true to
oneself. In fifteen years the syndrome has gone from an obscure psychological condition known to just a handful of scientists to the persona of a lawyer on *Boston Legal*. The inability to get inside someone
else's head, and to care what they think, is made to seem honest, liber-
ating—even fun. But the reality is that Asperger syndrome is usually a
source of frustration for those affected by it. At the same time, it can
also contribute to goal-driven behavior and mastery of complex systems of knowledge. The result is a form of male hyperbole: a focus on
facts, combined with a neglect of the often hidden emotional world.
Nine to ten times more common among males than females, Asperger
syndrome can be seen as an extreme on the male continuum. Shading
into normal geekiness, the menu of Asperger-like skills is tilted toward
fields that are popular with men: computer science, engineering, mathematics, physics, and economics.

A lack of empathy is certainly a handicap. But what would happen if Bob could find a niche where solitary, highly focused, and systematic problem solvers are prized? And what if more men than
women have a mild version of what we see in Bob? This chapter is
about extreme males whose social difficulties are counterbalanced by
their strengths in the technical or physical world. Like the dyslexic
men we met in chapter 2, whose spatial skills and single-mindedness
outstripped their reading and writing, men with Asperger syndrome
might be examples of what happens when certain male tendencies are
taken to their limit.

Let's look at competitive basketball as an example of how an
extreme biological trait might promote one type of success. One doesn't
have to be more than seven feet tall to be a basketball star. In fact, the
average height of the NBA's twenty all-time leaders is six feet six inches,
and talented players such as Bob Cousy can be as short as six one. But
many star players literally graze the top of the charts: Wilt Chamber-
lain was seven one, as is Shaquille O'Neal. Kareem Abdul-Jabbar is
seven two and my favorite, Yao Ming, is seven feet five inches. Those
at the extremes tell us something about what it takes to succeed, and

illustrate the prerequisites for success *in that activity*. In the case of men with Asperger syndrome, their isolated talents and their blind spot for people's inner workings make them particularly gifted at certain types of work.

"This failure [of social integration] is compensated for by particular originality of thought and experience, which may well lead to exceptional achievements in later life," Uta Frith wrote when first describing Asperger syndrome.[5] When I finally met the perceptive neuroscientist in her University of London office in 2006, we talked about the missed human connections in Asperger syndrome—the small smattering of friends, the poignant and unwanted social isolation. I'd had a preview of the professor's own social skills—she had scheduled our meeting to accommodate my travel arrangements, anticipating whatever I'd need to get to her office and still make my flight a few hours later. Still, upon meeting her, I was struck by her benevolent outlook, one that combined a firm grasp of the facts with sympathy for the Asperger experience. Even the few women with the disorder seem to have better social skills than the men, Dr. Frith remarked. Her sense that men and women with autistic spectrum disorders are somehow distinct is consistent with new evidence pointing to different genetic mechanisms underlying autism in males and females. Data on seven hundred children with autistic features subsequently collected by her University of London colleague, psychiatry professor David Skuse, has echoed Professor Frith's observation. Despite their outsider status in the complex social sphere of teenage girls, within the Asperger world the girls are the better communicators and have more conventional interests. "Girls with autism are rarely fascinated with numbers and rarely have stores of arcane knowledge," Dr. Skuse said.[6]

Even within the parameters of a social disorder, men are more extreme. Yet no matter how weird the juxtaposition of their strengths and weaknesses, no matter how narrow their expertise, people at the top of their game are compelling to watch. Are Bob and other men like him more likely than the average Joe to become the Yao Ming of computers? We'll now meet several highly gifted men whose contributions changed the landscape of physical science, music, and mathematics. Suspected of having Asperger-like traits, their flaws are linked to unusual gifts.

The Prodigies

In the late 1700s British scientist Henry Cavendish was the first to isolate hydrogen and to reveal the chemical composition of water and air. Working alone in a home laboratory in a manse in rural England, he elucidated the workings of electrical charges and the conductivity of solutions. A brilliant inventor, Cavendish was solitary and socially awkward "to a degree bordering on disease," wrote one of his biographers. Working alone, he tried to figure out what the world was made of, and he seems to have succeeded. As Bill Bryson notes in *A Short History of Nearly Everything,* "Among much else, and without telling anyone, Cavendish discovered or anticipated the law of the conservation of energy, Ohm's law, Dalton's Law of Partial Pressures, Richter's Law of Reciprocal Proportions, Charles's Law of Gases, and the principles of electrical conductivity." Yet Cavendish "was on no account to be approached or even looked at. Those who sought his views were advised to wander into his vicinity as if by accident and to 'talk as it were into vacancy.'"[7] The parallels with Asperger syndrome did not escape neurologist Oliver Sacks, who in 2001 marshaled biographers' descriptions into a clinical portrait that included "a striking literalness and directness of mind, extreme single-mindedness, a passion for calculation and quantitative exactitude, unconventional, stubbornly held ideas, and a disposition to use rigorously exact language—even in his rare nonscientific communication—coupled with a virtual incomprehension of social behaviors and human relationships."[8] Combined with obvious intelligence, being highly systematic, solitary, and heedless of others' nay-saying created the conditions for a lonely existence, but also for remarkable contributions to science.

This social obliviousness also characterized the brilliant but eccentric Canadian pianist Glenn Gould, who died in 1982. Pegged an Asperger candidate by his biographer, psychiatrist Peter Ostwald, and in an introduction to the book by Oliver Sacks, Gould was well loved by the public but well known for being a socially awkward recluse and a hypochondriac. Retrospective diagnosis is by nature a flawed exercise, and Gould was such an oddball and so outwardly anxious that more than one diagnosis may have applied. Still, his highly mathematical take on Bach combined with a tenuous grasp of social situations—

his exquisite musical precision yet horror of shaking hands, chatting, or any unpredictable event—bring Asperger syndrome to mind.

Gould's take on the Webern's Saxophone Quartet shows his systemizing approach to music at age twenty. "The first movement is ternary in shape and canonic in texture. It opens with a five-bar introduction which lays bare the interval properties of this row in four three-tone groups which are echoed in inverted canon by a row transposed down two semi-tones." In contrast to this acute perception of patterns, in a letter to his agent Gould recounts his horror of the unpredictable nature of the social world, "What's really alarming is that the whole area of this thing seems to be spreading. Where it used to be just a fear of eating in public, now it's a fear of being trapped anywhere with people, even having any kind of dealings with people."[9] Gould found other people's emotions confusing and irrelevant, and couldn't intuit their thoughts and feelings well enough to feel comfortable around them. As a result he seemed brusque, even rude, and his fears led him to truncate the range of normal social interaction.

It's easy to give diagnoses to people who are dead. What about today's world of achievement? A person with Asperger syndrome who has currently achieved recognition is the gifted mathematician Richard Borcherds, who won the Fields Medal for Mathematics in 1998, his discipline's highest accolade. In a profile in *The Guardian,* Borcherds mentioned that he suspected he had Asperger syndrome, and Simon Baron-Cohen subsequently included him as an example of the "extreme male brain" in his book *The Essential Difference.* A professor of mathematics at Cambridge University, Borcherds is flummoxed by other people, whom he finds "complex, mysterious beings who were hard to comprehend because they did not conform to the laws of physics or math."[10] He lives in the hyperconnected cell phone and e-mail universe but he doesn't use these media for chatting and can't imagine why any one would. His obliviousness to social niceties and his narrow interests made him an outcast as a child, but paradoxically created the conditions for excellence in his field as an adult. There is no question of getting distracted by family, e-mail, or social events, of getting tied in knots about office politics or graduate students' problems. He doesn't care what people think of him because he doesn't usually consider other people's thoughts and feelings. Here Baron-Cohen writes about the impact of such insouciance on his family. "His [Borcherd's] mother sat worrying one night when, as a teenager, he didn't come home until late. When he finally arrived home she said to him in an anxious state, 'Oh, Richard. Why didn't you phone me to let me know where you were?' to which he replied, 'What for? *I* knew where I was.' "[11] To Borcherds, only his own perspective mattered. His success as an adult seemed less a matter of adapting to others' goals and more a question of finding an environment where his single-mindedness and egocentrism had currency.

If you had to choose just such a world, you could do no worse than academic science and math. As we saw in chapter 2, the lack of human interaction and the laser focus needed for success in academic science can drive gifted women with broader interests away. But the high-tech world, too, has attractions for those with an extreme male brain. It's a truism that the field is a magnet for men, and despite huge budgets and institutional incentives to attract women to computer science, women's interest in IT has been slim and declining. It hasn't made a huge difference to female enrollments that the National Science Foundation, the National Physical Science Consortium, Google, IBM, Lucent, L'Oréal, the Association for Women in Science, and other groups offer millions of dollars in financial incentives to attract women to physical and computer science. (Undergraduate computer science degrees awarded to women in 2004 hovered at about 17 percent, down from 19 percent in 2000.)[12] At the other end of the extreme, men with Asperger syndrome hardly need incentives to be attracted to the predictability of computers. Many see operating systems as a stand-in for their own and other people's brains, and try to use computing algorithms to decode human emotion. (You will soon meet an IT expert who thought anger is what happens when someone's internal timer goes off, and a brilliant young man who prefers e-mail to social interaction because emoticons are more transparent to him than facial expressions.)

Not everyone with an affinity to intelligent machines has a disorder, of course. Craig Newmark, the founder of craigslist.org, is a likable, high-tech superachiever, though not a person with Asperger syndrome per se. As a child he may have struggled on the social margins, but as an adult he is hardly an odd man out. His website has offered free classified ads for the past twelve years, allowing people all over the world to find apartments, pets, and dates at a moment's notice. It is the seventh most visited site on the Net, not far behind Google and eBay.[13] With ten million users a month in 190 cities around the world, craigslist.org has chilled newspaper empires' advertising revenues, and many media conglomerates are scrambling to infuse their broadsheets with its honesty, spontaneity, and communitarian values. Yet the iconoclast founder describes himself this way: "I was academically smart, emotionally stupid. I can't read people and I take them too literally." He confesses to having a lifelong ambition to master quantum physics, and was described by Philip Weiss in *New York* magazine as "one of the most socially impaired people this side of a high-school reunion."[14] The online phenomenon he founded is at least partially an offshoot of his unique brand of socializing. He was one of the first to link people together in cyberspace on a grand scale, and it all started with his own group of contacts. One blogger called him "the catalyst of connection," an ironic title for someone who describes himself as unable to read people. He may find others inscrutable, but *he* is refreshingly lacking in artifice or conceit. When I called him to get his feedback about including him in this book, he immediately responded, "Sure, if it helps someone." Newmark was able to write his own ticket using his particular combination of technical skills, finely honed interests, and as I discovered, a lack of self-consciousness. A sophomoric eighties film may have lampooned the idea, but there is really such a thing as revenge of the nerds. The question is, are there a lot more of them now than there used to be?

The Disorder du Jour

Autism has always existed, but it is now in the public eye. Cultural references to autistic spectrum disorders are everywhere—on Oprah, on bookshelves, and in movie theaters—the films *Snow Cake, Autism, The Musical,* and *Mozart and the Whale* were released within a few months of one another in 2007, and socially inept Asperger-style leads such as Napoleon Dynamite quickly boost a film's cult appeal. Closer to the clinical reality, including the milder Asperger syndrome in the autistic spectrum has increased its visibility and made the prototype more recognizable, swelling diagnosis rates at the same time. But the idea of a more subtle version of autism has also created confusion.

Unlike the classic autistic savants that the public has come to know, like Dustin Hoffman's Raymond Babbitt in *Rain Man,* or British author Mark Haddon's real-world-challenged Christopher Boone in *The Curious Incident of the Dog in the Night-Time,* people with Asperger syndrome don't flap their hands, have tantrums, or repeat themselves. Even if their highly developed intellectual abilities are often strangely offset by a childlike social naïveté, their language skills are fine, and they can function in the real world.[15]

Autistic spectrum disorders used to be extremely rare—perhaps one in 10,000 births. But now that there is better awareness of the signs and symptoms, as well as its milder forms, the rate has been recalculated as one in two hundred, although some argue the numbers are increasing for other reasons. One is the relatively recent entry of women into the world of paying work and the inevitability of mutual attraction. Since systems-oriented men *and* women now find themselves in work environments where they are likely to meet people like themselves, there's a hypothesis that with intense "systemizing" on both sides of the family, any children who result are more likely to have even more profound systemizing (and less cognitive empathy), than either of their parents. Bob is one example of someone with Asperger syndrome with one parent who is a computer scientist and the other an engineer, a phenomenon Simon Baron-Cohen has documented in other children of engineers, physicists, and computer scientists.[16] In the not so distant past there *was* no high-tech mecca, there was no software aristocracy—in short, there were fewer niches where extreme systemizers might exploit their skills so publicly. And their increased status has burnished their appeal to future romantic partners. On a recent walk on the McGill University campus, an attractive young woman was spotted wearing a T-shirt with the words "Talk Nerdy to Me" emblazoned across the chest. Most women who have heard this story say they want one just like it.

The tech boom may have boosted awareness of the disorder, especially in California's computer heartland, Silicon Valley, where the rate of autism diagnoses, including Asperger syndrome, has increased twenty fold in the past fifteen years.[17] It's an intriguing sociological phenomenon that has looked to some like an epidemic. But fears about environmental triggers have not panned out. In fact there seems to be no place in the world that *doesn't* have autism, and its downstream correlate, extreme males. It's not a cultural happening as much as a biological one, as I learned when I met up with one of the more oblique men I've ever encountered, Daniel Tammet. With extreme gifts and more than a few idiosyncracies, this was no vanilla male. And he lived as far from the concrete plazas of Silicon Valley as I could possibly imagine.

A British savant with Asperger syndrome whom I had first read about in the *Guardian,* Daniel Tammet can compute 37 to the power of 6 in his head, divide 13 by 97 to 100 decimal places, and recall and recite 22,514 places of pi, establishing a European record. "I memorized pi to 22,514 decimal places, and I am technically disabled. I just wanted to show people that disability needn't get in the way," he said with typical understatement while we chatted in his cozy living room in seaside Kent. He was referring to his Asperger syndrome, which had him counting the stitches on his interviewer's shirt instead of making eye contact. His focus on detail means that multitasking is impossible, so he can't drive a car and depends on other people to get around. Daniel can memorize an almost infinite string of numbers or learn a new foreign language within a week—both outcroppings of his prodigious visual memory. Yet the gulf between his abilities and his disabilities made me wonder how he functions in the real world. Aside from establishing mathematical records, what could his outsized numeracy and systemizing abilities actually do for him?

I wanted to know if Daniel would be personable enough to look me in the eye and shake my hand. With ten languages to his credit, the mechanics of expressing himself would be no problem. But could he have a conversation that flowed naturally from one topic to another, or would he be derailed by interruptions and a literal understanding of common idioms? Because if he could exploit his gifts while suppressing the unintentional social obtuseness of Asperger syndrome, the traditional indices of success—money, recognition, and choice—would be within his grasp. He'd be an example of an extreme male who had succeeded despite—or as a result of—his male-linked fragilities.

*   *   *

My train from London to Kent to interview Daniel rolled past miles of narrow gardens unwinding briskly like bolts of green fabric, a greenhouse fastened on the back of almost every one. People who write about Asperger syndrome often use outer-space vocabulary, like "Martian," "alien," or "android" to describe the feeling of being so distant from others that you feel you're from another planet or species.[18] In Daniel's case he was isolated, all right, I thought as I passed the hundredth verdant mile from central London. He had instructed me to take a taxi from the train station because his house was so remote. "It's too far to walk," he said when I called to warn him I might be a bit late. Was he really walking a mile in my shoes? Or was he worried that his routine would be disrupted? Later he told me he *was* anxious about such unpredictable events, and as much as he could, tried to cloister himself and stick to a highly regimented routine. "I enjoy the solitary life. I like it very, very quiet."

The taxi left me off in front of a modest cottage with lacy curtains at the end of a lane, on the outskirts of a provincial seaside hamlet. A moddish, blue-eyed young man with wire-frame glasses and closely cropped hair came to the screen door soon after I rang, smiled shyly, and when I extended my hand, he shook it. I took in his quiet, tidy surroundings, including purring cat, books, and videos. Outside I saw an expansive stretch of grass and empty garden bed, with a cleared area for a greenhouse, which was scheduled to arrive the following day. His kitchen table was filled with potted seedlings he had started indoors and was waiting to plant. Clearly, Daniel was no "Rain Man." He made eye contact, had outside interests, chatted amiably, and offered to make me a cup of tea, the sine qua non of British hospitality. On his home turf the features of his social disorder were almost invisible. I didn't notice his five-o'clock shadow—he later told me that his fine motor skills are so iffy he can't shave himself. There were other subtle clues to his Asperger syndrome, but I had to really search for them. Daniel had mastered the social give-and-take so well by rote that unless I asked I would never have known how exhausting he found it to parse out exactly what he should say and do and what he should avoid—second by second.

I learned that his childhood was marked by poignant disconnects. But as an adult, Daniel seemed to have mastered his environment, marshaling his unusual skills to rack up extraordinary achievements. He ran a successful online language tutoring business he had established based on his mastery of foreign languages, had written an autobiography, and was earning a good living from his writing, he said. He was becoming a minor celebrity after having appeared on television demonstrating his prodigious computation and language skills, and his book *Born on a Blue Day,* had been featured on Richard and Judy, the British version of Oprah. Strangers on the street were starting to ask for his autograph, a recent development that pleased him. He was now able to converse with strangers, a type of social interaction he had only conquered as an adult. As a result, his contact with the outside world had increased. Daniel had met his partner online and with Neil's help and his recent forays into the media spotlight had established a small circle of friends.

Being the oldest of nine children had been helpful in acquiring these social skills, he told me. As a child he had no friends of his own. He had no interest in people and was preoccupied by narrow interests in ladybirds, "conkers" (horse chestnuts), and math. Daniel shared a room with his brother but says, "We lived parallel lives. He often played in the garden while I stayed in my room and we hardly ever played together. When we did, it was not mutual play—I never felt any sense of wanting to share my toys or experiences with him. . . . I became an increasingly quiet child and spent most of my time in my room, sitting on my own in a particular spot on the floor, absorbed in the silence." Blocking his ears intensified the aloneness, a sensation he found soothing. Classroom noise, too, was so bothersome that he sat with his fingers in his ears to block it out, so his isolation was almost complete. And although well loved by his parents, Daniel didn't enjoy physical contact, and when feeling upset, hid under his bed. If he needed comfort during school hours, he pressed his index finger lightly on the side of one of his siblings' necks as soon as he could. "Like this," he said, showing me with his two fingers on his own neck, as if taking his pulse (I could see that a gesture like this might not fly in the school yard).

Life became easier during adolescence, "when I started to have feelings for people other than myself." Daniel seemed to have become more socially aware as he matured, as if shadowing the increasing social competence in normal children as they develop—but just a few beats off the mark. "When I was a child," he said, "I would talk and talk and talk and brothers and sisters would interrupt me and tell me to stop." This perseveration, or inability to stop an activity once it's started, is common in the average preschool child, but it persists in children who have Asperger syndrome and it's a trait that still surfaces when Daniel lets down his guard with familiar people in familiar surroundings.[19] As with many other successful men with Asperger, his mother had coached him intensely as a child, so he knew what behaviors to suppress in polite company. Noticing that he always watched the visual pattern of his feet hitting the ground as he walked and thus tended to bump into things, his mother taught him to lift his head and fix his gaze on a point in the distance and to readjust his focal point as he progressed. This anecdote brought home the reversal of easy and hard that makes Asperger syndrome so intriguing to us neurotypicals. How is it that someone finds it difficult to do something so simple, yet can do 4-by-4 multiplications in his head? No matter how well he could do complex calculations or how perfectly he mastered social routines by rote, Daniel was still affected by a pervasive sense of separateness that he said was like "living behind a glass wall."

One feature of that separateness is his desire for rigid routine—he always likes his cup of tea the same way and at the same time, his morning oatmeal precisely measured and eaten on schedule. He doesn't like novelty or surprises. Yet his perceptions are so flexible that his senses jump their usual boundaries. Mysterious connections between his senses boost his memory into the range of the paranormal. Daniel can see numbers as vivid shapes and colors and thus can read off seemingly interminable sequences as if scanning an ever-changing visual landscape. Calling off thousands of decimal places of pi is just like watching and describing a travel documentary in his mind's eye, he told me. Psychologists call the ability to experience one sense as another synesthesia, and suspect that it is a form of idiosyncratic brain wiring, or an unexpected degree of neural flexibility that runs in families. It was yet another factor in Daniel's highly unusual neurological picture. With a one in two hundred chance of having an autism spectrum disorder, as one of a hundred people alive who is an autistic savant—and among 1 in 2,000 who experience synesthesia—Daniel is one of the most extreme males around.[20]

The Science of Opposites

Daniel's family history and early development tell us something about the biological origins of his extreme male brain. He was different from birth, an infant who cried inconsolably during his first year of life and who was more comforted by rigid, repetitive routines than by cuddling and interaction. As he was the first child his parents didn't know that his constant distress and lack of eye contact and interest in them were the first signs of a biologically based disorder and outside the norm for healthy babies. Daniel's language skills developed well enough, but as he got older, numbers and systems were what piqued his interest, not the imaginary, interactive, or athletic games of childhood. Transformers, Power Rangers, Pogs, and soccer—the preoccupations of his peers—held no sway at all. Instead Daniel had obsessive interests in discerning patterns in the natural world: clouds drifting by, the tide coming in, his feet rhythmically hitting the pavement, and the systematic world of numbers. When Daniel was diagnosed with Asperger syndrome as an adult, these clues fell into place, but until then he was like Bob, an odd, gifted child who didn't fit in.

There is increasing evidence for a strong genetic component to Asperger syndrome, and Daniel's family history make it all the more likely that genes are at the root of his Asperger traits. One of Daniel's brothers also has an autistic spectrum disorder, and his father had experienced a severe clinical depression. Depression and autism often occur together in members of the same family—indeed, sometimes in the same person (there is not only a biological predisposition, but there are also ample environmental triggers; having an autistic spectrum disorder is no walk in the park). One study showed that 60 percent of people diagnosed with Asperger syndrome have a family history of depression, while their siblings have a thirty-five-fold chance of being on the autistic spectrum.[21] If one member of a pair of identical twins has a form of autism, there is a 60 to 90 percent chance that his twin will have it, too; and researchers from different labs are getting close to isolating the genes involved.[22] It is likely to be a combination of candidate genes on several locations as opposed to a single gene that is responsible, and the effects on brain development are wide-ranging, affecting neural connectivity as well as the brain's architecture and rate of growth.

But something else distinguished Daniel's childhood: he had temporal lobe epilepsy. Epilepsy combined with Asperger syndrome and savant abilities are more than a confounding coincidence. The three syndromes are tied together by a neurological thread, and being male plays a role in binding them together. Epilepsy is a family of disorders resulting from a glitch in the transmission of the electrical or chemical signals the brain uses to communicate. The seizures that ensue can have multiple causes: strange and unusual brain architecture, short circuits in its feedback loops, or tiny cerebral lesions or scars. In animal studies, an abnormal level of testosterone produced when the fetus is developing is suspected as causing some of these microscopic disconnects. One experiment that rejigged rats' hormonal exposure found that the more testosterone in the blood of a rat, the more susceptible to epileptic seizures and the more powerful the seizures would be, affecting the rat's full limbic system (a region regulating emotions). Experiments like this can't be conducted on humans, of course, but they demonstrate a possible link between androgens and the higher rate of temporal lobe seizures in men. The question is what role testosterone might play in laying down the specific brain architecture of autistic disorders. A hormonal link may explain why 40 percent of children with autism also have epilepsy.[23] And at least half of all known savants also have some type of autism. So Daniel is at the center of a Venn diagram where epilepsy, Asperger, and savant syndromes intersect, and all three circles are dominated by men. This is one men's club women may not want to join. In all three, abilities largely localized in the right hemisphere dominate, fostering stellar abilities in mathematics, music, mechanics, or computing. Meanwhile, there are countervailing deficits in left-hemisphere skills that affect the symbolic use of language and global problem solving.[24] I, for one, would not want to make the trade.

Indeed, they were once called idiot savants. The label is offensive and no longer used, but it captures the dichotomy of men whose skills graze the top of the chart in one area and scrape the bottom of the barrel in another. Some theorists say this two-part relationship reflects uneven prenatal development of the two hemispheres of the brain. In a series of publications, psychiatrist Darold Treffert and psychologist Gregory Wallace explain how skills associated with the left hemisphere of the brain are compromised in savants like Daniel, while the right hemisphere develops more neural connections to compensate, as if sending out colonizing shoots in a neural land grab. That's how opposing areas of ability might emerge: holes in symbolic language, social comprehension, and global problem solving linked to the left hemisphere, overshadowed by stellar visual memory and systemizing abilities linked to the right hemisphere. (Similar mechanisms may be at work in the "compensating advantages" discussed in chapter 2, on dyslexia.) In explaining the phenomenon, Treffert and Wallace refer to a theory by Harvard neurologists Norman Geschwind and Albert M. Galaburda that attempts to explain why boys are more vulnerable not only to savant syndrome, but to developmental problems of all kinds. By calling it the "pathology of superiority," Geschwind and Galaburda capture its paradoxical extremes.

> The left hemisphere of the brain normally completes its development later than the right and is therefore subject to prenatal influences—some of them detrimental—for a longer period. In the male fetus, circulating testosterone can act as one of these detrimental influences by slowing growth and impairing neuronal function in the more vulnerable left hemisphere. As a result, the right brain often compensates, becoming larger and more dominant in males. The greater male-to-female ratio is seen not just in savant syndrome but in other forms of central nervous system dysfunction, such as dyslexia, delayed speech, stuttering, hyperactivity and autism."[25]

But how the two hemispheres of the brain develop at different rates is not the whole story. As we've seen, other biological factors, such as one's genetic inheritance, skew one's abilities in the same direction as Bob's and Daniel's—toward more focused interests in systematic knowledge and away from the unpredictable world of social interaction. The question is whether there is a continuum between these extreme cases and the average male. If we think of the features of Asperger syndrome as an extreme male brain, as does Baron-Cohen, then understanding how this brain works would tell us something about why men are drawn to fields where an understanding of data and systems is at a premium.

Growth, Overgrowth, and Pruning

Taking another train out of central London, I went to the University of Cambridge to ask Simon Baron-Cohen this question. As I crossed the campus to his office, I admired the gothic buildings that were both monumental and graceful, ornamented with heraldry, lions, and turrets that now sadly say Hogwarts instead of Henry VIII. I was in Trinity College, Cambridge, where Isaac Newton, Bertrand Russell, and Ludwig Wittgenstein were educated, I reminded myself as I climbed the well-trodden wooden staircase to Professor Baron-Cohen's fourth-floor office. It looked like penitents had worn down the treads.

Baron-Cohen is in his late forties and has a placid manner that belies the controversial nature of his work. Tall, clean-shaven, and wearing wire-framed glasses, he turned out to be as genteel as his surroundings, and gently eliding dozens of studies, speculated about how the pieces might fit into the Asperger puzzle. "There is a hyperconnectivity among neurons that is more common in autism," he said. This hyperconnectivity of local networks would allow someone to link a mass of details in one area without seeing the big picture or the alternative view. Meanwhile, other long-range connectors of the brain are missing or underdeveloped, leaving some brain functions turbocharged and others underpowered, isolated from other parts of the brain, as if marooned.

But here's the interesting part. If, as Baron-Cohen suggests, the autistic male is the extreme on a continuum, then extrapolating to the general population of men one might find fewer long-range connections from the areas that process stimuli in the real world—to the regions in the brain where emotion is processed. Hypothetically, there would be more local connections, allowing men, *on average,* a more intense focus on systemizing details, but fewer neural networks dedicated to processing other people's emotions. Taking individual differences into account, the reverse would be true of women—more long-range connections that would allow the perception of emotion to be more immediate and more connected to other areas of the brain. As we learned in the previous chapters, this is what Professors Canli, Gur, Shaywitz, and Witelson have found: a thicker corpus callosum connecting the two hemispheres in women, and women's brains being less lopsided in the way emotion and language are processed. There are other differences, too, in the subtly different ways women's brains demand oxygen, and how neurotransmitters function in women that favor integration over a "detailed scrutiny of narrowly characterized process," as the Gurs describe it.[26] These, then, could be the neural underpinnings for what Baron-Cohen has unearthed in his research— that profound empathizing is more commonly found among women— and that an implacable drive to construct lawful systems is more commonly found among men. Individual differences determine the proportion: there are women who are systemizers and men who are empathizers, and people of both sexes with a nice balance between the two. But in principle, the two ways of approaching the world would be reflected in the allocation of neural resources.[27]

I'm simplifying the complex and delicate anatomy and physiology involved. But in those with autistic spectrum disorders in particular, the theory is that the communication lines to other areas of the brain appear to be truncated, resulting in a detail-driven type of intelligence with very little coherence or big-picture comprehension—little ability to see the forest for the trees. This might be why Bob listed all of Homer Simpson's negative traits in alphabetical order ("being a child-abuser is one of them") while not getting the big picture of Homer as ironic archetype: the laughable, paunchy, middle-aged father as seen from a kid's point of view. It's also why Daniel could recall thousands of decimal places of pi yet could not understand the overriding principles of algebra. It's why he said to me, "I'll remember your colorful scarf. I'll remember your earrings dangling down. I'll remember your curly hair and your square glasses. But in one hour I won't remember what you look like."

This overgrowth of short-range connections and pruning of long-range connections might also be reflected in the early history of uncoordinated brain development now being documented in children with autism. You can even see it in the size of their heads, because their brains grow unevenly, Baron-Cohen said, pointing me to the work of Eric Courchesne, a neuroscientist at the University of California at San Diego. "He's studied growth rates of the brain," he added, as we headed out for lunch.

Researching this reference when I got back to my hotel, I discovered that Dr. Courchesne had found an early, external sign of autism. Using the humble tape measure (combined with the more sophisticated anatomical MRI), he found that most children with autistic disorders have abnormal brain growth that starts in the first year of life and continues for another one to three years, reaching the size of a teenager's brain six to eight years prematurely. Thus a three-year-old with an autistic disorder has such a big head he can wear his father's baseball cap, and a five-year-old has the same size brain and head as a sixteen-year-old.[28] Dr. Courchesne and his team are now figuring out why this happens, tracking an unusual buildup of white and gray matter in the frontal lobe: the seat of planning and social interpretation, and in the cerebellum: a central switching station for attention and goal-directed movement. They're also looking into how the disorder's genetic signals might jump-start any miswiring between the hemispheres or any periods of inflammation that might wax and wane. After decades of studies looking for an environmental trigger, there has been no reliable evidence that vaccines or food allergies are causes of autism. Instead, new evidence is pointing to genes and hormones as the catalysts in the growth and shrinking of the neural networks involved. These two players would explain the higher male-to-female ratios of Asperger syndrome and provide clues as to why Asperger-like traits might be on a continuum with average male traits.

The T Factor

As I exited the turnstiles at the station after returning from Cambridge, I saw what looked like giant testicles towering above the rush-hour crowd. Two flesh-colored spheres with rubbery hairs sprouting out at odd angles bobbed unsteadily above a pair of jeans-clad legs. A smiley face was plastered on the front. It advanced toward me, holding out a white plastic bucket with the words "Bollocks to Male Cancer." Aha—this was a fund-raising ploy for research in testicular cancer. People were smiling and throwing in coins and as I followed suit, I thought, of course. I had been thinking about why many boys and men in general, but particularly those with Asperger syndrome, might have such dramatically opposing tendencies: a propensity toward systems-based knowledge and single-minded pursuits and away from a more expansive, people-oriented, verbally connected worldview. Bollocks, or hormones from the testes, were the clue. Professor Baron-Cohen had discussed the effects of prenatal testosterone on the neural networks that underlie social skills. I would have to delve a bit deeper into the role of testosterone if I were to understand why many men gravitate toward careers in engineering, computing, and physics and many women toward careers where their superior social skills could be deployed.

Earlier in this book we saw how male hormones do much of the work of establishing male traits during prenatal development, irreversibly masculinizing the male brain. Doreen Kimura, a Canadian neuroscientist now working at the mountaintop Simon Fraser University just outside of Vancouver, has documented how testosterone acts on laying down these circuits during three critical periods of human development. Now retired, Dr. Kimura is still working and writing, and though she told me she was frankly "tired of writing about sex differences," she nonetheless agreed to meet to discuss testosterone's effects on the developing brain.

Having spent the past four decades meticulously documenting sex differences in skills as diverse as listening and ball throwing, Dr. Kimura seemed baffled as to how any serious scientist could deny the biological triggers of male-female differences. And it all begins, she explained, with hormones. From two months to six months before birth, as an infant of five months, and again during puberty, an infusion of male hormones spurs the development of spatial skills like navigation, aiming at targets, and imagining how three-dimensional objects will look as they move around in space—all areas that show an average male advantage.[29] These advantages appear as early as age three, are stable as boys grow, and exist in different cultures. In contrast, girls—who have not been exposed to the same amount of male hormones during their development—are, on average, better at computation, verbal memory, and fluency, and at remembering landmarks, all strengths that influence their occupational choices, in Dr. Kimura's view. Evidence from animal *and* human studies shows how early exposure to male hormones influences male typical behavior, she said, reminding me of the famous "natural" experiments with humans that she had written about extensively. Girls with congenital adrenal hyperplasia (CAH), who are genetically female, have a genetic defect that leads them to produce high levels of androgens. These girls have a female gender identity—they think of themselves as girls and are raised as girls—but their bodies produce more androgens than they should. As a result, they end up with more masculine psychological and cognitive traits. They perform better on some spatial tasks, prefer masculine toys such as vehicles more often than other girls (though not as often as boys), show less interest in babies, and prefer more male-typical careers as adults, such as engineer and airline pilot. This research by Sheri Berenbaum and Susan Resnick, two more women investigating sex differences, has been buttressed by many more studies of the effects of testosterone in animals, said Dr. Kimura, all of which point to testosterone "helping to turn people into boys."[30]

That Dr. Kimura finds biologically determined sex differences "uncontroversial" probably stems from how carefully she has tracked testosterone's varying effects over time. Levels of testosterone in men fluctuate according to the seasons and time of day, and amazingly, their spatial abilities follow suit. So men do best on spatial tasks in the spring, when their blood levels of testosterone are perfect, neither too low nor too high. Men's performance on mental rotation tasks—imagining what three-dimensional objects look like as they move—is worst in early morning, when their testosterone levels are high.[31] This made me wonder if testosterone is influential not only in career choices but also on the domestic front. Who should pack the car, who should read the map, and who should talk to the tetchy contractor before an early-morning road trip in spring? Was the fact that I ended up with the delicate negotiation and my husband ended up packing the trunk by himself a reflection of our marriage or our testosterone levels? Whatever it was, it was history. This kind of division of labor was laid down long ago.

More recently, though, Baron-Cohen and his research team published a study linking higher levels of fetal testosterone to restricted interests and poor social skills. The team had measured the levels of fetal testosterone in fifty-eight pregnant mothers, then followed their healthy children after they were born and as they developed, watching for links between testosterone, language development, eye contact, and social skills. Although there were no sex differences in their language skills, there were links between the sex of the children, their levels of fetal testosterone, and their social development. Specifically, the higher the level of fetal testosterone measured in amniotic fluid during the second trimester, the less frequently a healthy one-year-old baby maintained eye contact with a parent. A higher level of fetal testosterone also predicted weaker social skills and narrower interests when the children were four. There was a sex difference favoring the girls in social relationships, girls who, of course also had lower levels of fetal testosterone in utero.[32]

We can't say that fetal testosterone causes these differences. When two factors coexist, we don't know what comes first. Still, common sense suggests that higher testosterone levels may be tipping the developing brain toward data-driven, spatial problem solving and away from understanding emotion and intention in others. So not only does testosterone influence male-dominated developmental disorders, it also could be the elixir that skews the direction of our interests—wiring together the areas of the brain that help us decide where we should focus our attention and how, exactly, we should spend our time.

The remarkable way in which Asperger syndrome can focus one's attention hit home the day I was hunkered down outside Georges Huard's office door. This would be the third time someone with this social blind spot had stood me up. While I stared at a picture of the North Korean president Kim Il Sung ripped from a magazine and pasted where Georges' name should have been, I pressed redial on my phone and heard it ringing away behind his locked door. Unlike the other offices in the Physics Department, there was no plaque with name and title above it, just a number: PK2470.

Forty minutes later Georges answered his cell phone—the fourth time I tried it. "Did you forget about our appointment?" I tried to suppress my irritation. But Georges sounded cheery, even lighthearted. He explained that while intent on restoring his colleague's Mac G4 866 MHZ hard drive, he had not only forgotten our meeting, he hadn't noticed the vibrations of his cell phone. "I need to focus on one thing at a time. I'm not like you neurotypicals, I don't multitask." He was at another university building seven blocks away and asked me to meet him there.

The forty-eight-year-old works as a technology consultant for a climate change lab run by four universities and two government ministries. He tweaks their Cray-SX-6 supercomputers, helps with scientists' software glitches, and is the technology troubleshooter. His single-minded focus on systems suits his employers just fine, and their focus on science—not conformity—suits Georges, too. "In a scientific milieu people tend to be more calm. And that's where I fit in. I'm glad I'm not in a business milieu, where people are always tearing their hair out. I find it hard to know people's moods," Georges told me as we walked to a café for lunch. Although a bit apologetic about our initial snafu, he was more interested in the state of my parking meter. Did I realize that if I punched in a code, I could feed a parking meter anywhere in the vicinity and not get a ticket?

With his aviator glasses, mustache, and long salt-and-pepper hair pulled back in a ponytail, Georges is a Frank Zappa look-alike, but taller. Georges' face is open, usually smiling, and refreshingly unconflicted. "Cynicism demotivates me. I prefer a state of wonderment," he later told me without irony. I had asked about friends; he has a few faithful chums he's known a long time, he told me. "I meet them in situations where wonderment gets people together, like at university open houses, where you get to see the new technology." There isn't much ambivalence about Georges. Sticking to strict rules defines his work, his identity—even his appearance. He has altered nothing about his style of grooming or wardrobe in thirty years, buying his trousers from the same store and wearing his hair the same way. That's because he identifies with the counterculture movement of the seventies, he told me, seeing it as a time when individual differences were tolerated and respected. So he has adopted the style of the era, telling me he'd refuse to work anywhere there was a dress code or that required him to wear his hair short, a rare sensitive point. Georges is firm about not cutting his long hair, not because he wants to stick it to the man but because he likes the way it looks and is loath to change any aspect of his appearance or his routine.

Georges Huard, a gadget junkie,
at his favorite café

Georges sees the world in black and white, and machines as ciphers for mental states. "People's values are like computer languages," he explained. "Cobol is like all old-fashioned, complicated value systems. Basic is like freethinking. And Fortran is like scientific thinking." Unable to comprehend others' emotions as a child, he thought his mother's angry outbursts at his nonstop talking about arachnids— known as spiders to neurotypicals—were because a preset timer had gone off in her head. From the first time he saw a computer, he used its vocabulary to describe his activities and mental states, seeing little difference between machines and humans. "I would say 'syntax error' each time I made a social faux pas, or 'system error!' if it was bad enough to foul up an evening and result in rejection. If I wasn't allowed to do something I liked, I used 'protection violation.' I would log out from school and log in to my house." Georges knew early on that he was different from most people and now maintains a website so that others can understand his Asperger traits and his brother's. Like Daniel Tammet, he's the firstborn of a large family and has a brother with autism. One entry about Georges' adolescence touches on the painful aspects of being unable to read subtle social cues. If you can't imagine how others perceive you, it's hard to tailor your behavior so you'll fit in. But the flip side of unadulterated curiosity is that it's a surefire way to develop an area of expertise.

My special interests and differences (gait, monotone speech, and still my weakness in processing nonverbal cues) made me the butt of many jokes. . . . I had an obsession with time, and loved to set egg timers, play with stopwatches, and enjoyed looking at watches in jewelry store windows. I also liked calculators and especially liked the HP-55 because it had a 100-hour stopwatch. I knew the whole line of Hewlett-Packard calculators by heart. I even owned an HP-55. In my teenage years I had one interest that would eventually land me a few jobs. That was computers. On my HP-55 I learned the rudiments of programming with its 49 steps of programming memory and 20 registers. In high school I learned BASIC on an HP-2000 time-sharing minicomputer (we were linked with a 300-baud acoustic modem and a used Decwriter 2 printing terminal).[33]

This fascination with computers has been good for Georges, launching a stable, successful career, and creating a circle of like-minded people, who as it happens, are all male. Is it possible that this lifelong obsession with smart machines is the result of gender typing by Georges' parents and teachers? I think the answer is no. There is something in Georges' biological makeup that had him pull out his WIFI-enabled PDA over lunch and excitedly download a picture of the programmable calculator I had in 1979. There it was, the bulky Texas Instruments box plastered with the same fake wood grain as my father's old station wagon, with its impossibly tiny square keys that made a satisfying mechanical click. I feigned interest—after all, this was Georges' way of finding common ground. It occurred to me then that men with Asperger syndrome are the perfect foil for setting most women's strengths in relief. While I was focused on capturing the human experience of Asperger syndrome, its impact on Georges' relationships, his family, and his work, he was hell-bent on showing me all his portable electronic devices and how they were programmed—one to count down the minutes and seconds until the weekend, another to count the minutes and seconds that had passed since the moment of his birth, a third to record the milliseconds until his lease was up. He told me, "I'm sure that statistically speaking, nothing bad will happen to me for the next one hundred hours. So I hacked my Ironman [his watch] to count down from one hundred hours, and then I reset it. This makes me feel like a neurotypical who is calmed by smoking a cigarette." His determination to deconstruct his thought processes for me was not just instructive but endearing. Like Bob and Daniel, Georges was trying to forge a connection and enjoyed human contact. That it didn't come naturally didn't mean they didn't want it. Explaining how their brains worked to others was their way to connect.

Still, Georges lives alone by choice. "It takes a lot of effort to deal with people on a day-to-day basis. I need a few pauses between social interactions so I can face people at work," he said. But it would be a mistake to think of him or the other men profiled here as not interested in socializing or in making friends. Georges told me he enjoys people "as long as they're not cranky." But a job requiring him to read other people's emotional states and intentions would be impossible. "If I was at a job where I had to watch my social interactions and people's impressions of me . . ." Here there was a pause as he struggled to find the words to express just how bad this would be. "That would be like being a rocket scientist for you. You work with people on a day-to-day basis—connecting. I call it people processing. I need a lot of time off to do just a little bit of that." We chatted a bit more about the rarity of people with Asperger syndrome finding life partners. The need for protracted solitude or their difficulties with empathy might jinx a relationship, I suggested. Not judging how and where your comments might land could cause friction with a loved one. There's less reciprocity, no? Well, yes, Georges said. But there was something else. He reminded me that most people with Asperger syndrome are male. With a ratio of nine or ten men to one woman, unless they're gay, the chances of a person with Asperger syndrome finding a partner like himself would be very slim.

We had looked at the same problem with two different lenses. The color and texture of the human experience was my focus. I wanted to describe its variability and infinite shadings. An application of the numbers was his. Similarly, Georges hoped to dispatch with any uncertainty through his understanding of systems—his computer, timekeeping, and measurement devices. We seemed to be at opposite extremes and there was no changing places. No matter how much programmable calculator and computer experience I had, I was no more interested in these devices for their own sake than I was in the mechanics of my parking meter. They were systems I learned to use as means to specific ends. And no matter how much human contact Bob, Daniel, and Georges had as children in large families, other people's emotional worlds were still inscrutable to them. They needed to be coached in human interaction the way I needed to learn Fortran, step by step. And aside from a single-minded focus in their area of interest, each one succeeded in their systems-based jobs, in part because they had adults to teach them human relations skills explicitly and the intelligence to apply them in new situations.

Bob, Daniel, and Georges are examples of what happens when certain characteristics more common in men are exaggerated.[34] When it comes to their ability to understand systems versus people's motivations, these men are male hyperbole. With practice and assistance they have learned the essential social routines, and they gravitated to disciplines where their strengths are valued and their social weaknesses overlooked. Plus, many of their symptoms dissipated as they got older, not disappearing as much as becoming less extreme.[35] This is how many of these men experience a greater acceptance of their foibles in certain work environments than they experienced as children at school. They are able to make a contribution through a single-minded, concrete, and highly systematic approach. To succeed at work, they needed to find solitary jobs where an understanding of complex systems, not social finesse, is the ticket. Careers in math, physics, and computers are the perfect fit, disciplines where it just so happens they found other men like themselves.

It would be so much simpler if men and women were identical, with the same biological influences on their development and their interests. Yet the more closely we look at the biologically rigged extremes, the better we can see some of the same tendencies subtly reflected in the middle ranges, too. I've tried to convey the affecting way a more limited understanding of social signals makes the world seem concrete, with a literal understanding of language and shorter antennae for other people's reactions. With less awareness of the other point of view, there's less emphasis on other people's needs. There are fewer options—and less ambivalence—as these men seek out disciplines where their single-minded emphasis on systems is prized. A reduced capacity for empathy may not be much fun, but it sure clarifies life's choices.

We've seen how extreme men with dramatic gaps between their strengths and weaknesses gravitate to jobs that exploit a narrow field of expertise. But what of the reverse? What of women with more balanced profiles? As large numbers of women with powerful verbal and social skills, good systematic problem solving, broad ambitions and interests, *and* finely tuned empathy move into demanding, high-status jobs, one would expect few obstacles to material success. From extreme men working in narrowly defined fields, let's now return to the world of gifted women as they find themselves working in extreme jobs.

CHAPTER 6

No One Ever Asked Me
If I Wanted to Be the Daddy

I first met Sandra at a small dinner party she and her husband were hosting in honor of recently married colleagues. The food was perfect, the conversation was perfect, her elegant wool suit was perfect. Her two boys, one a toddler, the other a fair-headed preschooler, made a just-bathed, slicked-hair appearance before bedtime and then quietly disappeared with the babysitter. More help was in the kitchen, and as the courses kept coming it became clear that this evening had been planned by a pro. No one was left out, nothing forgotten. The wedding gift was a carved wooden box that was passed around so each guest could insert his or her good wishes, and it conveyed a sense of cere-mony, as if this were not just a small gathering for working buddies but a rite of passage. As a corporate litigation lawyer with two children under five, Sandra had to be organized, but this was more than just making a few lists. Everyone's needs were considered. Sandra seated like-minded people together, launched their first conversations, and interjected at critical moments to keep the social interaction flowing. As the evening rolled on, she leaned back in her chair with one leg tucked under her and cracked a private grin.

When I met her again a few years later, she had opted out of a dozen years of excellent suits and fourteen-hour-long days as a corpo-rate litigator. Her coterie of professional and domestic helpers was let go, and she'd foresworn planning perfect social evenings. When I asked why, Sandra explained that she'd felt conflicted about her work for years. At first she didn't mind pulling all-nighters, and enjoyed the rush that came after an intense push to get a legal problem solved. But after 12 years of extreme hours, after managing a recent case with 112 plaintiffs and 11 defendants, she felt dragged down. One of her boys, a fragile child, was showing signs of strain, with crying jags and behavior problems in school. She felt he was acting out the pressures of their family life, and she had been advised by her doctor to take a little time off to shore up her own resources. That was the beginning of a longer hiatus—one she was still assessing. She wanted to keep working, but something essential wasn't quite right—there was something off-kilter that she couldn't name.

Sandra had tried everything she could think of to find a fulfilling position in which she could reconcile the demands of a law career with family life. She'd moved from a big firm to a boutique firm back to a big firm and then to a position as in-house counsel. This peripatetic route finally convinced her that there was no perfect job for her in corporate law. It took her two years to make up her mind to quit; staying home with children was never part of her plan. "It was a surprise, even to me. I grew up thinking the workplace was so marvelous. After watching my mother at home, I felt so lucky to be working. I thought work would be a place where you could realize yourself. But I was naive. Work is just work."

Sandra thought hers was a unique, singular experience. But when she had invited eight female lawyers who had left practice to a social event, she discovered how similar their experiences were. The half hour she'd pegged for introductions took four hours as each of the female lawyers, all with more than ten years of experience, talked volubly about why they had ditched their jobs. Fed up with the hours and unable to meet brutal work demands even after making partner or after choosing in-house positions that would allow them to work a little less, like Sandra, they'd eventually tossed it all to stay home with fragile children, to start businesses or university degrees that would allow them more control of their time. All successful women, they wanted to work but found law practice unforgiving. One former lawyer in her late forties avowed that if her nineteen-year-old daughter chose to go into law, she'd go into mourning. "It's not a life," she said.

*   *   *

In 2001 the American Bar Association estimated the average salary of a law partner at $806,000, which is 33.5 times the average American's annual income. It's likely to be much more now, but even at half that sum the financial rewards are compelling. Yet many women routinely reject the chance to pull in these astronomical earnings. In fact, they decamp law firms 60 percent more often than men do.[1] No matter how much money they offer and how many work-life consultants they hire, law firms can't seem to hang on to the lion's share of their talented female associates past the first few years. A study of Harvard law graduates found that women were more likely than men to be hired at elite firms, but ten years later only a quarter of the women had stayed on to become partners (meanwhile, half the men did). Women now comprise 16.8 percent of large law-firm partners in the United States, where the attitude can be summarized by this question from high-stakes New York litigator David Boies: "Would you rather sleep or win?"[2]

Women aspiring to be partners "are back faster than a speeding bullet after childbirth" and feel the pressure to log even more hours than they did before children were born, according to Fiona Kay, a sociologist who studies lawyers. The need to conceal their physical and emotional needs so as to appear more like men seems understood. Linda Robertson, a veteran Vancouver lawyer, told attendees at the Canadian Bar Association annual convention in 2007 that female lawyers working in law firms are so terrified about appearing unproductive that they keep their cancer diagnoses and heart attacks a secret. "I have too many friends who have been diagnosed with cancer who won't tell their work colleagues because they are so afraid of being judged weak," she said.[3] Needless to say, many women find they can't sustain this rhythm. In Canada, where 60 percent of the law students are women, 26 percent of lawyers in private practice are female, and the ratio is similar in Britain.[4] This ratio is partly due to the "gendered generation," now in their sixties and mostly male. But it's also affected by the number of women who entered law practice since the seventies and who have since chosen to work in education, government, or industry.[5] Louise Ackers, a Leeds University law professor, had a no-nonsense answer when asked by the *Sunday Times* about the remarkable influx of female lawyers to university teaching in the United

Jubilant members of the Harvard Law School graduating class,
June 2006

Kingdom, where the average salary is about £35,000, or U.S. $70,000, about as much as a flight attendant might earn. "Many women like me—I have four children—find the long hours of law firms not suited to family life."[6] The motivation to find something more suitable must be powerful to take an 86 percent cut in pay. This chapter examines why so many women make that trade-off, looking specifically at women who seem to be the opposite of the extreme men I've profiled so far. These women are highly verbal, educated, literate, and most have superb social skills. They can do just about any job they please. So why don't they choose one that will net them $800,000 a year?

"I don't attribute this decision to being a woman or a mother. I see it as my personality, my values," Sandra said as we settled into the pillows on her pale green living-room couches. Regal even in track pants and nursing a cold, this forty-five-year-old had wrestled with her choices, especially as she felt she'd be disappointing her family by quitting. Her husband, a physician, was dead set against her leaving her job. Among other concerns, he thought she'd be bored. A former congressman, her father had always had the highest expectations of her. She waited until he was dying before telling him she was leaving her job. Even working as a corporate lawyer was seen as "my form of rebellion," as he didn't see that as a way for his daughter to burnish the intellectual landscape. As was true of the high-achieving women with science backgrounds, Sandra's family and the men in particular badly wanted her to achieve in the public sphere. She was clearly capable. As a law school gold medalist and with an Ivy League graduate degree, the best clerkships at the bench were hers and blue-chip law firms had clamored to hire her. She had tried both and now wanted out—at least for a while.

The exodus of women like Sandra is usually attributed to a hostile male culture, discrimination, and a dearth of female mentors. Thirty years ago these explanations had thrust, but now two others are more compelling. A good proportion of these high-achieving women have discovered that they have goals other than making pots of money. And many are in a position to act on their priorities, having married people similar to themselves. In the previous chapter we learned about assortative mating, which begins with like-minded people marrying each other. The same principle holds true for hardworking, high-earning lawyers, half of whom are women who are marrying professionals much like themselves. High six-figure salaries are very nice, but many families find they don't need two of these incomes to live comfortably. So why don't the male lawyers opt out instead? Many do. But not being "vanilla males," far more women discover they *want* to decamp or look for alternatives, especially when law presents such stark choices.

When Linda Hirshman wrote that "half the wealthiest, most-privileged, best-educated females in the country stay home with their babies rather than work in the market economy" because "the glass ceiling is at home," she wasn't writing about corporate lawyers like Sandra.[7] These so-called elite women can not only afford the best educations with multiple, prestigious degrees, but also the best household help. Since someone else was folding the laundry at Sandra's house, the truth was much more shaded than the marital chore roster. Instead, Sandra was motivated by the existential qualities of work and her priorities. Like many of the women profiled in previous chapters, Sandra expects her career to be consistent with her values. She did a master's degree in philosophy, Sandra said with a laugh, because she was looking for "the meaning of life." When she entered law school it was "to make the world a better place." Was she really going to hunker down indefinitely for fifteen hours a day when she felt there was no significance to her efforts except another buck in the bank?

Ultimately there was a conflict between Sandra's market value as a lawyer and the kind of work that resonated with *her* values. "As a good student, I got drawn into corporate practice," she said, and soon she found herself taking corporate jobs at high pay. After she had to sack an employee, she felt that she was "not living my values, that there was no loyalty." Adding to her disillusionment was empathy for her children, whom she felt deserved more time than she could give them while she was working in such an extreme job. Intelligent, ambitious, and hardworking, well educated and well connected, Sandra was not being stymied by external factors—she didn't feel that a glass ceiling was preventing her from achieving her goals. She simply felt that there was a mismatch between the corporate model and what she wanted from her work life. "I was not self-promoting. Those weren't my values. I was modest. And I didn't have a plan." The corporate world had derailed her from making a difference because "that's what happens when you don't have a plan."

Although she felt alone in her experience, Sandra's feeling of dislocation was one feature of the mass movement of women into male-typical careers in the 1970s and 1980s. For the most part these work environments made no adjustments for women—and were not expected to. Yet a huge transformation was taking place, one that would dramatically affect the legal profession. Between 1971 and 1991 the proportion of female lawyers grew more than 800 percent. More women have entered law than any other formerly male profession since equal-rights legislation changed the work landscape. Yet not much was done to alter the formula for promotion and partnership in law. Billable hours and demands stayed static and have even increased as the international business environment has become more competitive, with expectations of 1,800 to 2,000 hours a year now the standard in high-status jobs. In this atmosphere, and without the force of goodwill behind them, recent adjustments such as nonpartnership tracks, part-time, and flextime are often code words for a dead end to your career.

Many women discovered a lack of fit they didn't anticipate. Studies of women in corporate law show that they are more unhappy with their work than men and thus twice as likely to leave it.[8] Even in their first five years of practice, young female lawyers say that they are less satisfied with the social value of their work and its setting than are men, according to Ronit Dinovitzer, a Toronto sociologist who surveyed 9,200 American lawyers who graduated from law school in 2002. Her report reflects a pattern seen all over the developed world: higher numbers of men in private practice, but twice to three times as many women working in education or in nonprofit agencies, choosing to earn less than a third of their colleagues' private-sector salaries. Dinovitzer sees no sign that this money versus meaning gender gap is abating and predicts that it will soon yawn even wider.[9]

The fact that these women are educated, highly literate, and have a number of attractive options makes them a perfect group to stand in for other well-educated professional women. And as there are a number of large-scale studies tracking corporate lawyers' decisions, the field is an excellent test case for the vanilla male hypothesis. With an edge in verbal and social skills, most of these women are at an advantage. Women who enter law are eminently capable of doing the work; the pay is excellent; and law firms want them. But many women belatedly discover that the attraction is not mutual.

Adaptive Women

Sandra's epiphany is not unique to her but part of a social trend. Not having a fixed plan is the rule for 60 percent of women in developed societies, according to the British sociologist Catherine Hakim. In fact, given the choice, 60 to 80 percent of American and European women choose part-time work over full-time schedules or staying home full-time—even if they had initially intended to work full-time and even if the decision will cost them in job security and earnings.[10] "The vast majority of women who claim to be career-oriented discover that their priorities change after they have children," writes Hakim. Eroding the idea of a united sisterhood, Hakim has amassed data from European and American census and national surveys that clearly show that women in modern societies are hardly homogeneous. Instead, they separate fairly cleanly into three groups. There are those who want to stay home full-time, whom she calls "home-centered" (approximately 20 percent). There are those whose careers take precedence, whom she calls "work-centered" (approximately 20 percent). These career-oriented women experience few disadvantages to being female; if they have the same credentials and put in the same hours, they achieve the same rewards as men.

The majority, the remaining 60 percent, are women who try to combine children and career, drifting between various work schedules and positions, looking for the perfect arrangement.[11] These "adaptive" women adjust their careers to accommodate their families' needs and their own values, a trend as powerful in socially progressive Sweden and Norway as it is in the United States. Like Sandra, many of these "adaptive" women don't have a firm plan when they start out, or find that it changes the minute they see their baby's face. Many end up working part-time, have patchwork résumés, and ultimately work in less lofty positions than they would if their families had not been their priority.

Adapting one's career to one's family is axiomatic for this group, whether they're lawyers, nurses, or salesclerks. Having bounced between college teaching, clinical work, and writing, taking various positions in varying combinations of full-time and part-time work over the twenty years I was raising a family, this characterization was faithful to my experience. It also described Sandra's leapfrogging through four or five different legal positions in twelve years—a pattern not likely to be the best route to the highest number of partnership points. Calling it "Preference Theory," Hakim nailed two realities. Not all women want the same thing. And when women have choices, only about 20 percent will choose what men choose.

When I went to meet Hakim for lunch at the London School of Economics, the slight, colorfully dressed sociologist was already there waiting for me among the noisy throngs of students. She immediately picked me out from the crowd, extending her delicate, braceleted hand as we made eye contact. For years Hakim has pricked the ire of the European feminist establishment by asserting that persisting gender gaps in pay were the result of women's deep-seated preferences. As a result, she has an iron lady reputation that has rivaled Margaret Thatcher's. Hakim called the idea that one-size-fits-all social policies would alter pay gaps "true lies." Her worst sin, according to her critics, was asserting that social policy could never allow the majority of women to have it all, since a measurable slice of the population—10 to 30 percent—never wanted it all, anyway, and another 60 percent adapt their ambitions to their family's needs.

Hakim believes that one reason why women haven't made greater inroads into the more homogeneous male phalanx is that women aren't clones of one another, but a heterogeneous group with competing interests and goals. "If you are seriously interested in a career, you don't have time for children and if you are seriously interested in bringing up more than one child, you don't have the time, effort, and imagination for getting to the top of a career," she said. Dem's fightin' words. You'd hardly expect this whippet-thin woman in a brilliant royal blue dress, brass beads, and sparkly gold jacket to take on all comers. But appearances can fool you. "If someone tested me, I'm sure I'd have the highest level of testosterone," she said mildly as we chose our lunch plates in the sunny LSE cafeteria, adding "the pudding here is just smashing" as she put one on her tray.

That people can be other than what they seem is not that hard to grasp. But the notion that professional women can feel emotionally conflicted once children are born is seen as letting down the side. And women themselves often feel betrayed by their expectation that high-level jobs and children can be seamlessly combined. "Most of us thought we would work and have kids, at least that was what we were brought up thinking we would do—no problem. But really we were duped. None of us realized how hard it is," said a former high tech executive to a *New York Times* reporter in 2006. The article documented women's declining participation in the labor force as of 2000, a trend most acute in highly educated, high-earning mothers, many of whom delayed parenthood until their careers were established.[12] This subset of "adaptive" women often want work that can accommodate their families, but find high-level part-time or nine-to-five jobs rare.

And what about women who share the typically "male" view that commitment to a career takes precedence over the vicissitudes of family life and therefore remain childless—as is true of Hakim herself?

Such exclusively career-oriented women are a minority, Hakim says, and much like the majority of men, their histories are characterized by a fair degree of foresight and strategizing to get them where they want to go. Half of all women in the top professional and managerial grades are childless, Hakim reports, which is similar to women in academic science and engineering.[13] Reliable contraception has allowed them to choose how they want to direct their energies and to plan their ascent. In Hakim's case, over the past eight years she has written six books and says, "there's no way I could have done that if I had had children. The fact is that children are a twenty-year project and a career is a twenty-to-forty-year project and there is an incompatibility there."[14]

And there's the rub. Women who plan their careers are the ones netting dramatic advantages in earnings and promotions. But they're in the minority. One of the data sets Hakim looked at was the American National Longitudinal Survey, which examined women's career aspirations over a fifteen-year span. Young women were asked about their plans for their careers in 1968, and then interviewed again every year until 1983, when they were twenty-nine to thirty-nine years old. What did they expect to be doing at age thirty-five? Female career planners turned out to be a small group. The majority of the women were either home-centered or were drifters who ended up working but hadn't had a firm plan of what they would do when they started out. Compared to the planners, these undecideds were ultimately 30 percent less likely to be working than women who planned a career as a trial lawyer, for instance. Eighty-two percent of women who planned their careers were working as anticipated at age thirty-five, and their planning netted them salary premiums.[15] Still, planners comprise only a quarter of all women. The majority of women drift from job to job, from full-time to part-time or not working at all for a spell, and their earnings and upward mobility take a hit. This contributes mightily to the gender gap in earnings.

Now that women have choices, their values and preferences have turned out to be driving forces in their careers. In Sandra's case, having earned a high salary for years as well as marrying a professional like herself, those choices were amplified, giving her the freedom to decide what she wanted to do next. George Bernard Shaw quipped,

"That is the use of money: it enables us to get what we want instead of what other people think we want."

Sandra followed opportunities as they presented themselves, moving from one job to another, to a two-year hiatus, and then to a part-time position as a university law teacher—her next step. This uncharted approach is consistent with Stanford professor Charles O'Reilly's research findings about male and female MBA students' careers. "Typically, the men would have a vision of where they were going to be and what kind of job they were going to have." Although the women were ambitious and good at playing the game, their plans were more diffuse," said O'Reilly.[16] Two female CEOs profiled by *The New York Times* in 2006 confirm this serendipitous approach. "It was never about wanting to be a CEO. I didn't know what a CEO was. It was about getting the As and getting the education," said Carol Bartz, the former chief executive of Autodesk, a software company. Maggie Wilderotter, the chief executive of Citizens Communications, commented, "I never sat down and said, 'I'm going to be a doctor when I grow up.' I just had opportunities present themselves to me in my career."[17] Here Hakim describes the organic quality of women's histories:

There is a remarkable difference between men and women in the way they tell the story of their lives. The masculine life story typically emphasizes decisiveness, "doing it my way," refusing to accept situations that were belittling or boring, overcoming obstacles and enemies, highlighting achievements and the attainment of goals. The feminine life story typically presents a smoothly integrated stream of events in which everything they did was the "natural" outcome of the situation at the time, the actions of others, chance events. . . . It appears that many women have difficulty in openly expressing their work-lifestyle preferences. Intentions, plans, motivations, and preferences can disappear into the stories women tell about their lives, like water into sand.[18]

This lyrical passage captures not just two career approaches, but two ways of recounting your career story. More men than women start out with a goal, then keep their heads down and their eyes on the prize. The more swashbuckling male story also conceals the costs of slogging away at jobs that suit long-term goals but not necessarily personal happiness, a theme I'll return to shortly. They may get you to your destination, but at a price. The flexibility inherent in the female story includes the tendency to incorporate alternative points of view, which has different costs. It's not so much a question of women feeling it's not "nice" to own up to their ambitions as it is of looking at their careers from multiple vantage points, constantly reevaluating where they are. For many women, the goal is a moving target.

That's What Happens When You Don't Have a Plan

If you had asked me before my first child was born to choose from Hakim's three groups, I wouldn't have hesitated before placing myself with career-oriented women. I didn't expect to feel any differently after my baby was born than I did before—or much differently than her father would. But my plans for a swift return were shot to hell when a wrinkly, underweight, and squalling baby appeared instead of the placid, pink-cheeked, robust infant I'd imagined cheerily handing off to a babysitter. She needed to gain weight rapidly and I had to nurse her on demand so her tiny limbs would plump up and she would be comforted. Work demands seemed remote as I spent the first few weeks of her life feeding and walking her around our apartment just to soothe her. The isolation was a contrast to my former life of shoulder-padded suits and agenda control.

I was shocked by my protective feelings. I needed to be with her. I needed her to be healthy. So what was I thinking when I said yes to a physician who called me one afternoon for help? He was one of my colleagues at the pediatric clinic where I worked, and a prominent family in his practice was in trouble. As a favor, could I come in to assess the situation? As I propped the baby high up on my shoulder to answer the phone, I heard his undertone of dismay. In the past this colleague had been kind to me. I wanted to be of assistance, and thought, would I refuse this request if I were a man? It would be unprofessional, uncollegial, to withdraw from my work life completely just because I had *a baby*. The small favor turned into days spent researching a new area— as I was soon called to court as a witness, and would spend even more time preparing and testifying. It's a slow dance any lawyer knows well. My father, a lawyer whose advice I had sought about testifying, said, "This will be good for you." My husband said, "It will be refreshing to get out," and my male colleague was urging me to assist. My personal patriarchy was rooting for me to get out and work. While I was at the clinic other families requested assistance as well, some urgently, others insistently. Soon enough I was back at the office—even though the longing to be with my infant was fierce—and any baby's cry from the waiting room would trigger my letdown response and soak the front of my blouse, discreetly concealed beneath my all-purpose blazer. I had submitted to external pressures to participate in the economy. Like Sandra, I was among the majority—an "adaptive" woman who belatedly discovered she would rather adjust career to family than the other way around.

In the early eighties I was not alone in thinking that men and women had nearly identical brains, but that we had been socialized to take on different roles. If my husband, a doting father, could leave his scrawny newborn after two weeks at home and go to work for ten hours a day without a backward glance or a blip in his concentration, the script dictated that this was because he had learned that his role was to be the provider. And if I felt physical distress about tearing myself away from a six-week-old baby—notwithstanding the monotony and isolation of new motherhood—I had internalized mine as maternal caregiver. Never mind that my mother and both grandmothers worked outside the home, as well as in it. Many of us thought that if only women could tame their outdated sentimentality, if only men were present and willing to offer their babies more bottles, then our parental roles could be reversed. I was amused but admiring when a male friend strapped on a device at a dinner party that allowed him to simulate breast-feeding. The vinyl reservoir lay flat and deflated against his white torso like a colostomy bag. Even if he seemed a bit sheepish, he was also proud that with four children and a working wife he could whistle this familiar tune: "I can do anything better than you can. I can do anything better than you." At the time we assumed that men and women were equals—not just in rights and opportunities, as they should be, but also in underlying psychology and behavior. Any differences, including physical differences, could be fixed via technology, policy, or force of will. This is how social ideals clouded attitudes toward the intersection of nurturing and work, an issue as personal and often as biologically driven as sex itself.

This is the vanilla gender assumption: that female is just a variation of male. But more than two decades after my daughter was born, brain imaging and neuroendocrinology have unveiled many of the biological networks underlying mothers' specific longing for their infants and their drive to nurture them. Breast-feeding in particular releases hormones and neurotransmitters that induce euphoria in mothers, so funneling nutrients into a newborn through retrofitted surgical tubing just gets half the job done.

I'm not suggesting that only mothers can feed babies, but the word euphoria provides a little hint as to why they might want to. The hormone prolactin, produced in males *and* females, is the messenger that turns on breast-feeding in females and circulates any time feeding, nurturing, or protecting is on the agenda. And the opiatelike hormone oxytocin, which the anthropologist Sarah Blaffer Hrdy calls "the elixir of contentment," surges during breast-feeding, too (not to mention during childbirth, sex, and cuddling), which is evolution's way of making proximity to infants and being tied down to feeding them attractive. The hormone is likely in breast milk as well, so the baby enjoys not only physical closeness but pleasure along with her meal in a compelling pas de deux.[19] The resulting give-and-take causes reciprocal changes at the cellular, hormonal, and even the epigenetic levels of the mother and child, reinforcing their attachment to each other through nursing and skin-to-skin contact. These baroque interactions are difficult to tease apart, but one certainty emerges. There are distinctive design elements in female brains that evolved to promote the survival of infants. Triggered by an avalanche of hormones at childbirth and during nursing, the behavioral and emotional interactions that ensue don't vanish because social and economic factors require new mothers to work. In fact, separation from their babies can induce anxiety and panic in nursing mothers that Louann Brizendine, a neuropsychiatrist in San Francisco, describes in *The Female Brain* as much like the symptoms of drug withdrawal. Regular intimate contact is not simply a cultural imperative, but a physiological one. After infusing their brains with the analgesic and pleasure-inducing effects of oxytocin every few hours when they nurse their babies, a mother is suddenly cut off from her supply. That's why nursing mothers newly returned to full-time work can't wait to get home. Nursing doesn't just release milk that's been building up all day. As we saw in the chapter on empathy, it also produces a natural drug that reduces stress.

Now, human fathers also care for infants, so why didn't they evolve to grow breasts? It *would* be handy. Pigeons, doves, emperor penguins, and flamingos of both sexes regurgitate a unique recipe of digested food mixed with mucus called "crop milk," so why not human males? The evolutionary answer is that when mammals first evolved they weren't monogamous. As babies were gestated internally males didn't know which infants were theirs, and so didn't invest anything in their survival. Females evolved to be able to feed their offspring solo with a high-calorie diet that would allow mothers to keep foraging, all the while shielding their offspring from having to compete for food before they were ready. The genes for breast growth and lactation—as well as for the sex hormones that regulate the whole process—were laid down at that time and are still with the species. The only male mammal that has breasts is the Dyak fruit bat in Malaysia, but evolutionary psychologist Linda Mealey notes that no one knows whether they develop breasts after eating fruit with phytoestrogens, or whether these male bats really do nurse their young. If they do, they'd be the only male mammals—other than my friend Michael—to try it.[20]

Whether birds or bats do it, the connection between nursing and maternal attachment is affectingly described by Hrdy as central to the evolutionary roots of empathy. But it starts off very slowly. Instead of the raucous joy North Americans are expected to feel as soon as a baby is born, many cultures are initially more guarded. The real emotional response comes when the dangerous hours after birth are past and the mother puts baby to breast, thus kicking more hormonal circuits into gear.

Among the Machinguenga and other peoples of lowland South America, the newborn is set aside after the midwife cuts the umbilical cord, almost ignored, till the mother has been bathed. Only after the mother begins to nurse the child, hours later, or perhaps the next day, does the mother become concerned about the infant.[21]

Anthropologists have described Mayan women in Yucatán reacting "indifferently" to their newborns at first—"no smiles, no talk or exclamations," according to Hrdy. Another slow-to-warm-up group of mothers was a sample of mostly married, healthy, well-off British mothers whose affection for their babies developed only in the days and weeks after they were born. Mothers with older children at home were less likely to have this delayed reaction, possibly because prolactin is in greater supply among experienced parents and jump-starts the attachment process earlier. Prolactin and oxytocin are not unique to females, but the delicate interplay between hormones and behavior seems perfectly rigged when nursing is one of the hubs in the circuit.

The Female Rat Race

Anyone who has ever watched *Wild Kingdom* knows that a female's behavior toward its offspring can trump all else, including feeding and protecting itself. Why would a female killdeer—a ploverlike bird that nests on the ground—limp pathetically across the baseball field as if it were mortally wounded and a marauding dog's next Happy Meal? High levels of prolactin prompt not only nurturing behavior, but these defensive antics, too. Prolactin activates neural networks that spur the bird to entice away a predator who gets dangerously close to her nest. Her defense of the chicks then boosts her prolactin levels even more.

In mammals, such surges of hormones during pregnancy, birth, lactation, and caretaking have been found to remodel neural circuits in the female brain, not only fostering nurturing but also enhancing learning and memory. More simply, there's evidence that motherhood makes mammals smarter. Roughly the same hormone circuits involved in the killdeer's dissimulation also allow mother rats to negotiate mazes better than nonmothers, according to two neuroscientists at the University of Richmond, Craig Howard Kinsley and Kelly Lambert. The researchers showed how young female rats that had either been pregnant or had just been provided with foster pups were able to find food hidden in mazes better than virgin rats. Simply the presence of young ones—even around females that had never been pregnant—boosted spatial memory by delivering oxytocin and altering neural circuits.[22] These newly developed spatial skills are permanent and permit them to forage and hunt better. This seems to contradict the folk wisdom that pregnancy and motherhood addle one's brain—likely through the sedative effects of some of the very same hormones. But there seems to be an ancillary benefit. Motherhood increases certain types of problem solving, especially when offspring are vulnerable.

Clearly, males and females do not have interchangeable brains, and motherhood confers cognitive advantages. Kinsley and Lambert's research brought to mind the resources marshaled by the mothers of the vulnerable males profiled in this book. Daniel Tammet's mother tutored him in the nuts and bolts of social interaction; Daniel Paley's and Andrew's mothers took an acute interest in their reading and made sure they had the assistance they needed; and Sandra's awareness of her son's emotional needs prompted her to reassess her work schedule. We often attribute this kind of support to cultural expectations of mothers, that they'll be the ones to step up to the plate when their children need help. But perhaps there's a biological thread, too, making them more vigilant to their children's distress and more apt to apply their problem-solving skills to relieving it. This hypersensitivity to the needs of offspring is evident in brain studies of parents' reactions to their infants' crying. When Italian researchers at the University of Milan-Bicocca compared the brain activation of parents and nonparents responding to the pictures of distressed or placid babies, both men and women reacted to the unhappy infants. "But the female parents showed the greatest and earliest response," wrote Alice Proverbio.

There are limitations to generalizing from rats to humans, of course, one of which is that hormones play a stronger role in the behavior of animals, whereas culture means more to humans. Still, there is a shared maternal neural pathway in mammals' brains that has been clearly delineated in animal *and* in human studies. These regions in the brain are rife with hormone receptors, and include a part of the hypothalamus deep in the middle of the brain called the medial preoptic area (mPOA). The mPOA and its connections to the cingulate cortex, a ridge of infolded neurons that surround the corpus callosum, help regulate mood and emotions. The whole pathway is not just exquisitely sensitive to stimulation by oxytocin and prolactin; estrogen and progesterone also enlarge neurons in these areas and increase connections to other regions of the brain linking motherhood to problem solving and rewards.[23] There's a heavy cost to becoming a mother in pure energy and the freedom to move around. The neurochemically induced feeling of being rewarded by nurturing might have evolved to counteract those costs.

We see the evidence in the pleasure pathways lit up by holding and feeding babies—a phenomenon I noticed whenever a newborn was in my clinic waiting room. I could hear from the chords of high-pitched cooing that the female family physicians and office staff had gathered yet again around a new mother, admiring her baby and waiting for their "fix"—the opportunity to hold it close. All these women had chosen work that would bring them into contact with children, but babies under four months of age continued to exert a magnetic pull that never wore off. In animals, the nurturing relationship is so inherently rewarding to mothers that when given the choice, new mother rats choose newborn pups over cocaine. Before they had babies or once their pups were older, female rats definitely preferred the drugs. But this small window affecting the choices of new mothers seems evolutionarily wise, as even a single dose of cocaine disrupts maternal behavior. Joan Morrell, the neuroendocrinologist at Rutgers University who did this clever study, discovered that cocaine interferes with the neural pathways that govern maternal behavior, specifically the mPOA. If this part of the maternal neural circuit is damaged by these drugs or by surgery, maternal behavior disappears entirely.[24]

Moving from rats back to humans, when neuroimaging is used to peek behind the curtain of mother-child interaction, we see that motherly love is tightly linked to its predecessor, romantic love. Andreas Bartels at the Max Planck Institute and Semir Zeki at University College London studied neural mechanisms activated by couples in love, and hypothesized that the same neural regions might form a core network of human attachment. After all, both have evolutionary benefits—lovers perpetuate the species and maternal attachment ensures its survival. So the neuroscientists expected the two psychological phenomena to share neural and hormonal circuitry. When mothers looked at pictures of their own infants, the parts of their brains that govern pleasure and reward lit up on fMRIs in ways that were distinct from their reactions to pictures of other infants they knew. And the regions of the brain that were activated by these maternal feelings overlapped significantly with the areas that the scientists had previously found to be activated by feelings of romantic love. So the bonds between lovers and those between mothers and children share some of the same hardware, networks, and hormonal binding sites. But there were some routes specific to maternal love—specifically the lateral orbito-frontal cortex and the periaqueductal gray matter, or PAG—that were activated only when women were looking at pictures of their own children. Based on previous studies, the scientists expected these overlapping attachment networks to feature lots of receptores for hormones like oxytocin and a related peptide, vasopressin. Not only were these core attachment areas dense in hormone receptors, but stimulating these areas elicited pleasure in the mother and suppressed negative feelings and judgments about the object of her affection—her child.[25] This explains why every child is beautiful to his or her mother. (I have seen mothers look adoringly at their children while they kick and spit—at me.) Romantic love is indeed blind, and the chemicals that sweeten lovers' perceptions of each other put similar blinders on mothers.

This is a good thing for infants, who can be smelly, noisy, and outrageously demanding and who don't ever say thank you. Yet as we've seen, when environmental conditions are right, hormonal priming prompts mothers to feed and nurture them, to be keenly attuned to their distress, and to exploit every neural connection that will allow them to solve problems related to their survival. These behaviors release the same pleasure-inducing hormones responsible for the feeling of well-being after orgasm. Clearly maternal behavior prompts feel-good circuits in the brain.

Does it do the same in fathers? All the information we have is from animal studies, which show that the PAG, one of the sites activated in the maternal attachment circuit, is involved in nurturing behavior only in females, according to Andreas Bartels. While there are plenty of studies showing large sex differences linked to maternal behavior in animals' brains, the human fMRI studies on attachment haven't yet included any males. As I mentioned earlier, there is preliminary evidence that oxytocin in nasal spray boosts men's trust in social situations and their ability to read hard-to-decipher facial expressions. Oxytocin, more readily produced and "taken up" by women during childbirth, breast-feeding, and ongoing nurturing, is likely the chemical glue that bonds mothers and babies together after birth, amplifying their preexisting advantage in empathy.

In previous chapters we saw how testosterone acts on neural circuitry to rejig spatial and social skills—pushing these areas to extremes in some men. The hormonal influences on female nurturing are similarly profound. These biological factors can't help but influence women's attitudes to their work, including the more common desire among women to work part-time or reasonable hours. Gifted women in male-typical careers feel these pressures no less than women in so-called gender-typical jobs. To put it baldly, high-achieving, high-billing female law partners also want to nurse their babies and spend time with them and if they can't, many quit. The demands on female lawyers who have children are not only in thousands of billable hours and administrative duties, but also in the cascading physiological conditions of motherhood. These unique hormonal-genetic-environmental interactions make mothers smarter, more responsive to their infants, and more communicative about their shared environment—including its stresses. But this combination of factors puts lawyers who are mothers in a unique crucible that no male lawyer experiences. Their internal drivers are different, and their infants respond to them and their stresses in unique ways. It shouldn't be any surprise that on average, female lawyers who have children view their supercharged careers through a different lens than men do.

Still, individual differences mean that there will be some fathers with a stronger desire to stay home with their children, and some mothers with a stronger desire to work at just this kind of extreme job. Does that mean that their roles are easily reversed? Let's meet a family where this seems, from afar, to be true.

The So-Called Glass Ceiling

Nothing could be more different from Sandra's elegant house than the inner-city breakfast spot where I met Caroline. When I showed up at

8:00 A.M. dragging my briefcase and overnight bag, she was already waiting, sitting with a drained coffee cup and the newspaper open to the legal page. She pointed out the headline with mild amusement. "At some firms can lawyers be too gay?" All around us were the bleary-eyed trying to jar themselves awake. The government buildings were nearby—that's where Caroline worked as a lawyer—and the bureaucrats in suits and oxford shirts were joined by office workers and a couple of men who looked like they had spent their night on the street. Caroline's white cardigan and tidy school-girl appearance screamed teacher! librarian! mild-mannered nice person! Underestimating her would be a grave mistake, however. As soon as we started chatting I decided that if I were in serious legal trouble, I would want her at my side, softly intoning instructions in my ear. But as she had left corporate law practice soon after becoming a partner, this would not be possible.

Caroline was interesting to me because, like Sandra, she was a top-tier lawyer and searingly smart. She could have chosen any type of work—and indeed had tried several options before settling on the public service. With a Ph.D. in the arts she could have opted for academe but decided she wanted to change the world, she told me, with a wry grin. She "was lucky enough" to be hired by a blue-chip law firm, where she stayed for ten years, making partner even after two long maternity leaves. Taking almost a year off after a baby reflected a recent shift in the corporate climate, she said as just a few years earlier women were taking two months maximum. Caroline also had a stay-at-home husband when her children were babies. Now that they were a bit older he was working part-time, but his primary job was to cover the home front: ferry the children to and from school, look after them when they were sick, make sure the fridge was stocked, fill all the countless invisible gaps that a parent at home fills. Child care and domestic duties were phantom problems, she said. Her spouse had the major child responsibilities in her case, and "it makes no difference at this income level, anyway," she said flatly about lawyers and child care. For most, nannies are the rule. But even with the much-envied proverbial "wife" at home—the preexisting condition for men's success, according to most professional women—Caroline had still abandoned corporate law for a salary that was a fraction of what she had been earning before.

"I wasn't forced out. It was the opposite." Her firm begged her to stay. "I never felt that the work I was given was different. I was never treated badly as a woman. The environment was very supportive. On the contrary, at the big firms they bend over backward. I think firms have worked really hard to move away from discriminatory practices, to welcome women." Caroline had mentors, and she liked the files she worked on. It was a systems problem and not a gender issue at all, she said, referring to the expectation that every lawyer—male or female—would be available 24/7 if necessary, not just to meet billing targets but also to meet clients' demands. "It's about providing service to the clients, being available to them anytime, keeping the profits high," she said of the draconian hours of the standard law practice. In the global environment all the big firms were angling for the same clients and hoped to snag them by providing the best service, she said—not an environment where part-time, flextime, or working a nine-to-five day would be an asset to one's career.

At her firm Caroline routinely worked from 7:30 A.M. to 6:00 P.M., plus an evening and two weekends a month to make her target of 1,800 billable hours. "It wasn't just the hours, but that was part of it," she said with a mild upward shift in volume. "I would leave the house before my son was awake. And come home after 6:00 P.M. I felt I was turning into a 1950s dad, a dad who comes home when the kids' day is over and just plays with them for fifteen minutes before bed. Here we had an arrangement that worked. I had a partner who was happy to work part-time. But I was missing out. I was never going to get that back." She repeated the sentence, this time with more emphasis. "And it would never get better. I'd always be busy. No one ever asked me if I wanted to be the daddy."

Caroline did not see herself as a victim of discrimination, but as an agent of her own decisions, as someone who had made a considered choice. And in fact she hadn't opted out of full-time work but had taken a full-time job in the public service that reflected her social values and gave her more flexibility. Caroline still puts in long hours—she's dedicated, and she likes to work. But she no longer comes in to work at the crack of dawn unless there is a special deadline. Round-the-clock availability and face time are less crucial in government than in private practice. Her choice to sacrifice phenomenally high pay and corporate status was driven by her desire to spend more time with her children and to work on projects that reflect her values. For her, the change was good news. But those at her former firm hoping to add a bright, motivated woman to the corps of senior partners just lost another one. And the statistics would reveal another female lawyer earning less than a man.

Sandra and Caroline are not unusually altruistic. On average, female lawyers everywhere are more likely than men to migrate to meaningful but less well-paid work that is more closely aligned with their values. When they do, the glass ceiling is self-imposed. "My impression is that more women are motivated by social justice issues," observed Caroline, remarking on her friends' reasons for going to law school and her own switch from private practice to public service. Her impression is supported by the number of women who say they go into law "to promote social fairness," according to author Mona Harrington, and who then opt to work in legal aid, or in the nonprofit sector, both areas dominated by women.[26]

At least ten studies show that women, on average, find social aspects of the job more important than men, whereas men find pay and advancement the big carrots.[27] Described in chapter 3, the recent 500 Family Study found that intrinsic rewards, such as a job's inherent challenges, one's interest in the work, the social support it offers, and its humanitarian mission are powerful motivators for the majority of women and outweigh extrinsic rewards such as salary and benefits. Of course, men are also motivated by a job's challenges and the ability to contribute knowledge. But the men in the study were less driven by a job's social aspects and by the opportunity to help people. Interestingly, women's motivations vary according to their occupations and education. Female managers were most likely to be motivated by salary and benefit plans, whereas female lawyers and judges were least likely to be motivated by these things, which may explain why throwing more money at them may not keep them in their jobs. As we saw in chapter 3, the higher a woman's education, the less likely she is to be motivated by extrinsic rewards. College-educated women are 37 percent less likely than less-educated women to be lured by the salary and status of the occupation. This was true even when the researchers controlled for their husbands' occupations. Women didn't feel any more drawn to high-paying jobs when their spouses earned less.[28] And there is evidence that there is good reason to take mothers' work motivations seriously. There is a closer link between a mother's work satisfaction and her adolescents' happiness than there is with a father's. To put it simply, a mother's motivations and feelings about her work are contagious to her teenagers in a way that a father's are not.[29]

The Gender Paradox

We know that women have varying goals—career, home, or both—and that 60 to 80 percent of women are in the last two categories; they adapt their careers to accommodate children. We also know that female law partners are twice as likely as men to be dissatisfied with their corporate careers, one factor that hastens their exit.[30] And finally, we know that female lawyers choose socially meaningful jobs over money and status twice as often as men do.[31] The question is what relationship these factors have to women's happiness.

No one expects women to be happier with their work. Yet when career satisfaction is measured, women beat men hands down. Economists call this the gender paradox. Women earn less as a group and are still sparse at the top of the hierarchy. Yet in countries including the United States, Japan, Korea, Switzerland, Sweden, Canada, and Britain, they have consistently rated themselves to be more satisfied with their work lives than men.[32] It's assumed that women will want the same things as men and be very unhappy if they don't get them. But what if women have different goals? If women view their work as an isolated element to be evaluated on its own, then the "vanilla male" view makes sense, as it does to 20 to 30 percent of women. But if the majority of women see work as only one factor that fits into a complex pastiche, they might rate themselves as happier if their jobs allow them to succeed in other spheres, too. One British study that supports that idea was conducted by the sociologist, Michael Rose, at the University of Bath. Based on surveys of 25,000 female public service employees, Rose showed that British women's rates of job satisfaction have fallen since the early nineties, while men's work satisfaction has stayed the same. Thus, as women's work values and pressures approach the male standard, their satisfaction drops to the male level, too. Clearly, a significant proportion of women don't want to work long hours at intense jobs and are doing so reluctantly.[33]

In his book *Happiness,* the British economist Richard Layard explains why he thinks women's levels of happiness have dropped while their pay and job opportunities have improved. Their happiness has not kept pace with their increasing salaries and job opportunities because they can't keep up with the Joneses, Layard writes. Women used to measure themselves against other women. Now they look at both men and women, so there are more ways to feel that they don't make the grade.[34] But there's more to it than that, I think. For the most part women have stepped into positions defined by male ambition. By turning on their heels, more than half of all female lawyers are saying they reject this picture of success.

More typical male single-mindedness may come at a cost to happiness and personal health. The laser focus required of some high-level jobs requires employees to behave as if they work in a vacuum. At the highest levels, work can supersede all other interests and concerns. If career success is your primary goal, this will create no dissonance. But multiple goals require trade-offs—another way to understand the gender paradox. If women opt for a job that's less extreme or one that offers a chance to have a social impact, they're applying their preferences and exerting some control over their lives. This may detract from their earnings but add to their satisfaction.

Whatever the reason, the complex relationship between women's happiness and their work also hinges on the much-vaunted balance between work and family. A British research team led by Anne McMunn, an epidemiologist at University College London, interviewed 1,171 women born in 1946 every decade after they turned twenty. They found that women who had taken on multiple roles as mothers, wives, and at work were the healthiest—and the thinnest—compared to women who filled only one role. Meanwhile, a similarly large Canadian study led by Heather McLean at the University of Toronto found that successfully balancing work and family can reduce women's rates of depression, just as long as the hours are not too long and they don't work too hard.[35]

The two lawyers I profiled made trade-offs that enabled them to combine three priorities: professional work, a commitment to social values, and time for family life. But what about the 55 percent of men and 20 percent of women who make no such adjustments? They're unabashedly career-driven and reap the rewards in upward mobility and pay. Charles O'Reilly, the Stanford business professor I quoted earlier about men's single-mindedness, compares it to a tennis tournament. "If you think about performance in organizations as being a function of motivation times ability—how smart you are and how hard you work—what makes a difference at the top level is effort. If somebody does five hundred backhands a day and somebody else does only a hundred, then in the long term, the person who does more backhands is more likely to win." This subgroup, which O'Reilly calls the "masculine-identified," is willing to compete at all costs, put in extremely long hours, relocate frequently, and favor work over family life. They are the ones who end up at the top of the pay scale. The poet and essayist Samuel Johnson wrote that "those who attain any excellence commonly spend life in one pursuit; for excellence is not often gained upon easier terms."

Let us now turn to a group of women who are excellent. They have spent their life in one pursuit. They have done what was expected of them all along and are successful. But for some reason they don't feel as if they've earned it. Meet the imposters.

CHAPTER 7

Hiding the Imposter Within

In 1997, when Dr. Margaret Chan was head of Hong Kong's Health Department, she ordered 1.4 million chickens and ducks slaughtered to control contagion from the very first cases of a new strain of avian flu. Then she purchased U.S. $1.3 million in vaccines. These were unpopular decisions at a time when the world didn't quite believe that bad things could come from birds. When Dr. Chan was criticized by government auditors, she stood her ground. "The cost was peanuts, and it was an insurance policy for which I was happy not to have to make a claim," she said. No one knew how perspicacious she was, Dr. Chan least of all. That year the H5N1 strain of avian influenza killed a total of six people in Hong Kong. Closely related to the 1918 Spanish flu that killed forty million people in a single year—the most devastating pandemic in world history—H5N1 could have been a global disaster. Dr. Chan went on to lead Hong Kong's SARS investigation, and after controlling that outbreak, joined the World Health Organization. Within a few years she became its director general, in January 2007. Yet she attributes her success to luck, not talent. When asked how she came to be one of the most respected public health officials in the world, Dr. Chan told a *New York Times* reporter that she always happens to be in the right place at the right time.[1]

Her ability, conviction, and good judgment saved countless lives. But Dr. Chan discounted her native smarts—and the opportunity to promote herself—attributing it all to luck. Another public health expert and physician, an acquaintance of mine, once told me that her

expertise in tuberculosis is "a fluke." She travels the world to give lectures. She talks to the media and helps draft policy. Yet the diminutive,
sharply dressed doctor has wondered aloud why people treat her with
deference. "There are an awful lot of people out there who think I'm
an expert. How do these people believe all this about me? I'm so much
aware of all the things I don't know."

Objectively, these people *are* experts. Yet like many high-achieving
women, they chalk up their successes to chance. No matter how much
recognition they get, they feel that they have to try even harder.[2] It's not
so much a fear of failure. That's universal—both men and women
worry that they might not make the grade. What is particular to many
successful women is that their hard-won successes don't feel genuine.
The belief that one's achievements are illusions, that one's professional
position is due to luck or someone's colossal mistake characterizes the
internal work experience of many women and has been dubbed "the
imposter syndrome." Persisting well past the first few weeks of a job,
the idea that one is playing at the role of doctor, engineer, or executive
transforms work into a race to avoid discovery. This can have a paradoxical effect, pulling some women irrevocably upward as they try to
prove themselves—to themselves—every time there's a challenge, while
pushing other women to opt out. This chapter explores these opposite
effects. Why are some women haunted by their success to the point
that they abandon their pursuits? As we shall see, the same self-doubt
drives other women's achievement, as they keep on plugging to prove
themselves and to avoid detection.

Will the Real Woman Please Stand Up?

In 1978 two psychologists at Oberlin, Pauline Rose Clance and
Suzanne Imes, happened on an unexpected finding in a study of 150
highly successful professional women in law, medicine, nursing, social
work, and academe. Despite accolades, rank, and salary, these women
felt like phonies. They didn't believe in their own accomplishments;
they felt they were scamming everyone about their skills.[3] So how did
they rise to their position, achieve high scores on standardized tests,
receive those awards? As Clance, now a professor emeritus in Atlanta,
Georgia, puts it, each of them thinks she's the one Harvard mistake.

They feel they've done a great con job and that eventually they'll be unmasked.

You'd think this wouldn't matter if they succeed anyway. But many women acknowledge that self-doubt reins in their ambitions. "Lots of times imposter syndrome limits how high people can go. Sometimes when people have been offered promotions—and search committees, bosses, team leaders, and supervisors predict they'll excel at the next level—they turn them down because they feel they won't be able to succeed. People will find out what they don't know," Clance explained in her soft southern drawl. Clance went on to describe a real estate agent whose scores on a standardized scale of imposter feelings were high. The agent had just clinched a big deal, but still avoided making the next call, the one that might close a lucrative commercial contract and boost her to the next sales level. She thought that this time she might not be so lucky. Imposters internalize negative feedback but discount positive events; no proof is ever enough. As a result, many so-called imposters self-select themselves out of a race, leaving gaps in high places that leave the impression they've been expressly excluded. "It kept me from putting myself in situations where my fears could be proved true. I would only apply for positions when I knew I was going to get it. It was only when I knew I could deal with failure that I started to take risks," said the tuberculosis expert. She learned about imposter syndrome when a nurse, hearing her talk about her anxieties about taking on a new role, handed her a pile of articles. "For those people it was a syndrome. For me it was real," she joked, implying the participants in the studies may have *thought* they were fakes. But she really was one.

When Clance and Imes published their first article about this group of high-achieving women with self-doubts in the seventies, "People said, 'that's me they're writing about,'" Clance told me. The interest has not abated since. The increasing number of interview and workshop requests tells her the issue isn't just an artifact of the era. "I wish it weren't still relevant," Clance said. Indeed, with most women now in the workforce and work pressures mounting, imposter feelings may be increasing. In 2003, Susan Vinnicombe and Val Singh, two social scientists at the Center for Developing Women Business Leaders in the United Kingdom, set out to look at what distinguished the career paths of twelve directors in a major international telecommunications company. They found that the senior executives—six women and six men—had remarkably similar career paths. The women did not report facing different barriers than the men, and all described challenges offered early on that helped them clinch their careers. The differences were internal, having to do with their sense of agency and the appeal of risky opportunities. The male directors described themselves actively seeking out mentors or sponsors, whereas the female directors remember having been picked out by superiors for special assignments. The men reported unquestioningly accepting the chance to prove themselves, while the women talked about having to be persuaded. One female director described her rise thus:

> I was not at all happy about making this move, although it was a promotion. I didn't want to do it; I didn't know how to do it. I didn't know what it would entail. . . . In the end he made it clear to me that I didn't have too much choice. So at that point I gave in. He said: "I want you to do the job. I really want you to do the job." I said "I can't do it" and he said "You can, you know." I thought, he must know better than I did.

Another female director credited her opportunities to factors having little to do with her qualifications.

> I would say a very strong bit of why I got the job was X's positive discrimination. He wanted a woman general manager.[4]

While reading the clips from the research interviews I could see the men pulling down the air with a triumphant "yes!" when offered a promotion, while the women whipped their heads around as if to say, "Who, me?" Notwithstanding these different attitudes, both male and female directors accepted the challenges, continued to rise, and ended up in the same spot. But the ambivalence in many of the women was clear. Instead of feeling exultant, many were reluctant as was this professor of biomedical engineering, Monique Frize. In an interview for a newspaper feature in 2002 she told me that her reaction to the offer of a prestigious research chair was a feeling of foreboding. Despite a string of past successes she felt unprepared. "I told my husband that I'd be an imposter to accept this job. But when I succeeded so incredibly, the men around me began asking me, 'When is enough going to be enough?'" Since that appointment, she has been awarded four honorary degrees. Yet self-doubt still haunts her. "I've always had fears of being unmasked before a new responsibility. After six months I would start to feel better. But the feelings came back every time there was a new challenge."

The issue is rarely discussed. The disconnect between the public persona—actually living out the vanilla male model of success—and the private experience of self-doubt keeps the phenomenon concealed from public view. After all, if you're trying to mask what you consider a hidden defect, you're not likely to divulge it unless prompted. This is one of the ground rules in a society that considers a positive self-image a prerequisite for success. One female dean of engineering, a highly placed, self-described imposter who didn't want to be identified by name, described her aha! feeling upon hearing another university administrator admit her self-doubts. "When a female president of a university talked about feeling like an imposter in a public speech to two hundred women scientists, we were all nodding, thinking of ourselves, thinking, oh my God, even her!"

Cosi Fan Tutti

But are imposter feelings universal? They are certainly familiar. My own recollection of being a neophyte psychologist is like a double exposure: the challenge of the job in the foreground, anxiety about being unmasked in the background. I remember listening to a married mother of two toddlers describe her anguished ambivalence about her sexual identity one hour, and the next, to an articulate young couple concerned about a just-adopted child with a dubious family history. "This is a real problem. Maybe you should see a *real* psychologist," I recall thinking. I was listening carefully. I appeared to be saying the right things. People were emerging with an understanding and a plan. But I spent my leisure hours trying to find definitive answers in journals, getting clinical supervision, and listening to taped conference sessions, desperate to outrace the discovery that I felt I was flying by the seat of my pants.

I didn't know that I had lots of company. A study of randomly selected American psychologists reported that 69 percent of them felt like imposters.[5] And a league of successful professional women, some of them celebrities, share this underlying fear of being discovered. Michelle Pfeiffer had been nominated for three Academy Awards and six Golden Globe awards when she described her self-doubts in an interview in 2002. When asked how she had developed her gifts, Pfeiffer responded, "I still think people will find out that I'm really not very talented. I'm really not very good. It's all been a big sham." Kate Winslet, too, has been frank about doubting her talents. "Sometimes I wake up in the morning before going off to a shoot, and I think, I can't do this. I'm a fraud."[6]

Many people feel that they're not smart enough or expert enough, especially in a new job. Testing has shown that intermittent, fleeting imposter feelings exist in 70 percent of the general population.[7] What differentiates imposter syndrome from garden-variety self-doubt is that the feelings may wane but never entirely disappear, regardless of accolades. The other difference is that like depression, arthritis, and osteoporosis, it's more often women who find that it's chronic. When men feel self-doubt, especially in a new job, these feelings are transient, less internalized. When researchers ask people whether they believe they can achieve a desired outcome, the studies reveal that women have lower perceptions of their agency—a belief in their mastery and control—than men.[8] This doesn't mean that they are less effective, only that they *think* they are. Men are less likely to talk about these doubts or allow them to influence their behavior, according to the researchers. "Men are more comfortable bluffing," says Valerie Young, an expert on the imposter phenomenon. "Before women will apply for a job or raise their hand, they feel they have to know 100 percent, whereas men feel they only have to know 50 percent and can fake the rest."[9]

In science especially, expecting 100 percent certainty can slow you down if not offside you completely. Many women are "more cautious and careful in their research and more hesitant to make statements until they feel they can really 'prove' them," said a female scientist when asked about differing approaches to scientific methodology in a large Harvard study. In interviews both sexes commented on the perfectionism that often characterizes female scientists' work. That was one of several gender differences found by two Harvard professors, Gerhard Sonnert, a sociologist, and his colleague, Gerald Holton, a physicist and historian of science, when they followed the progress of all the postdoctoral research fellows who received National Science Foundation funding between 1952 and 1985, almost seven hundred scientists in all. When two hundred of them were interviewed face-to-face, both men and women commented that women were more meticulous and thorough, often because they feared failure or criticism. Their publications tended to be broader in range, longer, and better documented, and as a result there were fewer of them, contributing to a narrowing but still noticeable female productivity gap that is well known in academic science.[10] As we've seen, family and maternity leaves help explain this gap, but a desire to be bulletproof also plays a part.

If they felt like imposters, women might be worried that neglecting something might reveal that they weren't real scientists after all. The contrast between blustery self-confidence and an almost paranoid commitment to doing one's homework is a subplot in *Intuition*, Allegra Goodman's 2006 novel about envy and scientific discovery. Sandy Glass, a senior male scientist, is one of the protagonists who is desperate to be the first to nail a finding—and is ready to go out on a limb to do it. "He had a good temperament for grand discoveries and impending fame. The grant proposal for the NIH would be a knockout, an utter masterpiece. How could he be sure of this? He'd already written it. Marion didn't know. She would have been scandalized, but Sandy had drafted the whole thing. He'd left out the numbers, of course, the actual tables and figures. The data were still to come, but secretly, Sandy had crafted all the filigree for the proposal. He'd extrapolated from Cliff's preliminary results, and discussed their significance at length." And his female scientific collaborator, Marion? She's depicted as cool, cautious, and highly conservative. "I'm not going to let you jump to conclusions for me. I won't stake the reputation of this lab on half-baked results," she responds.[11]

This is fiction, of course, but the conflict between Sandy's desire to take a risk to be the first up at bat, and Marion's guarded perfectionism captures a gender divide that seems to come from within. Call it hubris or nerve, but whatever you call it, many female high achievers admit they don't have it. "My male classmates from MIT will say that no one ever doubted that they would succeed. They go through their entire lives with everyone assuming they can do what they set out to do. And no woman scientist has that experience, no matter how capable she is," wrote one psychology professor (who described herself as "paranoid" when I asked if I could use her name). To be sure, some of this self-assuredness stems from their perception of others' expectations of them. But are perfectionism and self-doubt really women's work?

Flawed Optimism and the Externalizers

A mountain of evidence points to women reporting that they experience more anxiety and guilt than men. Among other studies, a huge meta-analysis by Alan Feingold confirms it, as does the most comprehensive study of mental states in the United States, directed by Ronald Kessler at Harvard. His data show that women have much higher rates of mood and anxiety disorders than men. In psychology lingo, the evidence points to males, on average, "externalizing," meaning their negative behaviors are directed to the world at large through aggression, anger, or substance abuse, whereas women, on average, are more likely to "internalize," meaning their negative thoughts are more likely to be turned inward, through sadness, guilt, anxiety, or shame.[12] One group of researchers, led by psychologist Stephanie van Goozen, now at Cardiff University, looked at how people responded to negative feedback about their performance. The men were more likely to be angry about criticism, whereas the women were more likely to feel sad and ashamed. (The women got angry just as often, but in response to perceived interpersonal slights, not negative assessments of their achievement).[13] No matter the context, women are more likely to self-reflect, ruminate, and search for causes of events within themselves.

When bad things happen are women more likely to look inward while men look outside themselves? This seems to be true in literature and popular culture, which are populated by male figures who try valiantly but can't make the grade, from Willy Loman in *Death of a Salesman* to *Curb Your Enthusiasm*'s Larry David. Poignant or absurd, their failures resonate as reminders of our fallibility. Yet even if the world is full of obstacles for these guys, they never see their problems as self-imposed. They do battle with external factors: changing urban or social landscapes, supernatural powers, deadbeat sons, and the nincompoops of this world, never looking inward. Their problems are out there, not within themselves.

This literary view lines up nicely with the empirical one. Many studies show that men who sense that success is eluding them chalk it up to external factors, such as unfair competition (the other team cheated, the test was hard, the road was icy). Women, on average, focus on themselves (I should have tried harder, I studied the wrong chapter, I should have been more careful). These studies confirm that while women are more prone to internalize failure, they often attribute their successes to external factors.[14] This is especially true when success is unexpected. One classic study from the early 1970s, titled "What Is Skill for the Male Is Luck for the Female," looked at how men and women understand their successes. The hypothesis was that people would automatically rate men as better at certain tasks due to stereotypes (this was the seventies, after all). An unexpected finding was that when asked to rate their own performance, men expected to do better than an observed model on *both* masculine-typed and feminine-typed tasks, whereas women only expected to do better on feminine-typed tasks. When women performed well across the board, they thought it was a fluke.

Know Thyself?

Since then a lot of research has confirmed two sobering facts about self-assessment. The first is that none of us is very good at it. We're even bad at evaluating ourselves when it comes to matters of life and death. Nurses are poor predictors of how well they've mastered their basic life-support skills, and adolescent boys think they're more savvy about condoms than they really are. Gun owners don't know if they've really grasped firearm safety, and medical students and surgical residents are not good at predicting how they'll fare on tests of their surgical skills. In other words, self-confidence is vastly overrated—it's only loosely connected to performance, if at all.[15] In areas in which feedback is vague, rare, or comes too late, the connection between self-confidence and performance is even more tenuous. People who think they are intelligent aren't necessarily; college students have little idea how they're doing at school; and managers often rate themselves as having more competence and better people skills than they actually demonstrate.[16] Despite the maxim about knowing thyself, most people don't. Most overestimate how smart they are and how well they've done, so it's no use asking them. To be blunt, self-confidence *feels* good, but it doesn't mean you *are* good.

The second fact is that there are indeed sex differences in self-assessment on cognitive tasks. More women than men think they'll do poorly, even when they perform very well.[17] Their predictions don't determine their performance but can affect what they decide to try next. Cornell University psychologists Joyce Ehrlinger and David Dunning found that women who thought they had done badly on a science quiz—even though they had actually done well—then declined to enter a competition. Their self-perceptions didn't affect their performance on the quiz. It wasn't the classic self-fulfilling prophesy. But their self-perceptions influenced their desire to compete in the future.[18] In the competitive sphere, this can look like discrimination when in fact women may be withdrawing from the race of their own accord, based on their faulty self-assessments. Carol Bartz, the CEO we met in the previous chapter discussing her serendipitous career, reflected that some women in business resist entering the race to the executive suite because they think they won't win. "There is a whole lot of hand-wringing going on with women. They get the high-power degrees and then they drop back because they tell themselves they're not going to get very far anyway." By misjudging their own competence, women withdraw from opportunities or hang back. In the interim, those with flawed optimism can step forward.

Less willing than women to expose their vulnerabilities on record, the men I interviewed who admitted to self-doubt felt strongly that feelings of inadequacy are to be expected as one goes about the task of proving oneself. They attributed any doubt to a concrete piece missing from their background or education. Their imposter feelings were not due to a psychological flaw but to a temporary material gap. In other words, it wasn't their fault. Instead of feeling shame and isolation, in most men the imposter phenomenon was either a nonissue or fodder for jokes, as in this confession from actor Mike Myers: "I still believe that at any time the no-talent police will come and arrest me." The subtext? Notwithstanding thoughts that go bump in the night, the world acknowledges my achievements. The evidence is there. Why question it in front of others? Or as Mort Zuckerman, billionaire, publisher, commentator, and political mover and shaker, cast his swift rise to CEO at his first real estate job in 1962: "They thought I knew something. I did not disabuse them of that notion."[19]

Even the young, fragile men in this book seemed at ease when talking about their achievements, in contrast to the jittery lack of self-assuredness in many of the professional women with decades of experience and accomplishment behind them. Harry, whom I followed for several years to help him manage his ADHD and Tourette's symptoms, described his first days as a high school teacher this way: "When it comes to teaching, I never have any doubts or worries. I'm confident in front of students." But what about his flighty attention and intermittent tics? Did they affect his ability to feel self-possessed as a new teacher? Still taking three medications a day to keep his symptoms at bay, Harry felt these difficulties were unimportant. "I know all eyes are on me, but it doesn't even cross my mind," he told me. What about Andrew, now working as a chef? Did his school history or the fact that he was a new arrival in the kitchen make him feel like a poseur? Did he secretly feel he was fooling everyone about his competence? "I never felt that way because I was rushed in and given a lot of responsibility. I didn't feel like I was faking it because they put me in charge right away, so I knew they had confidence in me." Andrew internalized his successes and put his small failures in context. "I used to be yelled at all the time, but it's part of the job. Everyone makes mistakes. You just learn from it. If you don't learn from it, then people will really think you're a fake." Harold, a talented young African American, first thought he didn't have the right background and skills when he began his new job as an analyst in a think tank. "But then looking back at my work and what I was able to accomplish—tasks other people hadn't been able to do—I was reassured. There was a problem and I was able to solve it, and I thought, I can do this." Whatever feelings of inadequacy he faced at the beginning evaporated by the three-month mark.

He took credit for his accomplishments and attributed any obstacles to factors outside his control. His story was in striking contrast to a study that found that 93 percent of African American female college students continue to feel like imposters, attributing their success to luck instead of to their own abilities.[20]

Pessimism with a Punch

Not everyone agrees that imposter feelings affect mostly women. But it's no coincidence that one of the few people researching the phenomenon teaches at an all-female Ivy League college, a high-achieving population where these feelings are common. Julie Norem, a psychology professor at Wellesley, has incorporated the notion of imposter syndrome into her studies on negative thinking, and said this of imposters: "They're not enjoying themselves, they're not getting much satisfaction, even though they're performing well. And their fear that they'll be discovered really interferes with their friendships." What interests her is how they cope. Even though they're not getting much satisfaction from their achievements, the second-guessing, self-critical, and pessimistic thought patterns of imposters do not always set the stage for failure. Instead, the strategies imposters use to compensate for their feelings of inadequacy—overpreparing and outcredentialing their peers—reduce their anxiety and promote their strong performance. She calls this "defensive pessimism." Unrealistically low expectations lead to time and energy spent anticipating everything that could go wrong. Mentally playing through every negative outcome, then addressing it help imposters reduce anxiety, Norem says, because this kind of planning allows people to move from anxiety to concrete action. "The imposters who use this strategy are more satisfied with their lives."

Even more compelling, though, is the idea that self-doubt drives a person to try harder. Research on chess masters by two cognitive scientists, Michelle Cowley and Ruth Byrne, at Trinity College in Dublin, shows that the most proficient players second-guess themselves, look eight moves ahead, and try to counter their own hypotheses. In contrast to this "negative" strategy, novices were more likely to be optimistic and then experience a crushing defeat.[21] This is the paradox of self-doubters; they're constantly testing the hypothesis that they might not know what they're doing. In the process of trying to fill the gaps in their knowledge they master their field. As an example, consider the TB expert who attributed everything she achieved to "a fluke." She told me that she thinks she should always be doing more research, more reading, to prove herself. "I'm always carrying around a pile of articles I have to read. I'm only slowly getting used to giving talks. I absolutely overprepare and look up every reference." As a result she has moved from promotion to promotion.

The Internalizers

Asking people if they feel like fakers is hardly polite. Yet when I mentioned I was writing about imposter syndrome, highly accomplished women made unbidden confessions. "I felt it for years, it's the weirdest feeling—that it can't really be me making those decisions," said a female hospital CEO who had risen quickly through administrative ranks to head a series of acute-care hospitals. The fact that she was responsible for more than a thousand health professionals and their patients and had been systematically promoted to positions of more responsibility hadn't made a dent in the feeling that she is just faking it. Similarly, a doctor who had earned several university degrees and academic and community service awards, all while carrying a full clinical practice in a university teaching hospital and raising four children, waved a limp hand and looked at me meaningfully over her reading glasses. "I guess I fooled you, too. I'm still waiting for the big 'they' to figure it out. When I went to Harvard the first time, I was always ready for someone to say 'You're not who you think you are!'" The feeling of never knowing enough may be why this physician is now writing yet another university admissions essay. Twenty years of experience, a full clinical practice, and a series of publications and awards are not enough. She decided she wants another degree to follow up the fellowship she just completed at Harvard. "I do want to do it, but I'm scared. These new people don't know me, and they're going to figure it out and say, 'Fraud, get out! You don't deserve to be here.'"

Strongest when they start a job, imposter feelings vary with new challenges. As workplace and performance pressures escalate, imposter feelings rise in tandem. The result is more anxiety about work and less appetite for risk. Imposter feelings may prompt women to move to ever higher rungs through perfectionism and fear of failure, but discounting one's own talent hardly contributes to an overweening sense of personal accomplishment. It's this lack of satisfaction that can precipitate the exit of a high-achieving, high-earning professional or sour her enjoyment of work. "A high proportion of people have experienced these feelings now and then, but about 30 percent have it to the degree that it interferes with their work and their life," says Pauline Clance. When that happens imposter syndrome inches closer to depression, another condition characterized by distorted attributions, and twice as common in women as in men.

The Other Problem with No Name

There are no published studies that measure the relationship between imposter feelings and depression. But there's a cognitive style that's common to both. Primed by biological triggers as well as environmental stresses, depression is marked by a distortion of thinking that focuses on the negative and discounts the positive. People who are depressed often generalize from a few bad experiences, think things are worse than they are, and imagine that unlikely-to-happen risks apply to themselves. No matter their capabilities, much like Joe Btfsplk in *L'il Abner,* they view themselves and the future through a cloud.[22] Compare this to imposter-type thinking, where real-life experience of success has only a limited effect on one's expectation of the future. No matter how high the imposter climbs, she doesn't think she'll succeed the next time, and fears being discovered as a fraud. Indeed, the pioneer of the positive psychology movement, Martin Seligman (whom we met in chapter 1, investigating self-discipline), sees the perception of having no control over one's fate as a mental state related to depression. According to his theory, people who attribute negative events to internal factors (it's all my fault) and positive events to external ones (I was just lucky) are at a higher risk of depression when faced with stress.[23] If you can't control positive events you might see your situation as hopeless.

Despite the overlap, imposter syndrome and depression shouldn't be confused. Depression is a disorder that persists over time and disrupts one's daily life. "Imposters" may not feel satisfied with their work in a breezy, happy-go-lucky way. But by working actively to change their outcome, they're less likely to become incapacitated by doubt. Imposter feelings resemble depression only when someone has few coping skills and rumination takes over. This creates an undercurrent of chronic stress, which, combined with genetic and biochemical factors, could turn into a clinical depression if not recognized and treated. Depression affects 9.5 percent of the population—twelve million women in the United States alone—and is the most common mental health problem in women. Although there is almost always a precipitating event, biological factors are key.[24] Familiar reasons— genes, hormones, and brain-based sex differences—explain why women have a higher incidence of the disorder than men and are more vulnerable at certain points in their lives. It's not as if work causes depression. But work is more likely to offside women when they experience chronic stress and think they can do nothing to control it.[25]

The paradox of imposter syndrome is that second-guessing can either lead women to withdraw, or prompt them to try harder. An undercurrent of self-doubt is the flip side of achievement in many women. When they do conform to the vanilla male model of success, a subset of women continue to question the fit. Grooming their status through self-promotion and bluffing is not high on the list of these women's priorities; being taken seriously for their skills, values, and inner qualities comes first. The effect is not that *less* capable women select themselves out, but that many gifted women may not throw their hats in the ring. At a moment of hesitation other more confident but perhaps less qualified candidates can step forward. On that bracing note, let us now turn back to men and whether, on average, they're more eager to compete and win than the opposite sex.

CHAPTER 8

Competition: Is It a Guy Thing?

The afternoon I went to fetch my three-year-old nephew after his nap was when I started to think about male competition as bred in the bone. Wearing a wet diaper and a soaked onesie, Jack was gripping the bars of his crib and eyeing the crack of light between the door and the frame when I appeared. He was expecting his mother, so I decided to chat with him a bit before I scooped him up in my arms and kissed him. "I hear you just had a birthday," I ventured. He nodded warily. "And you got a big present. A tricycle!" He nodded again. "What a great present," I blabbed on. "I got a bicycle for my birthday and I ride it all the time." I took one step closer to his crib as he looked at me steadily. "Mine's faster than yours," he said. He locked his dark eyes on mine, challenging me. "I can go faster than you."

The male tendency to challenge all comers is the subject of this chapter. Like Jack, not all have what it takes to triumph over bigger, stronger, and more experienced opponents. But an eagerness to compete and to use aggression to cement status have been documented in males from an early age and in almost every culture. To get what they want, to be top dog, or just for the fun of it, three- to twelve-year-old boys have been observed pushing, poking, hitting, play-fighting, exchanging insults, challenging, attacking, and counterattacking significantly more often than girls all over the world.[1] The sheer volume of data on male status-seeking and aggression has created a rare consensus. Almost all social scientists agree that on average, males are more aggressive and aggressively competitive than women, and the evidence is plain in every context—from the nursery to the playing field, from the battlefield to the boardroom.

Both males and females compete. But to enter any classroom is to be disabused of the idea that males and females compete in exactly the same ways. One study showed how four- and five-year-old boys and girls were motivated by the same goal but reached it through different means. When these preschoolers needed to work together to watch a cartoon, boys used competition and physical tactics fifty times more often than girls. Meanwhile, girls used talking and turn-taking twenty times more often than boys.[2] When given the choice, nine- and ten-year-old boys compete overtly 50 percent of their play time, while girls choose to compete only 1 percent of theirs. Boys choose games with winners and losers most often; girls prefer turn-taking games, with pauses built in for social interaction.[3] These styles of play diverge to the degree that boys and girls stick to playing in same-sex groups so they can play the games they prefer. But do boys simply ape competitive, macho behavior after watching other guys? We'll soon see how biological forces impel males to play rough games and seek out competition, allowing them plenty of practice at grandstanding, turf-defending, winning, and losing. More aggressive and competitive males hone their skills further through cultural forms of aggression that have natural appeal, such as violent computer games or paintball. These activities don't make them aggressive—they're fun to those who already are.

But the male edge in aggressive competition doesn't mean that women are passive, or that all women will withdraw from a fight. Individual women can easily be more competitive than individual men. But on average, girls' and women's style of competing looks different, involving subtle social signals, gossip, and mean comments more than physical challenges. And as the goals are often social, it's harder to track who's ahead through points, dollars, or scores. Simply having to compete boosts male performance, while it lowers females'. This is what the American economists Uri Gneezy and Aldo Rustichini found when they looked at how fourth-grade Israeli schoolchildren fared when running races during gym class. When the children were timed while running alone on a forty-meter-long track, there were no measurable sex differences. The girls ran just as fast as the boys. Then children were either matched to another child of comparable speed and asked to run a race, or they ran a second trial alone. Gneezy and Rustichini discovered that boys ran faster when they competed against an opponent, whereas girls ran slower when they were asked to compete than when they ran alone. And if girls had to compete, the sex of their opponent mattered. Boys' performance improved whether they competed against boys *or* girls. But girls performed better when running against boys.[4]

This suggests that coed schools might not be such a bad idea after all, as long as teachers are sensitive to naturally occurring variations in students' appetites for competition. Even when their athletic skills are well matched, boys are more eager to defeat an opponent, psychologist Carol Weisfeld found. When she matched students of similar skill in mixed-sex games of dodgeball, boys dodged the ball more, aggressively snagged loose balls, and whacked other players with the ball more often than girls did. This is how boys beat usually high-scoring girls by a margin of 67 to 4.[5] If the ways in which men and women compete look different, their goals diverge, and their appetites for unbridled competition vary, enforcing a level playing field becomes a slippery task. Neither male nor female works as the standard for the other sex.

Most boys structure their activities so that there's a clear champion, and if there isn't, where's the fun? For years I used a therapeutic board game with some children in my practice aptly called *The Ungame* because there are no winners or losers. Players pick up cards that prompted them to talk about themselves and learn about others' motives as they move their plastic pieces around the board. Until I added tokens as rewards, the boys were perplexed. If you couldn't keep score, what was the point? Even reserved boys were less driven by "the journey" than by former coach Vince Lombardi's maxim "Winning isn't everything. It's the only thing." As we shall see, differing approaches to competition can have surprising effects, influencing the types of jobs men and women want, and their earnings and status once they get them.

Penny Candy or Making a Deal by the Gross

It's a truism that women have always worked, even if their labor was more scattershot than men's. At least three generations of women in my family slotted their work around family or found work near home, starting with my grandmother, who attended medical school in Europe but ended up immigrating in the 1920s before completing her degree. Once in Canada, she did factory work. Then, after coming home to discover that a babysitter had ditched the children while she was at work, she sewed neckties at home by the piece. Disassembled ties were draped over every doorknob and door of her flat, and these little sewing jobs slid around bigger ones, presaging the 24/7 work hours we think of as new. Women still do more freelance and contract work than men. More women opt for the flexibility, getting paid by the word, the call, the hour, the lesson, the report, the course, or the project, in the process becoming invisible teleworkers, neither subject to labor norms nor counted as official employees with a chance to move up.

The willingness of many women to trade a stable salary for flexible hours adds to the global wage gap. Other than a desire to have time for family, is there something about women's approach to competition that fosters such trade-offs? Muriel Niederle, a Stanford economist, and her colleague Lise Vesterlund posed just this question in a research project in 2006. Their experiment was designed to explore why there are so few women in executive and leadership positions where competition is rife.[6] They proposed that if women like competition less than men, then even if they are equally capable and have equal opportunities, they will compete less often for promotions and lucrative jobs.

The two economists tested this hypothesis by gathering groups of four volunteers, each composed of two women and two men. Every group had to find the correct sum of as many two-digit numbers as they could in five minutes. At first everyone was paid 50 cents for every correct answer. But the second time around they had to compete for a prize. The person in each group with the most correct answers would get $2 for each one. The losers would get nothing.

The results showed that women and men answered the same number of problems correctly under each system. But when given the choice about what they wanted the third time around, 75 percent of the men chose the tournament (or winner-takes-all model) over the piece rate, compared to only 35 percent of the women. Even comparing men and women who did equally well, women were 38 percent less likely to enter the tournament than men. It wasn't about skill. Even men who couldn't add well were more eager to compete, displaying a confidence that didn't reflect their abilities, and in the end earning much less than they could have. Where abilities are balanced, where discrimination is absent, and where everyone spends an equal amount of time on each task, the majority of women still shied away from competition. Why?

Niederle and Vesterlund suggest two possible explanations: less confidence and aversion to risk. Even comparing men and women who believed they could win, men were still 30 percent more likely to choose the tournament style of compensation than women, so self-confidence is not the whole story. It was risk—the possibility that they might not get paid at all if their performance was not the best—that scared women off. The authors found this all-or-nothing approach unappealing to most of the women, regardless of their abilities. Hesitating to put all their eggs in one basket might explain why fewer women compete in zero-sum games like politics, where they can win big, but if they lose they get nothing. Or why fewer women inhabit the aeries of science, where the investment in training is intense but where only a tiny minority are awarded the prestigious grants and enjoy spectacular success. With this elegant study, two economists proved that fewer women than men are willing to risk all to gain all.

But what about just asking for what they want instead of competing for it? A reduced appetite for risk means that women are also less willing to negotiate on their own behalf. Another economist, Linda Babcock at Carnegie Mellon University, designed a compelling study after a group of female graduate students approached her to ask why male graduate students got to teach their own courses while female grad students were mostly given teaching assistantships. "The women just don't ask," was the response she got from the dean. This inspired Babcock to design an experiment in which students were offered between $3 to $10 to play Boggle, a word game. After the game they were told, "Here's three dollars. Is three dollars okay?" Nine times more men than women asked for more money.

Even though the women rated their game-playing skills equal to men's and complained bitterly about being underpaid, they were willing to accept less compensation as long as they did not have to negotiate—a competitive act with risks attached (the main risk being that they'd be turned down). Babcock presents this example. "Suppose that at age twenty-two an equally qualified man and woman receive job offers for $25,000 a year. The man negotiates and gets his offer raised to $30,000. The woman does not negotiate and accepts the job for $25,000. Even if each of them receives identical 3 percent raises every year throughout their careers, by the time they reach the age of sixty the gap between their salaries will have widened to more than $15,000 a year."[7] Women don't like to negotiate, and don't like it when their subordinates try to negotiate with them, either. Female bosses penalized both men and women who tried, whereas men were more averse to women negotiating.[8] Even so, the act of negotiating prompted bigger rewards. Yet when women do negotiate, they tend to set less aggressive goals and therefore net less, Babcock writes. Those on the other side of the table may sense this, setting up a feedback loop in which candidates are offered less as a challenge to negotiate. They ask for less, and therefore get less, Babcock told me over the phone. Although the intention is not discriminatory, the effect is.[9] But the roots are in women's reluctance to thump their chests and aggressively compete for more resources.

Aggression

In 1938 Virginia Woolf wrote a scathing response in the *Atlantic* to a letter asking "the daughters of educated men" to join the antiwar cause. The men had a lot of nerve to expect women to get involved, she wrote.

> The fact is indisputable—scarcely a human being in the course of history has fallen to a woman's rifle; the vast majority of birds and beasts have been killed by you, not us. How then, are we to understand your problem, and if we cannot, how can we answer your question, how to prevent war? The answer based upon our experience and our psychology—why fight?—is not an answer that would be of the least use to you."[10]

Woolf was right. Participants in turf wars, religious wars, gang wars, hand-to-hand combat, seizing property by force, duels, jousting, boxing, or shoot-outs are almost always men fighting other men.[11] Even if aggression, criminal behavior, and relentless striving are not the same as competition, their underlying drivers are linked.[12] The drive to win the biggest prize, the most sought-after sexual partner, the highest score in a game, or the most powerful position that garners the most acclaim no longer requires weapons, or physical size and strength. But it still requires the mettle flaunted by my three-year-old nephew when he challenged me. You have to believe that you're faster, bigger, more, or most, and be prepared to prove it by displacing someone else.

A frank desire to compete is required for seeking political office or winning any zero-sum game. An example is Sam Sullivan, who was elected major of Vancouver in 2005, and was wryly described by a *Globe and Mail* journalist as "a guileless, aw-shucks, Howdy Doody–like quadriplegic who was seemingly amazed even one person would ever vote for him." Sullivan may project that persona but that is not his self-perception, baldly revealed in a documentary film. "I love it when people underestimate me. They pat me on the head and then I rip their throats out," Sullivan said about himself. "I'm going to keep my foot on his goddamn throat and I'm going to just keep pressing and see if the guy can breathe at the end of it all." More than scrappiness, such aggressive drive—even if concealed—may be what it takes to prevail in winner-takes-all competitions. This may be the reason why women seek leadership positions less often. Women comprise about 5 percent of the highest-paid executives in the United States and only about 15 percent of the seats in the U.S. Congress, in part because more women are interested in proving themselves than in smashing their opponents into the ground.[13]

New York Times columnist David Brooks calls this blend of aggressive competitiveness and striving *thymos*, after Plato's division of the soul into three parts: reason, eros, and thymos (thymos being the hunger for recognition). "Thymos is what motivates the best and worst things men do. It drives them to seek glory and assert themselves aggressively for noble causes. It drives them to rage if others don't recognize their worth. Sometimes it even causes them to kill over a trifle if they feel disrespected," Brooks wrote in 2006. Injured male pride is taken to an extreme in men who go on shooting rampages when they feel slighted. Hardly a made-in-America phenomenon, in *How the*

Mind Works, my brother Steve describes the universality of injured thymos in cultures as diverse as small-town Scotland and Papua New Guinea, where men have wantonly killed others after suffering "a loss of love, a loss of money, or a loss of faith."[14]

The *Random House Webster's Dictionary* defines the word aggressive as "vigorously energetic, especially in the use of initiative,"[15] while popular culture often blurs the criminal and the heroic—think Tony Soprano or Tupac—who blend modern swashbuckling with a winner-takes-all blind spot for the rules. It's this pairing of hubris and risk-taking that creates the paradox of the fragile male. Aggressive, competitive boys and men can be vilified as bullies, and some might find it a stretch to call them fragile. But a heightened appetite for competition and risk, paired with poor impulse control, results in a much higher rate of accidents, behavior problems, school failure, violence, and imprisonment in men. Yet a controlled channeling of the same competitive urge can push men to pursue a discovery or a goal with the same horsepower as they pursue a rival. How far they will go, and why, is where the story takes us next.

J. Craig Venter wins his bet with Cambridge University geneticist Michael Ashburner. "We made a bet at the start of the jamboree that if in the end he thought it [sequencing the genome] was successful, he would pose for a photo on his hands and knees with my foot on his back," Venter recalled.

Punishment and Revenge

"Sweet is revenge—especially to women," wrote the romantic poet Lord Byron, but that was two hundred years before MRIs and assays of sex hormones came on the scene. We now know that an eagerness to punish and seek revenge feels more fun to men, and is tied to the increase of adrenaline and testosterone during the flush of competition. Adrenaline increases in competitive situations in men but decreases in most women, according to studies by Swedish psychologist Marianne Frankenhaeuser, which show how women's neuroendocrine systems set them up to experience competition differently from men.[16] In fact, many men don't need to get mad to get even. All they need is some neurochemical priming in a competitive environment. In Britain, soccer fans are more likely to become violent when their home team wins than when it loses. Their assaults on other spectators are more closely related to their general state of arousal—or excited engagement—than by anger, shame, or disappointment.[17] And all male college students need to do to feel inclined to punish a stranger is to handle a gun. In 2006 the American researchers Jennifer Klinesmith, Tim Kasser, and Francis McAndrew discovered that average, happy-go-lucky college students would be more likely to mix a brutally spicy drink for a stranger after handling a gun than after playing a board game. Their urge to punish was related to a rise in testosterone, which spiked in the men who had touched the gun.[18]

Charting how hormones affect cognition is new, but the link between males and punishment is not. In the 1970s, several studies showed how easily boys administered electric shocks to other children who gave wrong answers on a mock teaching task. The boys were more likely than girls to increase the intensity and hold the shock button down longer. More recent experiments using neural imaging have shown how much more quickly men will resort to physical punishment and take pleasure in exacting revenge. Tania Singer, Klaas Enno Stephan, and their colleagues at University College London taught men and women how to play a strategy game in which players could share their profits with others. The game included the researchers' accomplices—actors who played selfishly and hoarded their rewards. The psychologists expected that their test subjects would empathize with someone who played fairly and dislike the selfish players, and tested this idea by administering painful electric shocks to the hands of all the players. Brain imaging revealed the extent to which sex differences affected empathy for the person getting shocked. When the male participants observed the "bad guys" being given a punishing electric shock, the part of their brains that registers pleasure—the nucleus accumbens—became activated. But the centers engaged by empathy remained dull. Women, in contrast, showed neural evidence of empathy when either nice guys or bad guys got zapped.[19] Far from making them look like ogres, such neural responses probably evolved in men to make them more likely to punish the cheaters in their midst, Dr. Singer wrote in an e-mail. Males may have evolved to police the behavior of those in their group—and to feel less aversion to getting rid of free-riders, or those who don't play fair.

That's the long, evolutionary view. In the present it means that male brains are wired to be more trigger-happy and to feel pleasure when rivals get their due. Could this have an impact on how men experience competition in the workplace? Less empathy for one's opponents means less ambivalence about offsiding them. That might be what it takes to win.

Whatever Doesn't Kill You . . .

With fewer internal brakes to curb their competitive, aggressive, and vengeful impulses, more men end up incarcerated (the ratio of male to female prisoners is ten to one),[20] committing suicide (four times as many men as women take their own lives),[21] and killing or being killed on the job (93 percent of workplace shootings are carried out by men, and 90 percent of occupational fatalities are men).[22] School shooters, who risk their lives to take revenge for real or imagined slights, are always male. Accidents are the fourth cause of death in men, and occur twice as often in men as in women.[23] But the outcomes are not always catastrophic. Websites such as YouTube and XXXL feature video clips of daring men, including those who crack open watermelons with their heads, snort a line of black pepper, skateboard off apartment roofs, or hit a homemade Molotov cocktail with a baseball bat.[24] People who take absurd chances are almost always males.

When the architects of such tricks land up in the hospital or the morgue, they become candidates for the Darwin Awards, which laud the dubious achievements of those who unwittingly engineer, or nearly engineer, their own demise through outsized ambition and poor impulse control. Some Darwin tales are funny, others are tragic, and almost all involve men taking mortal risks. Out of the 403 Darwin Awards that have removed individuals from the human gene pool, 90 percent involve men.[25] An unquestioning approach to risk is personified by Darwin Award winner Larry Walters, a former truck driver from Los Angeles who decided that he wanted to fulfill his boyhood dream of flying. After watching jets fly from his backyard he came up with a plan. He purchased forty-five weather balloons from an Army-Navy surplus store, tied them to his tethered lawn chair, and filled the four-foot-diameter balloons with helium. Then he strapped himself in with sandwiches, beer, and a pellet gun. The plan was to float up to about thirty feet above his backyard, fly around up there while enjoying the view and a brew, then shoot a few of the balloons with his pellet gun when he'd had enough so he could float back down.

> When his friends cut the cord anchoring the lawn chair to his Jeep, he did not float lazily up to thirty feet. Instead, he streaked into the LA sky as if shot from a cannon, pulled by a lift of forty-five helium balloons holding thirty-three cubic feet of helium each. He didn't level off at a hundred feet, nor did he level off at a thousand feet. After climbing and climbing, he leveled off at sixteen thousand feet. At that height he felt he couldn't risk shooting any of the balloons, lest he unbalance the load and really find himself in trouble. So he stayed there, drifting with his beer and sandwiches for several hours while he considered his options. At one point he crossed the primary approach of Los Angeles LAX airspace, and Delta and Trans World airline pilots radioed in incredulous reports of the strange sight. Eventually he gathered the nerve to shoot a few balloons and slowly descended through the night sky. The hanging tethers tangled and caught in a power line, blacking out a Long Beach neighborhood for twenty minutes. Larry climbed to safety, where he was arrested by waiting members of the Los Angeles Police Department. As he was led away in handcuffs, a reporter

dispatched to cover the daring rescue asked him why he had done it. Larry replied nonchalantly, "A man can't just sit around."[26]

Evolutionary psychologists Margo Wilson and Martin Daly suggest that such risk-taking is "an attribute of the masculine psychology," and in 1999 three psychologists from the University of Maryland decided to assess if this statement is true. James Byrnes, David Miller, and William Schafer analyzed 150 studies in which male and female risk-taking were compared and crunched the results in a meta-analysis. They found that in nearly every study, males were more likely to take risks than females, and that the size of the sex differences was not small. The biggest differences were in gambling, undertaking risky experiments, intellectual risk-taking, and physical skills—which would explain Carol Weisfeld's finding about dodgeball. The smallest differences in risk-taking included social behaviors like smoking, drinking, and sex. In one of their analyses they found that males took risks "even when it was clear that it was a bad idea," while the opposite was true for women and girls, who avoided risk even in harmless situations when they should have taken a gamble, such as practice SAT tests. "Whereas the former finding suggests that men and boys would tend to encounter failure or other negative consequences more often than women and girls, the latter finding suggests that women and girls would tend to experience success less often than they should," the authors write—an interesting observation given that women's lower rates of material success are usually attributed to outside forces. Unlike aggression, which normally decreases as children age, the researchers found that risk-taking increases as boys reach adolescence and young adulthood.[27] This would contribute to the widening gender gap just as men and women are choosing their careers—creating the paradox of young men who drink, party, and drop out of school at one extreme, versus men who go into highly competitive careers at the other.

Why Do Men Take Risks?

Why do some men put themselves at risk with thrill-seeking stunts, iffy wagers, or physically dangerous occupations, while others devote outrageous hours and psychic energy to compete aggressively in their work, often to the detriment of their health and the exclusion of all else? There are two related reasons why males are more eager than females to take such chances. The first is a gloss on evolutionary theory dreamed up in the early 1970s by the evolutionary biologist and onetime sixties radical Robert Trivers. In 1972 Trivers, then a young Harvard professor, wrote a paper that sought to clarify a conundrum that Charles Darwin left unanswered. Darwin's theory of sexual selection proposed that males and females of each species choose mates with whom to reproduce, and that the interaction between the pair's traits and the environment they find themselves in determines the survival of their offspring. At the time, biologists had observed that males compete fiercely with one another for females—sometimes to the death—and that females choose certain males over others.[28] But there was a big piece missing. On what basis, exactly, did females choose?

Trivers, then twenty-nine, added the following idea: it's not just genetic traits and the host environment that matter. The mate's relative investment in the offspring's survival is part of the equation. This would include the metabolic investment in producing the sex cells (sperm and ova), as well as the cost of gestating, bearing, feeding, and guarding any new arrivals. If females invest more in their young through pregnancy, lactation, and ongoing solicitous care, then the number of offspring are limited by how many babies a female could have in a single year—normally one. But males could literally play the field. Their reproductive success would be limited by two factors: how many other competitive males were out there, and how many females would have them. Highly aggressive and larger males could knock off the competition through brute force, sometimes grabbing females the same way. Meanwhile, good-looking show-offs and risk-takers could garner more female attention, gathering a harem to themselves. More cautious men were the wallflowers left out of the fun. Ultimately there would be fewer of their genetic signatures around.

Trivers' theory suggests that competitive risk-taking is wired into males. Due to her own unique wiring, a female invests greatly in her future offspring, feeding them, nurturing them, and raising them to maturity, all at significant cost to herself. Plus, once pregnant, that's it. She's committed. No matter how many one-night stands she has, a female will only have a given number of offspring during her lifetime—

which she's programmed to guard with her life—while a successful, competitive male striver can father ten, twelve, or even a hundred. Given these stakes, a female would be mighty selective about her partners. She'd also be conservative about taking on risk, because if she dies, her offspring wouldn't survive. A more extreme, risk-taking male with hundreds of millions of sperm could compete for the attention of multiple partners, fathering many mini-risk-takers and investing little in what happens to them afterward (inspiring evolutionary anthropologist Donald Symons' phrase "sperm is cheap").

The math was demonstrated by Lucky Moulay Ismail the Bloodthirsty of Morocco (1646–1727), who fathered 888 children with multiple wives. Meanwhile, the female record holder, Madalena Carnauba of Brazil, married at 13 and gave birth to 32 children. The evolutionary anthropologist Sarah Hrdy points out that the context is missing. We don't know how many children from each family survived, or how many of their rivals' offspring were done in by Moulay's more competitive wives. But the difference in output between Lucky and Madalena is still 856 children. More recent accounts of ambitious males include a one-legged sixty-year-old from the United Arab Emirates, Daad Mohammed Murad Abdul Rahman, who has fathered seventy-eight children and set a target of one hundred children by 2015, and Nanu Ram Jogi, a ninety-year-old farmer from Rajasthan who became the world's oldest dad when he fathered his twenty-first child with his fourth wife. "Women love me," he told relatives who came to see his two-week-old daughter, Girija Rajkumari, who was born in August 2007. "I want to have more children. I can survive another few decades and want to have children until I am one hundred. Then maybe it will be time to stop."[29]

According to Trivers, the parent who invests more in their offspring is the one who ultimately limits how many there are—namely the mothers. Females get to choose with whom they will mate, and it's the males who take risks—or who aggressively knock off their rivals—who get chosen and whose genes have survived.[30] It's a harsh assessment, to be sure, but based on data from fruit flies, dragonflies, frogs, prairie chickens, grouse, elephant seals, dung flies, lizards, and baboons, not to mention other primates and Renaissance rulers like Lucky, it works. Males show more variation; they compete fiercely against rivals and for females' attention, and only some men score. Does this hold true for contemporary human beings? It does, although less as a conscious strategy than as a backbeat to human motivation. As a bass line it blends with other riffs, such as cultural pressures to be successful, to earn well, or to best others. Men don't hang glide, parachute-jump, compete in mountain bike races, or negotiate aggressively for the highest salary as conscious—or even unconscious—strategies to lure the most fertile women into their beds. The biochemical mechanisms that make these activities feel fun evolved when taking risks reaped big dividends. The surge of hormones following such stunts makes them feel like their own reward.

Of course, not all men are reckless show-offs. Nor do all women avoid risk, while pointing imperiously from their safe perches, as if to say, "I'll take that one." Such rigid visions violate the nature of human variation, not to mention the complex interplay of other factors that affect female choice, such as the state of her health, how much pressure is being exerted by other males or females in her circle, who else is around to help with her offspring, and whether environmental conditions are right for an infant's survival.[31] Plus, the power of Trivers' theory of parental investment is that it is gender-blind. Where one sex invests in offspring, the other competes and vice versa. In species where males invest much more in their offsprings' survival than females, like phalaropes (a sandpiper-like bird), it's the males who brood the eggs and the females who do the competing. Female phalaropes have dramatic black masks set against their white and orange throats. They're unlike most female birds, which as "choosers" tend to be little brown jobs—LBJs in birder lingo—who go for the more brightly hued males. The brown female cardinal who chooses a brilliant scarlet mate trilling a beautiful song is an example of a chooser, not a competer. The reverse is the brown and white male phalarope, sitting on the nest trying to look inconspicuous, who has chosen his mate from among the black and orange female beauties.

And in humans, where both mothers and fathers invest in their offspring, albeit differently, both compete, albeit differently. Women still invest more as they bear and usually nurture their infants. But the fact that often both parents look after their children over the very long apprenticeship toward adulthood means that females also compete—mainly with one another. In humans it's not only the females who choose. But as parental investment is optional for men—think of deadbeat dads—there is still more competition between men and more choice among women, who find signs of men's ability to invest in their offspring attractive. Thus males compete overtly through dominance, beauty, or kindness contests that make them appealing to women, either as good genetic bets or as good providers.

Competing in the Dating Game

When it comes to sexual attraction, the power of female choice is not just prehistory. On April 9, 2006, a British professor of psychology, Richard Wiseman, engineered a large public experiment. One hundred people attending the Edinburgh International Science Festival took part in ten speed dates each, or one thousand face-to-face encounters. After every three-minute date, participants rated the sex appeal of each new partner and decided if they wanted to meet that person again. Half the women made their decisions in less than thirty seconds. Less than a quarter of the men made up their minds that fast. Yet even if women were quicker to decide, they were twice as choosy as men—rejecting many more candidates right off the bat. As it happens, most of the men's pickup lines fell flat. The top-rated conversation topic was travel—not books or movies, about which few unacquainted men and women could find common ground. But women were unanimous about the most attractive man.[32]

If the sexes were exactly the same, then men and women would be suckers for the same characteristics in their mates. But for women in particular, the magnetic pull of male competition and achievement is undeniable and universal. In 1995 the psychologist Alice Eagly looked at how women's romantic preferences might vary in different societies, and charted how a woman's attitudes might be related to her country's record of gender equality. She expected that as women participated more equally in a society's political and economic life, their lust for good providers would wane. As per the 1970s bumper sticker, they'd need men as much as a fish needs a bicycle. Yet the traits women found alluring in a mate didn't change much from country to country, no matter how many women were running its government or were active in business.[33] Even in the Netherlands, where gender equality is highly prized, Dutch women place 35 percent more emphasis on a mate's ability to earn than Dutch men do. Highly paid professional women and ambitious female college students also prefer men with excellent career prospects.[34] As Robert Trivers would predict, men who can somehow communicate what great parents and providers they'll be possess ineffable sex appeal. This is what David Buss, an evolutionary psychologist from the University of Texas, found when he surveyed women's tastes in thirty-seven societies. In sub-Saharan villages, towns all over the United States, and cities in northern Europe, women find high-status, high-earning men the most attractive. Having analyzed the results from studies spanning fifty-seven years, Buss and his colleagues found that twice as many women as men everywhere see earning power, industriousness, and ambition as highly appealing. Of course, women also value education, kindness, maturity, and intelligence in a mate. But unlike men, when women have to choose between a man's appearance and his resources, resources always win.[35] In a literal gloss on Mark Twain's quip that clothes make the man, when anthropologists John Marshall Townsend and Gary Levy showed women pictures of men wearing Burger King uniforms, the women were never willing to date, have sex with, or marry the men in the fast-food outfits. Yet when the same men were pictured wearing suits and fancy watches, the women changed their minds.[36]

When choosing a romantic partner, men placed more importance on a woman's beauty and youth; they didn't care whether women were wearing fast-food uniforms. "Men are from Mars, women are from Deloitte & Touche," crowed a newspaper article about a survey of 1,022 adults that showed that on average, women prefer a man with a steady job who pays his bills on time, while men choose an attractive woman with a good sense of humor. Even if men are starting to be affected by women's earning power, according to David Buss, it's not their top priority. Men now rate its importance thirteenth on the list, up from seventeenth in 1939. We're left with the finding that primal drivers affect women's preferences when it comes to love. And primal drivers still motivate men to strive and compete.

The sex differences in male injury, mortality rates, and competition for high-paying executive positions still tell that story. But human females compete for males, too; covert social manipulation and harassment tell the female competition story. High-ranking nonhuman female primates can harass subordinate females to the point where mating is impossible. Or if she has managed to choose a mate, the pestered lower-ranking female is in no shape to conceive or raise her own offspring.[37] This, of course, is the ultimate evolutionary put-down.

Trivers had several early flashes of brilliance that irrevocably changed the direction of research in behavioral science. His theories were powerful enough to explain greater male risk-taking, and how some extreme male traits might serve as advertisements of a man's genetic pedigree. Several decades later many of Trivers' predictions have been borne out by data collected by hundreds of other scientists. Yet instability and brushes with the law also marked Trivers' life, nearly offsiding him.[38] His own story would make the perfect allegory about the tension between self-destructive risk and its first cousin, spectacular success.

The Magic Elixir

We saw how Robert Trivers' theory might explain why males compete. Testosterone explains how. While I was writing this chapter yet another male career was boosted to the stratosphere, then just as swiftly torpedoed by testosterone. In the summer of 2006 Floyd Landis, an American cyclist from Pennsylvania Dutch country, was briefly the Tour de France champion. Midway through the race he collapsed in exhaustion and fell off his bike during a steep ascent. The following day he made a breathtaking recovery, overtaking his rivals and coming in first—that is, until his second blood test came back positive for synthetic testosterone and he was stripped of his title. Landis defended himself and his title by exposing irregularities in the lab reports that nailed him. Still, the U.S. Anti-Doping Agency sanctioned the cyclist with a two-year suspension in September 2007. The lesson is clear: even a whiff of testosterone can make you or break you.

This is just one instance of testosterone's paradoxical effects. It's associated with toughness, dominance, assertiveness, endurance, and winning. Yet it can also prompt aggressive and antisocial behavior. As we've seen, naturally occurring testosterone masculinizes the brain in utero, organizing it for rough-and-tumble play, fighting, and threat behavior in childhood, and sensitizing the brain to the later effects of the same hormone during puberty. In young adulthood it can help certain men achieve the social dominance that Trivers predicts.[39]

A host of animal studies shows that administering testosterone prompts animals of both sexes to behave more aggressively. Testosterone injections shift hens up on the pecking order and ramp up the aggression and status of female rhesus monkeys, while also reducing their nurturing behavior.[40] In young men testosterone levels steadily increase, reaching levels twenty times higher in boys than in girls by the end of their teenage years. But as much as people fear teenage boys, it's not as if aggression simply kicks in at puberty. Aggression comes naturally to boys early in childhood—as any parent of a hitting, biting, and scratching two-year-old knows. But in some children it never dies down. By following more than a thousand children from kindergarten until late adolescence, Richard Tremblay and his colleagues at the University of Montréal and Carnegie Mellon University found that early aggression in a very small group of boys accurately predicts violent behaviors about a dozen years later. In this high-risk group of boys, aggression doesn't abate as they get older, as it does in most children who learn self-control early on and increasingly apply it as they mature.[41] Testosterone may be one reason why these boys (about 4 percent) don't learn how to inhibit their aggressive impulses. In this small subset of boys, aggression just increased as these boys grew smarter and stronger.

Yet as we shall soon see, administering testosterone to adolescent girls doesn't have the same effect as it does on boys who are primed with it in utero. The prenatal environment is critical in setting up later receptiveness to the hormone's behavioral effects. Average girls and adult women who take synthetic testosterone as adults don't bulk up and act more like men just because they've suddenly swallowed the magic elixir. But as we learned in chapter 5, girls with congenital adrenal hyperplasia, or CAH, have the XX female genetic signature but were exposed to abnormally high levels of male hormones in utero, so they are indeed primed. Lacking an enzyme that converts androgens to cortisol, their adrenal glands produce an excess of male hormones that work their organizational effects early on, virilizing their bodies while masculinizing their brains.[42] Compared to average girls, twice as many of these young CAH girls prefer the rough-and-tumble play more typical of boys their age. They have better spatial skills and are more competitive, aggressive, and self-confident than other girls, including their sisters.[43] As adolescents, they are much more likely than other girls their age to use aggression to solve problems.[44] Not only do they prefer playing with boys, but as they mature these girls are also less interested in babies and in marrying and having children. They also choose more characteristically male careers than their sisters and female peers, such as airplane pilot, engineer, or architect.[45] Clearly, prenatal androgens do more than create the obvious physical sex differences—male genitalia in the fetus and a more muscular and hairy adult physique. A prenatal saturation with male hormones also affects children's preferences and behavior, making CAH girls *psychologically* less like typical girls and women. There is no evidence that their parents or teachers treat them any differently than they would other girls; the transformative element is their early exposure to androgens.

There are new studies showing that oxytocin may have similar effects, influencing prenatal cell growth related to social skills and empathy. Several studies have found lower levels of prenatal oxytocin and its precursor, OT-X, in autistic children than in normally developing children. Administering oxytocin during a critical period in development may be exploited as one aspect of treatment in the future.[46] In the meantime, we know that prenatal sex hormones transform our brains so that we can't help but think with our gonads.[47]

Bo-Hogs and Trial Lawyers : Testosterone and Careers

If testosterone affects thinking and an appetite for risk, does more of it make certain careers more appealing? James McBride Dabbs, a professor of psychology at Georgia State University, tested the testosterone levels of 8,000 men and women in different jobs. Unlike athletes like Floyd Landis, they didn't have to give urine samples. They just had to spit in a cup. So it was easy to get a variety of people in different occupations to participate in what they nicknamed the Testosterone Olympics. Associating the hormone with youth and virility, the participants assumed that scoring high was good and scoring low was bad. But what Dabbs found was not at all what the participants expected. At the high testosterone end were actors, football players, construction workers, and unemployed men on the street (whom Dabbs conjectured were not really unemployed but unable or unwilling to stay at one job for very long). Blue-collar workers were higher in testosterone than white-collar workers. Managers were 46 percent higher in testosterone than computer programmers, salespeople 24 percent higher than teachers, and construction workers 24 percent higher than lawyers, though male trial lawyers were higher than all other legal types. At the low end of measured testosterone were ministers, farmers, and academics. Dabbs tested Vietnam veterans twenty years after the war and found the higher the testosterone level, the more combat exposure a veteran had experienced. Even criminals have a testosterone hierarchy. Violent, obstreperous prisoners had higher levels of testosterone than nonviolent ones who hewed to prison rules. The more edgy, aggressive male risk-takers—called "bo-hogs" by the other prisoners—were at testosterone's upper limits.[48]

In men, high testosterone is not necessarily linked with money or prestige, as the subjects' egos might predict, but with lower levels of education and blue-collar work. These are male-dominated ghettos, whose denizens have struggled mightily in North America since the manufacturing and agricultural sectors have dwindled. This might account for the large number of unemployed among them.

But androgens—including testosterone—are not just for men. They're also produced by women, albeit in smaller amounts. So do androgens affect women the same way? To understand why the answer is no, consider this paradox. If women are versions of men, you'd see exactly the same pattern as we see in men. High levels of testosterone would be tied to low levels of education and lower-status work. But research on women and testosterone shows just the opposite. In Dabbs' study, all female lawyers were higher in testosterone than female athletes, nurses, or teachers. And when New Mexico researchers Frances Purifoy and Lambert Koopmans took blood samples from women of various ages and linked their hormone levels to their occupations, they found that high blood levels of androstenedione (which converts to testosterone) and testosterone were found in those women who had lofty ambitions and high job status: university students, professionals, managers, and those with technical backgrounds. Lower levels of circulating androgens were found in homemakers and clerical workers, who had less professional training before marrying and having children. This is the opposite of what we would expect if men and women were clones. It's intriguing that higher levels of androstenedione were more commonly found in women with people-oriented jobs, and higher levels of testosterone were found in women who had jobs related to things.[49] The level and type of hormones circulating in the bloodstream are linked with how well you solve spatial tasks, how expertly you read others' emotions, how easily you trust other people, and, not surprisingly, the types of jobs you choose.

Still, there is an aversion to thinking about our choices as having a biological life of their own, especially among women who feel wrongly pegged by "the biology is destiny" and "must be her time of the month" assumptions of the past. Just try asking women if they feel aggressive as a result of fluctuating hormones in their menstrual cycle; they're likely to tell you to get lost. Utah anthropologist Elizabeth Cashdan got around this problem by measuring the same fluctuating hormones (testosterone and androstenedione plus estradiol, the most potent of estrogens) in young adult women, then asking them to rank their own status and the status of their peers. She found that women with higher levels of these hormones felt mighty fine about themselves. Women with high androgens thought they were very popular with other women. Interestingly, their peers did not agree.

As they do in men, higher androgen levels in women meant greater assertiveness and toughness. But women's self-perceptions as leaders and popularity queens were not reflected in how others saw them. Cashdan interprets this disconnect in an evolutionary context. If women are competing among themselves for men who will support them and their children, then an assertive, competitive streak will hardly earn them brownie points with other women. (Nor will it with men, who'd want proof that their investment is needed. In situations where women don't expect much paternal investment—where men don't often stick around to support families, for example—then toughness and assertiveness might be more valued among other women.)

Higher androgens are also linked to having a higher than average number of sexual partners, perhaps one of several reasons why other women don't quite agree that these highly assertive women should be leaders.[50] Lack of confidence in other women and censure are just what Rocio Garcia-Retamero, a psychologist from the Max Planck Institute in Berlin, discovered in 2006 when looking at how female leaders in "nonfeminine" industries were viewed by other women. Basing their expectations on gender role theory, Garcia-Retamero and her colleague Esther Lopez-Zafra expected that there would be more prejudice against female leaders who work in traditionally male roles in traditionally male industries, like car manufacturing—where people expect to see men—than there would be in more female-typed environments, such as clothing manufacturing. They were surprised by what they found. Both men and women thought female candidates would be promoted in "feminine" industries. But men had fewer prejudices about female leaders rising in "male" industries than women did. Women were much more likely than men to discriminate against female leaders.[51] As with same-sex mentoring, gender bias is more likely to come from other women.

In a later study about hormones and competition, Cashdan asked the women to keep diaries about their competitive and aggressive feelings during school activities, sports, friendship, and dating, all the while keeping track of their hormone levels. Women whose diaries documented more verbal aggression turned out to have higher levels of both testosterone and androstenedione. As in men, these male hormones reduced their inhibitions, which gives us a hint as to why other women might not like them all that much. Women with high levels of androstenedione were more likely to express their competitive feelings overtly through verbal aggression. Those women with lower levels had competitive feelings but were unlikely to act on them. Individual differences in the ebb and flow of male hormones influence whether men act on their aggressive or competitive impulses. In women, this aggression is verbal.[52]

Blowing the Lid off Female Aggression

Regardless of cultural background, women compete with other women more than they do with men.[53] Their style is to take on contenders subtly, indirectly, and covertly. Studies of children showed that girls are less physically aggressive but more cutting, excluding newcomers more than boys—often within the first four minutes of an interaction.[54] As they get older, adolescent boys continue to be more physically aggressive and keenly competitive than women, trying to dispatch rivals directly, while women use covert maneuvering to cement their status. Social exclusion, mean remarks, trying to win over a competitor's friends and allies are the "female" ways to jockey for power. Less overt and more socially sophisticated, female aggression is harder to observe.[55] Women who are targets of female aggression are more likely to slink away quietly than to fight back, thus adding to the number of female defectors from the workplace. But until recently it has also been politically incorrect to suggest that women may undermine one another instead of shoring one another up. A cooperative female network is the ideal and is often the case, but by no means the rule.[56]

But the lid is starting to come off female aggression. After I wrote a newspaper column about aggression among academic women in universities, I was inundated with mail from readers. Some applauded my courage for dealing with a taboo topic, others wanted to tell their own stories. One e-mail I received in 2005 read as follows:

> I am a female Ph.D. student from the University of Oxbridge, and have just gone through a traumatic academic divorce from my Ph.D. supervisor of four years. In my case my supervisor was more than disrespectful. She was verbally abusive to female staff and students and utterly exploitative. She would work her students into the ground and scream and yell twenty-four hours a day. Her female Ph.D. students were exploited as unpaid lab assistants and their work and ideas were confiscated and published in her own name. Due to stressful working conditions in our lab, many staff and students ended up getting ill, and were on antidepressants or in counseling. But the many complaints filed against this university professor were largely ignored by the university.

It was only when a new generation of younger women surged into the workforce in the nineties and were supervised by the first cohort of female supervisors that cases of covert female-female aggression started to see the light of day. In corporate environments cases of female aggression were being outed and training programs had even been devised to soften the edges of competitive women, whose behind-the-scenes maneuverings were perceived as too cutthroat.[57] In the early 2000s, books started appearing with titles like *Mean Girls Grown Up, Odd Girl Out,* and *Tripping the Prom Queen: The Truth about Women and Rivalry.* After being viewed as a male issue for decades, competition between women had come out of the closet. And according to evolutionary psychologist David Geary, female-female competition is to be expected in every generation, especially over prized resources. Now that women have gained status in the workplace, they compete with one another over desired promotions and recognition, not just for mates. "The bigger the potential promotion or job, or the better the guy, the more there is at stake and thus the more likely jealousy and envy are triggered," he wrote in an e-mail. Clearly competition is not just for men.

But men still dominate tournaments, races, and zero-sum games. They continue to fill the prisons—and positions of political and corporate leadership. Of the twentieth century's 1,941 government heads, 1,914 were men and 27 were women. Outside democracies, 85 percent of these male rulers were violently deposed or left office in a casket; within democracies male leaders faced a 10 percent chance of being assassinated.[58] But women have their own ways of establishing a hierarchy, ways that are less likely to kill other people or themselves.

Criminals and Geniuses

Women are not only less likely to kill, they're also less likely to commit crimes of any kind. For every fifteen robberies by an American man, a woman commits one. A woman is three times less likely to assault someone than a man, to use a gun, or to start a domestic brawl.[59] In an unusual paper, psychologist Satoshi Kanazawa of the London School of Economics explored the connection between crime and achievement in men. He charted the biographies of 280 scientists, jazz musicians, painters, and authors and mapped the ages of their great achievements against the age-crime curves of criminals. He found that male geniuses peaked early, achieving most impressively at about ages twenty-five to thirty. After that, their accomplishments dropped off sharply, especially if they got married. He writes, "Paul McCartney has not written a hit song in years, and now spends his time painting. J. D. Salinger now lives as a total recluse and has not published anything in more than three decades. Orson Welles was a mere twenty-six when he wrote, produced, directed, and starred in *Citizen Kane,* which many consider to be the greatest movie ever made. The relationship between age and genius appears to be the same in science." Kanazawa goes on to show that John von Neumann, James Watson, and other Nobel Prize winners made their discoveries by age twenty-five. By charting the age of these scientific and artistic achievements against the age that criminal behavior peaks in men—in their early twenties—he discovered the same precipitous rise, sudden burst of activity, then dramatic fall-off, as both male criminals and creators settle down. The men's distributions had the shape of a peaked witch's hat. In comparison, women's achievement distribution looked more like a Stetson, with a delayed, albeit squatter and flatter top reached at about age forty-five that extended into their late fifties, reflecting the diverted energies of their childbearing years.

What does this mean for men? Kanazawa uses evolutionary theory to explain that the psychological mechanism that compels men to commit crimes also pushes them to make great contributions. The achievement window coincides with a burst of testosterone-linked courting and competition. If men's brains evolved millennia ago, then they would have been competing for reproductive success—fighting off competitors for the loveliest, healthiest, most nurturing woman who would bear and raise their children to maturity. The genes of those who succeeded through violence, drive, or cunning would be alive and well in men today (in a law-abiding context, competing to produce artistic or scientific discoveries would be forms of "cultural display designed to attract mates," according to Kanazawa).[60] That male genetic inheritance would foster success in highly competitive arenas, while also increasing the risk of injury or early death. Hence the standard youthful debut of gangs, often training grounds for more audacious crimes.

Summarizing the research literature on criminals' careers, Canadian criminologists Carlo Morselli and Pierre Tremblay have indeed found that young adults were more motivated and successful at crime than older adults. Not only did young adults possess the same characteristics as high achievers in other lines of work, but "male offenders were more likely to take advantage of monetary opportunities than female offenders."[61] If violence and competition are the genetic legacy of young men competing for women between male adolescence and the birth of their first offspring, then it would make sense that men's efforts diminish once their children are born. The costs of continuing to compete are too great. They could die trying—and their children would be left fatherless and without resources. Kanazawa asserts that this is why men are more aggressively competitive when they're young. Just as married men's scientific and artistic achievements diminish by midlife, violent crimes fall off by age forty.

As far-fetched as this sounds, the careers of "successful" high-earning criminals follow the same trajectory as the careers of high-achieving scientists. Both areas are primarily filled with young men who start their training as adolescents, apprentice themselves in larger organizations in their early twenties, travel some distance to champion their work, and have mentors to tutor them. In a study of 268 male inmates from five penitentiaries, Morselli, Tremblay, and an American investigator, Bill McCarthy, found that the criminals who made the most money from the fewest crimes (incomes of $105,000 versus $12,000) had older mentors who had selected their protégés based on their personal characteristics. The mentor then educated his student about how to plan projects and avoid getting caught. He also provided the opportunity to network with people in the same line of work.[62] This sounds an awful lot like graduate school to me.

The difference is that many highly competitive men manage to succeed outside the structure of school, whereas, as we've seen in chapter 1, women are more likely than men to succeed within it. Among men who've made their fortunes through high-octane smarts combined with high-octane risk, there's a sense that school is for sissies. Some with learning or attention difficulties don't do well in a school context. But those with intelligence and an appetite for risk can apply other countervailing strengths—self-confidence and a profound drive to compete and win.

Playing with the Big Boys

When Mark Twain wrote "I have never let my schooling interfere with my education," he captured the life histories of most eminent men until the mid-twentieth century, and many beyond. Henry Cavendish, the oddball scientist we met in chapter 5, identified hydrogen, described the composition of water, and measured the density of the Earth but never managed to graduate from Cambridge. Einstein's original thesis didn't qualify as a doctoral dissertation at the University of Zurich, as he had hoped. He was finally granted a Ph.D. after four thesis attempts and five years of trying. Charles Darwin tried studying medicine at Edinburgh University but dropped out and found studying law too dull to complete that degree, too. His father considered his passion for natural history useless noodling. "You care for nothing but shooting dogs, and rat-catching, and you will be a disgrace to yourself and all your family." He ended up studying divinity, and Bill Bryson writes in *A Short History of Nearly Everything* that Darwin's lackluster academic performance was a constant worry to his parents.[63] Looking in the rearview mirror, the peripatetic school histories of many leaders and luminaries seem trivial compared to three other prerequisites for spectacular achievement: native smarts, investing at least a decade of hard labor to master a discipline, and a monomaniacal preoccupation with a subject. United by an ineffable drive to achieve, these qualities can eclipse formal credentials, according to research psychologist Dean Keith Simonton in his book *Greatness: Who Makes History and Why*.

Neither George Washington nor Abraham Lincoln had much formal education. Michael Faraday had to leave school when he was 14 years old, and even Isaac Newton never advanced beyond the bachelor's degree. In the 20th century, Harvard saw three of its students leave its hallowed halls to triumph without a diploma. Edwin Land dropped out, and proceeded to invent Polaroid lenses and the Polaroid Land Camera. Buckminster Fuller left under less pleasant circumstances, but still managed to devise the geodesic dome and a host of other inventions. Bill Gates, the third and most recent Harvard dropout, founded Microsoft Corporation, the goliath among computer software companies.

To advance beyond mere storytelling, we can cite the educational statistics gathered on more than 300 distinguished creators, leaders, and celebrities born between 1841 and 1948: 15% had an eighth grade education or less, 11% had some high school, 19% completed high school, 9% endured some college, 19% actually earned an undergraduate degree, 4% acquired some knowledge in graduate school, and only 19% earned graduate degrees. In brief, the Ph.D.s were well outnumbered by those who never walked across the stage at a high school commencement ceremony![64]

I am not suggesting that dropping out of school promotes success as much as drawing attention to the staggering momentum of testosterone-fueled drive. Nowhere is this as evident as in the world of high-stakes competitive card and board games. A quick review of the thousands of online gaming sites reveals that most players are unschooled and that 96 percent of the top players are men. One celebrity player is Daniel Negreanu, a thirty-year-old originally from Canada who is one of the most successful tournament poker players in history. According to a 2005 profile in the *New Yorker*, Negreanu has earned $6 million in tournaments since 1997 and another $6 million in online games and at casinos. Despite being thrown out of high school for running a study-hall poker game, Negreanu now writes poker-related columns that run in twelve newspapers, has a website that attracts 100,000 visitors a month, has a book coming out, an instructional DVD, and earns even more money through lucrative endorsement contracts.

Like Mordecai Richler's protagonist Duddy Kravitz, Negreanu is an iconic North American self-made man. But his financial success, based on risk and drive, is hardly fiction. Harvard sociologist Christopher Jencks has documented how education explains only a minor part of the variance in people's incomes, and that "some men value money more than others and these men make unusual sacrifices to get it."[65] This is one reason why a woman with two graduate degrees would earn a fraction of Negreanu's income, an inequality tightly bound to the biology of risk-taking. Aggressively competitive men can succeed in school but also use their street smarts to excel outside it. *New Yorker* writer Kevin Conley described Negreanu as denigrating the "math guys" who rely on game theory and probability instead of intuition. With typical moxie Negreanu thinks these subjects can be learned outside of school.

> "I went to speak at Ohio State and I ended up jokingly saying that I'm starting my Stay Out of School program," he said. "I was totally kidding, but realistically, it's not that far-fetched an idea. For kids that are eighteen, nineteen years old, that are going to college, get a dead-end job where they make fifty or sixty thousand dollars a year, I can take that same kid, teach him how to play poker, and in three months show him how to make more money than he would ever make in that dead-end job. The stock market is gambling, right?" he continued. "This kid studies and he makes money in the stock market, and this is considered by society O.K. A poker player, a kid, sees all these idiots making poor investments and says, 'Wow, I could do a better job than they're doing,' and he studies, and he makes it."[66]

You can dismiss this as bravado, but there's no doubt that this kind of self-confidence helps to push men like Negreanu forward.[67] It is the feeling of invincibility, of superiority, and of inherent self-worth that people sometimes think of as self-esteem. On average, men have been found to have higher self-esteem than women, although the difference is not huge. Even if men have been found to have more of it, it's neither a necessary ingredient for success nor a force for good. People who report the highest self-esteem often act as bullies and enforcers.[68] Like aggression or an appetite for risk, self-esteem boasts a mixed bag of consequences. The concept is fuzzy. There's no real way to measure it other than asking people whether they have a lot of it, which is like asking whether people think they're smart or funny. People with high self-esteem often say they're highly intelligent, but as we've seen, there is no connection between their opinions of themselves and how they do on intelligence tests.[69] Meanwhile, the mountain of studies in the area are mostly correlations, meaning one never knows if someone has high self-esteem because he's a great poker player or if he's a great poker player because he has high self-esteem.

Social psychologist Roy Baumeister and his colleagues at Florida State University tried to strip away all the hype about self-esteem by examining the research. They looked at 15,000 articles on the subject and made the following discoveries. High self-esteem helps people persist longer when they think they might fail. They know better when to hold and when to fold, helpful in poker if not in one's career. People with high self-esteem speak up more often in groups. They get lost less often (although I wonder if a third factor like testosterone boosts both navigational abilities and confidence). Those with high self-esteem tend to be more uninhibited and adventurous, and are more likely to be early experimenters with sex, drugs, and rock and roll.[70] Contrary to popular belief, bullies and aggressors are more likely to have inflated views of themselves; their aggression is often a reaction to "defensive high self-esteem," commonly known as wounded pride.[71]

An Appetite for Risk

We've seen how Daniel Negreanu's type of moxie is associated with adventurousness in gaming. It seems that no one has researched it systematically but I suspect that such moxie is more common in men. The few women who reach the top in this highly competitive world are likely to have the same characteristics along with a superb ability to calculate mathematical probabilities. They'd succeed in the upper echelons of business, too, although they're probably earning more at high-stakes poker.

Just as there are positive and negative aspects of self-esteem, the same holds true for risk-taking. Earlier in this chapter I touched on the higher rates of mortality in men. Adolescents and men in their twenties in particular are more susceptible to reckless driving and fatal car crashes, dying in the military after volunteering for it, or shortening their life spans through violence, avoidable accidents, drug or alcohol use.[72] Currently three young adult men die for every young woman. The pattern of high-risk behavior begins in adolescence, reaches a maximum during a man's early twenties, and declines thereafter. So the peaked witch's hat–shaped distribution of male death via accidents or homicide follows Satoshi Kanazawa's arc of male achievement for scientists, artists, and criminals. It also traces the career trajectory of high-risk, male-dominated careers such as entry into the military, police, and fire-fighting work. Just when their testosterone levels are peaking, men seek out the adrenaline rush of high-risk pursuits—for better or for worse.[73]

Frank Farley, a Temple University psychologist who has devoted his career to studying risk-taking, calls this the T factor. For Farley, T stands for thrill. But T also stands for testosterone. Farley says Type Ts deny that they take risks because they are confident that everything is under their control. He divides them into two groups: Type T positives—entrepreneurs, inventors, explorers, racing car drivers—and Type T negatives—gamblers, criminals, and people who engage in unsafe sex. It would be an appealing dichotomy, if only the two sub-types didn't overlap. When the twenty-four-year-old NFL quarterback for the Pittsburgh Steelers, Ben Roethlisberger, rode his motorcycle in traffic without a helmet and suffered head injuries in June 2006, he denied he was engaging in risky behavior. After all, his job involves aggressively rushing into play leading with his head, and the rewards are phenomenal: a $22 million contract and more than $17 million in bonuses and incentives. According to Farley, "as the quarterback, you are in a sense making your own rules. You live by your decisions, in real time, under the gun. The play starts and everything is moving fast."[74] So was the windshield Roethlisberger splintered with his skull.

Not only does Roethlisberger fit Kruger and Nesse's high-risk cat-egories for age and sex, he also embodies the male tendency toward extremes, including jobs that are extremely risky, dirty, or lethal. In his book *Biology at Work,* Wayne State University law professor Kingsley Browne lists the following ten occupations as the most dangerous, hav-ing compiled these numbers from the U.S. Bureau of Labor Statistics. The risk of death compared to the average worker is in parentheses beside it, so a fisherman would be 21.3 times more likely to die on the job than an office worker, teacher, accountant, or dentist. All of the fol-lowing occupations, with the exception of farmer, are 90 to 95 percent male: fisherman (21.3), logger (20.3), airplane pilot (19.9), metal-worker (13.1), taxi driver (9.5), construction worker (8.1), roofer (5.9), electric power installer (5.7), truck driver (5.3), and farmer (5.1).[75]

British labor statistics reveal a similar pattern. In the United King-dom, you're most likely to die on the job if you work in forestry, fish-ing, hunting, agriculture, metalworking, or truck driving.[76] All are male-dominated. Unpredictability—the exciting part of risk—is the common element, alongside the desire to work alone while ranging unsupervised over vast swaths of territory. These factors cluster together as a theme on the guidance surveys often given to high school students when they are choosing careers. The solitary, outdoors, high-risk jobs overwhelmingly appeal to men.[77]

Competing for Fun and Profit

Even without the chance to earn big bucks, the chance to compete and win is a big enough draw for many men. So far, Joel Wapnick's earnings in Scrabble championships have netted him $63,305. Amortized over twenty-five years of games and travel to tournaments, this is not a way to get rich, he admits. One of the world's top Scrabble players, he ranked first in the world in 1999 and second in 1993 and 2001.

"It's a compelling game. It's a beautiful game. It's about knowledge. It's about strategy." This is how the soft-spoken, frizzy-haired, sixty-year-old professor of music rhapsodized about all the ways he loves competitive Scrabble. Sitting in his cramped McGill office, with its rotating desk fan and surrounded by piles of books and yellowed papers, Professor Wapnick hardly looks like a hard-bitten thrill-seeker. The window behind Wapnick's head was crosshatched with protective grillwork and was so grimy that the midday summer sun looked faded out. But the huge computer screen with a Scrabble board screen saver provided just enough illumination for us to see each other.

"What distinguishes a champion from mere Scrabble junkies?" I asked him.

"How competitive you are is very important."

"And why so few women?"

"The small sample of top women players form a pretty small comparison group." Then Professor Wapnick offers an educated guess. "It takes a certain ruthlessness. When you sit down to play, you've got to want to win very badly. The impression I get from women is that when they sit down to play, at some point they give up."

According to Wapnick, Scrabble is essentially "a spatial game, a math game, a probability game." You need to be able to calculate the probabilities of the tiles that are left and what's on your opponent's rack from what's displayed on the board. But what's most important is being hell-bent on winning. "When I first started I just wanted to be one of the best players. I knew I had it in me. It was something I felt I could be really great at. The most important thing is the tournaments you've won and in that I'm pretty good." He spent hours a day memorizing lists of words like "kabaya," "guaiac," "barye," not exactly as spelled, but as variations on nonsense alphagrams, like "aabkya," "aaicgu," and "abery"—in the order they might appear in Scrabble. Wapnick estimates he knows jumbled-up spellings of about 120,000 words—about 100,000 more than the average person—with meanings so obscure the words might as well be gibberish.

Most years, about 45 percent of the total number of players who qualify to compete in the North American and World Scrabble championships are female. But at the highest-scoring division only 5 percent are. So competitive Scrabble looks exactly like the executive pyramid, as 46 percent of the workforce is female yet only 5 percent of the most senior management is.[78] It's also a lot like the top levels of competitive poker and chess. The former has a handful of world-class female champs, and the latter has none at all.[79] In Scrabble there was one female world champion in 1987: Rita Norr. Currently a Canadian woman from Toronto, Robin Pollock Daniel, is the highest-ranked female Scrabble player in the world, having finished twenty-first out of 635 players at the 2006 U.S. Scrabble Open, in Phoenix. But Scrabble divas are an anomaly. Do the Scrabble brainiacs, whom Pollock Daniel says are mostly male "musicians, computer geniuses, or math people," really care what sex their opponent is? "If you can play and hold a decent conversation, you're in. I'm accepted very well by the men. I've always been one of the guys."

She goes on to support Wapnick's contention. "I care a lot about winning," she says. "That's what distinguishes me from a lot of women. I hate to lose. When I'm playing Joel—who has two Masters and a Ph.D. and is just brilliant—I so expect to beat him. Still, I go into every game and there's a small female voice that says, You don't belong here. You're fraudulent. It's the female thing. I'm happy to be corroborated by a Scrabble writer as one of the top players. I need that corroboration. I'm always in the top group and I need that proof that I belong there. I wonder if the men feel that. A lot of the men feel very deserving."

Once Pollock Daniel, a psychotherapist who gave up her practice for her kids and Scrabble, was asked to act out her secret alter ego during a Gestalt therapy training session. "I chose Rain Man. We both have the ability to do things mentally—it's my idiot savant type of talent. He did it without shame." She thinks that women have not been given permission by society to consecrate six hours a day to activities like memorizing alphagrams and high-probability bingos—seven-letter words with fifty-point bonuses. But I'd wager that even if they had her prodigious memory, few women would want to. They have other things to do. John D. Williams, the executive director of the National Scrabble Association, agrees. "Women are too busy with the business of life, whereas men are more focused and obsessive than women," he told me. "I've met few women who know who played second base for the Blue Jays in 1987, or the difference in engine size between a 1968 Chevrolet and a 1969 Buick. It's the same thing. Who would sit around learning 100,000 words that no one would use in real life? Males tend to gravitate to esoterica. Go to a *Star Trek* convention—it's 90 percent male." Terrence Tao, the young math wizard, Fields Medal winner, and UCLA math professor who is an expert on oscillatory integrals, nonlinear dispersive equations, and multilinear operators, and Daniel Tammet's ability and desire to memorize 22,500 digits of pi reveal how far the tendency to absorb mountains of data can take someone when the drive to compete is thrown into the mix.

"Women are more sensible than guys are. To expend a lot of effort on Scrabble a lot of women would say, Why do it? There's not a lot of payoff. To get the adulation of a few hundred people?" Wapnick asks rhetorically. Yet when he was younger and won the world championship, he remembers "going back to my room and jumping up and down." Now that he's in his sixties, winning would be kind of nice, but he tells me that it's not as important as it used to be. As I scribble this in my notebook, I recall Kanazawa's youthful spikes of testosterone and their link to early genius. I think of Dabbs' testosterone surveys and wonder whether someone should ask the top Scrabble and poker players to spit in a cup.

If they did, I'd hazard they'd discover why males are on average more aggressive and competitive. Biochemical drivers of behavior, released under stress and refined over millennia, signal to men that other guys are in their crosshairs. These hormones make competition feel invigorating and fun. Meanwhile, females are more likely to consider the long haul. Due to their own hormonal influences, more women than men are judicious about risking everything to win one bet. They find competition less inherently appealing and most perform better without it. Men and women, on average, have different neuroendocrine responses to stress. Men release greater quantities of adrenaline and cortisol when they compete, which casts a psychological glow on their experience. "This may be why females tend to respond more selectively to challenge, and more economically in the sense that they master many stressful situations without calling upon their bodily reserves to the same extent as males," wrote Marianne Frankenhaeuser, the psychologist at the University of Stockholm cited earlier in this chapter in the discussion of punishment and revenge. Even under extraordinary pressure women's output of adrenaline is much the same as it is day-to-day, she discovered, while men's always increases under stress. This chemical boost makes the experience of competing feel different. Women report more intense negative feelings and discomfort in competitive situations, even while performing just as well as the men.[80] For most women it's less a question of who's able to win. It's whether competing feels good and is worth the cost.

If males are more competitive by nature, is this a problem that should be fixed? It's tempting to see it that way if we expect men and women to be identical and to want the same things. More men than women strive to win the game, no matter the investment. More men than women choose to work the eighty to a hundred hours a week required to win the jackpot, or to be the top dog. There are lots of highly competitive women and lots of men who hate to compete. But on average, sex differences in aggressive competition suggest that the male and female teams are playing by two sets of rules.

It's also tempting to try to tame the male penchant for competition and risk-taking given the costs to men's longevity and happiness. I, for one, would like to see my sons and nephews live as long as the girls in their classrooms. The fact that male risk-taking and restless striving are twinned with fragility is a feature of the sexual paradox. A competitive advantage comes with a trade-off, and nowhere is this more obvious than in impulsive men with short attention spans. As exaggerations of the average male, men with attention deficit disorder often take big chances. But that means that they can win big, too.

CHAPTER 9

Turbocharged:
Men with ADHD Who Succeed

Ron Randolph Wall, the chairman of an international marketing firm based in Nevada, could be a poster boy for ADHD. Silver-haired, Wall is a lanky six feet two, has a tidy salt-and pepper mustache, and sounds a lot like James Bond. He has the same British vowels and sartorial style, the same impeccable manners, and a gleaming European sports coupe he uses to tool around town. What's missing is that split second of British reserve. Wall never hesitates. He strides into a room with confidence and zeal. After meeting me, he immediately wants to tell me about his latest idea, reaching out warmly as if we're old chums.

An immigrant with attention deficit disorder and a ninth-grade education, Wall is why I'm standing in a Lake Tahoe hotel lobby at eight thirty in the morning. Or more precisely, I'm waiting for Brooke, Wall's twenty-one-year-old personal assistant, to pick me up in her aging SUV, acquired to plow through the Sierra Nevada snowdrifts and to accommodate her snowboard and Wall's dogs, she tells me after instructing me to hop in. The ornate tattoo crawling up Brooke's wrist and arm and the large gray poodle sleeping in the back of the car are signs that this won't be the standard interview: hushed boardroom, scripted comments. Apparently Wall has his own way of doing business. One of them is to delegate to a clutch of trusted minions, whether or not they have the standard credentials. After all, when he started he didn't have any.

* * *

Wall's offices, a sanctuary with large windows framing the Tahoe pines, are packed with dozens of Generation Y employees like Brooke, all facing computer terminals, calculating reward ratios, and mapping the demographics of each movie theater in the United States. They're working out a formula that puts free movie tickets in boxes of cereal, toothpaste, and disposable diapers. "If you deliver more to someone than what's expected, you'll get more in return," is Wall's mantra. Putting it into practice means that nearly every North American consumer can now see the latest blockbuster free while becoming a loyal user of Crest. Wall knows who is likely to take him up on the offer better than anyone. His company uses the mere possibility of incentives to attract consumers to a brand. By putting movie tickets worth $15 in a $3 box of breakfast cereal, or by branding credit cards that rack up electronic points, Wall instills loyalty in deal-hungry buyers. And with a shrewd grasp of the probabilities, he banks on his hunch that a good percentage of people won't bother to cash in on their gifts. Motivating consumers to buy the product without always having to pay out on their rewards turned out to be a marketing coup.

Forty years ago Wall was the first to think of linking freebies to plastic credit cards—now called loyalty cards—thus offering the consumer something for nothing and co-branding two distinct products in the buyer's consciousness. A generation ago, if you bought enough groceries, you could trade in your Pinkie or Green stamps for a few bowls, or maybe a toaster. Now purchases charged to your card can earn you a flat-screen TV, or a trip for two to Vegas. That there's no licking and sticking is a bonus. The corporations get loyal clients who have invested something and only occasionally return to collect on it. The banks get to lend money at the boosted credit-card rate. And Ron, who thought up the idea, gets a premium at each end of the transaction. Consumer, retailer, and manufacturer—everyone thinks they're getting something special out of the deal. Combined with his outsized gregariousness, this belief in the power of freebies built his multinational operation. Wall used the idea to spin off international franchises until his company was generating $50 million a year. Having amassed a small fortune, he is now considering philanthropy as his next new thing. But before he does, I want to get a glimpse of how a successful man with ADHD goes about his day.

*   *   *

After stopping to pick up lattes, Brooke and I pull up to a low-rise office building set into a stand of pines. Wall, smiling and in a workout suit, is suddenly there, greeting us with hugs in the sunny parking lot. Then he bounds up the stairs two at a time with his poodle, Loki, in tow. He talks steadily to me as we head toward his office, pausing to engage with every staff member we walk past, his cell phone vibrating and pasted flat against his ear. "I can't cut myself off from ideas," he says, turning back to me, then "I don't want to be outside myself" a moment later. Finally we close the door to his office and I ask him to tell me how he got to this point—head of a multimillion-dollar enterprise with franchises on several continents. Wall begins to review his career, beginning with the car washing business he started as a teenager, on to a stint as an underage croupier in a London casino, followed by a gig developing advertising for a condom company, and eventually, hopping across vast landscapes of time and place, landing up as CEO of this marketing enterprise. Suddenly he segues to his family history, his parents' postwar immigration to London, interweaving his own and his son's personal stories with assorted references to his ex-wife and his personal philosophy. I struggle to keep up with the thematic changes, phone interruptions, and doggy demands, clicking my digital tape recorder on and off and riffling backward and forward in my notes. He can't keep to one topic, and I can't keep up.

The Paradox of ADHD

Wall is a grown version of many boys I had assessed with ADHD—restless, distractible, voluble, quick to react. Easily frustrated and frustrating the adults around them, the boys were brought to the psychologist's office so their problem could be named and with any luck "fixed."

An attention deficit disorder is not usually considered an advantage. The speediness, fluid attention, impulsivity, and compulsion to seek novelty are symptoms, that is, they're signs of a disorder. Research on men with ADHD attests to their fragility—their frequent job changes, sleep disorders, and marital problems.[1] We expect those with this condition to struggle and perhaps fail, and many do, especially in school.[2] But the ones who succeed often do so in a spectacular way, raising two interesting questions: Are there features of the disorder that are catalysts for success? And as there are at least three times as many males as females with ADHD, is the disorder an exaggeration of more common male traits? We know that increased male variability means there are more extreme men—the athletes, criminals, and inventors you met in the previous chapter, and the multimillionaires you'll meet in this one. Their extreme male traits boost them forward, violating our expectations of how fragile men should turn out.

This is the paradox, and the inconsistency begins with a long-standing skepticism about whether ADHD is a disorder in the first place. Called ADD for short, it is mainly characterized by inattention, especially in repetitive situations where there's little chance of novelty. "Dreamy," "forgetful," and "not on the ball" are expressions often used to describe those with the disorder, who also tend to be restless and impulsive—blurting out unedited thoughts or taking untested risks. Those with ADHD often feel incapable of waiting. Nor can they easily and patiently listen to others for very long, execute elaborate plans, inhibit their urges or ideas indefinitely, or be coolheaded about boredom. Often hyperactivity goes along with these symptoms, creating a maelstrom of energy and disorganization that's hard to ignore.[3] Only when there are multiple symptoms that affect someone in different situations and over many years is a diagnosis made, and even then, only when the symptoms interfere with daily life: school, work, or relationships.[4] Affecting from 7 to 12 percent of children worldwide and 4.4 percent of adults, along with depression it is one of the most common psychological disorders in the world.[5] But whereas depression is primarily a female disorder, men are three times as likely as women to have ADHD and boys are three to ten times as likely to have it as girls.[6]

A disorder is a deviation from the norm, and this one has always carried moral overtones. ADHD was first identified as a biologically based "defect of moral control" of childhood at the beginning of the twentieth century, although mythology and literature offer clues that it existed long before.[7] In Shakespeare's *King Henry IV*, a chief justice tries to get Falstaff's attention in an exchange that would ring true to anyone who has interacted with someone with ADHD. "You would not come when I sent for you," the judge complains to Falstaff, who replies that his inattention is due to "much grief from study and a perturbation of the brain. . . . It is the disease of not listening, the malady of not marking that I am troubled withal."[8] When Shakespeare attributes this to deafness, drunkenness, or a deficit of attention that requires a doctor's attention, he sets up the moral question that still dogs the disorder: Are people who don't concentrate able to do otherwise? Although the scientific consensus is that they can't, for centuries the hallmarks of ADHD have been linked to a lack of self-control and moral lassitude. Trickster stories from various cultures feature a diminutive male figure who wanders around aimlessly, drawn by his impulses, by restlessness, and by curiosity.[9] The trickster creates chaos around him while escaping from it unscathed. Anansi, the spider in West African stories, Brer Rabbit in American folklore, and the coyote in Native American myths are a few of the trickster figures who won't submit to the rules and who live by their wits. Like the boy with ADHD who quietly reprogrammed my office clock so that the alarm went off long after he was gone, the trickster's gift is to escape the mundane. His problem is not being able to rein in his behavior to conform to expectations, often demonstrating universal truths while breaking all the rules. He's sly, quick, and charming. But is he normal?

Is It Really Disorder?

One reason why ADHD is controversial is that its symptoms shade into run-of-the-mill dreaminess and recklessness. And as diagnosis rates vary widely among countries and even among regions within countries, there's continuing suspicion that ADHD is just an artifact of culture, or the brainchild of an alliance between drug companies and physicians. Just the fact that eighteen times as many boys are treated for it in the United States as in the United Kingdom, that Scotland has higher rates than England, and Alabama has twice the rates of Colorado, creates skepticism about whether the disorder is "real."[10] Despite the public debate, there's a growing consensus among researchers that ADHD exists everywhere in the world and that regional variations reflect a society's tolerance of unfocused behavior and its willingness to face up to mental health issues. There are also demographics that skew developmental problems of all types—from premature births to asthma—and a better awareness of the symptoms in some places. Like burnout or traumatic stress disorder, once the profile is known it's identified more frequently.

While Europe was quicker to recognize autism as a disorder, the United States, Australia, and Canada had a thirty-year head start in research on ADHD and came out with evidence-based treatment plans a decade earlier (the American Academy of Child and Adolescent Psychiatry published its first treatment guidelines in 1997, whereas the United Kingdom's clinical guidelines will be published in 2008). In addition, a broader diagnostic category in the United States and Canada means that persisting inattentiveness merits a diagnosis there—even without hyperactivity—whereas in Europe one has to be inattentive and hyperactive to meet the criteria. Despite these nuances, there's burgeoning recognition of a condition that until recently was considered an American fad. Now 5 percent of schoolboys in the United Kingdom have been diagnosed with ADHD—half the rate in North America, but still well below Switzerland, the Netherlands, and Iceland. Hundreds of research articles documenting its genetic origins and pharmacological treatments have appeared in scientific journals since the early 1970s—evidence that has been largely ignored by the British psychiatric establishment until recently.[11] As a result, there's still tension between parents and teachers about whether a child's restlessness and inattention are due to lax parenting, bad teaching, poor diet, underfunded schools, or a bona fide brain disorder with biological roots. A scandal ensued when the BBC reported in 2006 that teachers told parents of children with ADHD that their children cannot attend school if they are not being treated for the disorder. Meanwhile, in the litigious United States, there are ongoing lawsuits about who is responsible for diagnosing and educating these children.[12] Much like autism—which was first blamed on "refrigerator mothers"—there has been a slow evolution from seeing ADHD as a symptom of a sick environment to a recognition that biological factors are at play.

Unfortunately for those who want concrete proof of the diagnosis, there is no lab test. But there are standardized rating scales, and the

diagnostic signs of ADHD are described in the North American psychologist's bible *The Diagnostic and Statistical Manual of Mental Disorders* and in its slightly stricter European equivalent, *The International
Classification of Diseases.*

The Biological Evidence

Even if the symptoms sometimes overlap with run-of-the-mill flight-
iness or obstreperousness, when the inattention, impulsivity, and
hyperactivity persist across different situations and over time, the
evidence for the biological roots of the disorder is unmistakable.
Although some children seem to grow out of the hyperactivity part
at adolescence, the more symptoms persist into adulthood the greater
the likelihood that close relatives will also have the disorder.[13] There
are also brain imaging studies that reveal ADHD's anatomical and
biochemical markers. Those with ADHD have a smaller caudate, a
C-shaped strip buried deep in the center of the brain, that is involved
in controlling voluntary movement. Some researchers have found the
splenium, the back band of the corpus callosum, to be smaller in people with ADHD.[14] Other neuroscientists pinpoint anomalies in the
prefrontal cortex—the part of the brain that regulates its supervisory
functions—harnessing behavior so that it's deliberate and focused.
The prefrontal cortex has been compared to a police force that keeps
unruly factions in line. But inhibiting urges is not simply a matter of
neural anatomy. The flush of neurotransmitters that governs the ability to prioritize and stop and start activities is also out of kilter in people with ADHD.[15]

Two genes that significantly increase the risk of developing the disorder, DRD4 and DAT-1, the first a dopamine receptor gene and the
second a dopamine transporter gene, have been found to be susceptibility genes for ADHD. Still, it's not just a case of cause and effect.
These gene loci are also implicated in reading disabilities and autism.
As we've seen, all three are more common in males, with two of the
three disorders often occurring together.[16] Multiple genes are involved
in a child inheriting any one or a combination of these conditions. Not
all the candidate genes have been identified yet, all the more reason to
be obsessive about teasing apart the family history. Being accident-

prone, dropping out of school early, drifting from job to job, depending on other people to be organized, being unable to complete projects, self-medicating with alcohol, and a hair-trigger response to conflict— all are clues of a possible attention deficit disorder, especially in those born before the 1970s, before the disorder was understood. These problems surface because people with ADHD have brains with distinct features, and these features emerge due to their genes, not one but several genes that work together. Environmental factors determine how severely someone will be affected but the basic pattern is laid down before birth. In fact, successive generations of people with ADHD are common, with males predominating in the family tree. Half of all adults with ADHD have an ADHD child, while a third of their siblings also has the disorder. Compare these probabilities to the 6 to 8 percent chance of unrelated people having ADHD and its genetic origins become clear.[17] Bolstering the family connection, the heritability of the disorder in identical twins ranges from 40 to 88 percent, depending on the type of ADHD and who is rating the child's behavior (parents often underestimate the disorder in the less severely affected twin).[18]

In short, there is a collection of physiological and psychological clues attesting to ADHD's existence as a biological phenomenon. Genetic variations are at the root of the desultory attention and impulsivity that in a precubicle world may once have made evolutionary sense. Hair-trigger responses could have meant snagging food or mates before anyone else got to them. Studies show that impulsive adolescent baboons and monkeys become the dominant adult males in the troupe, presuming they are able to control their aggressive impulses long enough to live to adulthood.[19] The risk-taking and impulsivity common to many males are exaggerated in ADHD. Under the right circumstances these characteristics can promote their success. But they are also associated with a distinct vulnerability—a penchant for fights, accidents, and unanticipated snafus.

Getting the background of a child with ADHD can be a messy affair. As one parent is likely to have the disorder, he or she ricochets from topic to topic, all while being baited by the child's restlessness and impulsivity. My case notes attest to the chaos that ensues. "Child rocks back and forth in his chair, then flips backward; father erupts," "child

repeatedly out to reception (elevator, water fountain, bathroom),"
"child disconnects phone, parent unaware," "empties Kleenex box,"
and "reaches for Etch A Sketch, paper clips, stapler, stopwatch during
interview," "bolts after five minutes," "child doesn't plan, know where
to start on the page," "mother answers before question is asked." I
soon discovered that a tightly structured, speedy interview works best,
as the chemistry of the disorder is unforgiving of the briefest pause.
Even in a sprint, such family histories reveal that most children with
ADHD were fussy babies who didn't like to be cuddled or held and to
the annoyance of their parents, didn't sleep much. A minority are
simply inattentive, without the hyperactivity that drives others with the
disorder to move relentlessly, as if powered by a motor. It's not hard
to see why school, requiring children to sit immobile for hours, endure
lots of repetition, and inhibit their impulses, is usually anathema. This
is one reason why it was originally considered a disorder of childhood. Most adults with ADHD had checkered school histories but no
idea what was wrong until they brought their own children to a psychologist to investigate why they weren't learning or behaving like
their peers. Only then did they see their experiences reflected in their
children's.

That was Ron Wall's story. When he brought his preschool-age son
to a neurologist he discovered why he found school unbearable as a
child, and why as an adult he always felt like a maverick. "I didn't care
for schoolwork. I wasn't captivated by it. I was more interested in
looking out the window," he told me. But as he listened to his son's
doctor, Wall recognized his own pattern—the impulsivity, flighty attention, the attraction to risk. When he was a child, these behaviors
prompted his parents to take him to the Tavistock Clinic in London.
"That was when I learned I was different. I was a naughty boy and
couldn't concentrate on anything. I was six. The diagnosis was that my
parents had an unhappy marriage." But his parents' marital problems
had little to do with Wall's inattention. It was probably the other way
around—a child with a problem can easily widen any chinks in the
marital wall.

Ron's ADHD had biological origins, which combined with his personal history, forged his unmistakable drive. The son of German Jews
who were in displaced persons camps after the war, Wall grew up in

battered postwar London where his parents were attempting to make a fresh start. His father sold stationery to small businesses. His mother cleaned houses and rented out rooms to make ends meet. Whether Wall's ferocious ambition was due to feeling like an impoverished outsider in class-conscious England, his attention deficit disorder, or both, it was implacable. He wanted to make more money than his father did, to own his own home, to drive a nice car, or better still, to be chauffeured around town. He was going to make it if it killed him.

The Edge

It's called a disorder, has its own brain geography, and it derails children from succeeding in school. Men with ADHD are like Superman and Kryptonite. It can be their undoing. Yet under the right conditions ADHD seems to give them special powers. In David Neeleman, the founder and CEO of JetBlue and WestJet Airlines, ADHD fostered the ingenuity to compensate for his deficits. Neeleman lost his watch so often he bought replacements five at a time. He forgot his airline tickets so often that he thought up paperless tickets. At first there was universal scoffing, but he persistently championed the idea of electronic tickets—a convention people now take for granted. His e-tickets and electronic reservation system earned him $22 million when he sold it to Hewlett-Packard in 1999—commercial ideas he credits to the necessity of coming up with alternatives. "My ADD brain naturally searches for better ways of doing things. With the disorganization, procrastination, inability to focus, and all the other bad things that come with ADD, there also come creativity and the ability to take risks."[20]

The downside is that risks can be expensive, inconvenient, and dangerous. Boys and men with ADHD get into more car accidents, drink more, take more drugs, and have more explosive moods than average guys.[21] Yet a high tolerance for risk is a prerequisite for business success. High-risk business ventures generate higher margins of profit, even if they engender the possibility of greater losses. To test the connections between gender and entrepreneurial risk-taking, several European economists asked 20,000 Germans how they would invest €100,000 if they won a lottery. There was a 50 percent chance that they would double their money every two years if they invested it, but also a 50 percent like-lihood that they would lose half of it. Should they hold on to the original sum or invest it, and how much should they risk? The researchers discovered that men invested an average of €6,000 more than women; young people invested more than older ones; and taller people invested more than short ones (for every centimeter of height, the amount invested increased by €200). The kicker was that people who enjoyed taking risks saw themselves as happier and more optimistic, although it's not clear what came first—risk-taking or optimism. Not surprisingly, an appetite for risk draws people to self-employment, while less risk-prone people are attracted to the public service, which offers job security and benefits but lower earnings.[22] Like height, risk-taking related to entrepreneurship is on a continuum, with male risk-takers at the extreme. And like height, it's largely inherited, with about half of a person's propensity to become an entrepreneur due to one's genes, according to a British study comparing the employment history of more than 1,200 pairs of twins.[23]

Less aversion to risk is one salutary aspect of the ADHD profile. An expansive extroversion is another. Paul Orfalea, the founder of Kinko's, was "a weather pattern, a hurricane," with "nonlinear, out-of-the-box thinking," according to Ann Marsh, the journalist who cowrote his autobiography. Having ADHD as well as dyslexia, Orfalea had attended eight different schools as a child, was expelled four times, couldn't pass second grade the first time around, and never made it through college. If ever there was a fragile male you'd predict would strike out, it was Orfalea. Having failed plenty in school, he already felt like an outsider in university, where his friends aced their classes and his red Afro earned him names like Mohair, Carpethead, Pubehead, Brillo Pad, Kinkhead, and finally Kinko. The name stuck. He hated it, but used it to his advantage. The renegade applied the nickname to a tiny photocopy shop he opened as a student in 1970, that he gradually transformed into a 1,200-store empire netting $2 billion annually. "It didn't take me long to conclude that I was basically unemployable. I had to figure out my own way to do it," he told me in a phone call from his home in Santa Barbara.

Talking to Orfalea is like lifting off in a tornado. Before I knew what was happening he took control of the interview, firing off personal questions to establish "who I am talking to." Then he became disarmingly frank about himself. He immediately assumed common ground, demonstrating how easily he turns business associates into friends, and friends into associates. There seemed to be no barriers—Orfalea was patently aware of his vulnerabilities and was upfront about discussing them. "I was 100 percent frightened that I was going to wipe myself out. But I had so many reversals early on, I was prepared to make a lot of mistakes. That's part of the game. When everything goes perfectly, you're not resilient. And you won't see the opportunities in front of your nose." Orfalea understood intuitively that in business, his clients were just versions of himself—anxious, afraid of missing deadlines, disorganized, always rushing, and maybe in need of a little company at odd hours. "We were still setting up shop when a professor from the university came to us. Like every one of the subsequent millions of customers we would serve over the next three decades, he was stressed out and in a hurry. . . . Later on we would learn that we weren't so much selling copies as we were assuaging anxiety. He didn't know exactly what he wanted, but he wanted it done yesterday."[24]

Orfalea wanted things done yesterday, too, and was too restless and driven to do them himself. Opening stores 24/7 was his idea but he left the grunt work to others, and focused on what he did best: meeting people and coming up with new ideas. "I found that leaving headquarters got me away from the mundane, daily grind that left no space for insight, inspiration, or innovation. Here, as elsewhere, I was powerfully helped by my so-called disorders. I could never bear staying in one place for very long." But he wasn't just physically restless. His employees described him as "a walking brainstorm—exhausting and stimulating at the same time," and having so many ideas you "had to claw your way through them." One of his strengths was anticipating what clients wanted. Copies overnight? Okay. An artist wanted to photocopy dead birds? Sure. A conservationist wanted plasticized maps of the African rainforest? Fine. There were even those who dropped their pants to photocopy themselves nude. That was okay, too. If there was a niche related to copies, Orfalea was ready to fill it, using mutual trust

Paul Orfalea, then a student at the University of
Santa Barbara, at his first Kinko's in 1970

and enthusiasm to drive home what *he* wanted. An appetite for risk
combined with his ability to understand what people need drove his
bottom line.

The Fluid, Skip-Around Style

It's while connecting with other people and juggling concurrent activities that Ron Wall comes up with his best ideas. A typical moment in
his day has him snaking his Rolls-Royce backward up a hill at the same
time as he's relating a story and picking up calls on his BlackBerry.
Instead of engaging in highly focused, solitary problem solving that
goes on behind closed doors, Wall finds that his scattered, skip-around
style allows him to see new elements in the big picture, to see across
categories, he says, to see links that others don't. He attributes this fluidity to his ADHD, which he calls an "attention surplus." Once new
ideas surface, he uses Burke, his straitlaced CFO, to evaluate them and
"manage my risk," and another disciplined associate to put his ideas
into practice. "I dream, he executes," Wall says.

According to many scientists and creators, new ideas come easiest to a scattered, unfocused consciousness.[25] Only a detour from the expected can prompt an idea that's really new, wrote the late-nineteenth-century psychologist William James.

> Instead of thoughts of concrete things patiently following one another in a beaten track of habitual suggestion, we have the most abrupt cross-cuts and transitions from one idea to another, the most rarefied abstractions and discriminations, the most unheard-of combinations of elements, the subtlest associations of analogy; in a word, we seem suddenly introduced into a seething caldron of ideas, where everything is fizzling and bobbling about in a state of bewildering activity, where partnerships can be joined or loosened in an instant, treadmill routine is unknown, and the unexpected seems the only law.[26]

"Bewildering activity" is a good term for Wall's cognitive style. Uninhibited experimentation is a hallmark of ADHD—one reason why many with the disorder are accident-prone. They try ideas on for size and make plenty of mistakes. "They win some, they lose some," says Daniel Goleman, the psychologist who explained the concept of emotional intelligence to the world. He sees creative people as making more errors, not because they're less expert but because they come up with more possibilities. And in people with ADHD the internal critic that puts the brakes on harebrained schemes and innovative ideas is very often silent.

As if corroborating Wall's suspicion that his dilatory attention is a boon, in *Greatness,* Dean Keith Simonton describes the dreamlike associations that creators often credit as the source of their ideas. Once unexpected links are in place a second process kicks in to assess their merit. The English playwright John Dryden starts a play "when it is only a confused mass of thoughts tumbling over one another in the dark"; the architect August Kekulé famously discovers the structure of the benzene ring in a dream about snakes biting their tails; Thomas Edison comes up with his best inventions while drifting off to sleep or just waking up. Called "addled" by his teachers, Edison was a school dropout by age twelve. But he exploited any idea that came to him in this hypnagogic state, and even developed a technique to capture serendipitous ideas that might surface while he was half conscious. Here Goleman describes Edison's invention for creating inventions:

> He would doze off in a chair with his arms and hands draped over the armrests. In each hand he held a ball bearing. Below each hand on the floor were two pie plates. When he drifted into the state between waking and sleeping, his hands would naturally relax and the ball bearings would drop on the plate. Awakened by the noise Edison would immediately make notes on any ideas that had come to him.[27]

People with ADHD tend to alternate between periods of hyperfocusing and a diffuse style of attention that goes fishing, casting about for novelty. What is critical is not just coming up with ideas but recognizing if they have currency, and here, too, those with ADHD may have an advantage. One recent study compared a group of college students who reported they had ADHD with a control group. Psychologist Cecile Marczinski found that those with ADHD were faster to react to novelty than those with normal attention spans. The ADHD group was much quicker on the draw when discerning what was new and what was just the same old thing.[28]

New angles are indeed what is interesting to Wall—especially sussing out an unfilled niche. He has asked himself why banks should be the only ones to extend consumer credit. Why shouldn't potential incentives, like points or movie tickets, be processed like checks—allowing him to sell something that only gets redeemed at some point in the future—or maybe not at all? His math skills are key to calculating risks and margins of profit. But his ADHD kicks in when connecting disparate ideas. He is just impulsive enough not to let "what-ifs" stop him, and just cautious enough to have someone else apply the brakes when necessary. He mostly plows ahead, knowing that if he fails, he can just start over.

Several months after I met him in Lake Tahoe, Ron Wall breezed through Montréal and I invited him for brunch. Sharply dressed and flushed from the cold, he unwrapped his silk scarf, proffered a pot of paperwhites in my direction, and immediately turned the spotlight of his attention to my children. He asked my fourteen-year-old about himself, then proudly blurted, "At your age I'd left school and had started my first business." Eric raised his eyebrows but made no reply. Later he asked, "Why would he tell me that?" It was the first time he'd met an adult who championed going to work over staying in school. I explained how Wall was a quick study—he learned on his feet. But school had been a bad fit. It meant living up to someone else's notions of success. And his wandering attention and gumption have never been traits much prized in the standard classroom. The workplace—or at least certain types of work—is better suited to his appetite for novelty and risk.

Choosing high-risk work over the standard educational route is paradoxically one reason why men with ADHD can leave school earlier than their peers, yet ultimately earn as much as or more than they do.[29] With fewer educational options but more moxie, a third of them become entrepreneurs before age thirty.[30] Here, then, is another example of extreme men as male hyperbole—illuminating a trend that we see among more "standard" men. Notwithstanding their earning power, leaving school is hardly desirable, and a U.S. analyst named Thomas Mortenson is systematically monitoring school dropouts, publishing flinty, fact-laden reports that show how women are leaving men in the dust. I tracked him down to his cabin deep in the Minnesota north woods, where he was preparing hunting stands for the November deer season. A senior scholar at the Pell Institute for the Study for Opportunity in Higher Education, Mortenson examines which slices of society are less likely to go to college. Increasingly, one of these populations is boys, and Mortenson hopes that publishing the numbers will help reverse the trend. "In almost every country except sub-Saharan Africa there are more women in higher education than men," he said, quoting statistics from the OECD and UNESCO. "When attendance becomes voluntary, boys are hemorrhaging out of the system."

I soon learned one reason why Mortenson is so committed to figuring out who is getting derailed. As a boy with ADHD, it had nearly happened to him. Mortenson described himself as having been "a pistol to raise" whose best subjects in school were "running away and recess." What motivated him to stay was a teacher who told him he had the strongest scores in the class, who hammered home that he had unusual promise. Having a teacher and a family who believed in his abilities was what kept him on track, he said. As corny as it sounds, Mortenson's experience reflects what two researchers, Gabrielle Weiss and Lily Hechtman, discovered after following a large sample of ADHD children as they entered adulthood. The majority said they were boosted by discovering a special talent or gift pointed out by a parent or a teacher. "When the adults who had been hyperactive were asked what had helped them most to overcome their childhood difficulties, their most common reply was that someone had believed in them."[31]

The Debate about ADHD Women and Girls

Among the boys and men with ADHD I encountered, that person who believed in them was usually their mother. Many fully employed, overextended women took the time to bring their boys into my office, and while I insisted that fathers be present for the first and last interviews, it was invariably the mothers who accompanied their children for these sessions, as well as all the ones in between. Mothers were there to hear the disorder described. They were often the ones who advocated for their children at school. They were also more savvy about using psychologists for their troubled boys, and more likely than fathers to seek help for themselves.

Being more apt to ask for help may be one reason why the proportion of adult women with ADHD seems to be increasing. While the ratio of boys to girls is about eight to one, the ratio of adult men to women is now three to one.[32] Still, with three times as many men as women with ADHD, there's no evidence that previously documented sex differences in diagnosis rates were due to gender bias, or have since disappeared. On the contrary, one reason for the recent increase in the number of women with ADHD is that the category has become more elastic. In 1994, a new version of the *Diagnostic and Statistical Manual* was broadened to include a purely inattentive type of ADHD—without hyperactivity (in contrast, Ron Wall and Paul Orfalea would have the combined type).

Girls and women with fewer of the disorder's excesses started

receiving a diagnosis that would not have applied to them ten years earlier. This bumped up women's rates, as did new ways of finding women
with the disorder. As with dyslexia, researchers reasoned that if there
was a bias against diagnosing women, they couldn't depend on clinicians, workplaces, and teachers to identify the problem; they'd have to
unearth it themselves. So they went into the community and tested
women at random, where they indeed found more women with ADHD
symptoms than had ever surfaced before.[33] These women were less
affected by their symptoms but still met the new criteria for ADHD.

But is there really the same percentage of girls with ADHD? Has a
gender bias caused teachers, professionals, and even parents to over-
look inattentive girls? In my experience, girls with ADHD, like most
girls, are indeed less likely to steal, set things on fire, spit, swear in people's faces, or attack them with scissors. My clinical practice was
mostly comprised of educated parents who assiduously watched over
their children's progress—both boys or girls. At the slightest misstep in
their children's development they brought them in to be evaluated,
requesting a full psychological workup, just to be sure. Boys were
referred for assistance more than girls because more boys had developmental problems, including ADHD. And when questions were raised
about girls, the disorder was hardly overlooked.

This, too, was what a comprehensive study on girls and boys with
ADHD had discovered. There were fewer girls with the disorder, and
many of the ones who had its symptoms presented somewhat differently from most of the boys with ADHD. When comparing 280 boys
and girls with ADHD to 240 kids without it, Joseph Biederman and a
team of researchers at Harvard Medical School found that girls were
more likely than boys to have the inattentive subtype of ADHD, and
were less likely to have other serious problems alongside it. Although
less severely affected and fewer in number, they were just as likely to
be treated for it.[34] As with other biologically determined traits, there
were identifiable differences between boys and girls with ADHD that
could be subtle. But that didn't mean that girls were getting shortchanged.

One of the risks of studying psychological disorders is that you're more
likely to identify its foibles in yourself. Thus my concentration seemed

strangely compromised as I tried to navigate my way over Vancouver's Lion's Gate Bridge at dusk en route to interview Dr. Gabrielle Weiss, one of the first social scientists to research ADHD in adulthood. After driving thirty blocks into suburban North Vancouver and passing acres of ranch houses, it occurred to me that I might have misheard. Had she said North Vancouver or West Vancouver? I hadn't paid attention. I finally arrived on her dark, leafy street, where Dr. Weiss and her high-strung little dog were waiting. It was Sunday evening but the diminutive and dignified European-born psychiatrist, now in her seventies, was dressed in a tailored woolen suit. She greeted me warmly and we launched into a discussion of men with ADHD who succeed.

"The majority of them do well," she stated, immediately qualifying that 60 percent of adults still had some symptoms. But could these erstwhile symptoms give them a leg up in their careers? Dr. Weiss seemed doubtful. I mentioned what she already knew, that boys and men with ADHD usually have a hearty appetite for risk. Their ability to jump into new experiences might put them on the cutting edge of ideas in the arts or business, influencing the high numbers who become entrepreneurs, I suggested. "If you were brilliant and took risks, it could pan out very well," she conceded. "The negative is courting danger. The positive is exploration. And if you link creativity with more risk-taking, well . . . it would take risk-taking combined with good judgment." She was not completely convinced that ADHD could ever be a good thing. But she admitted that her era of psychiatry was more focused on deficits than on strengths. And that thinking was shifting. She suggested I call her daughter Margaret, also a psychiatrist, with whom she had written her most recent book about ADHD.

A few days later I called Dr. Margaret Weiss, director of the ADHD Clinic at the Children's and Women's Health Center in Vancouver. Her quick précis was that a diagnosis never tells the whole story. "If you were rich, smart, had a lot of talents and lots of support, you did well. But if you were dumb, unlikable, and abused, you didn't," she said in a rat-a-tat delivery. "Sometimes you have a match between an ADHD person and the perfect job. I had a guy with ADHD who took huge risks, focused on the long-term vision, learned how to delegate to everyone around him, and worked sixteen-hour days and never fatigued."

She could have been talking about Ron Wall or Paul Orfalea. Wall, though, was less forthcoming about his disappointments than about his successes. Despite his lackluster experiences in school, his account had been relentlessly upbeat. "I've seen it. I've created it. I've hired the right people. I've done all the hard work. But now the question is, how do I keep myself amused?" That was his big question. His search for stimulation had driven him to climb Mount Kilimanjaro, go dog-sledding in the Arctic, hike in Mongolia, create his own salon of speakers and luminaries, and take on ever riskier business ventures. Yet considering Gabrielle Weiss's reticence about ADHD's benefits, I decided to ask Wall about failure.

Expecting him to clam up, I was surprised by the force of his response. He had been through a divorce and had parented a child with ADHD. But he seemed to assume that such challenges are just part of the adult terrain. His true measure of failure was the idea of losing a race, and that *really* miffed him. He told me how a couple of previous colleagues had managed to snag one of his business ideas, taking credit—and a fair amount of profit—for his ideas after their business relationship had ended. "Every day, and I mean every day," he said, jabbing the air with his index finger, "I wake up and think how I can smash those guys into the ground." Wall had just put thirty-nine million movie tickets in boxes of Waffle Crisp and another fifty million in Pampers. There was no doubt he would soon eclipse these opponents in astronomical earnings. How could they possibly compete?

It was a game, Wall told me, and every day he woke up and vowed he would win it. "I love a good fight," he told me later. "I like to win big."

Most of the phenomenally successful women I'd met had reached a point where they had achieved enough material success, and had shifted their attention to other goals. Meanwhile, many of their male peers still wanted to climb higher.

CHAPTER 10

Things Are Not What They Seem

The science of sex differences is clearly a grab bag of surprises. There's a common understanding that males are the stronger sex and that historical and cultural advantages continue to give them a leg up. But a closer look reveals that males are vulnerable to all sorts of biological and psychological mishaps. As we've seen, learning and behavior problems of all kinds dog males. Meanwhile, a heightened appetite for competition and derring-do leads some boys and men to spectacular achievements—and others to tragically high rates of accidents and suicides. Closely acquainted with these numbers, insurers quote higher premiums when young men apply for car insurance, and psychologists like me expect to see many more boys' names in their agendas. Given these real-life observations, the puzzle is why the idea of sex differences continues to be so controversial.

One reason is that forty years of discounting biology have led us to a strange and discomfiting place, one where women are afraid to own up to their desires, and men—despite their foibles—are seen as standard issue. "We were sold a bill of goods," said one corporate lawyer who left her position after twenty years of working long and hard hours. The catalyst was a fragile son who required assistance and support, but it could just as easily have been a health or existential crisis of her own. Her desire to adjust her work life to accommodate other priorities is reflected in the research we've seen here that shows that about 60 percent of gifted women turn down promotions or take positions with lower pay so as to weave flexibility or a social purpose into their work lives. Such statistically based trends never speak for individuals. But they do tell us something about why men and women are often drawn to different jobs, and why after four decades of trying to stamp out gender differences some occupational discrepancies remain.

Some people find this picture disheartening, as they expected that all jobs would be divided 50–50 by now. Others find nothing wrong with this scenario, figuring that nothing can be done about it, anyway. I'm convinced that both views are mistaken. Instead of evincing hidden prejudices, some gender asymmetries in the workplace are signs of a free and educated society—one where individuals are able to make their own choices. And with an eye on both the science and the history, a recognition of sex differences is neither a retrograde step nor grounds for apathy. A more nuanced understanding of gender differences reveals the benefits of certain traits, and pinpoints exactly where we might direct our efforts for change.

Shouldn't a Woman Be More Like a Man?

We now know that many women and men diverge in interests, abilities, and desires. But is this a problem that should be fixed? All empirical analyses of sex differences crunch numbers to give us a glimpse of the big picture. These statistics can never speak for an individual person, or say anything about how she should live her life. Both male-typical and female-typical profiles—and all gradations in between—have virtues to recommend them. None is better or worse, or more valuable to society. The idea that women should emulate men was more compelling, I'd argue, when that was a way to gain access to resources and opportunities that were deemed off-limits. But now that girls and women are doing so well academically and that women's rights are protected—at least in Europe and North America—there should be a way to view sex differences more dispassionately, and even with optimism.

There are advantages to being less extreme. Women are healthier than men and live longer lives. And women's tendencies to empathize and connect with others confer cognitive benefits as well as health advantages. The act of nurturing releases hormones that damp down stress, and there is now evidence that other social behaviors also elicit physiological benefits. People who keep in close contact with friends and relatives are less likely to experience memory loss and to die young. And altruism—in short, helping other people—is now linked to better mental health.[1] Maintaining a close social network comes easily to many women, but until recently the skills required to keep people connected carried little weight in the larger world. As with the long-standing female edge in literacy or classroom learning, it wasn't talked about or valued much. Being a good listener, communicator, and "mind-reader" seemed invisible next to more quantifiable traits, such as gifts in math, science, or physics. Most of the women I've profiled here had balanced skills—they were good "systemizers" and good "empathizers"—but they were still forcefully encouraged to focus on their math, science, and business talents to the exclusion of their other interests and strengths, advice that backfired for many of them. What-ever was associated with the male model of success was considered to have more merit. But as scientific evidence builds to show how empa-thy, altruism, or early verbal skills have ancillary benefits, these attrib-utes may come to be seen as equally worthy. This is not just wishful thinking. Over the past decade there has been a shift in economics from an exclusive focus on measuring money and profit to examining what drives longevity, satisfaction, and happiness. The public's interest in such intangibles has turned books like *Freakonomics, Emotional Intelligence,* and *Stumbling on Happiness* into runaway bestsellers. Now that empathy, altruism, and happiness are being measured, what was once taken for granted may acquire new luster. If it's associated with living a longer, happier life, perhaps being more moderate, avoid-ing risk, or having a more finely tuned empathy rheostat may be not be so worthless after all.

I've shown how economists who measure work satisfaction have found that women are happier with their work lives than men. Researchers seem perplexed by this finding, especially given recent studies that show that as women's work hours and demands approach the male standard, their level of work satisfaction drops. If women and men have identical ambitions, then women's satisfaction should rise as their status does. Economists call this the gender paradox because it seems counterintuitive—our expectations are not confirmed by the data. Shifting vantage points may explain part of it. As women earn more and have working lives that more closely resemble men's, they may still feel like the poor cousins. They're earning more than they did before but they're still not keeping up with the male Joneses. But there may be more to this paradox than their comparison group. If the majority of women prefer altruistic or transformative pursuits over competing to earn the biggest paycheck, the extreme male model of work won't fit. It will make them feel miserable or disconnected, as it did for many of the women profiled in these pages. The fact that they could remedy their predicament by changing jobs to incorporate their wider-ranging interests, their desire to connect with people, or to make a difference, is one of the benefits of living in a postfeminist Western democracy. The ability to follow your inclinations instead of doing work that others think you *should* do is a feature of a free society.

Women with alternatives have modern liberalism and feminism to thank for such choices. Opting to work fewer hours, or at jobs that are more satisfying to them but that pay less doesn't mean they're victims of gender bias, even if their choices contribute to the pay gap. Consider the alternative. Societies where women's occupations and work hours are decided for them are not usually paragons of equal opportunity. Catherine Hakim notes that women are rarely denied access to productive labor in developing countries—and often do most of it—while Claudia Goldin writes that uneducated married women in the United States and poor countries work only until their family incomes rise sufficiently to allow them to stop.[2] Even without such economic pressures, the liberty to make such choices should not be taken lightly. In the Soviet system, engineering was a broad category referring to almost any type of science, technology, or administrative job, and one became an engineer if the central committee deemed more engineers were needed. Industrial and military objectives drove the number of university spots, and there were so few places in the arts and humanities that connections and deep pockets were needed for the years of private tutoring required to sit those university entrance exams. One young woman from Russia told me that her parents and grandparents were engineers—as were all the adults she knew—because male or female, their occupational choices were limited to engineering. Her mother trained and worked as an engineer, although her passion was to study and teach chemistry. Her aunt trained to be an engineer but had badly wanted to study Russian literature. The state achieved near gender parity in physical science and engineering by squelching individual choice. Thus a society that achieves a 50–50 gender divide in a field might appear to have eradicated discrimination. But a closer look reveals an abrogation of individual freedoms.

The problem is not women who have too many choices but women who have too few. When women have limited opportunities, when they have little access to education, medical care, or no maternity leave, and have to work incessantly or at multiple jobs to support their families, there are serious problems to be remedied. In contrast, women who make conscious decisions based on their interests, abilities, and options shouldn't be seen as deficient or pitiable, even if their choices don't look just like men's. "We stand here confronted by insurmountable opportunities," according to the comic strip possum, Pogo. Girls are excelling in school and attending graduate and professional schools in record numbers. Young women living in urban centers such as New York, Los Angeles, Dallas, Chicago, and Boston now earn more than men.[3] If women's natural propensities toward empathy and verbal fluency help produce gifted physicians, teachers, human rights lawyers, book editors, or day-care workers, and they choose these jobs in greater numbers than they choose careers in computer technology, firefighting, or traveling sales, this may benefit society as much as it contributes to their individual happiness.

The Real Problems

Still, there's a fear that if we recognize the existence of sex differences we'll become part of a conservative backlash that will send women back to the kitchen. I'd argue that a more nuanced understanding of the average differences between men and women can lead to progress instead. In fact, several problems arise from *not* acknowledging that sex differences exist. Workplaces and career schedules designed for a single, standard male approach to competition and success now discourage many women, notwithstanding their native smarts, their educational opportunities, and their impressive accomplishments. If more than two-thirds of working women are "adaptives" who want to mesh their work lives with time for family, then a one-size-fits-all promotion or evaluation schedule will mean that a good portion of talented women will opt out, work part-time, or choose to plateau. They'll make these trade-offs to accommodate their desire to spend time with their families, or to make a difference. Despite the recent negative press about opt-out women, most of them don't want to stay home indefinitely or live the life of the prototypical 1950s housewife.[4]

Workplaces that incorporate multiple tracks, that don't stigmatize or penalize women for taking time out for children, or that acknowledge sex differences by allowing dedicated maternity leaves, more elastic promotion schedules, and ways to reintegrate after time-out or part-time work will find more women on staff. Universities that put tenure clocks on hold after women give birth, or that grant dedicated maternity leaves to women (as opposed to generic parental leaves) are better at forestalling the women-come-back with a backlog, men-come-back-with-a-book phenomenon. In contrast, turning a blind eye to sex differences can have the unintended effect of punishing women for having families while rewarding men, perhaps one reason why academic men with children have more publications than childless men, while academic women with children have fewer publications than childless women.

Acknowledging that women are more likely to have nonlinear careers and formalizing ways for them to adjust the intensity of their work, or to opt back in after a hiatus are also offshoots of acknowledging sex differences. "At its core, this type of flexibility is all about reattachment without unfair penalties or punishments," Sylvia Ann Hewlett writes in her book *Off-Ramps and On-Ramps*. Recently, companies in the banking and financial industries that have designed flexible career trajectories or project-based remuneration are finding that women are responding and returning to work. These initiatives stem from acknowledging sex differences, not denying them.

In contrast, companies that hold to the vanilla gender assumption turn a blind eye to the way their corporate values collide with many women's goals. In recent years workplaces have become more extreme, competitive, and unyielding in their demands. Even while extolling the virtues of gender balance, companies that allow an inflation of the number of hours, publications, breakfast, dinner, and weekend meetings required to become a partner or to achieve tenure—or that rigidly insist on relocation to build one's career—will find that these policies winnow their female employees. There may be lip service paid to gender equality via task forces, reports, and gender consultants. But where women are expected to act like male clones there is sure to be a female exodus from the most time-greedy, demanding, and lucrative jobs. Of course, this leaves institutions with the task of devising a menu of alternatives, and many are leery of straying from by-the-book equal treatment. But more than political correctness, many management models offer no respectable alternatives to putting in extreme hours, as any diversion is seen as eating into profits or diluting the corporate culture. One blogger, management consultant and author David Maister, describes the object lesson of a firm that tried to combine the high-intensity, high-fee, fourteen-hour-workday and weekend-work model espoused by "the sharks" of the firm with a more balanced, relationship-oriented practice wanted by the self-described "flounders." The moral of the story, as he tells it, was that the firm imploded because the two styles of work were incompatible.[5]

But formally adopting the "shark" model—no exceptions—gives most women the message that they're not wanted. This high-intensity version of work means that some working parents only see their children when a spouse or a babysitter brings the pajama-clad children in to the office to say good night (as reported in *Fortune* magazine), while other parents employ 'round-the-clock day care. The absurdity of these scenarios is not lost on working women, at least two-thirds of whom are likely to have ambitions other than status and pay, and are more likely to say that if that's what it takes, I'd rather be a flounder. "Do we want everyone to have an equal chance to work 80 hours a week in their prime reproductive years? Yes, but we don't expect them to take that chance equally often," said the Harvard economist Claudia Goldin, commenting on the intransigence of the gender gap in pay. In a competitive, winner-takes-all model, people who work eighty hours a week will be more highly rewarded than those who work twenty, forty, or sixty hours a week. That's the current model in business and science, one undeniable reason why women are scarce at the top in both.

Embracing the winner-takes-all model means accepting that there will always be fewer women, as only 20 to 30 percent of women ascribe to it. But there are other ways of seeing this picture. Grueling hours do not always translate into productivity. Some of these hours are just "face time," such as obligatory late-afternoon meetings or weekend retreats, where there is an expectation that you will just show up. Like neckties and panty hose, these obligations are linked more to the business culture than to productivity per se. Still, no company wants to be the first to abandon them. But it might be worth reconsidering these dated tokens of commitment if it means retaining a brilliant female scientist or a gifted professional who instead of putting in "face time," wants to be home to do homework with her children and put them to bed.

Countries and their industries can set visionary objectives that go beyond asking their employees to work unlimited hours. When I lived in France in the 1990s, people worked shorter hours and took more holidays than they did elsewhere in Europe and in North America, spending more time with their families and less in the office. Nonetheless, the French GNP was on a par with that of the United Kingdom and was higher than all other countries in the European Union. In short, profits and productivity don't have to take a hit if companies put a brake on the careening pace of time and expectations at work—even at the highest executive levels. Turnover, burnout, and galloping health and mental health expenses are very likely to be reduced, outweighing the short-term costs, and more women might be attracted to higher-level positions as a secondary effect. A final note about sex differences and the winner-takes-all model: acknowledging the research that tells us that women are less likely to negotiate is a cue to exploring more equitable ways to establish salary levels. In contrast, ignoring powerful gender differences in competition and negotiation, and simply letting the chips fall where they may has a discriminatory effect.

Ignoring sex differences also has the unintended effect of devaluing women's cognitive strengths and preferences. As long as a significant proportion of women have a different, or broader range of interests than most men, many women will be attracted to different occupations. And as it happens, the people or language-oriented occupations that appeal to most women are not as well paid as the standard male career choices. Despite comparable levels of education, teachers and nurses earn less than computer analysts and engineers. Speech pathologists and social workers earn less than most draftsmen or sound technicians. And even within professions, the specialties that attract women—say, family medicine or pediatrics—command lower salaries than those more popular with men, such as surgery, pathology, or radiology. It's not clear what comes first—lower rates of pay in people-oriented jobs, or stagnant pay scales in occupations dominated by women, who are less likely to negotiate. Either scenario results in lower pay for the work women prefer. Market forces determine pay scales in the private sector, but even then, if there's a will to retain and pay women fairly, corporate policies could be drafted that pay senior managers in human resources and media relations—more likely to be female—as much as senior managers in finance or production—which attract more men. Instead of expecting women to take jobs that don't interest them, acknowledging sex differences in the careers people choose might stimulate a more fruitful discussion of ways to redress these imbalances. In the public sector, more transparency about both gender differences and pay scales might overcome the inertia that has professors of education and nursing with equal qualifications earning less than those teaching engineering and economics.

In fact, the tremendous emphasis and resources devoted to attracting women to careers in science, technology, engineering, and mathematics reinforce the cachet of fields that appeal more to men. There is no corresponding movement to draft men into nursing, comparative literature, or speech pathology, no incentives or special task forces to tutor men in empathy or interpersonal skills—even if several dozen men have written in to my column asking for help in precisely these areas. Currently the message is that disciplines that capitalize on strengths and interests more commonly found among men have greater prestige. Even if the cognitive processes required to intuit another person's motivations are no less complex than map reading or basic trigonometry—and in fact are harder to teach—institutions are devoting most efforts and resources to urging women to choose and hone a "male-typical" skill set. As a result, even with equal or even superior academic skills, many of the women featured in this book expressed the feeling that they were letting down the side if they didn't choose male typical careers. Devaluing women's preferences is an unintended aspect of expecting the sexes to be exactly the same. Learning about science and technology is a laudable goal. But a society truly committed to redressing pay gaps between the sexes would value and pay as much for skillful teaching and nursing as it does for great plumbing and condo repairs.

Exhorting women to make "male" choices is more pernicious than simply encouraging them to earn more. Educated women who forgo the highest paying or high-status jobs are usually aware of their options and have weighed the pros and cons. The finger-wagging about being influenced by the media, not knowing the consequences of their actions, or giving license to employers to discriminate against women (which is not only unethical but also illegal) follows in a long tradition of assuming that women don't know their own minds. The women profiled here agonized about their career decisions—they didn't take them lightly. They weren't acting on "Prince Charming" myths or copping out as much as pursuing a feminist ideal—to exercise their autonomy. Yet the prevailing message is that these women are either patsies or victims. The idea that women don't know what they want, or don't have the power, interest, or inclination to determine their own fate lends a feeling of déjà vu to the debate about men, women, and work. Telling women that they'd prefer computer science to a degree in English or history if only they weren't blindered by cultural norms, or that putting in fourteen-hour days when their children are toddlers is really what's in their best interests, is a form of infantilization. It's also a form of homogenization. The problem is not that some women choose to opt out, others to work part-time, or that other women prefer to keep working as long and as hard as they can. The problem is that only one choice is seen as the right one.

Finally, a lack of attention to basic sex differences means that biological fragility in boys will continue to get short shrift. The men I've profiled here are examples of extreme males who succeed, and their stories illustrate the way extreme male traits can affect achievement. Yet it's disingenuous to suggest that such male variability is a synonym for quirky genius, or that having these traits is always a good thing. Most fragile boys who drop out don't become celebrity chefs, poker wizards, prize-winning mathematicians, or brilliant entrepreneurs. Many of these boys drift away from school, in part because they don't receive the assistance of psychologists or of parents who have the time, will, and savvy to advocate for them. These boys need teachers and clinicians eager to understand the basic neuroscience and genetics underlying their disabilities. Turning a blind eye to the biological variability of males, or pretending that their behavioral or learning difficulties are due to male role models or the cultural ether deprives needy boys of the help they need. It also leaves parents and teachers stranded as they try to assist boys and young men who are struggling. When we thought that girls were not doing as well as boys in math and science, specific projects were created with their interests in mind. Books specially written for girls teach "tips, tricks, and secrets for making math more fun with no timed tests, and best of all, no grades!" The National Science Foundation consecrated $30 million a year to educational programs in math, science, and technology directed only to girls and women, and created graduate fellowships exclusively for women studying engineering or computers (as long as they weren't also studying medicine, law, public health, or any field that ordinarily appeals to women).[6] In the late 1990s a special bill was passed by the U.S. Congress to investigate women in science and engineering, and universities continue to pledge large amounts to promoting women in science, most famously Harvard, which set up a $50 million fund just for that purpose.[7] Industries and individual scientists, astronauts, and engineers have created their own foundations and awards dedicated to getting women involved in science and technology pursuits (grants to female scientists from the Christiane Nusslein-Volhard Foundation that pay for babysitters and household help are my favorites). Today, although there may still be fewer female engineers, fourth-grade students of both sexes say they are equally interested in science, and the majority of professional and advanced biology degrees go to women. It's too hard and too soon to say whether these initiatives deserve some of the credit. But if a fraction of the funding and political will behind these programs were directed to the question of failing boys, there would likely be more men on campus and fewer in prison. Now that girls are excelling in school, it's time to turn the spotlight on struggling boys and to put serious muscle into remedying male gaps in literacy, social awareness, and self-control.

Good-bye Youth, Hello Maturity

Earlier in this book I described how two anthropologists were surprised by the occupational preferences they observed among men and women living on a kibbutz. The kibbutz was a utopian community designed to erase any barriers of sex or class, and it was assumed that with time, all sex differences would fade away. Every type of job would be equally divided between men and women. But a neatly divided world was not at all what the anthropologists found.

I knew nothing about the study when as an idealistic young student eager to see the world, I tried kibbutz living in the mid-1970s. "The new assumption behind the discussion of the body is that everything that we may observe *could be otherwise*" I had read in *The Female Eunuch,* and though I believed it, I soon discovered that working in the kibbutz plastics factory or hauling nets in the fish ponds were not really for me (nor was working in the kitchen gutting chickens). I preferred to work in the library, or with the children, where I soon discovered I had lots of female company. By the time I experienced kibbutz life in 1976, seventy years after the utopian communities were first established, the only men working near the communal children's houses were two gardeners who came by to trim the dusty shrubbery and three armed guards patrolling the area to protect the children from terrorist attacks. By the late seventies the kibbutzniks had discovered that giving men and women the same opportunities doesn't mean they'll all want the same things. In a society where you want people to be happy and productive, it just wasn't feasible to dictate what jobs people should do. To survive and adapt, these communities had to give up some cherished bits of their founding ideology. And they had to shed the idea that the two sexes are exactly the same.

Such changes can make one feel wistful—nostalgic for ideas that were once crisp and new. These ideas not only changed the way we viewed the world, but forever altered its landscape. But we're not left peering into a vacuum. Exciting discoveries from the worlds of neuroscience, cognitive science, and economics are creating a complex and more sophisticated view of the terrain. New developments in these fields have been surfacing so rapidly that I've had to update this book several times during the two years it took to write it. MRI studies of the perception of emotions, the genetics of learning disabilities and autism, and the transformational effects of testosterone and oxytocin are just a few areas of discovery that give us a more nuanced view of sex differences than was available, or even imagined, in the seventies. And with a more shaded understanding of the statistical variation within any human trait, it no longer makes sense to see men and women in black and white. There is no such thing as one type of woman who makes a prototypical choice that represents the right one for her sex. There is no biological evidence that suggests that women should stay home and raise babies. Nor is there proof that men and women are indistinguishable, and with the same opportunities, will value the same things and behave the same way. Instead, the data reveal a handful of different catalysts for people's choices—many with neurological or hormonal roots, and others that reflect workplaces designed to fit the male standard—that mesh to create the real gender gap.

Statistical differences do exist between men and women. But statistics should never speak for individuals, restrict their choices, or justify unfair practices. Instead, discoveries about sex differences in human learning and development can offer insights into the best ways to help boys who need assistance. Acknowledging their preferences can help girls choose the lives and careers they want. Finally, recognizing sex differences is the only way to understand the paradoxical motivations and choices of men and women—even if they seem to be the opposite of what we expect.

ACKNOWLEDGMENTS

There is no book without a story. More than two dozen people trusted me to tell theirs. Some of them had no idea who I was when I first contacted them, or knew me long ago during awkward periods of their lives. I then asked them to reveal what are usually quite private thoughts about love, ambition, and work. Without their confidence and candor, not to mention their time and patience as I came back repeatedly to nail down details, these pages would have been lifeless compilations of statistics. Many kept in touch with me during the years this book was taking shape and I am indebted to them and to their generosity of spirit.

Science fleshes out their narratives and I am grateful to the following researchers and experts who read drafts or sections of chapters in their areas of expertise. I owe thanks to Kingsley Browne of Wayne State University, Simon Baron-Cohen at the University of Cambridge, Nancy Eisenberg of Arizona State University, Uta Frith of University College London, Jeffrey Gilger of Purdue University, Fiona Kay at Queen's University, Ilyana Kuziemko at Princeton University, Michael Lombardo at the University of Cambridge, Laura-Ann Pettito at the University of Toronto, Charles A. Pierce at the University of Memphis, Bernard Rosenblatt at the McGill University Health Centre, Darold Treffert of the University of Wisconsin Medical School, Elizabeth Walcot at the University of Sherbrooke, Gabrielle Weiss at the BC Children's Hospital, and Sandra Witelson of McMaster University. All were invaluable sources of information and inspiration.

Other scientists were kind enough to answer questions when I wrote to say, that's very interesting, but can you run that by me again? I appreciate the help of Lea Baider at Hadassah University Hospital,

Andreas Bartels of the Max Planck Institute, Turhan Canli of Stony Brook University, Sue Carter at the University of Chicago, Elizabeth Cashdan of the University of Utah, Eric Courchesne of University of California San Diego, John Evans of the Christchurch School of Medicine, Catherine Hakim of the London School of Economics, George Hynd of Purdue University, Ronald Kessler at Harvard Medical School, Doreen Kimura at Simon Fraser University, Michael Meaney of McGill University, Phyllis Moen of the University of Minnesota, Tom Mortenson of the Pell Institute for the Study of Opportunity in Higher Education, Saroj Saigal at the McMaster University School of Medicine, David Skuse of University College London, Laurel Ulrich of Harvard University, Margaret Weiss of the Children's and Women's Health Centre of British Columbia, and Harold Wiesenfeld of the Magee-Women's Research Institute at the University of Pittsburgh.

My editors at the *Globe and Mail* have been loyal supporters of this project. Without their kind words and tolerance for weeks off from my column, this book could not have been completed. The *Globe* is where I learned how to be an obsessive writer but an obsession with an idea is not a book, and I had two fine editors, Anne Collins at Random House Canada and Alexis Gargagliano at Scribner, who were the best tutors I could have had in the art. Having nearly committed first drafts to memory, they instinctively knew the book's contours and where it needed to be nipped and tucked. I am indebted to Katie Rizzo for stickhandling the copyediting process, thus ensuring that my i's were dotted and that I meant what I wrote at every stage. My literary agents, Jackie Joiner and Denise Bukowski, simply made the book possible and assisted in myriad ways, and for that I cannot thank them enough. Thanks also go to the Westmount Masters Swim Team, which provided the endorphins and collegiality necessary for a long haul.

I am profoundly grateful to Terri Foxman, a researcher who leaves no stone unturned, for providing indispensable assistance with facts, charts, and images during the last few months of the project. Before Terri, a tag team of students shoehorned tours of library stacks and arcane data bases between graduate school applications and trips to the Middle and Far East. With the help of Razielle Aigen, Eva Boodman, Sarah Pearson, Jacqueline Rowniak, and David Weinfeld, I was able to devote more time to writing and less to Boolean search terms.

Thanks are also due to statistics maven Martin Lysy, who helped me transform data into legible graphs at the eleventh hour, and to Benjamin Silver who ensured I read the *Science Times* in a timely fashion. When these supports were unavailable—and indeed at all times—an incomparable researcher pitched in. My mother, Roslyn Pinker, cast her sharp eye and mind on the popular press. Any article related to my interests was duly e-mailed, or clipped and inserted in a manila envelope, and if I mentioned what I was writing about, a tidy stack of computer printouts would appear within the week, often tucked between a few jars of homemade apricot jam. Combining intellectual rigor with TLC is a cherished recipe handed down by both parents and one that I hope to transmit to my own children.

My family and many friends generously read excerpts or whole chapters, all while providing moral support, including Martin Boodman, Roslyn Pinker, Harry Pinker, Steven Pinker, Robert Pinker, Kristine Whitehead, Rebecca Newberger Goldstein, Barbara Baker, and Stephanie Whittaker. Steve encouraged me in all ways. From the ins and outs of Endnote software to the subtleties of invisible signposting, the wise advice he provided about book-writing kept my fingers glued to the keyboard. In fact, I could not have asked for more assiduous supporters than the members of my family. My children, Eva, Carl, and Eric, tolerated my two years of distraction with inimitable good humor and gave me countless moments of unadulterated joy. Finally, I thank Martin for everything.

NOTES

Introduction: Female Puppets and Eunuchs

1. Susan Dominus, "A Girly-Girl Joins the Sesame Boys," *New York Times,* August 6, 2006.
2. Louis Menand, "Stand by Your Man: The Strange Liason of Sartre and Beauvoir," *New Yorker,* September 26, 2005.
3. Juliet B. Schor, *The Overworked American: The Unexpected Decline of Leisure* (New York: Basic Books, 1992), 86.
4. Using large data sets from the National Longitudinal Survey of Young Women, the Harvard economic historian Claudia Goldin tracked a sharp and rapid shift among women's occupational and educational plans that occurred in the early 1970s. A huge cohort of baby boomers, born in the late fifties and choosing undergraduate majors in the early seventies, opted for disciplines more similar to their male peers, and less "traditionally female" majors than the previous generation. She calls this generation "unwitting foot soldiers" who were unaware that they were part of a huge revolution in attitudes that would affect subsequent generations. For example, 40 percent of women graduating from college in 1966 were in education. Twenty percent were in 1980, and 12 percent were in 1998. The big break between women choosing female-intensive majors, such as education or social work, and more male-intensive majors, such as business and management, happened in the early seventies. Not only did women in this cohort change their educational plans to match their career aspirations, they also married later and stayed in school longer. This allowed them to break away from the model of isolated, solo achievers and make inroads as a social force.
5. The Pill was legal in the United States in 1960, although not in the state of Connecticut. By the time it was legalized in Canada, about thirteen million American women were already taking it and had seven different brands to choose from.
6. Not many women did this work in 1973 and not many want to now. One generation later, 97 percent of the people who spend their work lives on the road, selling on commission, are men. According to the 3,300 member American Manufacturers' Agents Association, the average annual income of manufacturers' agents in 2007 was U.S. $105,000, more than twice the average American household income of $44,389, according to the U.S. Census Bureau.
7. These brief outlines of women's work history were gleaned from the following sources, which offer rich detail on women's working lives in the nineteenth and twentieth centuries.

    Alice Kessler-Harris, *Out to Work: A History of Wage-Earning Women in the United States* (New York: Oxford University Press, 2003); Schor, *The Overworked American.*

Schor, *The Overworked American: The Unexpected Decline of Leisure,* 95.

Claudia Goldin, *Understanding the Gender Gap: An Economic History of American Women* (New York: Oxford University Press, 1990).

8. Claudia Goldin, "From the Valley to the Summit: The Quiet Revolution That Transformed Women's Employment, Education, and Family," National Bureau of Economic Research Working Paper 10335 (Cambridge, Mass.: 2004).

9. The recent statistics are from the websites of the U.S. Department of Labor and Statistics Canada. Historical data were culled from publications by Juliet Schor (1992), Alice Kessler-Harris (2003), and Claudia Goldin (2004).

10. Claudia Goldin, "The Quiet Revolution That Transformed Women's Employment, Education, and Family." Paper presented at the American Economic Association Meeting, Boston, 2006.

11. Natasha Walter, "Prejudice and Evolution," *Prospect* (June 2005).

12. Feminist Research Center, *Empowering Women in Business* (Feminist Majority Foundation, 2007 [cited March 30]; available from http://www.feminist.org/research/business/ewb_toc.html.

13. In her book *Selling Women Short* sociologist Louise Marie Roth describes a history of blatant gender discrimination on Wall Street that has resulted in millions of dollars being awarded to women in arbitration and settlements. Specifically, Merrill Lynch and Morgan Stanley awarded significant settlements to female brokers alleging discrimination as recently as 2004, and Roth argues that more subtle, less actionable discrimination exists in the work culture of Wall Street and the trading floor that work to depress women's earnings and advancement. Louise Marie Roth, *Selling Women Short: Gender and Money on Wall Street* (Princeton, N.J.: Princeton University Press, 2006).

14. Claudia Goldin, Lawrence F. Katz, and Ilyana Kuziemko, "The Homecoming of American College Women: The Reversal of the College Gender Gap" (Cambridge, Mass.: National Bureau of Economic Research, 2006).

15. Goldin, "From the Valley to the Summit: The Quiet Revolution That Transformed Women's Employment, Education, and Family."

16. U.S. Department of Labor, *Labor Day 2006: Profile of the American Worker* (cited September 4, 2006); available from http://communitydispatch.com/artman/publish/article_6293.shtml.

17. C. E. Helfat, D. Harris, and P. J. Wolfson, "The Pipeline to the Top: Women and Men in the Top Executive Ranks of U.S. Corporations," *The Academy of Management Perspectives* 20, no. 4 (2006).

18. Diane F. Halpern, *Sex Differences in Cognitive Abilities* (Mahwah, N.J.: Lawrence Erlbaum Associates, 2000); L. V. Hedges and A. Nowell, "Sex Differences in Mental Test Scores, Variability and Numbers of High-Scoring Individuals," *Science* 269 (1995); W. W. Willingham and N. S. Cole, *Gender and Fair Assessment* (Mahwah, N.J.: Lawrence Erlbaum Associates, 1997).

19. Lawrence H. Summers, "Remarks at NBER on Diversifying the Science and Engineering Workforce." Paper presented at the National Bureau of Economic Research, Cambridge, Mass., January 14, 2005.

20. This is illustrated in Deary's data: at the very low ranges of ability—IQ scores between 50 and 60—there were 17.2 percent more boys than girls. And at the very high ranges—IQ scores between 130 and 140—there were 15 percent more boys. "The gradation between the extremes appears regular: as the population moves away from the extremes the sex difference in proportions steadily lessens," Deary and his colleagues write. See Ian J. Deary et al., "Population Sex Differences in IQ at Age 11: The Scottish Mental Survey 1932," *Intelligence* 31 (2003).

In *The Blank Slate,* my brother Steve explains the phenomenon of increased male variability at the extremes this way:

> With some other traits the differences are small on average but can be large at the extremes. That happens for two reasons. When the bell curves partly overlap, the farther along the tail you go, the larger the discrepancies between groups. For example, men on average are taller than women, and the discrepancy is greater for more extreme values. At the height of five foot ten, men outnumber women by a ratio of two thousand to one. Also, confirming an expectation from evolutionary psychology, for many traits the bell curve for men is flatter and wider than the curve for females. That is, there are proportionally more males at the extremes.

Steven Pinker, *The Blank Slate: The Modern Denial of Human Nature* (New York: Viking, 2002), 344.

Chapter 1: Are Males the More Fragile Sex?

1. Jane E. Brody, "Easing the Trauma for the Tiniest in Intensive Care," *New York Times,* June 27, 2006; Jane E. Brody, "For Babies, an Ounce Can Alter Quality of Life," *New York Times,* October 1, 1991.
2. D. K. Stevenson, J. Verter, and A. A. Fanaroff, "Sex Differences in Outcomes of Very Low Birth Weight Infants: The Newborn Male Disadvantage," *Archives of Disease in Childhood* 83 (November 2000); M. Brothwood et al., "Prognosis of the Very Low Birth Weight Baby in Relation to Gender," *Archives of Disease in Childhood* 61 (1986); Maureen Hack et al., "Growth of Very Low Birth Weight Infants to Age 20 Years," *Pediatrics* 112, no. 1 (2003).
3. Steven B. Morse, "Racial and Gender Differences in the Viability of Extremely Low Birth Weight Infants: A Population-Based Study," *Pediatrics* 117, no. 1 (2006).
4. One of the most recent studies of a large group of very premature babies (born before twenty-six weeks of gestation) was done in the United Kingdom. In what was called the EPIcure study, a research team led by Neil Marlow at the University of Nottingham found that these preemie boys had a much higher risk of disability and lower cognitive function than the preemie girls when tested at age six. Neil Marlow et al., "Neurologic and Developmental Disability at Six Years of Age after Extremely Preterm Birth," *New England Journal of Medicine* 352, no. 1 (2005).
5. Allan Reiss, Helli Kesler, and Betty Vohr, "Sex Differences in Cerebral Volumes of 8-Year-Olds Born Pre-Term," *Pediatrics* 145, nos. 242–249 (2004). Encouraging long-term results have been found by a research team led by Dr. Saroj Saigal, a professor of pediatrics at McMaster University, who reported that a group of young adults born at extremely low birth weights had more disabilities, but positive self-perceptions and as good a quality of life compared to a control group born at normal birth weights. Dr. Saroj reported in an e-mail (September 7, 2006) that sex differences in school problems and ADHD that were apparent at earlier ages in her high-risk sample became less apparent as the sample reached adulthood. Saroj Saigal et al., "Transition of Extremely Low Birth Weight Infants from Adolescence to Young Adulthood," *Journal of the American Medical Association* 295, no. 6 (2006).
6. Male vulnerability to environmental stressors has become more obvious in the dramatically reduced proportion of boys born in high-industry areas over the past three decades in the United States, Canada, and Japan. Males are more suscepti-

ble to the damaging effects of industrial pollutants that mimic hormones, which lead to early fetal death in males. Although the Chemical Valley community in Sarnia, Ontario, has seen the most significant decline in boys' births ever recorded, in Japan and the United States there were significantly fewer baby boys born between 1970 and 2002. Martin Mittelstaedt, "The Mystery of the Missing Boys," *Globe and Mail,* April 11, 2007.

Sebastian Kraemer, "The Fragile Male," *British Medical Journal* 321 (2000).

Emmy E. Werner and Ruth S. Smith, *Vulnerable but Invincible. A Study of Resilient Children* (New York: McGraw-Hill, 1982), 36–49.

7. Nicholas Wade, "Pas De Deux of Sexuality Is Written in the Genes," *New York Times,* April 10, 2007.

8. One of the only exceptions to males' higher rate of chronic illness is Alzheimer's disease, which is more common among women. Roni Rabin, "Health Disparities Persist for Men, and Doctors Ask Why," *New York Times,* November 14, 2006.

An account of the effect of testosterone on women's health was recounted by Malcolm Gladwell in an article on doping in competitive sports. He reported that male steroids were commonly used to boost the performance of female athletes in the eighties, with disastrous effects: masculinized physiques and voices, inexplicable tumors, liver dysfunction, internal bleeding, and depression. Malcolm Gladwell, "The Sporting Scene," *New Yorker,* September 10, 2001.

9. Richard G. Bribiescas, *Men: Evolutionary and Life History* (Cambridge, Mass.: Harvard University Press, 2006).

10. Daniel J. Kruger and Randolph M. Nesse, "Sexual Selection and the Male: Female Mortality Ratio," *Evolutionary Psychology,* no. 2 (2004).

11. Isaac Mangena, "Soweto Youths on Wrong Track as Train Surfers Die Having Fun," *Montreal Gazette,* November 26, 2006.

12. Kruger and Nesse, "Sexual Selection and the Male: Female Mortality Ratio."

13. Bribiescas, *Men: Evolutionary and Life History.*

14. Arjan Gjonca, Cecilia Tomassini, and James W. Vaupel, "Male-Female Differences in Mortality in the Developed World," (Max Planck Institute for Demographic Research, 1999); Kraemer, "The Fragile Male"; Kruger and Nesse, "Sexual Selection and the Male: Female Mortality Ratio."

15. U.S. National Vital Statistics Reports 54, no. 19 (June 28, 2006); Center for Disease Control. Statistics Canada: Selected Leading Causes of Death, by Sex. http://www40.statcan.ca/101/cst01/health36.htm?sdi=mortality%20rates%male.

16. Statistics Canada, *The Gap in Achievement between Boys and Girls* (March 9, 2006); available from http://www.statcan.ca/english/freepub/81–004-XIE/200410/male.htm; Richard Whitmore, "Boy Trouble," *New Republic Online* (2006).

17. Wendy Berliner, "Where Have All the Young Men Gone?" *The Guardian,* May 18, 2004.

18. Gerry Garibaldi, "How the Schools Shortchange Boys: In the Newly Feminized Classroom, Boys Tune Out," *City Journal* (Summer 2006).

19. From *Time,* April 16, 1956, and quoted in Bill Bryson's chapter about his school days. Bill Bryson, *The Life and Times of the Thunderbolt Kid* (Toronto: Doubleday, 2006).

20. Goldin, Katz, and Kuziemko, "The Homecoming of American College Women: The Reversal of the College Gender Gap."

21. OECD, "Gender Differences in the Eighth Grade Performance on the IEA Timss Scale," in *IEA Trends in International Mathematics and Science Study 2003* (2005).

22. Camilla Persson Benbow and Julian Stanley, "Sex Differences in Mathematical Ability: Fact or Artifact?" *Science* 210 (1980); Camilla Persson Benbow and

Julian Stanley, "Sex Differences in Mathematical Reasoning Ability: More Facts," *Science* 222 (1983).

23. The comparison isn't perfect, however, as Benbow and Stanley's studies examined only high performers—both boys and girls who had already distinguished themselves as very strong students and who were applying for admission to a special program. The OECD data are based on a sample of all students in eighth grade in the thirty member countries, not just the ones at the upper margins.

24. Virginia Valian, "Women at the Top in Science—and Elsewhere," in *Why Aren't More Women in Science?* ed. Stephen J. Ceci and Wendy M. Williams (Washington, D.C.: American Psychological Association, 2007).

25. Judith Kleinfeld, "Student Performance: Males Versus Females," *Public Interest* 134 (1999).

26. Ilyana Kuziemko, "The Right Books, for Boys and Girls," *New York Times,* June 14, 2006. Goldin, Katz, and Kuziemko, "The Homecoming of American College Women." A median is the point at which half the data, or other scores, fall below and half above it.

27. Harvard economist Claudia Goldin and her colleagues have shown that although boys took more math and science courses in the 1950s, by 1992 there was no difference in math and science preparation between the sexes, a factor that influenced women's increasing college enrollment.

    Goldin, Katz, and Kuziemko, "The Homecoming of American College Women."

28. Tom Mortenson, "What's Wrong with the Guys" (Washington, D.C.: Pell Institute for the Study of Opportunity in Higher Education, 2003).

29. S. J. Ingels et al., *A Profile of the American High School Sophomore in 2002: Initial Results from the Base Year of the Education Longitudinal Study of 2002 (NCES 2005–338).* U.S. Department of Education, (Washington, D.C.: National Center for Education Statistics, 2005). http://nces.ed.gov/pubs2005/2005338_1.pdf.

30. The Search Survey of 99,000 was conducted by psychologist Nancy Leffert, now at the University of Minnesota, and was quoted by Christina Hoff Summers in "The War Against Boys," *Atlantic Monthly* (May 2000). National Assessment of Educational Progress (NEAP) 2006: http://www.ed.gov/programs/neap/index.html.

31. Since the early 1990s, when reports of the call-out gap and teachers' neglect of girls surfaced, applications to these mostly private all-girls' academies have increased by 40 percent. Enrollments have increased by only 23 percent, however (all statistics from the National Coalition of Girls Schools, www.ncgs.org). The selection of the best and brightest among children whose families can afford private school fees could be one reason why the association reports that their alumnae major in math and science at a higher rate than both girls and boys from coed public schools. And now that these schools are receiving a wider range of applicants, they are likely selecting a stronger corps of students from a larger pool.

32. Christina Hoff Summers, *The War Against Boys* (New York: Simon & Schuster, 2000).

33. J. E. Brophy and T. L. Good, "Teachers' Communication of Differential Expectations for Children's Classroom Performance: Some Behavioral Data," *Journal of Educational Psychology* 61 (1970); Carol S. Dweck and Ellen S. Bush, "Sex Differences in Learned Helplessness," *Developmental Psychology* 12, no. 2 (1976).

34. Sandy Baum and Eban Goodstein, "Gender Imbalance in College Applications: Does It Lead to a Preference for Men in the Admissions Process?" *Economics of Education Review* 24, no. 6 (2005).

35. Some of the efforts to attract more women are as bald as admissions quotas, whereas others are more subtle—for example, adding more human applications to the department's offerings of courses, replacing the male students featured on their websites with an all-female cast, and bringing high school girls in for intensive summer programs in computer science to attract them as future students. Brown University's exclusively female Artemis Project is one such initiative. Cornelia Dean, "Computer Science Takes Steps to Bring Women to the Fold," *New York Times,* April 17, 2007.

36. Sarah Karnasiewicz, "The Campus Crusade for Guys," *Salon,* February 15, 2006.

37. Jennifer Delahunty Britz, "To All the Girls I've Rejected," *New York Times,* March 23, 2006; Josh Gerstein, "Kenyon's Policy Against Women Stirs a Debate," *New York Sun,* March 28, 2006.

38. Martin Seligman's discovery that one can change the thought processes behind learned helplessness helped launch a new field called positive psychology, and boosted cognitive approaches to treating depression.

39. Angela Lee Duckworth and Martin E. P. Seligman, "Self-Discipline Gives Girls the Edge: Gender in Self-Discipline, Grades, and Achievement Test Scores," *Journal of Educational Psychology* 98, no. 1 (2006).

40. William R. Charlesworth and Claire Dzur, "Gender Comparisons of Preschoolers Behavior and Resource Utilization in Group Problem Solving," *Child Development* 58, no. 1 (1987); Eleanor Emmons Maccoby, *The Two Sexes: Growing Apart, Coming Together* (Cambridge, Mass.: Harvard University Press, Belknap Press, 1998); Eleanor Emmons Maccoby and Carol Nagy Jacklin, *The Psychology of Sex Differences* (Stanford, Calif.: Stanford University Press, 1974); Irwin Silverman, "Gender Differences in Delay of Gratification: A Meta-Analysis," *Sex Roles* 49, nos. 9–10 (2003).

41. A further comment about school from Steve Jobs: "They came close to really beating any curiosity out of me. . . . I know from my own education that if I hadn't encountered two or three individuals that spent extra time with me, I'm pretty sure I would have been in jail." Steve Jobs, "You've Got to Find the Job You Love," *Stanford Report,* June 14, 2005; Daniel Morrow, *Oral History Interview with Steve Jobs,* 1995 (cited April 26, 2006); available from http://american history.si.edu/collections/comphist/sj1.html.

42. Simon Baron-Cohen, *The Essential Difference: The Truth About the Male and Female Brain* (New York: Basic Books, 2003); Simon Baron-Cohen, *Mindblindness: An Essay on Autism and Theory of Mind* (Cambridge, Mass.: MIT Press, Bradford Books, 1995).

43. Jennifer Connellan, Simon Baron-Cohen, Sally Wheelwright, Anna Batki, and Jag Ahluwalia, "Sex Differences in Human Neonatal Social Perception," *Infant Behavior and Development* 23 (2000); Svetlana Lutchmaya and Simon Baron-Cohen, "Human Sex Differences in Social and Non-Social Looking Preferences, at 12 Months of Age," *Infant Behavior and Development* 25 (2002).

44. Simon Baron-Cohen, "Sex Differences in Mind: Keeping Science Distinct from Social Policy," in *Why Aren't More Women in Science?* ed. Stephen J. Ceci and Christine L. Williams (Washington, D.C.: American Psychological Association, 2007); Doreen Kimura, *Sex and Cognition* (Cambridge, Mass.: MIT Press, 2000).

45. M. A. Wittig and M. J. Allen, "Measurement of Adult Performance on Piaget's Water Horizontality Task," *Intelligence* 8 (1984).

46. J. T. E. Richardson, "Gender Differences in Imagery, Cognition, and Memory," in *Mental Images in Human Cognition,* ed. R.H. Logie and M. Denis (New York: Elsevier, 1991).

47. Kimura, *Sex and Cognition.*

48. Allan Mazur, *Biosociology of Dominance and Deference* (Oxford, U.K.: Rowman & Littlefield, 2005). Pinker, *The Blank Slate.*

49. Tim Molloy, "Woman's Rampage Leaves Six Dead in the U.S.," *Globe and Mail,* February 1, 2006.

   The rarity of female school killers makes the occasional incident of lethal violence among girls and women newsworthy and therefore more salient. My brother Steven Pinker writes about how the occasional incident of female violence gets played as evidence that the sexes are becoming more similar: "A similar disconnect between headline and fact appeared in a 1998 *Boston Globe* story entitled 'Girls Appear to Be Closing Aggression Gap with Boys.' How much have they 'closed this gap'? According to the story, they now commit murder at *one-tenth* the rate of boys." Pinker, *The Blank Slate,* 339.

50. American Psychiatric Association, *Diagnostic and Statistical Manual of Mental Disorders:* 4th ed. (Washington, D.C.: American Psychiatric Association, 1994); M. Daly and M. Wilson, *Homicide* (New York: Aldine de Gruyter, 1988); Martin Daly and Margo Wilson, *Sex, Evolution, and Behavior,* 2nd ed. (Boston: Willard Grant Press, 1983); Steven E. Rhoads, *Taking Sex Differences Seriously* (San Francisco: Encounter Books, 2004), 297–301; Baron-Cohen, "Sex Differences in Mind: Keeping Science Distinct from Social Policy."

51. Rhoads, *Taking Sex Differences Seriously*; Richard Tremblay and Daniel Nagin, "The Developmental Origins of Physical Aggression in Humans," *Developmental Origins of Aggression,* ed. Richard Tremblay, Willard Hartup, and John Archer (New York: Guilford Press, 2005).

52. E. Feldman et al., "Gender Differences in the Severity of Adult Familial Dyslexia," *Reading and Writing* 7, no. 2 (1995); J. M. Finucci and B. Childs, "Are There Really More Dyslexic Boys Than Girls?" in *Sex Differences in Dyslexia,* ed. A. Ansara et al. (Towson, Md.: Orton Dyslexia Society, 1981); T. R. Miles, M. N. Haslum, and T. J. Wheeler, "Gender Ratio in Dyslexia," *Annals of Dyslexia* 48 (1998).

53. B. A. Shaywitz et al., "Sex Differences in the Functional Organization of the Brain for Language," *Nature* 373 (1995).

54. Louann Brizendine, *The Female Brain* (New York: Morgan Road Books, 2006); Halpern, *Sex Differences in Cognitive Abilities*; Hedges and Nowell, "Sex Differences in Mental Test Scores, Variability and Numbers of High-Scoring Individuals"; J. Huttenlocher et al., "Early Vocabulary Growth: Relation to Language Input and Gender," *Developmental Psychology* 27 (1991); Janet Shibley-Hyde, "Women in Science: Gender Similarities in Abilities and Sociocultural Forces," in *Why Aren't More Women in Science,* ed. Stephen J. Ceci and Wendy M. Williams (Washington, D.C.: American Psychological Association, 2007).

55. I am indebted to Diane Halpern's inclusive summary of the research literature on sex differences in verbal skills. Halpern, *Sex Differences in Cognitive Abilities.*

56. Macdonald Critchley, *The Dyslexic Child* (Springfield, Ill.: Charles C. Thomas, 1970).

Chapter 2: Dyslexic Boys Who Make Good

1. As "Andrew" is still in his twenties, this is a pseudonym.

2. Uta Frith, "Brain, Mind and Behaviour in Dyslexia," in *Dyslexia: Biology, Cognition and Intervention,* ed. Charles Hulme and Margaret Snowling (San Diego: Singular Publishing Group, 1997); H. S. Scarborough, "Very Early Language Deficits in Dyslexic Children," *Child Development* 61 (1990); Margaret Snowling, *Dyslexia* (Oxford, U.K.: Blackwell, 2000); Margaret Snowling, Alison Gallagher, and Uta Frith, "Family Risk of Dyslexia Is Continuous: Individual

Differences in the Precursors of Reading Skill," *Child Development* 74, no. 2 (2003).

3. Iona and Peter Opie, experts on children's rhymes and their language of play, have documented the provenance of thousands of children's chants and ditties in their book *The Lore and Language of Schoolchildren* (London: Oxford University Press, 1959), and show how these rhymes evolve when children mishear words. The error often preserves the rhyme or sound of the original word, and is then repeated, changing the poem forever.

4. Margarita Bauza, "Boys Fall Behind Girls in Grades," *Detroit News,* January 9, 2005; Y. Gingras and Jeffrey Bowlby, *The Costs of Dropping Out of High School* (Ottawa: Human Resources Development Canada, 2000).

5. In an e-mail on October 19, 2006, Cathy Barr, a molecular geneticist specializing in reading disabilities at the University of Toronto, issued a caveat about the precise genes involved. Despite being convinced about the chromosome locations, the particular genes linked to various aspects of reading disability can be in slightly different areas in different people, and the fine mapping of the various genes is still in progress, she wrote. Cathy L. Barr and Jillian M. Couto, "Molecular Genetics of Reading," in *Single Word Reading: Cognitive, Behavioral and Biological Perspectives,* ed. E. L. Grigorenko and A. Naples (Mahwah, N.J.: Lawrence Erlbaum Associates, in press); L. R. Cardon et al., "Quantitative Trait Locus for Reading Disability on Chromosome 6," *Science* 266 (1994); A. M. Galaburda et al., "From Genes to Behavior in Developmental Dyslexia," *Nature Neuroscience* 9, no. 10 (2006).

6. J. C. DeFries, Maricela Alarcon, and Richard K. Olson, "Genetic Aetiologies of Reading and Spelling Deficits: Developmental Differences," in *Dyslexia: Biology, Cognition and Intervention,* ed. Charles Hulme and Margaret Snowling (San Diego: Singular Publishing Group, 1997).

7. While it's universal, the different subtypes mean that someone could be dyslexic in an alphabet-based language such as English, French, or Arabic, but not in a symbol-based one, such as Chinese or Kanji (ideographic Japanese). So the disorder isn't cultural, but it does mean that boys like Andrew, with the phonologically based disorder, would struggle more with a language such as English. Thus the disorder seems more common in the West—showing up in as much as 15 percent of the population, and more common among readers of phonetically irregular English, than among readers of more predictably spelled languages such as German and Italian. See Frith, "Brain, Mind and Behaviour in Dyslexia"; E. Paulesu et al., "Dyslexia: Cultural Diversity and Biological Unity," *Science* 291 (2001); Wai Ting Siok et al., "Biological Abnormality of Impaired Reading Is Constrained by Culture," *Nature* 431 (2004); A. Yamadori, "Ideogram Reading in Alexia," *Brain* 98 (1975).

8. There is a debate about whether the traditionally larger numbers of boys and men with dyslexia reflects a true sex difference or the bias of teachers and parents to award attention, care, and special education instruction to boys with problems but not to girls (see Shaywitz, 2003, 31). Some of the controversy swirls around studies that have found that in the general population, people with poor reading compared to their level of intelligence are as likely to be women as men. At least two factors confirm that sex differences in dyslexia are faithful to reality and biology. When the severity of the disability is taken into account, males outnumber females ten to one. Although there is also evidence that girls have protective factors that shield them from the effects of a reading disability—unless they are so highly loaded with predisposing genetic factors that they pass a critical threshold—thus the fewer females with dyslexia might be more severely affected (I am grateful to Jeff Gilger for elucidating the "sex threshold effect"). Still, when other

diagnostic markers are included, so that language delay, difficulties with syntax or naming, and short-term memory problems are included (as opposed to just weak reading), males outnumber females six to one.

Feldman et al., "Gender Differences in the Severity of Adult Familial Dyslexia"; Finucci and Childs, "Are There Really More Dyslexic Boys Than Girls?"; Halpern, *Sex Differences in Cognitive Abilities*; Miles, Haslum, and Wheeler, "Gender Ratio in Dyslexia."

9. K. G. Anderson, "Gender Bias and Special Education Referrals," *Annals of Dyslexia* 47 (1997); Rosalie Fink, "Gender and Imagination: Gender Conceptualization and Literacy Development in Successful Adults with Reading Disabilities," *Learning Disabilities* 10, no. 3 (2000); Sally Shaywitz, *Overcoming Dyslexia* (New York: Vintage Books, 2003). When I requested some statistics from the British Dyslexia Association on the prevalence of dyslexia among males in the United Kingdom, I received the following response: "It is estimated that around 10 percent of the population have dyslexic difficulties. This is probably an underestimate and could be nearer 15 percent. It used to be thought that dyslexia was more prevalent among males, but it is now thought that an equal number of females will have dyslexic tendencies. Girls are often better able to find coping strategies and better behaved, so are less likely to be picked up at school."

10. Shaywitz, *Overcoming Dyslexia,* 33.

11. Jeff Gilger, a researcher in the neurobiology of dyslexia at Purdue University, commented that the best screening devices for dyslexia are designed to have high "hit rates" so that few children who are at risk are missed. The assumption is that further in-depth psychological testing will then be done to confirm the diagnosis.

12. A. M. Galaburda, *Dyslexia and Development: Neurobiological Aspects of Extraordinary Brains* (Cambridge, Mass.: Harvard University Press, 1993); K. R. Pugh et al., "Cerebral Organization of Component Process in Reading," *Brain* 119 (1996); Shaywitz et al., "Sex Differences in the Functional Organization of the Brain for Language."

13. Shaywitz et al., "Sex Differences in the Functional Organization of the Brain for Language."

14. Sandra Witelson, I. Glezer, and D. L. Kigar, "Women Have Greater Density of Neurons in Posterior Temporal Cortex," *Journal of Neuroscience* 15 (1995).

15. J. Coney, "Lateral Asymmetry in Phonological Processing: Relating Behavioral Measures to Neuroimaged Structures," *Brain and Language* 80 (2002); J. Levy and W. Heller, "Gender Differences in Human Neuropsychological Function," in *Sexual Differentiation: Handbook of Behavioral Neurobiology*, ed. A. A. Gerall, M. Howard, and I. L. Ward (New York: Plenum Press, 1992); Shaywitz et al., "Sex Differences in the Functional Organization of the Brain for Language"; Haitham Taha, "Females' Superiority in Phonological and Lexical Processing," *The Reading Matrix* 6, no. 2 (2006); H. Wagemaker, "Are Girls Better Readers? Gender Differences in Reading Literacy in 32 Countries," *International Association for the Evaluation of Educational Achievement* (1996). Galaburda et al., "From Genes to Behavior in Developmental Dyslexia."

16. J. Stein, "The Magnocellular Theory of Developmental Dyslexia," *Dyslexia* 7, no. 1 (2001).

17. J. N. Zadina et al., "Heterogeneity of Dyslexia: Behavioral and Anatomical Differences in Dyslexia Subtypes." Available online at http://www.tc.umn.edu/~athe0007/BNEsig/papers/Zadina.pdf.

18. George W. Hynd and Jennifer R. Hiemenz, "Dyslexia and Gyral Morphology Variation," in *Dyslexia: Biology, Cognition and Intervention,* ed. Charles Hulme and Margaret Snowling (San Diego: Singular Publishing Group, 1997); E. J.

McCrory et al., "More Than Words: A Common Neural Basis for Reading and Naming Deficits in Developmental Dyslexia?" *Brain* 128 (2005); Shaywitz, *Overcoming Dyslexia*; Catya von Karolyi and Ellen Winner, "Dyslexia and Visual-Spatial Talents: Are They Connected?" in *Students with Both Gifts and Learning Disabilities: Identification, Assessment and Outcomes,* ed. Tina M. Newman and Robert J. Sternberg (New York: Kluwer Academic Plenum Publishers, 2004).

19. When the tumor or trauma had been on the right side, the boys had no problems with reading and spelling. Breaking down speech into its component parts—a prerequisite to literacy—was more firmly seated on the left side for the boys. See Uta Frith and Faraneh Vargha-Khadem, "Are There Sex Differences in the Basis of Literacy-Related Skills? Evidence from Reading and Spelling Impairments after Early Unilateral Brain Damage," *Neuropsychologia* 39 (2001).

20. Hynd and Hiemenz, "Dyslexia and Gyral Morphology Variation."

21. Cheryl L. Reed, "Few Women Warm to Chef Life," *Chicago Sun Times,* January 29, 2006.

22. Adam Gopnik, "Dining Out: The Food Critic at Table," *New Yorker,* April 4, 2005.

23. Anthony Bourdain, *Kitchen Confidential: Adventures in the Culinary Underbelly* (New York: Bloomsbury, 2000).

24. Bill Buford, *Heat (An Amateur's Adventures as Kitchen Slave, Line Cook, Pasta Maker, and Apprentice to a Dante-Quoting Butcher in Tuscany)* (Toronto: Doubleday, 2006), 90.

25. M. Wagner, "Youth with Disabilities: How Are They Doing?" in M. Wagner, C. Marder, J. Blackorby, R. Cameto, L. Newman, P. Levine, and E. Davies-Mercier (with M. Chorost, N. Garza, A. Guzman, and C. Sumi), *The Achievements of Youth with Disabilities during Secondary School: A Report from the National Longitudinal Transition Study-2 (NLTS2)* (Menlo Park, Calif.: SRI International, 2003). www.nlts2.org/reports/pdfs/achievements_ch7.pdf.

   Mary Wagner et al., "An Overview of Findings from Wave 2 of the National Longitudinal Transition Study-2 (NLTS2)" (Washington, D.C.: U.S. Department of Education, 2006).

26. Phyllis Levine and Eugene Edgar, "An Analysis by Gender of Long-Term Postschool Outcomes for Youth with and without Disabilities," *Exceptional Children* 61, no. 3 (1994).

27. Rosalie Fink, "Literacy Development in Successful Men and Women with Dyslexia," *Annals of Dyslexia* 48 (1998); Rosalie Fink, "Successful Careers: The Secrets of Adults with Dyslexia," *Career Planning and Adult Development Journal,* Spring 2002.

28. Lisa Zunshine, *Why We Read Fiction* (Columbus: Ohio State University Press, 2006).

29. Paul. J. Gerber, "Characteristics of Adults with Specific Learning Disabilities," in *Serving Adults with Learning Disabilities: Implications for Effective Practice,* ed. B. Keith Lenz, Neil A. Sturomski, and Mary Ann Corley (Washington, D.C.: U.S. Department of Education, 1998).

30. Shaywitz, *Overcoming Dyslexia.*

31. Anne Fadiman, *The Spirit Catches You and You Fall Down* (New York: Noonday Press, 1997).

32. A. M. Galaburda et al., "Developmental Dyslexia: Four Consecutive Cases with Cortical Abnormalities," *Annals of Neurology* 18 (1985). Sally Shaywitz explains the gifts of dyslexia as follows:

   "Dyslexics use the 'big picture' of theories, models and ideas as a framework to help them remember specific details . . ."

Then goes on:

"Rote memorization and rapid word retrieval are particularly difficult for dyslexics. On the other hand, dyslexics appear to be disproportionately represented in the upper echelons of creativity and in the people who, whether in business, finance, medicine, writing, law or science, have broken through a boundary and have made a real difference to society. I believe that this is because a dyslexic cannot simply memorize or do things by rote; she must get far underneath the concept and understand it at a fundamental level. This need often leads to a deeper understanding and a perspective that is different from what is achieved by some for whom things come easier because they just can memorize and repeat—without ever having to deeply and thoroughly understand."

Shaywitz, 2003, 57–58. See also Gerber, "Characteristics of Adults with Specific Learning Disabilities."

33. Stein, "The Magnocellular Theory of Developmental Dyslexia."
34. Von Karolyi and Winner, "Dyslexia and Visual-Spatial Talents: Are They Connected?" *Students with Both Gifts and Learning Disabilities,* ed. Tina M. Newan and Robert J. Sternberg (New York: Plenum, 2004).
35. Jeffrey W. Gilger, George W. Hynd, and Mike Wilkins, "Neurodevelopmental Variation as a Framework for Thinking About the Twice Exceptional," in press (2007).
36. *The Collected Papers of Albert Einstein,* trans. Anna Beck with consultation from Peter Havas (Princeton, N.J.: Princeton University Press, 1987).
37. P. Bucky, *The Private Albert Einstein.* (Kansas City, Mo.: Andrews & McMeal, 1992) as cited in Marlin Thomas, "Was Einstein Learning Disabled?: Anatomy of a Myth," *Skeptic* 10, no. 4, 40–48, and "Albert Einstein and LD: An Evaluation of the Evidence," *Journal of Learning Disabilities* 33, no. 2 (2000), 149–158.
38. Thomas, "Was Einstein Learning Disabled?" See also Albert Einstein, *Autobiographical Notes,* trans. and ed. Paul Arthur Schilpp (La Salle, Ill.: Open Court, 1979), and Albert Einstein, "A Testimonial from Professor Einstein," in *The Psychology of Invention in the Mathematical Field,* Jacques Hadamard (Princeton, N.J.: Princeton University Press, 1949).
39. J. Hadamard, *The Psychology of Invention in the Mathematical Field*; Steve C. Wang, "In Search of Einstein's Genius," *Science* 289, no. 5484 (2000); Sandra F. Witelson, Debra L. Kigar, and Thomas Harvey, "The Exceptional Brain of Albert Einstein," *Lancet* 353 (1999).
40. Roger Highfield and Paul Carter, *The Private Lives of Albert Einstein* (New York: St. Martin's Press, 1993).
41. John S. Rigden, *Einstein 1905: The Standard of Greatness* (Cambridge, Mass.: Harvard University Press, 2005).
42. Ibid.
43. Hynd and Hiemenz, "Dyslexia and Gyral Morphology Variation."
44. Witelson, Kigar, and Harvey, "The Exceptional Brain of Albert Einstein."
45. George Hynd, a researcher at Purdue University who examines the neurological evidence for dyslexia, wrote in an e-mail on November 7, 2006, that he looks for and never finds sex differences due to the commonly higher male-female ratio in the sample. The uneven size of the groups reduces the power of any statistical comparison.
46. A review of the research literature by Susan Vogel at Northern Illinois University showed that compared to boys with learning disabilities, the girls with learning

disabilities who are identified at school have lower IQs, more academic deficits with reading and math, yet are better at spelling, writing, and fine motor tasks than males with learning disabilities. A consistent finding is that the learning-disabled boys were better than the girls in mathematical reasoning. See S. A. Vogel, "Gender Differences in Intelligence, Language, Visual-Motor Abilities, and Academic Achievement in Students with Learning Disabilities: A Review of the Literature," *Learning Disabilities* 23, no. 1 (1990).

47. Rob Turner, "In Learning Hurdles, Lessons for Success," *New York Times,* November 23, 2003.

48. R. Cameto, "Employment of Youth with Disabilities after High School," in *After High School: A First Look at the Postschool Experiences of Youth with Disabilities*: A Report from the National Longitudinal Transition Study-2 (NLTS2), M. Wagner, L. Newman, R. Cameto, N. Garza, and P. Levine (Menlo Park, Calif.: SRI International, April 2005), available at www.nlts2.org/pdfs/afterhighschool _chp5.pdf. See also P. Levine and E. Edgar, "An Analysis by Gender of Long-Term Postschool Outcomes for Youth with and without Disabilities" in *Exceptional Children* 61.3 (Arlington, Va.: Council for Exceptional Children, 1994), 282–301.

49. According to a recent report, the average starting salary of college graduates with computer engineering degrees is $51,496. Teachers earn $29,733 to start. See Jeanne Sahadi, "Lucrative Degrees for College Grads," *CNNMoney,* April 19, 2005, available online at http://money.cnn.com/2005/04/15/pf/college/starting _salaries. According to the National Research Center for Women and Families, in 2000, child-care workers earned $24,600 per year. Diana Zuckerman, "Child Care Staff: The Lowdown and Salaries and Stability," June 2000, available online at http://www.center4research.org/wwf2.html.

50. In a discussion of women's career choices, Claude Montmarquette, an economist at the University of Montréal, mentioned that his data show that women may be less sensitive to the market value of their career choices than men, and more sensitive to the impact of child-related leaves of absence on their ability to keep their jobs. The authors also observe that "in every major, the table shows that the earnings of women are noticeably lower than those for men . . . with the average student entering the field of education facing the lowest earnings after graduation across all majors." Claude Montmarquette, Kathy Cannings, and Sophie Mahseredjian, "How Do Young People Choose College Majors?" in *Economics of Education Review* 21 (2002), 543–556.

Regardless of learning problems, a number of economists have shown that women often select more poorly paid jobs, but say they are more satisfied with their work. See A. Clark, "Job Satisfaction and Gender: Why Are Women So Happy at Work?" *Labour Economics* 4 (1997), 341–372; J. Oswald, "Happiness and Economic Performance," *Economic Journal* 107 (November 1997), 1815–1831.

51. Women earn 30 percent more bachelor's degrees and 50 percent more master's degrees than men, and the gender difference favoring women's academic success is more dramatic among minority groups. Black women earn twice as many college degrees as black men at every level. Ann Hulbert, "Boy Problems," *New York Times Magazine,* April 3, 2005.

One twenty-two-country study conducted by Canadian researchers showed that a quarter of the women had more education than their jobs required, while 17 percent of men had *less* education than the minimum required for their jobs. Daniel Bootheby, *International Adult Literacy Survey: Literacy Skills, Occupational Assignment and Returns to Over- and Under-Education* (Statistics

Canada/Human Resources Development Canada, 2002), available at http://www
.nald.ca/Fulltext/nls/inpub/litskill/litskill.pdf.

Chapter 3: Abandon Ship! Successful Women Who Opt Out of Science and Engineering Careers

1. Economist Anne Preston, who studied the phenomenon using statistics from the
   Survey of Natural and Social Scientists and Engineers from 1982 to 1989, con-
   cludes: "Women are more likely than men to leave the labor force within every
   age cohort. Furthermore, women are more likely than men to leave the labor force
   for reasons other than family within every age cohort. Therefore the conventional
   explanation that these differentials in exit behavior are a result of childbearing by
   women is incomplete. These relatively high rates of labor-force exit throughout
   the career by women in the sciences and engineering raise a serious question. Why
   are women with highly marketable and socially valuable skills leaving the labor
   force with very low probabilities of reentry?" Anne Preston, "Why Have All the
   Women Gone? A Study of Exit of Women from the Science and Engineering Professions," *American Economic Review* 84, no. 5 (1994).
2. Catherine Weinberger, ed., *A Labor Economist's Perspective on College-Educated
   Women in the Information Technology Workforce, Encyclopedia of Gender and
   Information* (Santa Barbara, Calif.: Information Science Publishing Group,
   2005).
3. Bryant Simon, a professor of history at Temple University in Philadelphia,
   researches social habits by observing how people behave in Starbucks cafés all
   over the world. He confirmed in an e-mail in January 2006 that mothers predom-
   inate in Starbucks in the late morning, and that many mid-career women seem to
   be using it as their meeting place and office later in the day.
4. Roughly one in four doctorates in economics is earned by women, who also make
   up only 12 percent of tenured faculty in the field. See Claudia Goldin and
   Lawrence F. Katz, "Summers Is Right," *Boston Globe*, January 23, 2005; Donna
   K. Ginther and Shulamit Kahn, "Women in Economics: Moving Up or Falling Off
   the Academic Ladder?" *Journal of Economic Perspectives* 18, no. 3 (August
   2000), 193–214.
5. Daniel S. Hamermesh, "An Old Male Economist's Advice to Young Female Economists" (May 2004), available at www.eco.utexas.edu/faculty/Hamermesh/
   FemAdviceCSWEP.pdf.
6. In an October 2004 article by Elizabeth Durant, "Plugging the Leaky Pipeline"
   (*Technology Review,* October 2004, online at www.technologyreview.com/
   articles/04/10/durant1004.asp), MIT biology professor Nancy Hopkins refers to
   this lack of women in traditionally male-dominated disciplines like math, physics,
   and computer science as a "cultural climate." Yet paradoxically the assumption
   that a male "cultural climate" scares off other women also puts pressure on those
   who have entered these fields to act as role models to other women. In the article,
   MIT assistant professor of mechanical engineering Simona Socrate was quoted as
   feeling divided between encouraging other women and being honest about how
   difficult it is to have a family and an academic science career. "There is a price to
   pay and you wonder, should you be quiet or should you let them know? I am trying to keep quiet." Many other books, essays, and university diversity reports
   attribute fewer women in science and engineering to a male cultural climate and a
   lack of female role models. There are too many to list here, but some recent ones
   include Jacqueline Stalker and Susan Prentice, eds., *The Illusion of Inclusion:
   Women in Post-Secondary Education*; Margaret A. Eisenhart and Elizabeth Finkel,
   Women's Science; Annmarie Adams and Peta Tancred, *Designing Women: Gender*

in the Architectural Profession; and Nelson and Rogers, *A National Analysis of Diversity in Science and Engineering Faculties at Research Universities*.

7. Belle Rose Ragins, "Understanding Diversified Mentoring Relationships," in *Mentoring and Diversity: An International Perspective*, ed. D. Clutterbuck and B. Ragins (Oxford, U.K.: Butterworth-Heinemann, 2002).

8. In a large study of an electronic mentorship program for undergraduate and graduate women studying engineering and related sciences, 68 percent reported positive relationships with their mentors (who were already working in the field), but the mentor's gender was not related to the student's satisfaction with the mentoring process. Carol B. Muller and Peg Boyle Single, "Benefits for Women Students from Industrial E-Mentoring," paper presented at the 2001 American Society for Engineering annual conference, 2001.

9. Ronald J. Burke and Carol A. McKeen, "Gender Effects in Mentoring Relationships," *Journal of Social Behavior and Personality* 11, no. 5 (1996).

10. Some female professors are more sanguine role models. The American historian, Pulitzer Prize winner, and Harvard scholar Laurel Ulrich is also a Mormon, mother of five children, and a feminist. When I read that she serves as a role model to young academic women by communicating that "You have the right to have a whole life. You don't have to take monastic vows in order to achieve," I contacted her. Her view is that women could indeed be inspired by male role models, even though it meant "dividing oneself in some way." She listed the following examples in an e-mail on October 11, 2006: "Of course a woman's role model can be a man! There are hundreds of examples in history. One of my favorites is in Christine de Pizan's *Book of the City of Ladies* (1405) when she describes the Amazon queen Penthesilea who modeled herself on the Trojan hero Hector. And how about centuries of women who attempted to behave as Jesus did? Or Elizabeth Cady Stanton, who drew upon the Declaration of Independence to draft the Seneca Falls declaration? They were surely modeling themselves on the 'Founding Fathers.'"

11. Virginia Valian, *Why So Slow? The Advancement of Women* (Cambridge, Mass.: MIT Press, 2000).

12. Frederick M. E. Grouzet et al., "Goal Contents across Cultures," *Journal of Personality and Social Psychology* 89 (2005).

13. Intrinsic rewards as a stronger driver for women is a robust, stable finding. But American researchers have found that women not covered by health insurance plans behave differently than women covered by their spouse's plans, or than women living in countries where there is national health insurance. They work longer hours than they would prefer, at different types of jobs than they would otherwise choose if they had health insurance coverage. See Jacobs, Shapiro, and Schulman, 1993, and Buchmueller and Valetta, 1998.

14. J. Bokemeier and P. Blanton, "Job Values, Rewards, and Work Conditions as Factors in Job Satisfaction among Men and Women," *Sociological Quarterly* 28 (1986); Sylvia Martinez, "Women's Intrinsic and Extrinsic Motivations for Working," in *Being Together, Working Apart*, ed. Barbara Schneider and Linda J. Waite (Cambridge, U.K.: Cambridge University Press, 2005); J. Phelan, "The Paradox of the Contented Female Worker: An Assessment of Alternative Explanations," *Social Psychology Quarterly* 57 (1994).

15. Marcia Barinaga, "Surprises across the Cultural Divide," *Science* 263 (1994).

16. An Independent Women's Forum/Pew poll asked women what hours they would choose "if you had enough money to live as comfortably as you would like." They found that 15 percent of women chose to work full-time and a third would opt to work part-time. The rest—52 percent—would not work at a paying job at all.

17. American Institute of Physics, "Percentages of Physics Degrees Awarded to Women in Selected Countries, 1997 and 1998 (2 Year Averages)" (International Study of Women in Physics, 2001). Rachel Ivie and Kim Nies Ray, "Women in Physics and Astronomy, 2005," American Institute of Physics (February 2005).

18. Although the Philippines has one of the highest levels of female physics faculty members in the world, it is also a developing country where 10 percent of the population is working outside the country at any time. About 7.9 million people are "Overseas Filipino Workers" sending remittances of $15 billion back to their extended families to support them. Jason DeParle, "A Good Provider Is One Who Leaves," *New York Times*, April 22, 2007; Pranjal Tiwari and Aurelio Estrada, "Worse Than Commodities," Report from the Asia Pacific Mission for Migrants, November 19, 2002.

19. Lucy Sherriff, "World's Cleverest Woman Needs a Job," *The Register* (November 5, 2004).

20. Kingsley R. Browne, *Biology at Work: Rethinking Sexual Equality* (New Brunswick, N.J.: Rutgers University Press, 2002), 61; Kenneth Chang, "Women in Physics Match Men in Success," *New York Times*, February 22, 2005; Catherine Hakim, *Work-Lifestyle Choices in the 21st Century* (New York: Oxford University Press, 2000); American Institute of Physics, "Percentages of Physics Degrees Awarded to Women in Selected Countries, 1997 and 1998 (2 Year Averages)" (International Study of Women in Physics, 2001); Doug Saunders, "Britain's New Working Class Speaks Polish," *Globe and Mail*, September 23, 2006.

21. One young woman, an immigrant to Canada from the former Soviet Union, switched her university major from engineering to law. When I asked about her parents and stepfather, all engineers from Russia, she related that when she was a small child she thought all children grew up to be engineers. This generalization came from the limited educational opportunities available to the adults she had met, all Russian Jews, who had not been permitted to study the arts and were given a limited selection of courses at university.

22. This e-mail message was received on September 24, 2006.

23. Alan Feingold, "Gender Differences in Personality: A Meta-Analysis," *Psychological Bulletin* 116, no. 3 (November 1994), 429–456; Baron-Cohen, *The Essential Difference: The Truth about the Male and Female Brain*; Claudia Strauss, "Is Empathy Gendered, and if So, Why? An Approach from Feminist Psychological Anthropology," *Ethos* 32, no. 4 (December 2004), 432–457.

24. Robert Plomin et al., "Genetic Influence on Language Delay in Two-Year-Old Children," *Nature Neuroscience* 1, no. 4 (1998), 324–328.

25. Camilla Persson Benbow et al., "Sex Differences in Mathematical Reasoning Ability at Age 13: Their Status 20 Years Later," *Psychological Science* 11, no. 6 (2000).

26. Kingsley R. Browne, "Women in Science: Biological Factors Should Not Be Ignored," *Cardozo Women's Law Journal* 11 (2005); David Lubinski, "Top 1 in 10,000: A 10-Year Follow-up of the Profoundly Gifted," *Journal of Applied Psychology* 86 (2001).

27. Kenneth Chang, "Journeys to the Distant Fields of Prime," *New York Times*, March 13, 2006.

28. For U.S. figures see National Center for Education Statistics, "Percentage of Bachelor's Degrees Earned by Women and Change in the Percentage Earned by Women from 1970–71 to 2001–02, by Field of Study: 1970–71, 1984–85, and 2001–02," available at http://nces.ed.gov/quicktables/Detail.asp?Key=1169. In Canada, in 2000, women earned 24 percent of postsecondary engineering degrees as well as 32 percent of math and physical science degrees. At the same time, they earned 58

percent of degrees in social sciences, 68 percent in fine and applied arts, 71 percent in education, 64 percent in the humanities, and 67 percent in the broad category of arts and sciences. They earned 62 percent of agricultural and biological science degrees and 73 percent of degrees in health-related professions. See "University Qualifications Granted by Field of Study, by Sex" (last modified February 17, 2005), from the Statistics Canada website, http://www40.statcan.ca/l01/cst01/healtheduc21.htm.

29. Edward Krupat, "Female Medical Students More Patient-Centered," *International Journal of Psychiatry in Medicine* (1999).

30. Margaret A. Eisenhart and Elizabeth Finkel, *Women's Science: Learning and Succeeding from the Margins* (Chicago: University of Chicago Press, 1998).

31. Robin Wilson, "How Babies Alter Careers for Academics," *Chronicle of Higher Education,* December 5, 2003.

32. Less than half of Britain's new fathers take the paternity leave they are entitled to. In Sweden, which offers the most generous parental leave programs of all—paying 80 to 100 percent of the parent's salary—only 5 to 8 percent of fathers took advantage of it at first.

     Brian Christmas, "Half of British Fathers Not Taking Full Paternity Leave," *Globe and Mail,* August 2, 2006; Hakim, *Work-Lifestyle Choices in the 21st Century.*

33. This anecdote was shared by a junior professor at the college in late 2006. Although initially willing to be quoted, she ultimately decided not to be identified lest any mention of gender differences in productivity or parental benefits at her institution affect her own upcoming tenure review. This was one of many instances that reveal that discussion of gender differences on university campuses is considered taboo. Even in science departments, faculty immediately become skittish when the topic is broached.

34. Rhoads, *Taking Sex Differences Seriously,* 9–13.

35. Anne E. Preston, *Leaving Science: Occupational Exit from Scientific Careers* (New York: Russell Sage Foundation, 2004), xiii. Preston also points out that marriage, especially if there are children, increases the probability of women exiting any full-time career, not just in science. Also, the more work the woman does on the domestic front, the higher the likelihood that she will leave an academic career.

36. Traditionally there has been a large gap in research productivity between male and female scientists, with women producing about half the number of publications as men when this phenomenon was first measured in the late 1960s and 1970s. When Xie and Shauman followed up with a study that spanned the decades between then and now, they found that the gap had narrowed: scientific women have now reached 75 to 80 percent of their male colleagues' productivity. And when other factors, like age and marital status, were filtered out, female scientists produced the same volume of research as men.

     Xie and Shauman, 115–177, and Jonathan R. Cole, *Fair Science: Women in the Scientific Community* (New York: Free Press, 1979); J. Scott Long, "Productivity and Academic Position in the Scientific Career," *American Sociological Review* 43, no. 6 (1978), 889–908; Jonathan R. Cole and Harriet Zuckerman, "The Productivity Puzzle: Persistence and Change in Patterns of Publication of Men and Women Scientists," *Advances in Motivation and Achievement* 2 (1984).

37. Mary Ann Mason and Marc Goulden, "Marriage and Baby Blues: Redefining Gender Equity in the Academy," *Annals of the American Academy of Political and Social Science* 596 (2004).

38. Ellen Goodman, "Of Pensions and Pacifiers," *Montreal Gazette,* January 26, 2005.

39. In *Leaving Science,* Anne Preston examines huge data sets and discusses how both men and women are abandoning science careers at alarming rates—15.5 percent among men and 31.5 percent among women. At every stage and in every context the rate of women leaving doubles that of men. Of 1,688 people who left science careers, 64 percent to 68 percent of men said they left science for better opportunities and pay, whereas only 33 to 34 percent of women stated those reasons, listing "other fields more interesting," or "preference for other positions" as equally if not more compelling reasons to choose other occupations. In Preston's survey, 21.4 percent of the women who have left science careers state that it is impossible to have a family and work in science and engineering. Only 4.5 percent of men describe this as a problem. Twenty percent of women who leave science careers state that the hours are too long. None of the men who leave science careers give the hours as a reason to exit science.

40. Kingsley R. Browne, "Evolved Sex Differences and Occupational Segregation," *Journal of Organizational Behavior* 26 (2005); David S. Lubinski and Camilla Persson Benbow, *Sex Differences in Personal Attributes for the Development of Scientific Expertise,* ed. Stephen J. Ceci and Wendy M. Williams, *Why Aren't More Women in Science?* (Washington, D.C.: American Psychological Association, 2007).

41. Joe Alper, "The Pipeline Is Leaking Women All the Way Along," *Science* 260 (1993).

42. Lucy W. Sells, "The Mathematics Filter and the Education of Women and Minorities," in *Women and the Mathematical Mystique,* ed. Lynn Fox, Linda Brody, and Dianne Tobin (Baltimore: Johns Hopkins University Press, 1980).

43. Yu Xie and Kimberlee Shauman, *Women in Science: Career Processes and Outcomes* (Cambridge, Mass.: Harvard University Press, 2003), 45.

44. "Choosing a Career: Labor Market Inequalities in the New Jersey Labor Market," paper prepared and published by the Center for Women and Work at Rutgers University and the State Employment and Training Commission of New Jersey (September 2002), available at http://www.cww.rutgers.edu/dataPages/choosingcareer.pdf.

    An American Institute of Physics report showed that there is no indication that women are being discriminated against in science, even if 82 percent of doctoral degrees are earned by men. Instead, despite having taken the prerequisites in high school, fewer women were choosing to study physics at the university level. Nor were high school girls less prepared for studying physics in university, if that's what they chose. Rachel Ivie, a sociologist and the author of the 2005 report, said, "I'm not saying it's easy for women." But even though they looked for evidence of discrimination, there was no sign that women were being kept out.

45. Claude Montmarquette, Kathy Cannings, and Sophie Mahseredjian, "How Do Young People Choose College Majors?" *Economics of Education Review* 21 (2002).

46. According to the Association of American Medical Colleges, in 2004, female applicants outnumbered male applicants 50.4 percent to 49.6 percent, but men had the same slight edge in admissions. Statistics available at www.aamc.org/data/facts/2004/2004summary.htm. In Canada, the numbers are similar. In 2004, 50.1 percent of medical school graduates were women. See Ian K. Wong, "A Force to Contend With: The Gender Gap Closes in Canadian Medical Schools," *Canadian Medical Association Journal* 170, no. 9 (April 27, 2004), 1385–1386, available online at www.cmaj.ca/cgi/reprint/170/9/1385. In England in 2003, 58.81 percent of applicants and 61.48 percent of all acceptances at medical schools were women. See "The Demography of Medical Schools: A Discussion Paper" (British

Medical Association, June 2004), 59, available at www.bma.org.uk/ap.nsf/Content/DemographyMedSchls.

47. Mark O. Baerlocher and Allan S. Detsky, "Are Applicants to Canadian Residency Programs Rejected Because of Their Sex?" *Canadian Medical Association Journal* 173, no. 12 (2005).

Chapter 4: The Empathy Advantage

1. E. Armstrong, "'My Glass Ceiling is Self-Imposed,'" *Globe and Mail,* December 15, 2004.
2. Catalyst, "Leaders in a Global Economy: A Study of Executive Women and Men" (2003). Anne E. Preston, *Leaving Science* (New York: Russell Sage Foundation, 2004), 70.

   For a debate about whether executive women have "wives" or are married to men who earn less than they do, see the passionate letters to the editor that followed Sylvia Ann Hewlett and Carolyn Buck Luce's *Harvard Business Review* article, "Off-Ramps and On-Ramps: Keeping Talented Women on the Road to Success" (March 2005). The letters to the editor appear in the July-August 2005 issue of the *Harvard Business Review.*

   J. Bokemeier and Blanton, "Job Values, Rewards, and Work Conditions as Factors in Job Satisfaction among Men and Women," *Sociological Quarterly* 28 (1986); R. Feldberg and E. Glenn, "Male and Female: Job Versus Gender Models in Sociology of Work," in *Women and Work,* ed. R. Kahn-Hut, A. Daniels, and R. Colvard (Oxford, U.K.: Oxford University Press, 1982).
3. Sylvia Ann Hewlett, "Extreme Jobs: The Dangerous Allure of the 70-Hour Workweek," *Harvard Business Review* (December 2006).

   Hewlett and Luce, "Off-Ramps and On-Ramps: Keeping Talented Women on the Road to Success" (Boston, Mass.: Harvard Business School Press, 2007).
4. The AARP and the National Alliance of Caregiving conducted a survey in 2004 showing that there are 44.4 million family caregivers to adults in the United States. While 61 percent of these caregivers are women at the beginning stages of an illness, this percentage increases to 84 percent as demands become intense. Women are more likely to make adjustments to their work schedules, take leaves of absence, or early retirement to look after aging parents or spouses. See Gross, 2005, and http://www.aarp.org/research/press-center/presscurrentnews/a2004-03-30-caregiving.html.
5. Lea Baider, "Gender Disparities and Cancer" (paper presented at the American Society of Clinical Oncology, Orlando, Fla., May 2005).
6. Jane Gross, "Forget the Career: My Parents Need Me at Home," *New York Times,* November 24, 2005.
7. Phyllis Moen, a sociologist from the University of Minnesota who analyzed repeated interviews from 762 men and women in the Cornell Retirement and Well-Being Study that took place from 1994 to 2000, also reports that men with sick wives tend to delay their retirement, perhaps to pay other people to do the caretaking. Men tended to do more financial planning for their retirement. Women tended to plan more for health-care needs.

   Phyllis Moen and Joyce Altobelli, *Strategic Selection as a Retirement Project, The Crown of Life: Dynamics of the Early Postretirement Period, Annual Review of Gerontology and Geriatrics,* ed. Jacqueline Boone James and Paul Wink, vol. 26 (New York: Springer, 2006).
8. Harold Bear, Frances Lovejoy, and Ann Daniel, "How Working Parents Cope with the Care of Sick Young Children," *Australian Journal of Early Childhood* 28, no. 4 (2003); Nancy L. Marshall and Rosalind C. Barnett, "Child Care, Divi-

sion of Labor, and Parental Emotional Well-Being among Two-Earner Couples" (Sloan Work and Family Research Network, 1992).

9. Louise Story, "Many Women at Elite Colleges Set Career Path to Motherhood," *New York Times,* September 20, 2005.

10. In the 2005 Ivy League study, young graduates are not the only ones who are opting for part-time work or out of paid work altogether. Of alumni in their forties, 56 percent of the women reported paid work as their primary activity, compared with 90 percent of men. The gap narrows for graduates in their thirties (65 percent of the women were working, compared with 88 percent of the men) but is growing once again. Rebecca Friedkin, of the Office of Institutional Research at Yale, forwarded these statistics on the university's graduates, with the proviso that the university had no data on whether the women who reported being "employed for pay as their primary activity" were working full-time or part-time, and that the data did not cover graduates from all classes. As these are internal survey data, there is no formal Yale University report, according to Ms. Friedkin in an e-mail exchange. Reticence was typical of the Ivy League universities I contacted when queried on the topic. Gender is such a hot topic that universities were reluctant to release statistics on what their female graduates were doing, nor would they reveal how much their institution was spending on gender equity programs.

   David Sloan Wilson and Mihaly Csikszentmihalyi, "Health and the Ecology of Altruism," in *Altruism and Health,* ed. Stephen G. Post (New York: Oxford, 2007).

11. Paul C. Light, "The Content of the Nonprofit Workforce," *Nonprofit Quarterly* 9, no. 3 (2002); Louise Mailloux, Heather Horak, and Colette Godin, "Motivation at the Margins: Gender Issues in the Canadian Voluntary Sector" (Human Resources Development Canada Voluntary Sector Secretariat, 2002); Ron Saunders, "Passion and Commitment under Stress: Human Resource Issues in Canada's Nonprofit Sector" (Canadian Policy Research Networks, 2005).

12. One of the founding female members of Kibbutz Tsvi described the following work/family conflict resulting from women and men being regarded as interchangeable work units. It's eerily similar to the problems of contemporary female executives: "I often worked in the cowshed, as did my husband. I had a small child, and often I worked on Shabbat, so I always had a headache about where my child was [on Saturday morning the children's houses were closed]. My child hated the cowshed, so he never came there, but other children did. When my turn came to work in the cowshed in the evening shift, I wasn't able to put him to bed for two or three months." From Lionel Tiger and J. Shepher, *Women in the Kibbutz* (New York: Harcourt Brace Jovanovich, 1975).

13. Research shows that men are more altruistic when there's heroism or risk involved, when it's a means to an end, or in public situations. In more anonymous or hidden types of altruism (organ donors, Holocaust rescuers), the percentage of women is either equal to or higher than that of men.

   S. W. Becker and Alice Eagly, "The Heroism of Women and Men," *American Psychologist* 59 (2004); Gustavo Carlo et al., "Sociocognitive and Behavioral Correlates of a Measure of Prosocial Tendencies for Adolescents," *Journal of Early Adolescence* 23 (2003); Alice Eagly and M. Crowley, "Gender and Helping Behavior: A Meta-Analytic Review of the Social Psychological Literature," *Psychological Bulletin* 100 (1986).

14. Stephanie Nolen, "Maggy's Children," *Globe and Mail,* May 15, 2006.

15. Nancy Eisenberg sees sympathy as stemming from empathy: sympathy starts with an emotional response that reflects someone else's state but also prompts a person to want to help.

16. Nancy Eisenberg et al., "Personality and Socialization Correlates of Vicarious

Emotional Responding," *Journal of Personality and Social Psychology* 61, no. 3 (1991).

17. Alan Feingold, "Gender Differences in Personality: A Meta-analysis," *Psychological Bulletin* 116, no. 3 (1994).

18. E. J. Lawrence et al., "Measuring Empathy: Reliability and Validity of the Empathy Quotient," *Psychological Medicine* 34 (2004).
     Eisenberg, et al. (1991).
     Simon Baron-Cohen, *The Essential Difference: The Truth About the Male and Female Brain*; R. Campbell et al., "The Classification of 'Fear' from Faces Is Associated with Face Recognition Skill in Women," *Neuropsychologia* 40 (2002); Eisenberg et al., "Personality and Socialization Correlates of Vicarious Emotional Responding"; S. Orozco and C. L. Ehlers, "Gender Differences in Electrophysiological Responses to Facial Stimuli," *Biological Psychiatry* 44 (1998).

19. Simon Baron-Cohen and Sally Wheelwright, "The Empathy Quotient: An Investigation of Adults with Asperger Syndrome or High Functioning Autism, and Normal Sex Differences," *Journal of Autism and Developmental Disorders* 34, no. 2 (2004); Emma Chapman et al., "Fetal Testosterone and Empathy: Evidence from the Empathy Quotient (EQ) and the 'Reading the Mind in the Eyes' Test," in press (2006).

20. Baron-Cohen, *The Essential Difference: The Truth About the Male and Female Brain*.

21. Lawrence, et al., "Measuring Empathy: Reliability and Validity of the Empathy Quotient."

22. Carol Gilligan considers women's sensitivity to others' needs a critical part of their moral sense but also problematic. She writes: "Sensitivity to the needs of others and the assumption of responsibility for taking care lead women to attend to voices other than their own and to include in their judgment other points of view. Women's moral weakness, manifest in an apparent diffusion and confusion of judgment, is thus inseparable from women's moral strength, and overriding concern with relationships and responsibilities." Carol Gilligan, *In a Different Voice* (Cambridge, Mass.: Harvard University Press, 1982).

23. J. A. Hall, *Nonverbal Sex Differences* (Baltimore: Johns Hopkins University Press, 1985).

24. R. F. Baumeister and K. L. Sommer, "What Do Men Want? Gender Differences in Two Spheres of Belongingness," *Psychological Bulletin* 122 (1997), 38–44.

25. J. J. Haviland and C. Z. Malatesta, "The Development of Sex Differences in Nonverbal Signals: Fallacies, Facts and Fantasies," in *Gender and Nonverbal Behavior,* ed. C. Mayo and N. M. Henley (New York: Springer-Verlag, 1981).

26. J. Scourfield et al., "Heritability of Social Cognitive Skills in Children and Adolescents," *British Journal of Psychiatry* 175 (1999).

27. In this study, 102 newborn babies just three days old were filmed while they looked at either a human face or a mobile designed to have similar features, much like a mechanical, cubist Picasso. Cambridge University graduate student Jennifer Connellan and the lead investigator, Simon Baron-Cohen, wanted to test their hypothesis that baby girls would look longer at a human face than they would at an object, and that baby boys would show the reverse: be more interested in the mechanics of a moving object than a human face. More newborn baby boys gazed longer at a mechanical mobile than at a face, while only 17 percent of the girls did. More baby girls than boys preferred to gaze at a human face. Connellan, et al., "Sex Differences in Human Neonatal Social Perception" (2000).

28. C. Zahn-Waxler et al., "Development of Concern for Others," *Developmental Psychology* 28 (1992); M. L. Hoffman, "Sex Differences in Empathy and Related

Behaviors," *Psychological Bulletin* 84 (1977); Rhoads, *Taking Sex Differences Seriously*; Connellan, "Sex Differences in Human Neonatal Social Perception"; Hall, *Nonverbal Sex Differences*; David C. Geary, *Male, Female: The Evolution of Human Sex Differences* (Washington, D.C.: American Psychological Association, 1998); Geoffry Hall, B. C., et al., "Sex Differences in Functional Activation Patterns Revealed by Increased Emotion Processing Demands," *Neuroreport* 15, no. 2 (2004).

29. Jill M. Goldstein, David N. Kennedy, and V. S. Caviness, "Brain Development and Sexual Dimorphism," *American Journal of Psychiatry* 156, no. 3 (1999).

30. Nancy Eisenberg, Richard A. Fabes, and Tracy L. Spinard, "Prosocial Development," in *Handbook of Child Psychology: Social, Emotional, and Personality Development*, ed. William Damon, Richard Lerner, and Nancy Eisenberg (New York: John Wiley & Sons, 2006); R. Koestner, C. Franz, and J. Weinberger, "The Family Origins of Empathic Concern: A 26-Year Longitudinal Study," *Journal of Personality and Social Psychology* 58 (1990).

31. Nancy Eisenberg et al., "The Relations of Empathy-Related Emotions and Maternal Practices to Children's Comforting Behavior," *Journal of Experimental Child Psychology* 55 (1993).

32. Lutchmaya and Baron-Cohen, "Human Sex Differences in Social and Non-Social Looking Preferences, at 12 Months of Age."

33. Rebecca Knickmeyer et al., "Foetal Testosterone, Social Relationships, and Restricted Interests in Children," *Journal of Child Psychology and Psychiatry* 46, no. 2 (2005). Koestner, Franz, and Weinberger, "The Family Origins of Empathic Concern: A 26-Year Longitudinal Study."

34. Chapman et al., "Fetal Testosterone and Empathy: Evidence from the Empathy Quotient (EQ) and the 'Reading the Mind in the Eyes' Test."

35. S. Coté et al., "The Development of Impulsivity, Fearfulness, and Helpfulness During Childhood: Patterns of Consistency and Change in the Trajectories of Boys and Girls," *Journal of Child Psychology and Psychiatry* 43 (2002).

36. Michael J. Meaney, "Maternal Care, Gene Expression, and the Transmission of Individual Differences in Stress Reactivity Across Generations," *Annual Review of Neuroscience* 24 (2001), 1161–1192.

37. Kathryn Shutt et al., "Grooming in Barbary Macaques: Better to Give Than to Receive?" *Biology Letters*, in press (2007).

38. Shelley E. Taylor, *The Tending Instinct: How Nurturing Is Essential to Who We Are and How We Live* (New York: Henry Holt, 2002).

39. David Dobbs, "The Gregarious Brain," *New York Times Magazine*, July 8, 2007. Kate Sullivan and Helen Tager-Flusberg, "Second-Order Belief Attribution in Williams Syndrome: Intact or Impaired?" *American Journal of Mental Retardation* 104 (1999), 523–532.

40. Helen Fisher, *The First Sex* (New York: Ballantine Books, 1999).

41. It's not that men don't secrete oxytocin under stress, but that their naturally higher level of androgens can counteract its effects. In addition, testosterone increases when males are under physiological and psychological stress (e.g., during extreme exercise, or when confronted), which makes them more hostile and aggressive under attack and also inhibits the effects of oxytocin. Finally, the effects of oxytocin are amplified by estrogen, making females not only less hostile but less fearful and also more maternal.

     Susan Pinker, "Women Naturally Tend and Befriend," *Globe and Mail*, September 20, 2006; Shelley E. Taylor et al., "Biobehavioral Responses to Stress in Females: Tend-and-Befriend, Not Fight or Flight," *Psychological Review* 107, no. 3 (2000).

42. Gregor Domes et al., "Oxytocin Improves 'Mind-Reading' in Humans," *Biological Psychiatry* 61, no. 6 (2006), 731–733.

43. Peter Kirsch et al., "Oxytocin Modulates Neural Circuitry for Social Cognition and Fear in Humans," *Journal of Neuroscience* 25, no. 49 (2005). I am grateful to Michael Lombardo, at the Autism Research Centre at the University of Cambridge, who elucidated some of the contradictory effects of oxytocin.

44. Dr. John Evans, a medical researcher in the Department of Obstetrics and Gynaecology at the Christchurch School of Medicine in New Zealand, forwarded the evidence that shows that women have four to five times the rate of circulating oxytocin compared to men. We don't know exactly how these differences affect their behavior, but we do know that women produce more oxytocin during their regular day-to-day activities, and not only when they have sex or have babies. L. Shukovski, D. L. Healy, and J. K. Findlay, "Circulating Immunotreactive Oxytocin during the Human Menstrual Cycle Comes from the Pituitary and Is Estradiol-Dependent," *Journal of Clinical Endocrinology and Metabolism* 68 (1989) and J. John Evans, "Oxytocin in the Human—Regulation of Derivations and Destinations," *European Journal of Endocrinology* 137 (1997). And I am grateful to my cousin Dr. Harold Wiesenfeld, a researcher in obstetrics and gynecology at the University of Pittsburgh, who pointed me to the animal studies that show that female prairie voles and rats secrete more oxytocin than males, and that these hormonal differences are linked to sex differences in the way these mammals bond with a member of the opposite sex, react to stress, and nurture their young. See Sue C. Carter, "Developmental Consequences of Oxytocin," *Physiology and Behavior* 79 (2003).

45. A. Luckow, A. Reifman, and D. N. McIntosh, "Gender Differences in Coping: A Meta-analysis" (paper presented at the Annual Convention of the American Psychological Association, San Francisco, August 1998); Taylor et al., "Biobehavioral Responses to Stress in Females: Tend-and-Befriend, Not Fight or Flight."

46. A. C. De Vries et al., "Stress Has Sexually Dimorphic Effects on Pair Bonding in Prairie Voles," *Proceedings of the National Academy of Science* 93 (1996). Sue C. Carter, "Monogamy, Motherhood and Health," in *Altruism and Health,* ed. Stephen G. Post (New York: Oxford University Press, 2007).

47. D. Belle, "Gender Differences in the Social Moderators of Stress," in *Gender and Stress,* ed. R. C. Barnett, L. Biener, and G. K. Baruch (New York: Free Press, 1987); J. T. Ptacek, R. E. Smith, and J. Zanas, "Gender, Appraisal, and Coping: A Longitudinal Analysis," *Journal of Personality* 60 (1992).

48. Hoffman, "Sex Differences in Empathy and Related Behaviors." Belle, "Gender Differences in the Social Moderators of Stress."

49. Douglas Coupland, *Terry* (Toronto: Douglas & McIntyre, 2005); Gary Mason, "Marathon Man," *Globe and Mail,* April 2, 2005.

50. Benedict Carey, "Message from Mouse to Mouse: I Feel Your Pain," *New York Times,* July 4, 2006; David Dobbs, "The Gregarious Brain," *New York Times,* July 8, 2007.

51. Stephanie D. Preston and Frans B. M. de Waal, "Empathy: Its Ultimate and Proximate Bases," *Behavior and Brain Sciences* 25 (2002).

52. Frans B. M. de Waal, *Our Inner Ape* (New York: Riverhead Books, 2005).

53. Tania Singer et al., "Empathy for Pain Involves the Affective but Not the Sensory Components of Pain," *Science* 303, no. 5661 (2004).

54. Anne McIlroy, "Why Do Females Feel More Pain Than Males Do?" *Globe and Mail,* October 23, 2006; Jeffrey S. Mogil and Mona Lisa Chanda, "The Case for the Inclusion of Female Subjects in Basic Science Studies of Pain," *Pain* 117 (2005).

55. Roger Dobson, "If You Don't Understand Women's Emotions, You Must Be a Man," *Independent on Sunday,* June 5, 2005; Michael Kesterton, "What Her Think Now?" *Globe and Mail,* June 9, 2005.

56. Hall, Witelson, et. al, 2004.

57. Turhan Canli et al., "Sex Differences in the Neural Basis of Emotional Memories," *Proceedings of the National Academy of Sciences* 99, no. 16 (2002): 10789–10794.

58. R. J. Erwin et al., "Facial Emotion Discrimination," *Psychiatry Research* 42, no. 3 (1992); Gina Kolata, "Man's World, Woman's World? Brain Studies Point to Differences," *New York Times,* February 28, 1995.

59. Hewlett, "Extreme Jobs: The Dangerous Allure of the 70-Hour Workweek." Sylvia Ann Hewlett, "Women and the New 'Extreme' Jobs," *Boston Globe,* December 2, 2006.

60. J. Mirowsky and C. E. Ross, "Sex Differences in Distress: Real or Artifact?" *American Sociological Review* 60 (1995).

61. Ronald C. Kessler, "The Epidemiology of Depression among Women," in *Women and Depression,* ed. Corey L. M. Keyes and Sherryl H. Goodman (New York: Cambridge University Press, 2006).

62. Ronald C. Kessler and Jane D. McLeod, "Sex Differences in Vulnerability to Undesirable Life Events," *American Sociological Review* 49, no. 5 (1984).

63. Roy Baumeister and K. L. Sommer, "What Do Men Want? Gender Differences in Two Spheres of Belongingness: Comment on Cross and Madson," *Psychological Bulletin* 122 (1997); Geary, *Male, Female: The Evolution of Human Sex Differences.*

64. Sarah Hampson, "Fonda Contradictions," *Globe and Mail,* April 23, 2005; Heather MacDonald, "Girl Problems," *National Review Online,* July 5, 2005.

65. Eva M. Pomerantz, Florrie Fei-Yin Ng, and Qian Wang, "Gender Socialization: A Parent X Child Model," in *The Psychology of Gender,* ed. Alice Eagly, Anne E. Beall, and Robert J. Sternberg (New York: Guilford Press, 2004).

66. Gilligan (1982), 17; and Fisher (1999).

67. Sandra Lee Bartky, "Feeding Egos and Tending Wounds: Deference and Disaffection in Women's Emotional Labor," in *Femininity and Domination: Studies in The Phenomenology of Oppression* (New York: Routledge, 1990), 109.

68. L. Fratiglioni, S. Paillard-Borg, and B. Winblad, "An Active and Socially Integrated Lifestyle in Late Life Might Protect against Dementia," *Lancet Neurology* (2004); L. Fratiglioni et al., "Influence of Social Network on Occurrence of Dementia: A Community-Based Longitudinal Study," *Lancet* 355, no. 9212 (2004); Thomas Glass et al., "Population-Based Study of Social and Productive Activities as Predictors of Survival among Elderly Americans," *British Medical Journal* (1999).

69. Browne, "Evolved Sex Differences and Occupational Segregation"; R. A. Josephs, H. R. Markus, and R. W. Tafarodi, "Gender and Self-Esteem," *Journal of Personality and Social Psychology* 63 (1992).

Chapter 5: Revenge of the Nerds

1. According to policy analyst Tom Mortenson of the Pell Institute, 72 percent of American men have left school without postsecondary degrees before age twenty. Seventy-five percent of British men have left school by that age; and the figures are 56 percent for Canada and 59 percent for Spain. Mortenson, "What's Wrong with the Guys," report from the Pell Institute for the Study of Opportunity in Higher Education, 2003, also presented at the European Access Network, Thessaloniki, Greece, September 2006.

2. Simon Baron-Cohen and his research team have shown that the fathers and grand-fathers of people with autistic spectrum disorders (of which Asperger syndrome is the mildest form) are twice as likely to be engineers as those in the general population. Looking at the situation in reverse, university students studying physics, engineering, or mathematics had a significantly higher number of relatives with autism than those studying literature. The common thread is a genetic predisposition for a certain cognitive profile: deficits in "folk psychology" or an innate understanding of how people interact, counterbalanced by superior skills in "folk physics," an innate understanding of inanimate objects and how they're organized in systems. Baron-Cohen hypothesizes that two parents with the latter profile are more likely to have a child with an autistic spectrum disorder. Indeed, this may be true of Bob.

    Simon Baron-Cohen, "Autism Occurs More Often in Families of Physicists, Engineers, and Mathematicians," *Autism* 2 (1998); Simon Baron-Cohen, "Is There a Link between Engineering and Autism?" *Autism* 1 (1997); Simon Baron-Cohen, "Two New Theories of Autism: Hyper-Systemising and Assortative Mating," *Archives of Disease in Childhood* 91 (2006).

3. *Diagnostic and Statistical Manual of Mental Disorders,* 4th edition (Washington, D.C.: American Psychiatric Association, 1994).

4. Baron-Cohen, *The Essential Difference*; Simon Baron-Cohen et al., "A Mathematician, a Physicist, and a Computer Scientist with Asperger Syndrome: Performance on Folk Psychology and Folk Physics Tests," *Neurocase* 5 (1999). Baron-Cohen coined the term "systemizers" to describe people who have an innate understanding of complex systems, whether technical, biological, mathematical, or social systems (such as law or economics). Although it exists in both men and women in varying degrees, he proposed that systemizing is more common among males, and in its extreme form, in males with autistic spectrum disorders.

5. Uta Frith, *Autism: Explaining the Enigma* (Cambridge, Mass.: Blackwell, 1989).

6. Emily Bazelon, "What Are Autistic Girls Made Of?" *New York Times Magazine,* August 5, 2007; David H. Skuse, "Rethinking the Nature of Genetic Vulnerability to Autistic Spectrum Disorders," *Trends in Genetics* 23, no. 8 (2007), 387–395.

7. Bill Bryson, *A Short History of Nearly Everything* (Toronto: Doubleday Canada, 2003).

8. Oliver Sacks, "Henry Cavendish: An Early Case of Asperger's Syndrome?" *Neurology* 57, no. 7 (2001).

9. Peter F. Ostwald, *Glenn Gould: The Ecstasy and the Tragedy of Genius* (New York: W. W. Norton & Company, 1997), 122.

10. Baron-Cohen, *The Essential Difference: The Truth About the Male and Female Brain.*

11. Ibid., 161.

12. "Male Female Enrollment patterns in Electrical Engineering at MIT and Other Schools." Final report of the EECS Women's Undergraduate Enrollment Committee, MIT, January 1995. Rachel Ivie and Kim Nies Ray, "Women in Physics and Astronomy, 2005," American Institute of Physics (February 2005). Donna J. Nelson and Diana C. Rogers, "A National Analysis of Diversity in Science and Engineering Faculties at Research Universities" (January 2004), available at http://www.now.org/issues/diverse/diversity_report.pdf.

13. The journalist Philip Weiss described Craig Newmark as an "action figure called the exploder of journalism." Philip Weiss, "A Guy Named Craig," *New York Times,* January 16, 2006.

14. Ibid.

15. Those with Asperger syndrome, perhaps 30 percent of all those diagnosed with autistic spectrum disorders, nonetheless function best with social coaching.

16. Baron-Cohen, "Autism Occurs More Often in Families of Physicists, Engineers, and Mathematicians"; Baron-Cohen, "Is There a Link between Engineering and Autism?"; Baron-Cohen, "Two New Theories of Autism: Hyper-Systemising and Assortative Mating."

17. Steve Silberman, "The Geek Syndrome," in *Wired* (2001).

18. Temple Grandin called herself "an anthropologist on Mars," which inspired the title of Oliver Sacks' book of essays. In her own autobiography, Grandin also identified with the android Data on *Star Trek,* while Claire Sainsbury described the feeling of having Asperger syndrome as a child as being a "Martian in the Playground."

19. This persistence of childhood traits in adults is similar to the concept of neoteny, described by Stephen Jay Gould in *Ontogeny and Phylogeny,* in 1977, and by Bruce Charlton, "The Rise of the Boy Genius: Psychological Neoteny, Science and the Modern Life," *Medical Hypotheses* 67 (2006), 674–681.

20. I am grateful to Dr. Darold Treffert for the figures on autistic savant syndrome.

21. Jules Asher, *Gene Linked to Autism in Families with More Than One Affected Child* (National Institute of Mental Health, 2006; available at http://www.nimh.nih.gov/press/autismmetgene.cfm); P. Bolton et al., "A Case Control Family History Study of Autism," *Journal of Child Psychology and Psychiatry* 35, no. 5 (1994); Mohammad Ghaziuddin, "A Family History of Asperger Syndrome," *Journal of Autism and Developmental Disorders* 35, no. 2 (2005). Baron-Cohen, *The Essential Difference,* 137.

22. Among other labs, Dr. Eric Courchesne's lab at the University of San Diego has shown duplication of the chromosome 15q11–13.

23. C. A. Mejias-Aponte, C. A. Jimenez-Rivera, and A. C. Segarra, "Sex Differences in Models of Temporal Lobe Epilepsy: Role of Testosterone," *Brain Research* 944, nos. 1–2 (2002); Lidia Gabis, John Pomeroy, and Mary R. Andriola, "Autism and Epilepsy: Cause, Consequence, Comorbidity, or Coincidence?" *Epilepsy & Behavior* 7 (2005).

24. Darold A. Treffert and Gregory L. Wallace, "Islands of Genius," *Scientific American* 286 (2002); Darold A. Treffert, *Extraordinary People* (Lincoln: iUniverse, 2006). According to Treffert and Wallace, savant syndrome disproportionately affects males, with a ratio of four to six male savants for every female. Their extreme talents favor right-hemisphere skills that are nonsymbolic, visual, or spatial, such as mathematics, mechanical skills, music, calculating, or computers, while they show deficits in left-hemisphere skills. Localization-related, symptomatic epileptic disorders are also more common in men, according to Christensen and colleagues in Denmark. It is hypothesized that an increased concentration of testosterone in the blood also increases susceptibility to seizures, at least in the temporal lobe. J. Christensen et al., "Gender Differences in Epilepsy," *Epilepsia* 46, no. 6 (2005); Mejias-Aponte, Jimenez-Rivera, and Segarra, "Sex Differences in Models of Temporal Lobe Epilepsy: Role of Testosterone."

25. Treffert and Wallace, "Islands of Genius"; Norman Geschwind and Albert Galaburda, *Cerebral Lateralization: Biological Mechanisms, Associations and Pathology* (Cambridge, Mass.: MIT Press, 1987).

26. Ruben C. Gur and Raquel E. Gur, "Neural Substrates for Sex Differences in Cognition," in *Why Aren't More Women in Science?* ed. Stephen J. Ceci and Wendy M. Williams (Washington, D. C.: American Psychological Association, 2007).

27. Nigel Goldenfeld, Simon Baron-Cohen, and Sally Wheelwright, "Empathizing and Systemizing in Males, Females, and Autism," *Clinical Neuropsychiatry* 2, no. 6 (2005).

28. Sandra Blakeslee, "Focus Narrows in Search for Autism's Cause," *New York Times,* February 8, 2005.

29. Kimura, *Sex and Cognition*.

30. One recent experiment found that male rhesus monkeys whose testosterone exposure had been blocked during prenatal development subsequently behaved more
like female monkeys, using landmarks when navigating in an open area looking
for food. Rebecca Herman, "Sex and Prenatal Hormone Exposure Affect Cognitive Performance," *Hormones and Behavior* (in press, 2007). For information on
girls with CAH see Sheri A. Berenbaum and Susan Resnick, "The Seeds of Career
Choices: Prenatal Sex Hormone Effects on Psychological Sex Differences," in
Why Aren't More Women in Science? ed. Stephen J. Ceci and Wendy M. Williams
(Washington, D.C.: American Psychological Association, 2007).

31. Doreen Kimura, "Sex Hormones Influence Human Cognitive Patterns," *Neuroendocrinology Letters* 23, no. 4 (2002).

32. The levels of uterine testosterone reflect the baby's, not the mother's, hormone levels. Simon Baron-Cohen, Svetlana Lutchmaya, and Rebecca Knickmeyer, *Prenatal Testosterone in Mind: Amniotic Fluid Studies* (Cambridge, Mass.: MIT Press,
2004); Knickmeyer et al., "Foetal Testosterone, Social Relationships, and
Restricted Interests in Children."

33. For examples of Georges Huard's early diary entries and pedantic language see his
website at http://people.sca.uqam.ca/~huard/asperger_pedant_e.html.

34. Neither are they representative of autistic men in general, whose handicaps may
be more limiting. I selected men whose intelligence and social networks are such
that they excel in their "islets" of ability, while being able to use their native intelligence and social supports to buttress their areas of weakness.

35. In a recent paper on Asperger syndrome, Uta Frith pointed out how Hans
Asperger himself considered the disorder biological in origin, yet predicted
improvement over the course of development (Frith, 2004).

Chapter 6: No One Ever Asked Me If I Wanted to Be the Daddy

1. Research by Fiona Kay, a Queen's University sociology of law professor, shows
that women leave law practice 60 percent more often than men. And Catalyst, an
organization that tracks women in business, issued a 2005 report that indicates
that 62 percent of female law associates (compared to 47 percent of men) do not
plan to stay at their law firms past the first five years and will migrate to other
positions or out of law entirely to gain more work-life balance. The report estimates a firm's average cost of losing a law associate as $315,000.

2. Jill Abramson and Barbara Franklin, *Where Are They Now: The Story of the
Women of Harvard Law* (New York: Doubleday, 1986); Wendy Werner, "Where
Have All the Women Attorneys Gone?" *Law Practice Today* (2005). As one of the
most successful litigators in the United States, David Boies has defended IBM,
AOL, CBS, and Napster, among others. The "sleep or win" quote is from Debo-
rah Rhode, "Searching for Balanced Lives" (American Bar Association, 2003).

3. Fiona Kay and John Hagan, "Raising the Bar: The Gender Stratification of
Law-Firm Capital," *American Sociological Review* 63 (1998). Kirk Makin,
"Female Lawyers Hiding Illness to Remain Competitive," *Globe and Mail*,
August 15, 2007.

4. A website that tracks the legal scene in the United Kingdom, http://www
.thelawyer.com, quoted Bar Council statistics showing that 48.9 percent of
lawyers called to the bar in 2005 were women, whereas 30 percent of lawyers in
private practice were. The same online publication issued a report on the top one
hundred law firms (http://www.thelawyer.com/euro100/2005). Of the thirty
European contenders, only three had more than 20 percent female partners. One
Dutch firm in the top hundred had a single female equity partner out of fifty-three.

5. Fiona Kay and Joan Brockman, "Barriers to Gender Equality in the Canadian Legal Establishment," *Feminist Legal Studies* (2000).
6. Claire Sanders, "Women Law Lecturers Pay the Price for Their Freedom," [London] *Times Online,* May 23, 2006.
7. Linda Hirshman, "Homeward Bound," in *American Prospect Online* (2005).
8. Charlotte Chiu, "Do Professional Women Have Lower Job Satisfaction Than Professional Men? Lawyers as a Case Study," *Sex Roles: A Journal of Research* (April 1998); John Hagan and Fiona Kay, *Gender in Practice: A Study in Lawyers Lives* (New York: Oxford University Press, 1995).
9. Ronit Dinovitzer, "After the J.D.: First Results of a National Study of Legal Careers" (NALP Foundation for Law Career Research and Education and American Bar Foundation, 2004).
10. Taking increasingly long maternity leaves with each successive child is the pattern of the average university-educated woman of the 1976 entering class, as quoted by the College and Beyond data set in Claudia Goldin's essay "The Quiet Revolution." In refuting the idea that educated women "opt out" of the workforce, she quotes four months as the average leave of absence taken after the first baby, and a little more than one year after the second child (although she does not state whether these women are returning to full-time or part-time work). By the time the third child arrives, the same woman, on average, had taken 2.84 years completely off paying work in the fifteen years since her graduation (compared to a total of two months off work for men of that graduating class, with three children). Goldin, "From the Valley to the Summit: The Quiet Revolution That Transformed Women's Employment, Education, and Family."

    Catherine Hakim, at the London School of Economics, points out that 80 percent of working women in the European Union choose neither full-time homemaking after the birth of a child nor full-time employment, but some combination of the two, usually a part-time, flexible job closer to home. She quotes surveys (by S. McRae published by the London Policy Institute) that show that of the 40 percent of women who were intending to go back to work in 1988, most returned to part-time jobs instead of their original full-time position. By 1999, 80 percent of mothers were working at flexible, part-time jobs. S. McRae, "Constraints and Choices in Mothers' Employment Careers: A Consideration of Hakim's Preference Theory," *British Journal of Sociology* 54 (2003).
11. Hakim, *Work-Lifestyle Choices in the 21st Century* (New York: Oxford University Press, 2000).
12. Eduardo Porter, "Stretched to the Limit, Women Stall March to Work," *New York Times,* March 2, 2006.
13. Fisher, *The First Sex.*
14. Joanna Moorhead, "For Decades We've Been Told Sweden Is a Great Place to Be a Working Parent. But We've Been Duped," *The Guardian,* September 22, 2004.
15. Catherine Hakim, "A New Approach to Explaining Fertility Patterns: Preference Theory," *Population and Development Review* 29, no. 3 (2003); S. Wyatt and C. Langridge, *Getting to the Top in the National Health Service,* ed. S. Ledwith and F. Colgan, *Women in Organizations: Challenging Gender Politics* (London: Macmillan, 1996).
16. Linda Tischler, "Winning the Career Tournament," *Fast Company,* 2004.
17. Julie Creswell, "How Suite It Isn't: A Dearth of Female Bosses," *New York Times,* December 17, 2006.
18. Hakim, *Work-Lifestyle Choices in the 21st Century,* 16.
19. Sarah Blaffer Hrdy, *Mother Nature: Maternal Instincts and How They Shape the Human Species* (New York: Random House, 1999).

20. Linda Mealey, *Sex Differences: Developmental and Evolutionary Strategies* (San Diego: Academic Press, 2000), 74.
21. Blaffer Hrdy, *Mother Nature: Maternal Instincts and How They Shape the Human Species.*
22. Craig Howard Kinsley and Kelly G. Lambert, "The Maternal Brain," *Scientific American,* January 2006.
23. B. J. Mattson et al., "Comparison of Two Positive Reinforcing Stimuli: Pups and Cocaine Throughout the Postpartum Period," *Behavioral Neuroscience* 115 (2001).
24. Mattson et al., "Comparison of Two Positive Reinforcing Stimuli: Pups and Cocaine Throughout the Postpartum Period."
25. Andreas Bartels and Semir Zeki, "The Neural Correlates of Maternal and Romantic Love," *Neuroimage* 21 (2004).
26. Mona Harrington, *Women Lawyers: Rewriting the Rules* (New York: Plume, 1995). Chiu, "Do Professional Women Have Lower Job Satisfaction Than Professional Men? Lawyers as a Case Study."
27. I. Gati, S. H. Osipow, and M. Givon, "Gender Differences in Career Decision Making: The Content and Structure of Preferences," *Journal of Counseling Psychology* 42 (1995); Halpern, *Sex Differences in Cognitive Abilities,* 267.
28. Martinez, "Women's Intrinsic and Extrinsic Motivations for Working," in *Being Together, Working Apart,* ed. Barbara Schneider and Linda J. Waite (Cambridge, U.K.: Cambridge University Press, 2005).
29. Jennifer Matjasko and Amy Feldman, "Emotional Transmission between Parents and Adolescents: The Importance of Work Characteristics and Relationship Quality," in *Being Together, Working Apart,* ed. Barbara Schneider and Linda J. Waite (Cambridge, U.K.: Cambridge University Press, 2005); Susan Pinker, "Looking Out for Number One," *Globe and Mail,* April 4, 2007.
30. Fiona Kay, "Flight from Law: A Competing Risks Model of Departures from Law Firms," *Law Society Review* 31, no. 2 (1997).
31. Werner, "Where Have All the Women Attorneys Gone?" *Law Practice Today,* November 2005.
32. Sara Beth Haviland, "Job Satisfaction and the Gender Paradox: An International Perspective" (paper presented at the American Sociological Association, August 16, 2004); Sangmook Kim, "Gender Differences in the Job Satisfaction of Public Employees," *Sex Roles* (May 2005); P. Sloane and H. Williams, "Are Overpaid Workers Really Unhappy? A Test of the Theory of Cognitive Dissonance," *Labour* 10 (1996); Alfonso Sousa-Poza, "Taking Another Look at the Gender/Job-Satisfaction Paradox," *Kyklos* 53, no. 2 (2000).
33. Michael Rose, " So Less Happy Too? Subjective Well-Being and the Vanishing Job Satisfaction Premium of British Women Employees," paper presented at the Social Policy Association's annual conference, June 27, 2005.
34. R. Richard Layard, *Happiness: Lessons from a New Science* (London: Penguin, 2005).
35. Heather MacLean, K. Glynn, and D. Ansara, "Multiple Roles and Women's Mental Health in Canada," in *Women's Health Surveillance Report* (Toronto: Centre for Research in Women's Health, 2003); A. McMunn et al., "Life Course Social Roles and Women's Health in Midlife: Causation or Selection," *Journal of Epidemiology and Community Health* 60, no. 6 (2006).

Chapter 7: Hiding the Imposter Within

1. Lawrence K. Altman, "Her Job: Helping Save the World from Bird Flu," *New York Times,* August 9, 2005.

2. Joan Harvey, a psychologist who researched imposter syndrome in the early 1980s, discovered that the highest-achieving female students—the strongest students in an honors program, for example—were more likely to have imposter feelings than the more average students. In other words, objective achievement was not the antidote, and by boosting these women to another category, could promote imposter feelings anew. Joan C. Harvey and Cynthia Katz, *If I'm So Successful, Why Do I Feel Like a Fake? The Imposter Phenomenon* (New York: St. Martin's Press, 1985).

3. Pauline Rose Clance and Suzanne Ament Imes, "The Impostor Phenomenon in High-Achieving Women: Dynamics and Therapeutic Intervention," *Psychotherapy: Theory, Research and Practice* 15, no. 3 (1978); Harvey and Katz, *If I'm So Successful, Why Do I Feel Like a Fake?*

4. Susan Vinnicombe and Val Singh, "Locks and Keys to the Boardroom," *Women in Management Review* 18, no. 5/6 (2003).

5. Margaret S. Gibbs, Karen Alter Reid, and Sharon De Vries, "Instrumentality and the Imposter Phenomenon." Paper presented at the meeting of the American Psychological Association, Toronto, 1984.

6. "Pfeiffer Still Fears Being Shown Up as a 'Sham,'" January 18, 2002: http://www.imdb.com/news/wenn/2002–01–18#celeb5. Mal Vincent "Pfeiffer Still Feels Being Shown Up as a 'Sham,'" *Virginian Pilot*, January, 25, 2002. The Kate Winslet quotes also appeared on the imdb.com website.

7. Gail M. Matthews, "Impostor Phenomenon: Attributions for Success and Failure," paper presented at the American Psychological Association, Toronto, 1984.

8. Joan S. Girgus and Susan Nolen-Hoeksema, "Cognition and Depression," in *Women and Depression,* ed. Corey L. M. Keyes and Sherryl H. Goodman (New York: Cambridge University Press, 2006); Susan Nolen-Hoeksema and B. Jackson, "Mediators of the Gender Differences in Rumination," *Psychology of Women Quarterly* 25 (2001); Susan Nolen-Hoeksema, J. Larson, and C. Grayson, "Explaining the Gender Difference in Depression," *Journal of Personality and Social Psychology* 77 (1999).

9. I am grateful to Valerie Young for background information and the celebrity quotes on the imposter syndrome.

10. Sonnert Gerhard and Gerald Holton, "Career Patterns of Women and Men in the Sciences," *American Scientist* 84, no. 1 (1996).

11. Allegra Goodman, *Intuition* (New York: Dial, 2006).

12. Feingold, "Gender Differences in Personality: A Meta-analysis"; Hall, *Nonverbal Sex Differences*; Kessler, "The Epidemiology of Depression among Women"; Susan Nolen-Hoeksema and Cheryl Rusting, "Gender Differences in Well-Being," in *Well-Being: The Foundations of Hedonic Psychology,* ed. D. Kahneman, Ed Diener, and N. Schwarz (New York: Russell Sage Foundation, 1999).

13. S. Van Goozen et al., "Anger Proneness in Women: Development and Validation of the Anger Situation Questionnaire," *Aggressive Behavior* 20 (1994).

14. L. Y. Abramson, Martin E. P. Seligman, and J. Teasdale, "Learned Helplessness in Humans," *Journal of Abnormal Psychology* 87 (1978), 49–74. Kay Deaux and T. Emswiller, "Explanations of Successful Performance on Sex-Linked Tasks: What Is Skill for the Male Is Luck for the Female," *Journal of Personality and Psychology* 29 (1974), 80–85.

15. Joyce Ehrlinger and David Dunning, "How Chronic Self-Views Influence (and Potentially Mislead) Estimates of Performance," *Journal of Personality and Social Psychology* 84, no. 1 (2003).

16. David Dunning, Chip Heath, and Jerry Suls, "Flawed Self-Assessment," *Psychological Science in the Public Interest* 5, no. 3 (2004).

17. Gerry Pallier, "Gender Differences in the Self-Assessment of Accuracy on Cognitive Tasks," *Sex Roles* 48, nos. 5–6 (2003).
18. Ehrlinger and Dunning, "Chronic Self-Views"; Jeanne M. Stahl et al., "The Impostor Phenomenon in High School and College Science Majors," paper presented at the American Psychological Association, Montréal, 1980.
19. Nick Paumgarten, "The Tycoon," *New Yorker,* July 23, 2007.
20. In a book about Ivy League strivers, author Alexandra Robbins profiles eight college applicants in a Washington suburb. While Julie "the superstar" is riddled with self-doubt, Sam runs out of time for a project and invents an entire transcript of a fictional interview to make a deadline for an assignment. See Alexandra Robbins, *The Overachievers: The Secret Lives of Driven Kids* (New York: Hyperion, 2006). Jeanne M. Stahl et al., "The Imposter Phenomenon in High School and College Science Majors."
21. Michelle Cowley and Ruth M. J. Byrne, "Chess Masters' Hypothesis Testing," *Cognitive Psychology,* in press. Julie Norem and N. Cantor, "Defensive Pessimism: Harnessing Anxiety as Motivation," *Journal of Personality and Social Psychology* 52 (1986), 1208–1217.
22. A. T. Beck, "Cognitive Models of Depression," *Journal of Cognitive Psychotherapy: An International Quarterly* 1 (1987), 5–37; Girgus and Nolen-Hoeksema, "Cognition and Depression."
23. Martin E. P. Seligman et al., "Depressive Attributional Style," *Journal of Abnormal Psychology* 88 (1979).
24. Ronald C. Kessler et al., "Prevalence, Severity and Comorbidity of Twelve-Month DSMIV Disorders in the National Comorbidity Survey Replication (NCS-R)," *Archives of General Psychiatry* 62, no. 6 (2005); Kessler, "The Epidemiology of Depression among Women"; Ania Korszun, Margaret Altemus, and Elizabeth Young, "The Biological Underpinnings of Depression," in *Women and Depression,* ed. Corey L. M. Keyes and Sherryl H. Goodman (New York: Cambridge University Press, 2006).
25. Yawen Cheng et al., "Association between Psychosocial Work Characteristics and Health Functioning in American Women," *British Medical Journal* 320 (2000); Mary Clare Lennon, "Women, Work, and Depression," in *Women and Depression,* ed. Corey L. M. Keyes and Sherryl H. Goodman (New York: Cambridge University Press, 2006).

Chapter 8: Competition: Is It a Guy Thing?

1. Janet S. Hyde, "Gender Differences in Aggression," in *The Psychology of Gender,* ed. J. S. Hyde and M. C. Linn (Baltimore: Johns Hopkins University Press, 1986); Maccoby and Jacklin, *The Psychology of Sex Differences.* Steven Pinker, *The Blank Slate: The Modern Denial of Human Nature* (New York: Viking, 2002).
2. Baron-Cohen, "Sex Differences in Mind: Keeping Science Distinct from Social Policy"; Charlesworth and Dzur, "Gender Comparisons of Preschoolers Behavior and Resource Utilization in Group Problem Solving."
3. Anne Campbell, *A Mind of Her Own: The Evolutionary Psychology of Women* (Oxford, U.K.: Oxford University Press, 2002); Maccoby, *The Two Sexes: Growing Apart, Coming Together.*
4. Uri Gneezy and Aldo Rustichini, "Gender and Competition at a Young Age," *American Economic Review* 94, no. 2 (2004).
5. Carol Cronin Weisfeld, "Female Behavior in Mixed Sex Competition: A Review of the Literature," *Developmental Review* 6 (1986).
6. Muriel Niederle and Lise Vesterlund, "Do Women Shy Away from Competition? Do Men Compete Too Much?" *Quarterly Journal of Economics,* in press (2006).

7. Linda Babcock and Sara Laschever, *Women Don't Ask: Negotiation and the Gender Divide* (Princeton, N.J.: Princeton University Press, 2003); Mirowsky and Ross, "Sex Differences in Distress: Real or Artifact?"

8. Hannah Riley Bowles, Linda Babcock, and Lei Lai, *It Depends Who Is Asking and Who You Ask: Social Incentives for Sex Differences in the Propensity to Initiate Negotiation* (Social Science Research Network, July 2005); available from http://ssrn.com/abstract=779506.

9. This corresponds to the legal concept of adverse effect discrimination, where the intent of an action is not to discriminate but the outcome has that impact. I am grateful to Martin Boodman for explaining this concept.

10. Virginia Woolf, "Equality, Opportunity and Pay," *Atlantic Monthly* (May-June 1938).

11. Maccoby and Jacklin, *The Psychology of Sex Differences.*

12. Richard Tremblay and Sylvana Coté, researchers in aggression at the University of Montréal, make a compelling argument that aggression, antisocial behavior, and risk-taking should never be lumped together, and that there's greater understanding in "splitting" versus "lumping" when it comes to scientific investigation of how these phenomena develop. I agree, and am only lining them up due to their common, sex-linked biological drivers.

13. Marianne Bertrand and Kevin F. Hallock, "The Gender Gap in Top Corporate Jobs," *Industrial and Labor Relations Review* 55 (2001); Elizabeth Cashdan, "Are Men More Competitive Than Women?" *British Journal of Social Psychology* 37 (1998); Alice Eagly and S. J. Karau, "Gender and the Emergence of Leaders: A Meta-analysis," *Journal of Personality and Social Psychology* 60 (1991), 685–710; Weisfeld, "Female Behavior in Mixed Sex Competition: A Review of the Literature."

14. David Brooks, "All Politics Are Thymotic," *New York Times,* March 16, 2006. Steven Pinker, *How the Mind Works* (New York: W. W. Norton, 1997), 364.

15. Sol Steinmetz and Carol G. Braham, eds., *Random House Webster's Dictionary* (Toronto: Random House, 1993).

16. M. Frankenhaeuser, "Challenge-Control Interaction as Reflected in Sympathetic-Adrenal and Pituitary-Adrenal Activity: Comparison between the Sexes," *Scandinavian Journal of Psychology* 23, no. 1 (1982).

17. Paul Taylor, "What's Nastier Than a Loser? A Winner,"*Globe and Mail,* April 1, 2005.

18. Jennifer Klinesmith, Tim Kasser, and Francis McAndrew, "Guns, Testosterone, and Aggression: An Experimental Test of a Mediational Hypothesis," *Psychological Science* 17, no. 7 (2006).

19. Tania Singer et al., "Empathic Neural Responses Are Modulated by the Perceived Fairness of Others," *Nature* (2006).

20. U.S. Census Bureau, "Population in Group Quarters by Type, Sex, and Age for the United States: 2000" (2000).

21. Centers for Disease Control and Prevention, National Center for Injury Prevention and Control. Web-based Injury Statistics Query and Reporting System (2004): http://www.cdc.gov/ncipc/wisqars/default.htm.
    G. McClure, "Changes in Suicide in England and Wales, 1960–1997," *British Journal of Psychiatry* 176 (2000).

22. Browne, *Biology at Work: Rethinking Sexual Equality,* 20.
    Northeastern University criminologist James Alan Fox has stated that out of 450 workplace shootings during the past thirty years, only 7 percent were carried out by women.Tim Molloy, "Women's Rampage Leaves Six Dead in the U.S.," *Globe and Mail,* February 1, 2006. In addition, men have a higher rate of mortal-

ity at work than women because women choose safer jobs, being more averse to fatal risk, according to a study at the National Bureau of Economic Research. Thomas DeLeire and Helen Levy, "Gender, Occupation Choice and the Risk of Death at Work" (National Bureau of Economic Research, 2001).

23. Kruger and Nesse, "Sexual Selection and the Male:Female Mortality Ratio."

24. A website that archives video clips of "stupid tricks": XXXL Games: http://xxxl games.com.

25. Wendy Northcutt, *The Darwin Awards: Survival of the Fittest* (New York: Plume, 2004); Wendy Northcutt, *The Darwin Awards: Unnatural Selection* (New York: Plume, 2003); Wendy Northcutt, *The Darwin Awards: Evolution in Action* (New York: Plume, 2002).

26. Northcutt, *The Darwin Awards: Unnatural Selection.*

27. James P. Byrnes, David C. Miller, and William D. Shafer, "Gender Differences in Risk Taking: A Meta-analysis," *Psychological Bulletin* 125, no. 3 (1999).

28. In a chapter on competition for mates, Martin Daly and Margo Wilson (1983) include dramatic graphs showing how male sheep on the Scottish Island of St. Kilda and male rhesus monkeys in Puerto Rico are twice as likely to die during mating season as females. The fierce fighting for females means that many of the males take combative risks and die young,

29. Blaffer Hrdy, *Mother Nature: Maternal Instincts and How They Shape the Human Species,* 84–85. Michael Kesterton, "Man with 78 Children Gearing Up for 100," *Globe and Mail,* August 21, 2007; Jeremy Page, "Father, 90, Shows Off New Baby—and Wants More," *Times of London,* August 22, 2007.

30. Robert L. Trivers, "Parental Investment and Sexual Selection," in *Sexual Selection and the Descent of Man 1871–1971,* ed. B. Campbell (Chicago: Aldine, 1972).

31. Sarah Blaffer Hrdy (1999) makes a convincing case that mothers in many species make "informed" choices about which male is a safe bet based on a complex web of factors. These might include the age, size, and sex ratio of her other offspring, the environmental factors that affect their survival and the number of helpers, or alloparents around—including the father—that would make her investment in offspring worthwhile.

32. Richard Wiseman, *Quirkology: The Curious Science of Everyday Lives* (London: Macmillan, 2007).

33. In the study, gender equality was measured by women's status as reported in the U. N. Development Program, 1995. See Alice H. Eagly, Wendy Wood, and Mary C. Johannesen-Schmidt, "Social Role Theory of Sex Differences and Similarities: Implications for the Partner Preferences of Women and Men," in *The Psychology of Gender,* 2nd ed., ed. Alice Eagly, Anne E. Beall, and Robert J. Sternberg (New York: Guilford Press, 2004).

34. Bojan Todosijevic, Snezana Ljubinkovic, and Aleksandra Arancic, "Mate Selection Criteria: A Trait Desirability Assessment Study of Sex Differences in Serbia," *Evolutionary Psychology* 1 (2003).

35. David M. Buss, "Sex Differences in Human Mate Preferences: Evolutionary Hypothesis Tested in 37 Cultures," *Behavioral and Brain Sciences* 12 (1989); David M. Buss et al., "A Half Century of Mate Preferences: The Cultural Evolution of Values," *Journal of Marriage and Family* 63 (2001).

36. Nancy Etcoff, *Survival of the Prettiest: The Science of Beauty* (New York: Doubleday, 1999); John Marshall Townsend, *What Women Want—What Men Want* (New York: Oxford University Press, 1998).

37. Mealey, *Sex Differences: Developmental and Evolutionary Strategies.*

38. Drake Bennett, "The Evolutionary Revolutionary," *Boston Globe,* March 27, 2005.

39. Sociologists Allan Mazur and Alan Booth studied endogenous testosterone in a large sample of air force veterans and conclude that it affects individuals' dominance in groups, dominance that can be antisocial but that is not always aggressive. They propose a feedback loop in which testosterone primes men to face a challenge, then rises in response to winning and declines as a result of losing, thus acting as both a cause and effect of behavior. Allan Mazur and Alan Booth, "Testosterone and Dominance in Men," *Behavioral and Brain Sciences* (2001).

40. Browne, *Biology at Work: Rethinking Sexual Equality,* 114.

41. Daniel Olweus, B. J. Mattson, and H. Low, "Circulating Testosterone Levels and Aggression in Adolescent Males: A Causal Analysis," *Psychosomatic Medicine* 50 (1988); Tremblay and Nagin, "The Developmental Origins of Physical Aggression in Humans."

42. Kimura, *Sex and Cognition.*

43. Rhoads, *Taking Sex Differences Seriously.*

44. Sheri A. Berenbaum and Susan M. Resnick, "Early Androgen Effects on Aggression in Children and Adults with Congenital Adrenal Hyperplasia," *Psychoneuroendocrinology* 22 (1997), as cited in Browne, *Biology at Work.*

45. Berenbaum and Resnick, "The Seeds of Career Choices: Prenatal Sex Hormone Effects on Psychological Sex Differences."

46. Carter, "Developmental Consequences of Oxytocin."

47. I borrowed this phrase from a scientific review article with that title. See Jeri S. Janowski, "Thinking with Your Gonads: Testosterone and Cognition," *Trends in Cognitive Sciences* 20, no. 20 (2005).

48. James McBride Dabbs and Mary Godwin Dabbs, *Heroes, Rogues, and Lovers: Testosterone and Behavior* (New York: McGraw-Hill, 2000).

49. Frances E. Purifoy and Lambert H. Koopmans, "Androstenedione, Testosterone, and Free Testosterone Concentration in Women of Various Occupations," *Social Biology* 26, no. 1 (1979).

50. Elizabeth Cashdan, "Hormones, Sex, and Status in Women," *Hormones and Behavior* 29 (1995).

51. Rocio Garcia-Retamero, "Prejudice Against Women in Male Congenial Environments: Perceptions of Gender Role Congruity in Leadership," *Sex Roles* 55 (2006).

52. Elizabeth Cashdan, "Hormones and Competitive Aggression in Women," *Aggressive Behavior* 29 (2003).

53. V. Burbank, "Female Aggression in Cross-Cultural Perspective," *Behavior Science Research* 21 (1987).

54. Kaj Bjorkqvist, "Sex Differences in Physical, Verbal, and Indirect Aggression: A Review of Recent Research," *Sex Roles* 30, no. 314 (1994); K. M. J. Lagerspetz, K. Bjorkqvist, and T. Peltonen, "Is Indirect Aggression Typical of Females? Gender Differences in Aggressiveness in 11–12-Year-Old Children," *Aggressive Behavior* 14 (1988).

55. Bjorkqvist, "Sex Differences in Physical, Verbal, and Indirect Aggression."

56. For accounts of female-female aggression in the postfeminist era see Cheryl Dellasega's 2005 book *Mean Girls Grown Up,* and an essay by Laura Miller, "Women's Ways of Bullying," *Salon* (1997).

57. Executive coach Jean Holland's training session for women, called Bully Broads Boot Camp at the Growth and Leadership Center in Silicon Valley, attracted a lot of negative press when it was launched in 2001. It was touted as a career aid for "exceptional women who want to share and learn from each other," but many critics saw it as a way to whitewash the type of competitive aggression that put executive women into positions of power in the first place. Reviews of the program and a documentary film seized on the old chestnut that the same behavior

that would be accepted in men is considered unfeminine and bad form for women. "Ninety percent of the women who are sent to us are sent because they are exhibiting behavior that is intimidating and aggressive and scaring people. We are not teaching women to be less aggressive, we aren't asking them to change their message, just the way their message is communicated," a Growth and Leadership spokesperson told a reporter from *BBC News Online*. While many critics castigated the program and Hollands' subsequent book *Same Game, Different Rules* as yet another exhortation for women to become "adorable doormats," many of the behaviors targeted by the program would not be acceptable in men, either. See "Bitchy Bosses Go to Boot Camp," *BBC News Online*, 2001, and Robin Gerber, "Bully Broads," James MacGregor/Burns Academy of Leadership (2006). http://www.academy.umd.edu/AboutUs/news/articles/09–12–01.htm.

58. Mazur, *Biosociology of Dominance and Deference*.
59. Deborah Blum, *Sex on the Brain* (New York: Penguin, 1997).
60. Satoshi Kanazawa, "Why Productivity Fades with Age: The Crime-Genius Connection," *Journal of Research in Personality* 37 (2003).
61. Carlo Morselli and Pierre Tremblay, "Criminal Achievement, Offender Networks, and the Benefits of Low Self-Control," *Criminology* 42, no. 3 (2004).
62. Carlo Morselli and Marie-Noele Royer, "Criminal Mobility and Criminal Achievement" (paper presented at the Environmental Criminology and Crime Analysis Meeting, Chilliwack, B.C., July 2006); Carlo Morselli, Pierre Tremblay, and Bill McCarthy, "Mentors and Criminal Achievement," *Criminology* 11, no. 1 (2006).
63. Bryson, *A Short History of Nearly Everything*. John S. Rigden, *Einstein 1905: The Standard of Greatness* (Cambridge, Mass.: Harvard University Press, 2005), 43–46. Walter Isaacson, *Einstein: His Life and Universe* (New York: Simon & Schuster, 2007), 149–54.
64. Dean Keith Simonton, *Greatness: Who Makes History and Why* (New York: Guilford Press, 1994), 163.
65. As quoted in Morselli, et al (2004). Christopher Jencks, *Inequality: Who Gets Ahead? The Determinants of Economic Success in America* (New York: Basic Books, 1979).
66. Kevin Conley, "The Players," *New Yorker,* July 11 and 18, 2005.
67. In an article exploring the relationship of egotistical high self-esteem to aggression, social psychologist Roy Baumeister and his colleagues write the following passage about "self-enhancement" as a motive to seek out competition:

> The quest for opportunities to prove oneself or to raise one's standing should therefore appeal mainly to people with high self-esteem. For example, a pattern of seeking out situations in which one's worth is challenged or disputed might strike a very confident person as a good chance to refute such threats and show oneself off to be a winner. In contrast, people with low self-esteem will probably tend to avoid such situations. [Baumeister, Smart, and Boden, 1996, 8].

68. Daniel Olweus, "Bullying at School: Long-Term Outcomes for the Victims and an Effective School-Based Intervention Program," in *Aggressive Behavior: Current Perspectives,* ed. R. Huesmann (New York: Plenum, 1994).
69. Ehrlinger and Dunning, "How Chronic Self-Views Influence (and Potentially Mislead) Estimates of Performance."
70. Roy Baumeister et al., "Does High Self-Esteem Cause Better Performance, Interpersonal Success, Happiness, or Healthier Lifestyles?" *Psychological Science in the Public Interest* 4, no. 1 (2003).

71. Roy Baumeister, Laura Smart, and Joseph M. Boden, "Relation of Threatened Egotism to Violence and Aggression: The Dark Side of Self-Esteem," *Psychological Review* 103, no. 1 (1996).

72. Daniel J. Kruger and Randolph M. Nesse, "An Evolutionary Life-History Framework for Understanding Sex Differences in Human Mortality Rates," *Human Nature* 17, no. 1 (2006); Kruger and Nesse, "Sexual Selection and the Male:Female Mortality Ratio."

Brian A. Jonah, "Accident Risk and Risk-Taking Behavior among Young Drivers," *Accident Analysis and Prevention* 18 (1986).

73. A study of 4,500 male army veterans has shown that single and divorced men have higher testosterone levels than married men the same age (Mazur and Michalek, 1998). Higher testosterone levels cause aggressive behavior in animal studies, and are linked to criminal behavior and spousal abuse in adult men.

74. Christina Rouvalis, "Risk-Taking Can Be a Two-Faced Monster," *Pittsburgh Post-Gazette,* June 14, 2006.

75. Browne, *Biology at Work.*

76. U.K. National Statistics, "Injuries to Workers by Industry and Severity of Injury: Great Britain" (2004).

77. Browne, *Biology at Work, 53.*

78. In the July 21, 2006, issue of the *Economist,* an article on women in business estimated that 46.5 percent of the American workforce is female and 95 percent of senior managers are male. The ratio was quoted as the same in Britain and France.

79. According to a 2006 *Scientific American* article by Philip Ross, "The Expert Mind," a Hungarian educator named Laszlo Polgar set out to create chess champions of his three home-schooled daughters. He assigned six hours of chess-related practice a day, and produced one international master and two grand masters who are "the strongest chess-playing siblings in history," according to Ross. Polgar's youngest daughter, thirty-year-old Judit, is now ranked fourteenth in the world.

80. Marianne Frankenhaeuser et al., "Sex Differences in Psychoneuroendocrine Reactions to Examination Stress," *Psychosomatic Medicine* 40, no. 4 (1978).

Chapter 9: Turbocharged: Men with ADHD Who Succeed

1. Russell A. Barkley et al., "The Persistence of Attention Deficit/Hyperactivity Disorder into Young Adulthood as a Function of Reporting Source and Definition of the Disorder," *Journal of Abnormal Psychology* 111 (2002); Joseph Biederman, "Impact of Comorbidity in Adults with Attention Deficit/Hyperactivity Disorder," *Journal of Clinical Psychiatry* 65, no. 3 (2004); Ronald C. Kessler et al., "The Prevalence and Effects of Adult Attention Deficit/Hyperactivity Disorder on Work Performance in a Nationally Representative Sample of Workers," *Journal of Occupational and Environmental Medicine* 47, no. 6 (2005); S. Mannuzza et al., "Educational Achievement, Occupational Rank, and Psychiatric Status," *Archives of General Psychiatry* 50 (1993).

2. Joseph Biederman, "Attention-Deficit/Hyperactivity Disorder: A Selective Overview," *Biological Psychiatry* 57 (2005). Academic failure is one of the most common impairments of ADHD, but there is also a high likelihood of social problems in childhood, an increased rate of substance abuse in adolescence and adulthood, and frequent job changes.

3. Thomas E. Brown, "DSM IV: ADHD and Executive Function Impairments," *Advanced Studies in Medicine* 2, no. 25 (2002). Instead of simply an attentional disorder, Thomas Brown, the associate director of the Yale Clinic for Attention and Related Disorders, makes the case that ADHD is a lack of coordination of various cognitive abilities, including the ability to decide when to start and stop

activities and how to prioritize them. He compares a person with the disorder to an orchestra with fine musicians who have no conductor to organize them and create a total sound.

4. American Psychological Association, *Diagnostic and Statistical Manual of Mental Disorders: 4th Edition.* Joseph Biederman and S. V. Faraone, "Attention Deficit Hyperactivity Disorder," *The Lancet* 366 (2005).

How much impairment is caused by the symptoms of ADHD is an intriguing question. According to studies cited by Joseph Biederman and Stephen Faraone in a 2005 article in *The Lancet,* when the symptoms are tracked in the general population, the prevalence of the disorder is over 16 percent in the United States, Germany, and Australia (three countries where large epidemiological studies have been done). Narrowing the holes in the net by limiting the diagnosis to those with functional impairment (meaning the symptoms interfere with daily living) reduces the rate to 6.8 percent, still a high rate. But the question is not just about numbers. Children, who are unable to control their environments, are likely to be more impaired by their symptoms, one reason why there is a higher rate of diagnosis in children than in adults. Adults with countervailing skills and resources may design their environments to reduce the impact of their symptoms and therefore will be less severely affected by them.

5. Ronald C. Kessler et al., "The Prevalence and Correlates of Adult ADHD in the United States: Results from the National Comorbidity Survey Replication," *American Journal of Psychiatry* (2004); Timothy E. Wilens, Stephen V. Faraone, and Joseph Biederman, "Attention Deficit/Hyperactivity Disorder in Adults," *Journal of the American Medical Association* 292, no. 5 (2004).

6. Joseph Biederman et al., "Influence of Gender on Attention Deficit Hyperactivity Disorder in Children Referred to a Psychiatric Clinic," *American Journal of Psychiatry* 159, no. 1 (2002); Ronald C. Kessler et al., "The Epidemiology of Major Depressive Disorder: Results from the National Comorbidity Survey Replication (NCS-R)," *Journal of the American Medical Association* 289, no. 23 (2003).

7. G. F. Still, "The Coulstonian Lectures on Some Abnormal Physical Conditions in Children," *The Lancet* 1 (1902).

8. William Shakespeare, "*Second Part of King Henry IV: The Complete Works of Shakespeare*" (New York: Spring, 1976).

9. Carl G. Jung, *Man and His Symbols* (Garden City, N.Y.: Doubleday, 1964); Paul Radin, *The Trickster: A Study in American Indian Mythology* (N.Y.: Schocken, 1956).

10. A small sample of books that question the validity of the disorder: Thomas Armstrong, *The Myth of the ADD Child* (New York: Dutton, 1995); Peter Breggin, *Toxic Psychiatry* (Irvine, Calif.: Griffin, 1994); J. Reichenberg-Ullman and Robert Ullman, *Ritalin Free Kids* (Rocklin, Calif.: Prima, 1996).

11. Hershel Jick, James A. Kaye, and Corri Black, "Incidence and Prevalence of Drug-Treated Attention Deficit Disorder among Boys in the U.K.," *British Journal of General Practice* 54, 502 (2004).

12. Cordelia Rayner, "The ADHD Dilemma for Parents," *BBC News Online:* http://news.bbc.co.uk/go/pr/fr/-/2/hi/uk_news/education/6071216.stm (2006).

13. Florence Levy, David A. Hay, and Kellie S. Bennett, "Genetics of Attention Deficit Hyperactivity Disorder: A Current Review and Future Prospects," *International Journal of Disability, Development and Education* 53, no. 1 (2006).

14. M. Clikeman Semrud et al., "Attention-Deficit Hyperactivity Disorder: Magnetic Resonance Imaging Morphometric Analysis of the Corpus Callosum," *Journal of American Academy of Child and Adolescent Psychiatry* 33, no. 6 (1994).

15. F. X. Castellanos, "Approaching a Scientific Understanding of What Happens in

the Brain in ADHD," *Attention* 4, no. 1 (1997), 30–43; A.J. Zametkin and J. L. Rapoport, "Neurobiology of Attention Deficit Disorder with Hyperactivity: Where Have We Come in 50 Years," *Journal of American Academic Child and Adolescent Psychiatry* 26 (1987), 676–686.

16. Michael Rutter, *Genes and Behavior: Nature-Nurture Interplay Explained* (Malden, Mass.: Blackwell, 2006).

17. S.V. Faraone, Joseph Biederman, and D. Friedman, "Validity of DSM-IV Subtypes of Attention-Deficit/Hyperactivity Disorder: A Family Study Perspective," *Journal of the American Academy of Child and Adolescent Psychiatry* 39 (2000); Jeannette Wasserstein, Lorraine E. Wolf, and Frank F.Lefever, eds., *Adult Attention Deficit Disorder: Brain Mechanisms and Life Outcomes, Annals of the New York Academy of Sciences* 931 (New York: New York Academy of Sciences, 2001).

18. Biederman, "Attention-Deficit/Hyperactivity Disorder: A Selective Overview"; Levy, Hay, and Bennett, "Genetics of Attention Deficit Hyperactivity Disorder: A Current Review and Future Prospects"; Rutter, *Genes and Behavior: Nature-Nurture Interplay Explained.*

19. Benedict Carey, "Living on Impulse," *New York Times,* April 4, 2006.

20. Lois Gilman, "ADD in the Corner Office," in *Additudemag.com* (2004); Chris Woodyard, "Jet Blue Soars on CEO's Creativity," *USA Today,* October 8, 2002.

21. Kessler et al., "The Prevalence and Correlates of Adult ADHD in the United States."

22. Thomas Dohmen et al., "Individual Risk Attitudes: New Evidence from a Large Representative Experimentally Validated Survey" (Bonn: Institute for the Study of Labor, 2005).

23. Lynn Cherkas et al., "Is the Tendency to Engage in Self-Employment Genetic?" (London Business School: 2006).

24. Paul Orfalea and Ann Marsh, *Copy This! Lessons from a Hyperactive Dyslexic Who Turned a Bright Idea into One of America's Best Companies* (New York: Workman Publishing, 2005).

25. R. Ochse, *Before the Gates of Excellence: The Determinants of Creative Genius* (New York: Cambridge University Press, 1990). Simonton, *Greatness: Who Makes History and Why.*

26. William James, "Great Men, Great Thoughts, and the Environment," *Atlantic Monthly,* 1880, quoted in Simonton, 1994.

27. D. Goleman, P. Kaufman, and Michael Ray, *The Creative Spirit* (New York: Dutton, 1992).

28. Cecile A. Marczinski, "Self-Report of ADHD Symptoms in College Students and Repetition Effects," *Journal of Attention Disorders* 8, no. 4 (2005).

29. Gabrielle Weiss and Lily Trokenberg Hechtman, *Hyperactive Children Grown Up,* 2nd ed. (New York: Guilford, 1993), 147.

30. Lynne Lamberg, "ADHD Often Undiagnosed in Adults: Appropriate Treatment May Benefit Work, Family, Social Life," *Journal of the American Medical Association* 290, no. 12 (2003).

31. Weiss and Hechtman, *Hyperactive Children Grown Up,* 2nd ed.

32. The child ratios are from Biederman et al., "Influence of Gender on Attention Deficit Hyperactivity Disorder in Children Referred to a Psychiatric Clinic." The adult ratios are close to 60 percent male, 40 percent female, an estimate provided by Canadian ADHD expert Dr. Margaret Weiss in a telephone interview on November 18, 2005

33. Joseph Biederman et al., "Absence of Gender Effects on Attention Deficit Hyperactivity Disorder: Findings in Nonreferred Subjects," *American Journal of Psychiatry* 162, no. 6 (2005). An epidemiological survey of 9,282 American adults in the

general population completed by a research group associated with Ronald Kessler at the Harvard Medical School and the NIMH found that 62 percent of those with ADHD in the community were male and 38 percent were female: Kessler et al., "The Prevalence and Effects of Adult Attention Deficit/Hyperactivity Disorder on Work Performance in a Nationally Representative Sample of Workers"; Kessler et al., "The Prevalence and Correlates of Adult ADHD in the United States." Results from the National Comorbidity Survey Replication.

34. Joseph Biederman et al., "Gender Effects on Attention Deficit/Hyperactivity Disorder in Adults, Revisited," *Biological Psychiatry* 55 (2004); Biederman et al., "Absence of Gender Effects on Attention Deficit Hyperactivity Disorder"; Biederman et al., "Influence of Gender on Attention Deficit Hyperactivity Disorder in Children Referred to a Psychiatric Clinic."

Chapter 10: Things Are Not What They Seem

1. Fratiglioni, Paillard-Borg, and Winblad, "An Active and Socially Integrated Lifestyle in Late Life Might Protect against Dementia"; Fratiglioni et al., "Influence of Social Network on Occurrence of Dementia: A Community Based Longitudinal Study"; C. Schwartz, J. B. Meisenhelder, Y. Ma, and G. Reed, "Altruistic Social Interest Behaviors Are Associated with Better Mental Health," *Psychosomatic Medicine* 65, no. 5 (2003), 778–785.

2. Hakim, *Work-Lifestyle Choices in the 21st Century*. Goldin, "From the Valley to the Summit: The Quiet Revolution That Transformed Women's Employment, Education, and Family."

3. Research by Andrew Beveridge, a demographer and sociologist at Queen's College in New York, shows that women under thirty in many American urban centers earn as much as 120 percent of men's wages in those locales. Sam Roberts, "Young Earners in Big City, a Gap in Women's Favor," *New York Times*, August 3, 2007.

4. The difficulty that many "opt-out" women have when making the transition back to work is described in Sylvia Ann Hewlett's *Off-Ramps and On-Ramps*. According to her surveys, 93 percent of "off-ramped" women want to return to paid work. Only 74 percent manage to, and only 40 percent return to full-time, mainstream jobs. The rest end up taking part-time jobs or seeking self-employment. Sylvia Ann Hewlett, *Off-Ramps and On-Ramps: Keeping Talented Women on the Road to Success* (Boston: Harvard Business School Press, 2007).

5. David Maister, *True Professionalism: The Courage to Care About Your People, Your Clients, and Your Career* (New York: Touchstone, 1997).

6. For more information on the National Science Foundation's awards for girls and women, see the Research on Gender in Science and Engineering (GSE) page on its website http://www.nsf.gov/funding/pgm_summ.jsp?pims_id=5475&org=NSF&sel_org=NSF&from=fund. Since 1993, the GSE (formerly called the Program for Women and Girls, or PWG) has set aside $10 million a year for girls' science and engineering education in their kindergarten though high school years. Another $20 million a year was added in 2001 to promote women in academic science and engineering careers through ADVANCE (Increasing the Participation and Advancement of Women in Academic Science and Engineering Careers: http://www.nsf.gov/funding/pgm_summ.jsp?pims_id=5383&from=fund).

7. Judith Kleinfeld, "The Morella Bill, My Daughter Rachel, and the Advancement of Women in Science," *Academic Questions* 12, no. 1 (1999); Lynette Long, *Math Smarts: Tips, Tricks, and Secrets for Making Math More Fun! American Girl Library* (Middleton, Wis.: Pleasant, 2004).

BIBLIOGRAPHY

Abramson, Jill, and Barbara Franklin. *Where Are They Now: The Story of the Women of Harvard Law*. New York: Doubleday, 1986.

Abramson, L. Y., Martin E. P. Seligman, and J. Teasdale. "Learned Helplessness in Humans." *Journal of Abnormal Psychology* 87 (1978): 49–74.

Alper, Joe. "The Pipeline Is Leaking Women All the Way Along." *Science* 260 (1993): 409–11.

Altman, Lawrence K. "Her Job: Helping Save the World from Bird Flu." *The New York Times,* August 9, 2005.

American Institute of Physics. "Percentages of Physics Degrees Awarded to Women in Selected Countries, 1997 and 1998 (2 Year Averages)." International Study of Women in Physics, 2001.

American Psychiatric Association. *Diagnostic and Statistical Manual of Mental Disorders,* 4th ed. Washington, D.C.: American Psychiatric Association, 1994.

Anderson, K. G. "Gender Bias and Special Education Referrals." *Annals of Dyslexia* 47 (1997): 151–62.

Asher, Jules. 2006. Gene Linked to Autism in Families with More Than One Affected Child. In National Institute of Mental Health, http://www.nimh.nih.gove/press/autismmetgene.cfm. (accessed October 18, 2006).

Babcock, Linda, and Sara Laschever. *Women Don't Ask: Negotiation and the Gender Divide*. Princeton, N.J.: Princeton University Press, 2003.

Baerlocher, Mark O., and Allan S. Detsky. "Are Applicants to Canadian Residency Programs Rejected Because of Their Sex?," *Canadian Medical Association Journal* 173, no. 12 (2005).

Baider, Lea. "Gender Disparities and Cancer." Paper presented at the American Society of Clinical Oncology, Orlando, Fla., May, 2005.

Barinaga, Marcia. "Surprises across the Cultural Divide." *Science* 263 (1994).

Barkley, Russell A., M. Fischer, L. Smallish, and K. Fletcher. "The Persistence of Attention Deficit/Hyperactivity Disorder into Young Adulthood as a Function of Reporting Source and Definition of the Disorder." *Journal of Abnormal Psychology* 111 (2002): 279–89.

Baron-Cohen, Simon. "Autism Occurs More Often in Families of Physicists, Engineers, and Mathematicians." *Autism* 2 (1998): 296–301.

———. *The Essential Difference: The Truth About the Male and Female Brain*. New York: Basic Books, 2003.

———, "Is There a Link between Engineering and Autism?" *Autism* 1 (1997): 153–63.

———. *Mindblindness: An Essay on Autism and Theory of Mind*. Cambridge, Mass.: MIT Press, Bradford Books, 1995.

————. "Sex Differences in Mind: Keeping Science Distinct from Social Policy." In *Why Aren't More Women in Science?*, edited by Stephen J. Ceci and Christine L. Williams. Washington, D.C.: American Psychological Association, 2007.

————. "Two New Theories of Autism: Hyper-Systemising and Assortative Mating." *Archives of Disease in Childhood* 91 (2006): 2–5.

Baron-Cohen, Simon, Svetlana Lutchmaya, and Rebecca Knickmeyer. *Prenatal Testosterone in Mind: Amniotic Fluid Studies.* Cambridge, Mass.: MIT Press, 2004.

Baron-Cohen, Simon, and Sally Wheelwright. "The Empathy Quotient: An Investigation of Adults with Asperger Syndrome or High Functioning Autism, and Normal Sex Differences." *Journal of Autism and Developmental Disorders* 34, no. 2 (2004): 163–75.

Baron-Cohen, Simon, Sally Wheelwright, Valerie Stone, and Melissa Rutherford. "A Mathematician, a Physicist, and a Computer Scientist with Asperger Syndrome: Performance on Folk Psychology and Folk Physics Tests." *Neurocase* 5 (1999): 475–83.

Barr, Cathy L., and Jillian M. Couto. "Molecular Genetics of Reading." In *Single Word Reading: Cognitive, Behavioral and Biological Perspectives,* edited by E. L. Grigorenko and A. Naples. Mahwah, N.J.: Lawrence Erlbaum Associates, in press.

Bartels, Andreas, and Semir Zeki. "The Neural Correlates of Maternal and Romantic Love." *Neuroimage* 21 (2004): 1155–66.

Bartky, Sandra Lee. "Feeding Egos and Tending Wounds: Deference and Disaffection in Women's Emotional Labour." In *Femininity and Domination: Studies in Teh Phenomenology of Oppression,* 99–119. New York: Routledge, 1990.

Baum, Sandy, and Eban Goodstein. "Gender Imbalance in College Applications: Does It Lead to a Preference for Men in the Admissions Process?" *Economics of Education Review* 24, no. 6 (2005): 611–704.

Baumeister, Roy, Jennifer D. Campbell, Joachim I. Krueger, and Kathleen D. Vohs. "Does High Self-Esteem Cause Better Performance, Interpersonal Success, Happiness, or Healthier Lifestyles?" *Psychological Science in the Public Interest* 4, no. 1 (2003).

Baumeister, Roy, Laura Smart, and Joseph M. Boden. "Relation of Threatened Egotism to Violence and Aggression: The Dark Side of Self-Esteem." *Psychological Review* 103, no. 1 (1996): 5–33.

Baumeister, Roy, and K. L. Sommer. "What Do Men Want? Gender Differences in Two Spheres of Belongingness: Comment on Cross and Madson." *Psychological Bulletin* 122 (1997): 38–44.

Bauza, Margarita. "Boys Fall Behind Girls in Grades." *The Detroit News,* January 9, 2005.

Bazelon, Emily. "What Are Autistic Girls Made Of?" *New York Times Magazine,* August 5, 2007.

Bear, Harold, Frances Lovejoy, and Ann Daniel. "How Working Parents Cope with the Care of Sick Young Children." *Australian Journal of Early Childhood* 28, no. 4 (2003): 53–57.

Beck, A. T. "Cognitive Models of Depression." *Journal of Cognitive Psychotherapy: An International Quarterly* 1, no. 5–37 (1987).

Becker, S. W., and Alice Eagly. "The Heroism of Women and Men." *American Psychologist* 59 (2004): 163–78.

Belle, D. "Gender Differences in the Social Moderators of Stress." In *Gender and Stress,* edited by R. C. Barnett, L. Biener, and G. K. Baruch, 257–77. New York: Free Press, 1987.

Bennett, Drake. "The Evolutionary Revolutionary." *Boston Globe,* March 27, 2005.

Berenbaum, Sheri A., and Susan M. Resnick. "Early Androgen Effects on Aggression in Children and Adults with Congenital Adrenal Hyperplasia." *Psychoneuroendocrinology* 22 (1997): 505–15.

———. "The Seeds of Career Choices: Prenatal Sex Hormone Effects on Psychological Sex Differences." In *Why Aren't More Women in Science?*, edited by Stephen J. Ceci and Wendy M. Williams, 147–57. Washington, D.C.: American Psychological Association, 2007.

Berliner, Wendy. "Where Have All the Young Men Gone?" *The Guardian*, May 18, 2004.

Bertrand, Marianne, and Kevin F. Hallock. "The Gender Gap in Top Corporate Jobs." *Industrial and Labor Relations Review* 55 (2001): 3–21.

Biederman, Joseph. "Attention-Deficit/Hyperactivity Disorder: A Selective Overview." *Biological Psychiatry* 57 (2005): 1215–120.

———. "Impact of Comorbidity in Adults with Attention Deficit/Hyperactivity Disorder." *Journal of Clinical Psychiatry* 65, no. 3 (2004): 3–7.

Biederman, Joseph, Anne Kwon, B. A. Aleardi, Virginie-Anne Chouinard, Teresa Marino, Heather Cole, Eric Mick, and S. V. Faraone. "Absence of Gender Effects on Attention Deficit Hyperactivity Disorder: Findings in Nonreferred Subjects." *American Journal of Psychiatry* 162, no. 6 (2005): 1083–89.

Biederman, Joseph, and S. V. Faraone. "Attention Deficit Hyperactivity Disorder." *Lancet* 366 (2005): 237–48.

Biederman, Joseph, S. V. Faraone, M. C. Monuteaux, Marie Bober, and Elizabeth Cadogen. "Gender Effects on Attention Deficit/Hyperactivity Disorder in Adults, Revisited." *Biological Psychiatry* 55 (2004): 692–700.

Biederman, Joseph, Eric Mick, Stephen V. Faraone, Ellen Braaten, Alysa Doyle, Thomas Spencer, Timothy E. Wilens, Elizabeth Frazier, and Mary Ann Johnson. "Influence of Gender on Attention Deficit Hyperactivity Disorder in Children Referred to a Psychiatric Clinic." *American Journal of Psychiatry* 159, no. 1 (2002): 36–42.

Bjorkqvist, Kaj. "Sex Differences in Physical, Verbal, and Indirect Aggression: A Review of Recent Research." *Sex Roles* 30, no. 314 (1994).

Blakeslee, Sandra. "Focus Narrows in Search for Autism's Cause." *New York Times*, February 8, 2005.

Blum, Deborah. *Sex on the Brain*. New York: Penguin, 1997.

Bokemeier, J., and P. Blanton. "Job Values, Rewards, and Work Conditions as Factors in Job Satisfaction among Men and Women." *Sociological Quarterly* 28 (1986): 189–204.

Bolton, P., H. Macdonald, A. Pickles, P. Rios, S. Goodes, M. Crowson, A. Bailey, and M. Rutter. "A Case-Control Family History Study of Autism." *Journal of Child Psychology and Psychiatry* 35, no. 5 (1994): 877–900.

Bowles, Hannah Riley, Linda Babcock, and Lei Lai. 2005. "It Depends Who Is Asking and Who You Ask: Social Incentives for Sex Differences in the Propensity to Initiate Negotiation." In Social Science Research Network, http://ssrn.com/abstract=779506 (accessed 2005).

Bribiescas, Richard G. *Men: Evolutionary and Life History*. Cambridge, Mass.: Harvard University Press, 2006.

Britz, Jennifer Delahunty. "To All the Girls I've Rejected." *The New York Times*, March 23, 2006.

Brizendine, Louann. *The Female Brain*. New York: Morgan Road, 2006.

Brody, Jane E. "Easing the Trauma for the Tiniest in Intensive Care." *The New York Times*, June 27, 2006.

———. "For Babies, an Ounce Can Alter Quality of Life." *New York Times*, October 1, 1991.

Brooks, David. "All Politics Are Thymotic." *New York Times,* March 16, 2006.

Brophy, J. E., and T. L. Good. "Teachers' Communication of Differential Expectations for Children's Classroom Performance: Some Behavioral Data." *Journal of Educational Psychology* 61 (1970): 365–74.

Brothwood, M., Dieter Wolke, H. Gamsu, J. Benson, and D. Cooper. "Prognosis of the Very Low Birthweight Baby in Relation to Gender." *Archives of Disease in Childhood* 61 (1986): 559–64.

Brown, Thomas E. "DSM IV: ADHD and Executive Function Impairments." *Advanced Studies in Medicine* 2, no. 25 (2002): 910–14.

Browne, Kingsley R. *Biology at Work: Rethinking Sexual Equality.* New Brunswick, N.J.: Rutgers University Press, 2002.

———. "Evolved Sex Differences and Occupational Segregation." *Journal of Organizational Behavior* 26 (2005): 1–20.

———. "Women in Science: Biological Factors Should Not Be Ignored." *Cardozo Women's Law Journal* 11 (2005): 509–28.

Bryson, Bill. *The Life and Times of the Thunderbolt Kid.* Toronto: Doubleday, 2006.

———. *A Short History of Nearly Everything.* Toronto, Canada: Doubleday Canada, 2003.

Buford, Bill. *Heat (An Amateur's Adventures as Kitchen Slave, Line Cook, Pasta Maker, and Apprentice to a Dante-Quoting Butcher in Tuscany).* Toronto: Doubleday, 2006.

Burbank, V. "Female Aggression in Cross-Cultural Perspective." *Behavior Science Research* 21 (1987): 70–100.

Burke, Ronald J., and Carol A. McKeen. "Gender Effects in Mentoring Relationships." *Journal of Social Behavior and Personality* 11, no. 5 (1996): 91–105.

Buss, David M. "Sex Differences in Human Mate Preferences: Evolutionary Hypothesis Tested in 37 Cultures." *Behavioral and Brain Sciences* 12 (1989): 1–49.

Buss, David M., Todd K. Shackelford, Lee A. Kirkpatrick, and Randy J. Larsen. "A Half Century of Mate Preferences: The Cultural Evolution of Values." *Journal of Marriage and Family* 63 (2001): 491–503.

Byrnes, James P., David C. Miller, and William D. Shafer. "Gender Differences in Risk Taking: A Meta-Analysis." *Psychological Bulletin* 125, no. 3 (1999): 367–83.

Campbell, Anne. *A Mind of Her Own: The Evolutionary Psychology of Women.* Oxford, U.K.: Oxford University Press, 2002.

Campbell, R., K. Elgar, J. Kuntsi, R. Akers, J. Terstegge, M. Coleman, and D. Skuse. "The Classification of 'Fear' from Faces Is Associated with Face Recognition Skill in Women." *Neuropsychologia* 40 (2002): 575–84.

Canada Statistics. "The Gap in Achievement between Boys and Girls." In *Education Matters,* http://www.statcan.ca/english/freepub/81–004-XIE/200410/mafe.htm (2004) (accessed March 9, 2006).

Cardon, L. R., S. D. Smith, D. W. Fulker, W. J. Kimberling, B. G. Pennington, and J. C. DeFries. "Quantitative Trait Locus for Reading Disability on Chromosome 6." *Science* 266 (1994): 276–79.

Carey, Benedict. "Living on Impulse." *New York Times,* April 4, 2006.

———. "Message from Mouse to Mouse: I Feel Your Pain." *New York Times,* July 4, 2006.

Carlo, Gustavo, A. Hausmann, S. Christiansen, and B. A. Randall. "Sociocognitive and Behavioral Correlates of a Measure of Prosocial Tendencies for Adolescents." *Journal of Early Adolescence* 23 (2003): 107–34.

Carter, Sue C. "Developmental Consequences of Oxytocin." *Physiology and Behavior* 79 (2003): 383–97.

———. "Monogamy, Motherhood and Health." In *Altruism and Health,* edited by Stephen G. Post. New York: Oxford University Press, 2007.

Cashdan, Elizabeth. "Are Men More Competitive Than Women?" *British Journal of Social Psychology* 37 (1998): 213–29.

———. "Hormones and Competitive Aggression in Women." *Aggressive Behavior* 29 (2003): 107–15.

———. "Hormones, Sex, and Status in Women." *Hormones and Behavior* 29 (1995): 354–66.

Castellanos, F. X. "Approaching a Scientific Understanding of What Happens in the Brain in ADHD." *Attention* 4, no. 1 (1997): 30–43.

Chang, Kenneth. "Journeys to the Distant Fields of Prime." *New York Times,* March 13, 2007.

———. "Women in Physics Match Men in Success." *New York Times,* February 22, 2005.

Chapman, Emma, Simon Baron-Cohen, Bonnie Auyeung, Rebecca Knickmeyer, Kevin Taylor, and Gerald Hackett. "Fetal Testosterone and Empathy: Evidence from the Empathy Quotient (Eq) and the 'Reading the Mind in the Eyes' Test." (2006).

Charlesworth, William R., and Claire Dzur. "Gender Comparisons of Preschoolers' Behavior and Resource Utilization in Group Problem-Solving." *Child Development* 58, no. 1 (1987): 191–200.

Cheng, Yawen, Ichiro Kawachi, Joel Schwartz, and Graham Colditz. "Association between Psychosocial Work Characteristics and Health Functioning in American Women." *British Medical Journal* 320 (2000): 1432–36.

Cherkas, Lynn, J. Hunkin, T. Spector, N. Nicolaou, and Scott Shane. "Is the Tendency to Engage in Self-Employment Genetic?" London Business School, 2006.

Chiu, Charlotte. "Do Professional Women Have Lower Job Satisfaction Than Professional Men? Lawyers as a Case Study." *Sex Roles: A Journal of Research* (April 1998).

Christensen, J., M. J. Kjeldsen, H. Anderson, M. L. Friis, and P. Sidenius. "Gender Differences in Epilepsy." *Epilepsia* 46, no. 6 (2005): 956–60.

Christmas, Brian. "Half of British Fathers Not Taking Full Paternity Leave." *Globe and Mail,* August 2, 2006.

Clance, Pauline Rose, and Suzanne Ament Imes. "The Imposter Phenomenon in High-Achieving Women: Dynamics and Therapeutic Intervention." *Psychotherapy: Theory, Research, and Practice* 15, no. 3 (1978).

Cole, Jonathan R., and Harriet Zuckerman. "The Productivity Puzzle: Persistence and Change in Patterns of Publication of Men and Women Scientists." *Advances in Motivation and Achievement* 2 (1984): 217–58.

Coney, J. "Lateral Asymmetry in Phonological Processing: Relating Behavioral Measures to Neuroimaged Structures." *Brain and Language* 80 (2002): 355–65.

Conley, Kevin. "The Players." *New Yorker* (July 11 and 18, 2005), 52–58.

Connellan, Jennifer, Simon Baron-Cohen, Sally Wheelwright, Anna Batki, and Jag Ahluwalia. "Sex Differences in Human Neonatal Social Perception." *Infant Behavior and Development* 23 (2000): 113–18.

Coté, S., Richard Tremblay, Daniel Nagin, Mark Zoccolillo, and Frank Vitaro. "The Development of Impulsivity, Fearfulness, and Helpfulness during Childhood: Patterns of Consistency and Change in the Trajectories of Boys and Girls." *Journal of Child Psychology and Psychiatry* 43 (2002): 609–18.

Coupland, Douglas. *Terry.* Toronto: Douglas & McIntyre, 2005.

Creswell, Julie. "How Suite It Isn't: A Dearth of Female Bosses." *New York Times,* December 17, 2006.

Critchley, Macdonald. *The Dyslexic Child.* Springfield, Ill.: Charles C. Thomas, 1970.

Dabbs, James McBride, and Mary Godwin Dabbs. *Heroes, Rogues, and Lovers: Testosterone and Behavior.* New York: McGraw-Hill, 2000.

Daly, Martin, and Margo Wilson. *Homicide.* New York: Aldine de Gruyter, 1988.

————. *Sex, Evolution, and Behavior.* 2nd ed. Boston: Willard Grant, 1983.

De Vries, A. C., M. B. DeVries, S.E. Taymans, and Sue C. Carter. "Stress Has Sexually Dimorphic Effects on Pair Bonding in Prairie Voles." *Proceedings of the National Academy of Science* 93 (1996): 11980–84.

Dean, Cornelia. "Computer Science Takes Steps to Bring Women to the Fold." *New York Times,* April 17, 2007.

Deary, Ian J., Graham Thorpe, Valerie Wilson, John M. Starr, and Lawrence Whalley. "Population Sex Differences in IQ at Age 11: The Scottish Mental Survey 1932." *Intelligence* 31 (2003): 533–42.

DeFries, J. C., Maricela Alarcon, and Richard K. Olson. "Genetic Aetiologies of Reading and Spelling Deficits: Developmental Differences." In *Dyslexia: Biology, Cognition and Intervention,* edited by Charles Hulme and Margaret Snowling. San Diego: Singular, 1997.

DeLeire, Thomas, and Helen Levy. "Gender, Occupation Choice and the Risk of Death at Work." National Bureau of Economic Research, 2001.

De Waal, Frans. *Our Inner Ape.* New York: Riverhead, 2005.

Dinovitzer, Ronit. "After the J.D.: First Results of a National Study of Legal Careers." The NALP Foundation for Law Career Research and Education and the American Bar Foundation, 2004.

Dobbs, David. "The Gregarious Brain." *New York Times,* July 8 2007.

Dobson, Roger. "If You Don't Understand Women's Emotions, You Must Be a Man." *Independent on Sunday,* June 5, 2005 2005.

Dohmen, Thomas, Armin Falk, David Huffman, Uwe Sunde, Jurgen Schupp, and Gert G. Wagner. "Individual Risk Attitudes: New Evidence from a Large Representative Experimentally Validated Survey." Bonn: Institute for the Study of Labor, 2005.

Domes, Gregor, Markus Heinrichs, Andre Michel, Chrstoph Berger, and Sabine Herpetz. "Oxytocin Improves 'Mind-Reading' in Humans." *Biological Psychiatry* (2006).

Dominus, Susan. "A Girly-Girl Joins the Sesame Boys." *New York Times,* August 6, 2006.

Duckworth, Angela Lee, and Martin E. P. Seligman. "Self-Discipline Gives Girls the Edge: Gender in Self-Discipline, Grades, and Achievement Test Scores." *Journal of Educational Psychology* 98, no. 1 (2006).

Dunning, David, Chip Heath, and Jerry Suls. "Flawed Self-Assessment." *Psychological Science in the Public Interest* 5, no. 3 (2004): 69–106.

Dweck, Carol S., and Ellen S. Bush. "Sex Differences in Learned Helplessness." *Developmental Psychology* 12, no. 2 (1976): 147–56.

Eagly, Alice, and M. Crowley. "Gender and Helping Behavior: A Meta-analytic Review of the Social Psychological Literature." *Psychological Bulletin* 100 (1986): 283–308.

Eagly, Alice, and S. J. Karau. "Gender and the Emergence of Leaders: A Meta-analysis." *Journal of Personality and Social Psychology* 60 (1991), 685–710.

Eagly, Alice H., Wendy Wood, and Mary C. Johannesen-Schmidt. "Social Role Theory of Sex Differences and Similarities: Implications for the Partner Preferences of Women and Men." In *The Psychology of Gender,* 2nd ed., edited by Alice Eagly, Anne E. Beall, and Robert J. Sternberg, 269–91. New York: Guilford, 2004.

Ehrlinger, Joyce, and David Dunning. "How Chronic Self-Views Influence (and Potentially Mislead) Estimates of Performance." *Journal of Personality and Social Psychology* 84, no. 1 (2003): 5–17.

Eisenberg, Nancy, Richard A. Fabes, Gustavo Carlo, A. L. Speer, G. Switzer, and M. Karbon. "The Relations of Empathy-Related Emotions and Maternal Practices to Children's Comforting Behavior." *Journal of Experimental Child Psychology* 55 (1993): 131–50.

Eisenberg, Nancy, Richard A. Fabes, Mark Schiller, Paul Miller, Gustavo Carlo, Rick Poulin, Cindy Shea, and Rita Shell. "Personality and Socialization Correlates of Vicarious Emotional Responding." *Journal of Personality and Social Psychology* 61, no. 3 (1991): 459–70.

Eisenberg, Nancy, Richard Fabes, A., and Tracy L. Spinard. "Prosocial Development." In *Handbook of Child Psychology: Social, Emotional, and Personality Development,* edited by William Damon, Richard Lerner, and Nancy Eisenberg. Hoboken, N.J.: John Wiley & Sons, 2006.

Erwin, R. J., R. C. Gur, R. E. Gur, B. Skolnick, M. Mawhinney-hee, and J. Smailis. "Facial Emotion Discrimination." *Psychiatry Research* 42, no. 3 (1992): 231–40.

Etcoff, Nancy. *Survival of the Prettiest: The Science of Beauty.* New York: Doubleday, 1999.

Evans, John J. "Oxytocin in the Human: Regulation of Derivations and Destinations." *European Journal of Endocrinology* 137 (1997): 559–71.

Fadiman, Anne. *The Spirit Catches You and You Fall Down.* New York: Noonday, 1997.

Faraone, S. V., Joseph Biederman, and D. Friedman. "Validity of DSM-IV Subtypes of Attention-Deficit/Hyperactivity Disorder: A Family Study Perspective." *Journal of the American Academy of Child and Adolescent Psychiatry* 39 (2000): 469–76.

Feingold, Alan. "Gender Differences in Personality: A Meta-analysis." *Psychological Bulletin* 116, no. 3 (1994): 429–56.

Feldberg, R., and E. Glenn. "Male and Female: Job Versus Gender Models in Sociology of Work." In *Women and Work,* edited by R. Kahn-Hut, A. Daniels, and R. Colvard, 65–80. Oxford, U.K.: Oxford University Press, 1982.

Feldman, E., B. E. Levin, B. Fleischmann, B. Jallad, A. Kushch, K. Gross-Glenn, M. Rabin, and H. A. Lubs. "Gender Differences in the Severity of Adult Familial Dyslexia." *Reading and Writing* 7, no. 2 (1995): 155–61.

Feminist Research Center. Empowering Women in Business. In Feminist Majority Foundation, http://www.feminist.org/research/business/ewb_toc.html (2007) (accessed March 30, 2007).

Fink, Rosalie. "Gender and Imagination: Gender Conceptualization and Literacy Development in Successful Adults with Reading Disabilities." *Learning Disabilities* 10, no. 3 (2000): 183–96.

———. "Literacy Development in Successful Men and Women with Dyslexia." *Annals of Dyslexia* 48 (1998): 311–46.

———. "Successful Careers: The Secrets of Adults with Dyslexia." *Career Planning and Adult Development Journal* (Spring 2002): 118–29.

Finucci, J. M., and B. Childs. "Are There Really More Dyslexic Boys Than Girls?" In *Sex Differences in Dyslexia,* edited by A. Ansara, N. Geschwind, A. M. Galaburda, and M. Gartrell. Towson, Md.: Orton Dyslexia Society, 1981.

Fisher, Helen. *The First Sex.* New York: Ballantine Books, 1999.

Frankenhaeuser, Marianne. "Challenge-Control Interaction as Reflected in Sympathetic-Adrenal and Pituitary-Adrenal Activity: Comparison between the Sexes." *Scandinavian Journal of Psychology* 23, no. 1 (1982): 158–64.

Frankenhaeuser, Marianne, Maijaliisa Rauste von Wright, Aila Collins, Johan von Wright, Goran Sedvall, and Carl-Gunnar Swahn. "Sex Differences in Psychoneuroendocrine Reactions to Examination Stress." *Psychosomatic Medicine* 40, no. 4 (1978): 334–42.

Fratiglioni, L., S. Paillard-Borg, and B. Winblad. "An Active and Socially Integrated Lifestyle in Late Life Might Protect against Dementia." *Lancet Neruology* (2004): 343–53.

Fratiglioni, L., H. Wang, K. Ericsson, M. Maytan, and B. Winblad. "Influence of Social Network on Occurrence of Dementia: A Community Based Longitudinal Study." *Lancet* 355, no. 9212 (2004): 1315–19.

Frith, Uta. *Autism: Explaining the Enigma*. Cambridge, Mass.: Blackwell, 1989.

———. "Brain, Mind, and Behavior in Dyslexia." In *Dyslexia: Biology, Cognition and Intervention*, edited by Charles Hulme and Margaret Snowling. San Diego: Singular Publishing Group, 1997.

Frith, Uta, and Faraneh Vargha-Khadem. "Are There Sex Differences in the Brain Basis of Literacy Related Skills? Evidence from Reading and Spelling Impairments after Early Unilateral Brain Damage." *Neuropsychologia* 39 (2001): 1485–88.

Gabis, Lidia, John Pomeroy, and Mary R. Andriola. "Autism and Epilepsy: Cause, Consequence, Comorbidity, or Coincidence?" *Epilepsy & Behavior* 7 (2005): 652–56.

Galaburda, A. M. *Dyslexia and Development: Neurobiological Aspects of Extraordinary Brains*. Cambridge, Mass.: Harvard University Press, 1993.

Galaburda, A. M., Joseph LoTurco, Franck Ramus, R. Holly Fitch, and Glenn Rosen. "From Genes to Behavior in Developmental Dyslexia." *Nature Neuroscience* 9, no. 10 (2006): 1213–17.

Galaburda, A. M., G. Sherman, G. Rosen, F. Aboitiz, and N. Geschwind. "Developmental Dyslexia: Four Consecutive Cases with Cortical Abnormalities." *Annals of Neurology* 18 (1985): 222–33.

Garcia-Retamero, Rocio. "Prejudice against Women in Male Congenial Environments: Perceptions of Gender Role Congruity in Leadership." *Sex Roles* 55 (2006): 51–61.

Garibaldi, Gerry. "How the Schools Shortchange Boys: In the Newly Feminized Classroom, Boys Tune Out." *City Journal,* 2006.

Gati, I., S. H. Osipow, and M. Givon. "Gender Differences in Career Decision-Making: The Content and Structure of Preferences." *Journal of Counseling Psychology* 42 (1995): 204–16.

Geary, David C. *Male, Female: The Evolution of Human Sex Differences*. Washington, D.C.: American Psychological Association, 1998.

Gerhard, Sonnert, and Gerald Holton. "Career Patterns of Women and Men in the Sciences." *American Scientist* 84, no. 1 (1996): 63–79.

Gerstein, Josh. "Kenyon's Policy against Women Stirs a Debate." *New York Sun,* March 28, 2006.

Ghaziuddin, Mohammad. "A Family History of Asperger Syndrome." *Journal of Autism and Developmental Disorders* 35, no. 2 (2005): 177–82.

Gilger, Jeffrey W., George W. Hynd, and Mike Wilkins. "Neurodevelopmental Variation as a Framework for Thinking About the Twice Exceptional," in press (2007).

Gilligan, Carol. *In a Different Voice*. Cambridge, Mass.: Harvard University Press, 1982.

Gilman, Lois. "Add in the Corner Office." In *Additudemag.com,* 2004.

Gingras, Y., and Jeffrey Bowlby. "The Costs of Dropping Out of High School." Ottawa: Human Resources Development Canada, 2000.

Girgus, Joan S., and Susan Nolen-Hoeksema. "Cognition and Depression." In *Women and Depression,* edited by Corey L. M. Keyes and Sherryl H. Goodman. New York: Cambridge University Press, 2006.

Gjonca, Arjan, Cecilia Tomassini, and James W. Vaupel. "Male-Female Differences in Mortality in the Developed World." Max-Planck Institute for Demographic Research, 1999.

Gladwell, Malcolm. "The Sporting Scene." *New Yorker,* September 10, 2001.

Glass, Thomas, Carlos Mendes de Leon, Richard Marottoli, and Lisa F. Berkman. "Population-Based Study of Social and Productive Activities as Predictors of Survival among Elderly Americans." *British Medical Journal* (1999).

Gneezy, Uri, and Aldo Rustichini. "Gender and Competition at a Young Age." *American Economic Review* 94, no. 2 (2004): 377–84.

Goldenfeld, Nigel, Simon Baron-Cohen, and Sally Wheelwright. "Empathizing and Systemizing in Males, Females, and Autism." *Clinical Neuropsychiatry* 2, no. 6 (2005).

Goldin, Claudia. "From the Valley to the Summit: The Quiet Revolution That Transformed Women's Employment, Education, and Family." In American Economic Association Meeting. Boston, 2004.

———. *Understanding the Gender Gap: An Economic History of American Women.* New York: Oxford University Press, 1990.

Goldin, Claudia, Lawrence F. Katz, and Ilyana Kuziemko. "The Homecoming of American College Women: The Reversal of the College Gender Gap." Cambridge, Mass.: National Bureau of Economic Research, 2006.

Goldstein, Jill M., David N. Kennedy, and V. S. Caviness. "Brain Development, Xi, Sexual Dimorphism." *American Journal of Psychiatry* 156, no. 3 (1999): 352.

Goleman, D., and P. Kaufman. "The Art of Creativity." *Psychology Today* (March 1992).

Goleman, D., P. Kaufman, and Michael Ray. *The Creative Spirit.* New York: Dutton, 1992.

Goodman, Allegra. *Intuition.* New York: Dial, 2006.

Goodman, Ellen. "Of Pensions and Pacifiers." *Gazette,* January 26, 2005.

Gross, Jane. "Forget the Career: My Parents Need Me at Home." *New York Times,* November 24, 2005.

Grouzet, Frederick M. E., Tim Kasser, Aaron Ahuvia, et al. "Goal Contents across Cultures." *Journal of Personality and Social Psychology* 89 (2005).

Gur, Ruben C., and Raquel E. Gur. "Neural Substrates for Sex Differences in Cognition." In *Why Aren't More Women in Science?* edited by Stephen J. Ceci and Wendy M. Williams, 189–98. Washington, D.C.: American Psychological Association, 2007.

Hack, Maureen, Mark Schluchter, Lydia Carter, Mahboob Rahman, Leona Cuttler, and Elaine Borawski. "Growth of Very Low Birthweight Infants to Age 20 Years." *Pediatrics* 112, no. 1 (2003): e30-e38.

Hadamard, J. *The Psychology of Invention in the Mathematical Field.* Princeton, N.J.: Princeton University Press, 1949.

Hagan, John, and Fiona Kay. *Gender in Practice: A Study in Lawyers' Lives.* New York: Oxford University Press, 1995.

Hakim, Catherine. "A New Approach to Explaining Fertility Patterns: Preference Theory." *Population and Development Review* 29, no. 3 (2003).

———. *Work-Lifestyle Choices in the 21st Century.* New York: Oxford University Press, 2000.

Hall, Geoffry B. C., Sandra Witelson, F. Henry Szechtman, and Claude Nhmias. "Sex Differences in Functional Activation Patterns Revealed by Increased Emotion Processing Demands." *Neuroreport* 15, no. 2 (2004): 219–23.

Hall, J. A. *Nonverbal Sex Differences.* Baltimore: Johns Hopkins University Press, 1985.

Halpern, Diane F. *Sex Differences in Cognitive Abilities.* Mahwah, N.J.: Lawrence Erlbaum Associates, 2000.

Hamby, Vickie. The Trickster. In http://www.create.org/myth/trick/htm (1996) (accessed November 21, 2005).

Hampson, Sarah. "Fonda Contradictions." *Globe and Mail,* April 23, 2005.

Harrington, Mona. *Women Lawyers: Rewriting the Rules.* New York: Plume, 1995.

Harvey, Joan C., and Cynthia Katz. *If I'm So Successful, Why Do I Feel Like a Fake? The Imposter Phenomenon.* New York: St. Martin's Press, 1985.

Haviland, Sara Beth. "Job Satisfaction and the Gender Paradox: An International Perspective." Paper presented at the American Sociological Association, August 16, 2004.

Hedges, L. V., and A. Nowell. "Sex Differences in Mental Test Scores, Variability, and Numbers of High-Scoring Individuals." *Science* 269 (1995): 41–45.

Helfat, C. E., D. Harris, and P. J. Wolfson. "The Pipeline to the Top: Women and Men in the Top Executive Ranks of U.S. Corporations." *Academy of Management Perspectives* (2006).

Herman, Rebecca. "Sex and Prenatal Hormone Exposure Affect Cognitive Performance." *Hormones and Behavior,* in press (2007).

Hewlett, Sylvia Ann. "Extreme Jobs: The Dangerous Allure of the 70-Hour Workweek." *Harvard Business Review* (December 2006): 49–58.

———. *Off-Ramps and on-Ramps: Keeping Talented Women on the Road to Success.* Boston: Harvard Business School Press, 2007.

———. "Women and the New 'Extreme' Jobs." *Boston Globe,* December 2, 2006.

Highfield, Roger, and Paul Carter. *The Private Lives of Albert Einstein.* New York: St. Martin's Press, 1993.

Hirshman, Linda. "Homeward Bound." In *American Prospect Online,* 2005.

Hoff Summers, Christina. "The War against Boys." *Atlantic Monthly* (May 2000).

———. *The War against Boys.* New York: Simon & Schuster, 2000.

Hoffman, M. L. "Sex Differences in Empathy and Related Behaviors." *Psychological Bulletin* 84 (1977): 712–22.

Hrdy, Sarah Blaffer. *Mother Nature: Maternal Instincts and How They Shape the Human Species.* New York: Random House, 1999.

Huttenlocher, J., W. Haight, A. Bryk, M. Seltzer, and T. Lyons. "Early Vocabulary Growth: Relation to Language Input and Gender." *Developmental Psychology* 27 (1991): 236–48.

Hyde, Janet S. "Gender Differences in Aggression." In *The Psychology of Gender,* edited by J. S. Hyde and M. C. Linn. Baltimore: Johns Hopkins University Press, 1986.

Hynd, George W., and Jennifer R. Hiemenz. "Dyslexia and Gyral Morphology Variation." In *Dyslexia: Biology, Cognition, and Intervention,* edited by Charles Hulme and Margaret Snowling. San Diego: Singular, 1997.

James, William. "Great Men, Great Thoughts, and the Environment." *The Atlantic Monthly* (1880): 441–59.

Janowski, Jeri S. "Thinking with Your Gonads: Testosterone and Cognition." *Trends in Cognitive Sciences* 20, no. 20 (2005).

Jencks, Christopher. *Inequality: Who Gets Ahead? The Determinants of Economic Success in America.* New York: Basic, 1979.

Jick, Hershel, James A. Kaye, and Corri Black. "Incidence and Prevalence of Drug-Treated Attention Deficit Disorder among Boys in the UK." *British Journal of General Practice* 54, no. 502 (2004): 345–47.

Jobs, Steve. "You've Got to Find the Job You Love." *Stanford Report,* June 14, 2005.

Jonah, Brian A. "Accident Risk and Risk-Taking Behavior among Young Drivers." *Accident Analysis and Prevention* 18 (1986): 255–71.

Josephs, R. A., H. R. Markus, R. W. Tafarodi. "Gender and Self-Esteem." *Journal of Personality and Social Psychology* 63 (1992): 391–402.

Jung, Carl G. *Man and His Symbols.* Garden City. N.Y.: Doubleday, 1964.

Kanazawa, Satoshi. "Why Productivity Fades with Age: The Crime-Genius Connection." *Journal of Research in Personality* 37 (2003): 257–72.

Karnasiewicz, Sarah. "The Campus Crusade for Guys." *Salon,* February 15, 2006.

Kay, Fiona. "Flight from Law: A Competing Risks Model of Departures from Law Firms." *Law Society Review* 31, no. 2 (1997): 301–35.

Kay, Fiona, and Joan Brockman. "Barriers to Gender Equality in the Canadian Legal Establishment." *Feminist Legal Studies* (2000): 169–98.

Kay, Fiona, and John Hagan. "Raising the Bar: The Gender Stratification of Law-Firm Capital." *American Sociological Review* 63 (1998): 728–43.

Kessler, Ronald C. "The Epidemiology of Depression among Women." In *Women and Depression,* edited by Corey L. M. Keyes and Sherryl H. Goodman. New York: Cambridge University Press, 2006.

Kessler, Ronald C., Lenard Adler, Russell A. Barkley, Joseph Biederman, C. Keith Conners, Olga Demler, S. V. Faraone, Laurence Greenhill, Mary Howes, Kristina Secnik, T. Spencer, T. Ustun, Ellen E. Walters, and Alan M. Zaslavsky. "The Prevalence and Correlates of Adult ADHD in the United States: Results from the National Comorbidity Survey Replication." *American Journal of Psychiatry* (2004).

Kessler, Ronald C., Lenard Adler, Minnie Ames, Russell A. Barkley, Howard Birnbaum, Paul Greenberg, Joseph A. Johnston, T. Spencer, T. Ustun, and T. Bedirhan. "The Prevalence and Effects of Adult Attention Deficit/Hyperactivity Disorder on Work Performance in a Nationally Representative Sample of Workers." *Journal of Occupational and Environmental Medicine* 47, no. 6 (2005).

Kessler, Ronald C., P. Berglund, O. Dernier, R. Jin, D. Koretz, K. R. Merikangas, A. J. Rush, E. E. Walters, and P. S. Wang. "The Epidemiology of Major Depressive Disorder: Results from the National Comorbidity Survey Replication (NCS-R)." *Journal of the American Medical Association* 289, no. 23 (2003): 3095–105.

Kessler, Ronald C., W. T. Chiu, Olga Demler, and E. E. Walter. "Prevalence, Severity and Comorbidity of Twelve-Month DSMIV Disorders in the National Comorbidity Survey Replication (NCS-R)." *Archives of General Psychiatry* 62, no. 6 (2005): 617–27.

Kessler, Ronald C., and Jane D. McLeod. "Sex Differences in Vulnerability to Undesirable Life Events." *American Sociological Review* 49, no. 5 (1984): 620–31.

Kessler-Harris, Alice. *Out to Work: A History of Wage-Earning Women in the United States.* New York: Oxford University Press, 2003.

Kesterton, Michael. "What Her Think Now?" *Globe and Mail,* June 9, 2005.

Kim, Sangmook. "Gender Differences in the Job Satisfaction of Public Employees." *Sex Roles* (2005).

Kimura, Doreen. *Sex and Cognition.* Cambridge, Mass.: MIT Press, 2000.

———. "Sex Hormones Influence Human Cognitive Pattern." *Neuroendocrinology Letters* 23, no. 4 (2002): 67–77.

Kinsley, Craig Howard, and Kelly G. Lambert. "The Maternal Brain." *Scientific American* (January 2006): 72–77.

Kirsch, Peter, Christine Esslinger, Qiang Chen, Daniela Mier, Stefanie Lis, and et al. "Oxytocin Modulates Neural Circuitry for Social Cognition and Fear in Humans." *Journal of Neuroscience* 25, no. 49 (2005): 11489–93.

Kleinfeld, Judith. "The Morella Bill, My Daughter Rachel, and the Advancement of Women in Science." *Academic Questions* 12, no. 1 (1999): 79–86.

———. "Student Performance: Males Versus Females." *Public Interest* 134 (1999): 3–20.

Klinesmith, Jennifer, Tim Kasser, and Francis McAndrew. "Guns, Testosterone, and Aggression: An Experimental Test of a Mediational Hypothesis." *Psychological Science* 17, no. 7 (2006): 568.

Knickmeyer, Rebecca, Simon Baron-Cohen, Peter Raggatt, and Kevin Taylor. "Foetal Testosterone, Social Relationships, and Restricted Interests in Children." *Journal of Child Psychology and Psychiatry* 46, no. 2 (2005): 198–210.

Koestner, R., C. Franz, and J. Weinberger. "The Family Origins of Empathic Concern: A 26-Year Longitudinal Study." *Journal of Personality and Social Psychology* 58 (1990): 709–17.

Kolata, Gina. "Man's World, Woman's World? Brain Studies Point to Differences." *New York Times,* February 28, 1995, C1.

Korszun, Ania, Margaret Altemus, and Elizabeth Young. "The Biological Underpinnings of Depression." In *Women and Depression,* edited by Corey L. M. Keyes and Sherryl H. Goodman. New York: Cambridge University Press, 2006.

Kraemer, Sebastian. "The Fragile Male." *British Medical Journal* 321 (2000): 1609–12.

Kruger, Daniel J., and Randolph M. Nesse. "An Evolutionary Life-History Framework for Understanding Sex Differences in Human Mortality Rates." *Human Nature* 17, no. 1 (2006): 74–97.

———. "Sexual Selection and the Male:Female Mortality Ratio." *Evolutionary Psychology,* no. 2 (2004): 66–85.

Krupat, Edward. "Female Medical Students More Patient-Centered." *International Journal of Psychiatry in Medicine* (1999).

Kuziemko, Ilyana. "The Right Books, for Boys and Girls." *New York Times,* June 14, 2006.

Lagerspetz, K. M. J., K. Bjorkqvist, and T. Peltonen. "Is Indirect Aggression Typical of Females? Gender Differences in Aggressiveness in 11–12-Year-Old Children." *Aggressive Behavior* 14 (1988): 303–15.

Lamberg, Lynne. "ADHD Often Undiagnosed in Adults: Appropriate Treatment May Benefit Work, Family, Social Life." *Journal of the American Medical Association* 290, no. 12 (2003).

Lawrence, E. J., P. Shaw, D. Baker, S. Baron-Cohen, and A. S. David. "Measuring Empathy: Reliability and Validity of the Empathy Quotient." *Psychological Medicine* 34 (2004): 911–24.

Layard, Richard. *Happiness: Lessons from a New Science.* London: Penguin, 2005.

Lennon, Mary Clare. "Women, Work, and Depression." In *Women and Depression,* edited by Corey L. M. Keyes and Sherryl H. Goodman, 309–27. New York: Cambridge University Press, 2006.

Levine, Phyllis, and Eugene Edgar. "An Analysis by Gender of Long-Term Postschool Outcomes for Youth with and without Disabilities." *Exceptional Children* 61, no. 3 (1994): 282–301.

Levy, Florence, David A. Hay, and Kellie S. Bennett. "Genetics of Attention Deficit Hyperactivity Disorder: A Current Review and Future Prospects." *International Journal of Disability, Development and Education* 53, no. 1 (2006).

Levy, J., and W. Heller. "Gender Differences in Human Neuropsychological Function." In *Sexual Differentiation: Handbook of Behavioral Neurobiology,* edited by A. A. Gerall, M. Howard, and I. L. Ward. New York: Plenum, 1992.

Light, Paul C. "The Content of the Nonprofit Workforce." *Nonprofit Quarterly* 9, no. 3 (2002).

Long, Lynette. *Math Smarts: Tips, Tricks, and Secrets for Making Math More Fun!* American Girl Library. Middleton, Wis.: Pleasant, 2004.

Lubinski, David. "Top 1 in 10,000: A 10-Year Follow-up of the Profoundly Gifted." *Journal of Applied Psychology* 86 (2001): 718.

Lubinski, David S., and Camilla Persson Benbow. *Sex Differences in Personal Attributes for the Development of Scientific Expertise.* Edited by Stephen J. Ceci and

Wendy M. Williams, *Why Aren't More Women in Science?* Washington, D.C.: American Psychological Association, 2007.

Luckow, A., A. Reifman, and D. N McIntosh. "Gender Differences in Coping: A Meta-analysis." Paper presented at the annual Convention of the American Psychological Association, San Francisco, August 1998.

Lutchmaya, Svetlana, and Simon Baron-Cohen. "Human Sex Differences in Social and Non-Social Looking Preferences, at 12 Months of Age." *Infant Behavior and Development* 25 (2002): 319–25.

Maccoby, Eleanor Emmons. *The Two Sexes: Growing Apart, Coming Together.* Cambridge, Mass.: University Press, Belknap Press, 1998.

Maccoby, Eleanor Emmons, and Carol Nagy Jacklin. *The Psychology of Sex Differences.* Stanford, Calif.: Stanford University Press, 1974.

MacDonald, Heather. "Girl Problems." *National Review Online,* July 5, 2005.

MacLean, Heather, K. Glynn, and D. Ansara. "Multiple Roles and Women's Mental Health in Canada." In *Women's Health Surveillance Report.* Toronto: Centre for Research in Women's Health, 2003.

Mailloux, Louise, Heather Horak, and Colette Godin. "Motivation at the Margins: Gender Issues in the Canadian Voluntary Sector." Human Resources Development Canada Voluntary Sector Secretariat, 2002.

Maister, David. *True Professionalism: The Courage to Care About Your People, Your Clients, and Your Career.* New York: Touchstone, 1997.

Makin, Kirk. "Female Lawyers Hiding Illness to Remain Competitive." *Globe and Mail,* August 15, 2007.

Malatesta, C. Z., and J. J. Haviland. "The Development of Sex Differences in Nonverbal Signals: Fallacies, Facts and Fantasies." In *Gender and Nonverbal Behavior,* ed. C. Mayo and N. M. Henley, 183–208. New York: Springer-Verlag, 1981.

Mangena, Isaac. "Soweto Youths on Wrong Track as Train Surfers Die Having Fun." *Gazette,* November 26, 2006.

Mannuzza, S., R. G. Klein, A. Bessler, P. Malloy, and M. LaPadula. "Educational Acheivement, Occupational Rank, and Psychiatric Status." *Archives of General Psychiatry* 50 (1993): 565–76.

Marczinski, Cecile A. "Self-Report of ADHD Symptoms in College Students and Repetition Effects." *Journal of Attention Disorders* 8, no. 4 (2005): 182–87.

Marlow, Neil, Dieter Wolke, Melanie Bracewell, and Muthanna Samara. "Neurologic and Developmental Disability at Six Years of Age after Extremely Preterm Birth." *New England Journal of Medicine* 352, no. 1 (2005): 9–19.

Marshall, Nancy L., and Rosalind C. Barnett. "Child Care, Division of Labor, and Parental Emotional Well-Being among Two-Earner Couples." Sloan Work and Family Research Network, 1992.

Martinez, Sylvia. "Women's Intrinsic and Extrinsic Motivations for Working." In *Being Together, Working Apart,* edited by Barbara Schneider and Linda J. Waite, 79–101. Cambridge, U.K.: Cambridge University Press, 2005.

Mason, Gary. "Marathon Man." *Globe and Mail,* April 2, 2005.

Mason, Mary Ann, and Marc Goulden. "Marriage and Baby Blues: Redefining Gender Equity in the Academy." *Annals of the American Academy of Political and Social Science* 596 (2004): 86–103.

Matjasko, Jennifer, and Amy Feldman. "Emotional Transmission between Parents and Adolescents: The Importance of Work Characteristics and Relationship Quality." In *Being Together, Working Apart,* edited by Barbara Schneider and Linda J. Waite. Cambridge, U.K.: Cambridge University Press, 2005.

Matthews, Gail M. "Imposter Phenomenon: Attributions for Success and Failure." Paper presented at the American Psychological Association, Toronto, 1984.

Mattson, B. J., S. Williams, J. S. Rosenblatt, and J. I. Morrell. "Comparison of Two Positive Reinforcing Stimuli: Pups and Cocaine throughout the Postpartum Period." *Behavioral Neuroscience* 115 (2001): 683–94.

Mazur, Allan. *Biosociology of Dominance and Deference.* Oxford, U.K.: Rowman & Littlefield, 2005.

Mazur, Allan, and Alan Booth. "Testosterone and Dominance in Men." *Behavioral and Brain Sciences* (2001).

McClure, G. "Changes in Suicide in England and Wales, 1960–1997." *British Journal of Psychiatry* 176 (2000): 247–62.

McCrory, E. J., A. Mechelli, U. Frith, and C. J. Price. "More Than Words: A Common Neural Basis for Reading and Naming Deficits in Developmental Dyslexia?" *Brain* 128 (2005): 261–67.

McIlroy, Anne. "Why Do Females Feel More Pain Than Males Do?" *Globe and Mail,* October 23, 2006.

McMunn, A., M. Bartley, R. Hardy, and D. Kuh. "Life Course Social Roles and Women's Health in Midlife: Causation or Selection." *Journal of Epidemiology and Community Health* 60, no. 6 (2006): 484–89.

McRae, S. "Constraints and Choices in Mothers' Employment Careers: A Consideration of Hakim's Preference Theory." *British Journal of Sociology* 54 (2003): 317–38.

Mealey, Linda. *Sex Differences: Developmental and Evolutionary Strategies.* San Diego: Academic, 2000.

Mejias-Aponte, C. A., C. A. Jimenez-Rivera, and A. C. Segarra. "Sex Differences in Models of Temporal Lobe Epilepsy: Role of Testosterone." *Brain Research* 944, nos. 1–2 (2002).

Menand, Louis. "Stand by Your Man: The Strange Liason of Sartre and Beauvoir." *New Yorker,* September 26, 2005.

Miles, T. R., M. N. Haslum, and T. J. Wheeler. "Gender Ratio in Dyslexia." *Annals of Dyslexia* 48 (1998): 27–56.

Mirowsky, J., and C. E. Ross. "Sex Differences in Distress: Real or Artifact?" *American Sociological Review* 60 (1995): 449–68.

Mittelstaedt, Martin. "The Mystery of the Missing Boys." *Globe and Mail,* April 11, 2007.

Moen, Phyllis, and Joyce Altobelli. *Strategic Selection as a Retirement Project.* Edited by Jacqueline Boone James and Paul Wink. Vol. 26, *The Crown of Life: Dynamics of the Early Postretirement Period, Annual Review of Gerontology and Geriatrics.* New York: Springer, 2006.

Mogil, Jeffrey S., and Mona Lisa Chanda. "The Case for the Inclusion of Female Subjects in Basic Science Studies of Pain." *Pain* 117 (2005): 1–5.

Molloy, Tim. "Woman's Rampage Leaves Six Dead in the U.S." *Globe and Mail,* February 1, 2006.

Montmarquette, Claude, Kathy Cannings, and Sophie Mahseredjian. "How Do Young People Choose College Majors?" *Economics of Education Review* 21 (2002): 543–56.

Moorhead, Joanna. "For Decades We've Been Told Sweden Is a Great Place to Be a Working Parent, but We've Been Duped." *The Guardian,* September 22, 2004.

Morrow, Daniel. Oral history interview with Steve Jobs. In *Smithsonian Institution Oral and Video Histories,* ed. J. Thomas Campanella (1995), http://americanhistory.si.edu/collections/comphist/sj1.html (accessed April 26, 2006).

Morse, Steven B. "Racial and Gender Differences in the Viability of Extremely Low Birthweight Infants: A Population-Based Study." *Pediatrics* 117, no. 1 (2006).

Morselli, Carlo, and Marie-Noele Royer. "Criminal Mobility and Criminal Achievement." Paper presented at the Environmental Criminology and Crime Analysis Meeting, Chilliwack, B.C., July 2006.

Morselli, Carlo, and Pierre Tremblay. "Criminal Achievement, Offender Networks, and the Benefits of Low Self-Control." *Criminology* 42, no. 3 (2004).

Morselli, Carlo, Pierre Tremblay, and Bill McCarthy. "Mentors and Criminal Achievement." *Criminology* 11, no. 1 (2006): 17–33.

Mortenson, Tom. "What's Wrong with the Guys." Washington, D.C.: Pell Institute for the Study of Opportunity in Higher Education, 2003.

Muller, Carol B., and Peg Boyle Single. "Benefits for Women Students from Industrial E-Mentoring." Paper presented at the Proceedings of the 2001 American Society for Engineering annual conference, 2001.

Nagin, Daniel, and Richard E. Tremblay. "Trajectories of Boys' Physical Aggression, Opposition, and Hyperactivity on the Path to Physically Violent and Nonviolent Juvenile Delinquency." *Child Development* 70, no. 5 (1999): 1181–96.

Niederle, Muriel, and Lise Vesterlund. "Do Women Shy Away from Competition? Do Men Compete Too Much?" *Quarterly Journal of Economics* (2006).

Nolen, Stephanie. "Maggy's Children." *Globe and Mail,* May 15, 2006 2006.

Nolen-Hoeksema, Susan, and B. Jackson. "Mediators of the Gender Differences in Rumination." *Psychology of Women Quarterly* 25 (2001): 37–47.

Nolen-Hoeksema, Susan, J. Larson, and C. Grayson. "Explaining the Gender Difference in Depression." *Journal of Personality and Social Psychology* 77 (1999): 1061–72.

Nolen-Hoeksema, Susan, and Cheryl Rusting. "Gender Differences in Well-Being." In *Well-Being: The Foundations of Hedonic Psychology,* edited by D. Kahneman, Ed Diener, and N. Schwarz. New York: Russell Sage Foundation, 1999.

Northcutt, Wendy. *The Darwin Awards: Evolution in Action.* New York: Plume, 2002.

———. *The Darwin Awards: Survival of the Fittest.* New York: Plume, 2004.

———. *The Darwin Awards: Unnatural Selection.* New York: Plume, 2003.

Ochse, R. *Before the Gates of Excellence: The Determinants of Creative Genius.* New York: Cambridge University Press, 1990.

OECD. "Gender Differences in the Eighth-Grade Performance on the IEA Timss Scale." In *IEA Trends in International Mathematics and Science Study 2003,* 2005.

Olweus, Daniel. "Bullying at School: Long-Term Outcomes for the Victims and an Effective School-Based Intervention Program." In *Aggressive Behavior: Current Perspectives,* edited by R. Huesmann. New York: Plenum Press, 1994.

Olweus, Daniel, B. J. Mattson, and H. Low. "Circulating Testosterone Levels and Aggression in Adolescent Males: A Causal Analysis." *Psychosomatic Medicine* 50 (1988): 262–72.

Orfalea, Paul, and Ann Marsh. *Copy This! Lessons from a Hyperactive Dyslexic Who Turned a Bright Idea into One of America's Best Companies.* New York: Workman, 2005.

Orozco, S., and C. L. Ehlers. "Gender Differences in Electrophysiological Responses to Facial Stimuli." *Biological Psychiatry* 44 (1998): 281–89.

Ostwald, Peter F. *Glenn Gould: The Ecstasy and the Tragedy of Genius.* New York: W. W. Norton, 1997.

Pallier, Gerry. "Gender Differences in The Self-Assessment of Accuracy on Cognitive Tasks." *Sex Roles* 48, nos. 5–6 (2003): 265–76.

Paulesu, E., J. F. Demonet, F. Fazio, E. McCrory, V. Chanoine, N. Brunswick, S. F. Cappa, G. Cossu, M. Habib, C. D. Frith, and U. Frith. "Dyslexia: Cultural Diversity and Biological Unity." *Science* 291 (2001): 2165–67.

Paumgarten, Nick. "The Tycoon: The Making of Mort Zuckerman." *New Yorker,* July 23, 2007, 44–57.

Persson Benbow, Camilla, David Lubinski, Daniel Shea, and Hossain Eftekhari-Sanjani. "Sex Differences in Mathematical Reasoning Ability at Age 13: Their Status 20 Years Later." *Psychological Science* 11, no. 6 (2000): 474–80.

Persson Benbow, Camilla, and Julian Stanley. "Sex Differences in Mathematical Ability: Fact or Artifact?" *Science* 210 (1980): 1262–64.

———. "Sex Differences in Mathematical Reasoning Ability: More Facts." *Science* 222 (1983): 1029–31.

Phelan, J. "The Paradox of the Contented Female Worker: An Assessment of Alternative Explanations." *Social Psychology Quarterly* 57 (1994): 95–107.

Pinker, Steven. *The Blank Slate: The Modern Denial of Human Nature.* New York: Viking, 2002.

———. *How the Mind Works.* New York: W. W. Norton, 1997.

Pinker, Susan. "Looking out for Number One." *Globe and Mail,* April 4, 2007.

———. "Women Naturally Tend and Befriend." *Globe and Mail,* September 20, 2006.

Pomerantz, Eva M., Fei-Yin Ng, Florrie, and Qian Wang. "Gender Socialization: A Parent X Child Model." In *The Psychology of Gender,* edited by Alice Eagly, Anne E. Beall, and Robert J. Sternberg. New York: Guilford, 2004.

Porter, Eduardo. "Stretched to the Limit, Women Stall March to Work." *New York Times,* March 2, 2006.

Preston, Anne. "Why Have All the Women Gone? A Study of Exit of Women from the Science and Engineering Professions." *American Economic Review* 84, no. 5 (1994): 1446–62.

Preston, Stephanie D., and Frans B. M. de Waal. "Empathy: Its Ultimate and Proximate Bases." *Behavior and Brain Sciences* 25 (2002): 1–72.

Ptacek, J. T., R. E. Smith, and J. Zanas. "Gender, Appraisal, and Coping: A Longitudinal Analysis." *Journal of Personality* 60 (1992): 747–70.

Pugh, K. R., B. A. Shaywitz, Sally Shaywitz, R. T. Constable, P. Skudlarski, R. K. Fulbright, R. A. Bronen, D. P. Shankweiler, L. Katz, J. M. Fletcher, and J. C. Gore. "Cerebral Organization of Component Process in Reading." *Brain* 119 (1996): 1221–38.

Purifoy, Frances E., and Lambert H. Koopmans. "Androstenedione, Testosterone, and Free Testosterone Concentration in Women of Various Occupations." *Social Biology* 26, no. 1 (1979): 179–88.

Rabin, Roni. "Health Disparities Persist for Men, and Doctors Ask Why." *New York Times,* November 14, 2006.

Radin, Paul. *The Trickster: A Study in American Indian Mythology.* New York: Schocken Books, 1956.

Ragins, Belle Rose. "Understanding Diversified Mentoring Relationships." In *Mentoring and Diversity: An International Perspective,* edited by D. Clutterbuck and B. Ragins, 23–53. Oxford, U.K.: Butterworth-Heinemann, 2002.

Rayner, Cordelia. "The ADHD Dilemma for Parents." 2006.

Reed, Cheryl L. "Few Women Warm to Chef Life." *Chicago Sun Times,* January 29, 2006.

Reiss, Allan, Helli Kesler, and Betty Vohr. "Sex Differences in Cerebral Volumes of 8-Year-Olds Born Preterm." *Pediatrics* 145, nos. 242–249 (2004).

Rhoads, Steven E. *Taking Sex Differences Seriously.* San Francisco: Encounter, 2004.

Richardson, J. T. E. "Gender Differences in Imagery, Cognition, and Memory." In *Mental Images in Human Cognition,* edited by R. H. Logie and M. Denis, 271–303. New York: Elsevier, 1991.

Rose, Michael. " So Less Happy Too? Subjective Well-Being and the Vanishing Job Satisfaction Premium of British Women Employees." Paper presented at the Social Policy Association Annual Conference, June 27, 2005.

Roth, Louise Marie. *Selling Women Short: Gender and Money on Wall Street.* Princeton, N.J.: Princeton University Press, 2006.

Rouvalis, Christina. "Risk-Taking Can Be a Two-Faced Monster." *Pittsburgh Post-Gazette,* June 14, 2006.

Rutter, Michael. *Genes and Behavior: Nature-Nurture Interplay Explained.* Malden, Mass.: Blackwell, 2006.

Sacks, Oliver. "Henry Cavendish: An Early Case of Asperger's Syndrome?" *Neurology* 57, no. 7 (2001).

Saigal, Saroj, Barbara Stoskopf, David Streiner, Michael Boyle, Janet Pinelli, Nigel Paneth, and John Goddeeris. "Transition of Extremely Low Birthweight Infants from Adolescence to Young Adulthood." *Journal of the American Medical Association* 295, no. 6 (2006): 667–75.

Sanders, Claire. "Women Law Lecturers Pay the Price for Their Freedom." (London)*Times Online,* May 23, 2006.

Saunders, Doug. "Britain's New Working Class Speaks Polish." *Globe and Mail,* September 23, 2006.

Saunders, Ron. "Passion and Commitment under Stress: Human Resource Issues in Canada's Nonprofit Sector." Canadian Policy Research Networks, 2005.

Scarborough, H. S. "Very Early Language Deficits in Dyslexic Children." *Child Development* 61 (1990): 1728–43.

Schor, Juliet B. *The Overworked American: The Unexpected Decline of Leisure.* New York: Basic, 1992.

Scourfield, J., N. Martin, G. Lewis, and P. McGuffin. "Heritability of Social Cognitive Skills in Children and Adolescents." *British Journal of Psychiatry* 175 (1999): 559–64.

Seligman, Martin E. P., L. Y. Abramson, A. Semmel, and C. von Baeyer. "Depressive Attributional Style." *Journal of Abnormal Psychology* 88 (1979): 242–47.

Semrud-Clikeman, M., P. A. Filipek, Joseph Biederman, R. Steingard, D. Kennedy, P. Renshaw, and K. Bekken. "Attention-Deficit Hyperactivity Disorder: Magnetic Resonance Imaging Morphometric Analysis of the Corpus Callosum." *Journal of American Academy of Child and Adolescent Psychiatry* 33, no. 6 (1994): 875–81.

Shakespeare, William. *Second Part of King Henry IV: The Complete Works of Shakespeare.* New York: Spring, 1976.

Shaywitz, B. A., Sally Shaywitz, K. R. Pugh, R. T. Constable, and P. Skurlarski. "Sex Differences in the Functional Organization of the Brain for Language." *Nature* 373 (1995): 607–9.

Shaywitz, Sally. *Overcoming Dyslexia.* New York: Vintage, 2003.

Sherriff, Lucy. "World's Cleverest Woman Needs a Job." *Register,* November 5, 2004.

Shibley-Hyde, Janet. "Women in Science: Gender Similarities in Abilities and Sociocultural Forces." In *Why Aren't More Women in Science?* edited by Stephen J. Ceci and Wendy M. Williams. Washington, D.C.: American Psychological Association, 2007.

Shukovski, L., D. L. Healy, and J. K. Findlay. "Circulating Immunotreactive Oxytocin during the Human Menstrual Cycle Comes from the Pituitary and Is Estradiol-Dependent." *Journal of Clinical Endocrinology and Metabolism* 68 (1989): 455–60.

Shutt, Kathryn, Ann MacLarnon, Michael Heistermann, and Stuart Semple. "Grooming in Barbary Macaques: Better to Give Than to Receive?" *Biology Letters* (2007).

Silberman, Steve. "The Geek Syndrome." In *Wired,* 2001.

Silverman, Irwin. "Gender Differences in Delay of Gratification: A Meta-analysis." *Sex Roles* 49, nos. 9–10 (2003): 451–63.

Simonton, Dean Keith. *Greatness: Who Makes History and Why.* New York: Guilford, 1994.

Singer, Tania, Ben Seymour, John P. O'Doherty, Holger Kaube, Raymond J. Dolan, and C. D. Frith. "Empathy for Pain Involves the Affective but Not the Sensory Components of Pain." *Science* 303, no. 5661 (2004): 1157–62.

Singer, Tania, Ben Seymour, John P. O'Doherty, Klaas E. Stephan, R. Dolan, and Chris D. Frith. "Empathic Neural Responses Are Modulated by the Perceived Fairness of Others." *Nature* (2006).

Siok, Wai Ting, Charles Perfetti, Ahen Jin, and Li Hai Tan. "Biological Abnormality of Impaired Reading Is Constrained by Culture." *Nature* 431 (2004): 71–76.

Sloan Wilson, David, and Mihaly Csikszentmihalyi. "Health and the Ecology of Altruism." In *Altruism and Health,* edited by Stephen G. Post. New York: Oxford, 2007.

Sloane, P., and H. Williams. "Are Overpaid Workers Really Unhappy? A Test of the Theory of Cognitive Dissonance." *Labour* 10 (1996): 3–15.

Snowling, Margaret. *Dyslexia.* Oxford, U.K.: Blackwell, 2000.

Snowling, Margaret, Alison Gallagher, and Uta Frith. "Family Risk of Dyslexia Is Continuous: Individual Differences in the Precursors of Reading Skill." *Child Development* 74, no. 2 (2003): 358–73.

Sousa-Poza, Alfonso. "Taking Another Look at the Gender/Job-Satisfaction Paradox." *Kyklos* 53, no. 2 (2000): 135–52.

Stahl, Jeanne M., Henrie M. Turner, Alfreeda Wheeler, and Phyllis Elbert. "The Imposter Phenomenon in High School and College Science Majors." Paper presented at the American Psychological Association, Montréal, 1980.

Stein, J. "The Magnocellular Theory of Developmental Dyslexia." *Dyslexia* 7, no. 1 (2001): 12–36.

Steinmetz, Sol, and Carol G. Braham, eds. *Random House Webster's Dictionary.* Toronto: Random House, 1993.

Stevenson, D. K., J. Verter, and A. A. Fanaroff. "Sex Differences in Outcomes of Very Low Birthweight Infants: The Newborn Male Disadvantage." *Archives of Disease in Childhood* 83 (November 2000): F182-F85.

Still, G. F. "The Coulstonian Lectures on Some Abnormal Physical Conditions in Children." *Lancet* 1 (1902): 1008–12.

Story, Louise. "Many Women at Elite Colleges Set Career Path to Motherhood." *New York Times,* September 20, 2005.

Summers, Lawrence H. "Remarks at NBER on Diversifying the Science and Engineering Workforce." Paper presented at the National Bureau of Economic Research, Cambridge, Mass., January 14, 2005.

Taha, Haitham. "Females' Superiority in Phonological and Lexical Processing." *Reading Matrix* 6, no. 2 (2006).

Taylor, Paul. "What's Nastier Than a Loser? A Winner." *Globe and Mail,* April 1, 2005.

Taylor, Shelley E. *The Tending Instinct: How Nurturing Is Essential to Who We Are and How We Live.* New York: Henry Holt, 2002.

Taylor, Shelley E., Laura Cousino Klein, Brian P. Lewis, Tara L. Gruenwald, Regan A. R. Gurung, and John A. Updegraff. "Biobehavioral Responses to Stress in Females: Tend-and-Befriend, Not Fight or Flight." *Psychological Review* 107, no. 3 (2000): 411–29.

Tiger, Lionel, and J. Shepher. *Women in the Kibbutz.* New York: Harcourt Brace Jovanovich, 1975.

Tischler, Linda. "Winning the Career Tournament." *Fast Company,* 2004.

Tiwari, Pranjal, and Aurelio Estrada. Worse Than Commodities. In *ZNet* (2002) (accessed 2006).

Todosijevic, Bojan, Snezana Ljubinkovic, and Aleksandra Arancic. "Mate Selection Criteria: A Trait Desirability Assessment Study of Sex Differences in Serbia." *Evolutionary Psychology* 1 (2003): 116–26.

Townsend, John Marshall. *What Women Want—What Men Want.* New York: Oxford University Press, 1998.

Treffert, Darold A., and Gregory L. Wallace. "Islands of Genius." *Scientific American* 286 (2002).

Tremblay, Richard, and Daniel Nagin. "The Developmental Origins of Physical Aggression in Humans." In *Developmental Origins of Aggression,* edited by Richard Tremblay, Willard Hartup, and John Archer, 83–105. New York: Guilford, 2005.

Trivers, Robert L. "Parental Investment and Sexual Selection." In *Sexual Selection and the Descent of Man 1871–1971,* edited by B. Campbell, 136–79. Chicago: Aldine, 1972.

Turner, Rob. "In Learning Hurdles, Lessons for Success." *New York Times,* November 23, 2003.

U.K. National Statistics. "Injuries to Workers by Industry and Severity of Injury: Great Britain." 2004.

U.S. Census Bureau. "Population in Group Quarters by Type, Sex, and Age for the United States: 2000."

U.S. Department of Labor. Labor Day 2006: Profile of the American Worker. In http://communitydispatch.com/artman/publish/article_6293.shtml (accessed September 4, 2006).

Valian, Virginia. *Why So Slow? The Advancement of Women.* Cambridge, Mass.: MIT Press, 2000.

———. "Women at the Top in Science—and Elsewhere." In *Why Aren't More Women in Science?* edited by Stephen J. Ceci and Wendy M. Williams. Washington, D.C.: American Psychological Association, 2007.

Van Goozen, S., N. Frijda, M. Kindt, and N. E. van de Poll. "Anger Proneness in Women: Development and Validation of the Anger Situation Questionnaire." *Aggressive Behavior* 20 (1994): 79–100.

Vinnicombe, Susan, and Val Singh. "Locks and Keys to the Boardroom." *Women in Management Review* 18, no. 5/6 (2003): 325–34.

Vogel, S. A. "Gender Differences in Intelligence, Language, Visual-Motor Abilities, and Academic Achievement in Students with Learning Disabilities: A Review of the Literature." *Learning Disabilities* 23, no. 1 (1990): 44–52.

Von Karolyi, Catya, and Ellen Winner. "Dyslexia and Visual-Spatial Talents: Are They Connected?" In *Students with Both Gifts and Learning Disabilities: Identification, Assessment and Outcomes,* edited by Tina M. Newman and Robert J. Sternberg, 95–115. New York: Kluwer Academic Plenum Publishers, 2004.

Wade, Nicholas. "Pas De Deux of Sexuality Is Written in the Genes." *New York Times,* April 10, 2007.

Wagemaker, H. "Are Girls Better Readers? Gender Differences in Reading Literacy in 32 Countries." *International Association for the Evaluation of Educational Achievement* (1996).

Wagner, Mary, Lynn Newman, Renée Cameto, Phyllis Levine, and Nicolle Garza. "An Overview of Findings from Wave 2 of the National Longitudinal Transition Study-2 (Nlts2)." Washington, D.C.: U.S. Department of Education, 2006.

Walter, Natasha. " Prejudice and Evolution." *Prospect,* June, 2005.

Wang, Steve C. "In Search of Einstein's Genius." *Science* 289, no. 5484 (2000): 1477.

Wasserstein, Jeannette, Lorraine E. Wolf, and Frank F. Lefever, eds. *Adult Attention Deficit Disorder: Brain Mechanisms and Life Outcomes, Annals of the New York Academy of Sciences.* vol. 931. New York: New York Academy of Sciences, 2001.

Weinberger, Catherine, ed. *A Labor Economist's Perspective on College-Educated Women in the Information Technology Workforce.* Edited by Eileen M. Trauth, *Encyclopedia of Gender and Information.* Santa Barbara, Calif.: Information Science, 2005.

Weisfeld, Carol Cronin. "Female Behavior in Mixed Sex Competition: A Review of the Literature." *Developmental Review* 6 (1986): 278–99.

Weiss, Gabrielle, and Lily Trokenberg Hechtman. *Hyperactive Children Grown Up,* 2nd ed. New York: Guilford, 1993.

Werner, Wendy. "Where Have All the Women Attorneys Gone?" *Law Practice Today* (2005).

Whitmore, Richard. "Boy Trouble." *New Republic Online* (2006).

Wilens, Timothy E., Stephen V. Faraone, and Joseph Biederman. "Attention Deficit/Hyperactivity Disorder in Adults." *Journal of the American Medical Association* 292, no. 5 (2004).

Willingham, W. W., and N. S. Cole. *Gender and Fair Assessment.* Mahwah, N.J.: Lawrence Erlbaum Associates, 1997.

Wilson, Robin. "How Babies Alter Careers for Academics." *Chronicle of Higher Education,* December 5, 2003.

Witelson, Sandra F., I. I. Glezer, and D. L. Kigar. "Women Have Greater Density of Neurons in Posterior Temporal Cortex." *Journal of Neuroscience* 15 (1995): 3418–28.

Witelson, Sandra F., Debra L. Kigar, and Thomas Harvey. "The Exceptional Brain of Albert Einstein." *Lancet* 353 (1999).

Wittig, M. A., and M. J. Allen. "Measurement of Adult Performance on Piaget's Water Horizontality Task." *Intelligence* 8 (1984): 305–13.

Woodyard, Chris. "Jet Blue Soars on CEO's Creativity." *USA Today,* October 8, 2002.

Woolf, Virginia. "Equality, Opportunity, and Pay." *The Atlantic Monthly* (May–June 1938): 585–94, 750–59.

Wyatt, S., and C. Langridge. *Getting to the Top in the National Health Service.* Edited by S. Ledwith and F. Colgan, *Women in Organizations: Challenging Gender Politics.* London: Macmillan, 1996.

Xie, Yu, and Kimberlee Shauman. *Women in Science: Career Processes and Outcomes.* Cambridge, Mass.: Harvard University Press, 2003.

Yamadori, A. "Ideogram Reading in Alexia." *Brain* 98 (1975): 231–38.

Zadina, J. N., T. A. Knaus, D. M. Corey, R. M. Casbergue, L. C. Lemen, and A. L. Foundas. "Heterogeneity of Dyslexia: Behavioral and Anatomical Differences in Dyslexia Subtypes."

Zahn-Waxler, C., M. Radke-Yarrow, E. Wagner, and M. Chapman. "Development of Concern for Others." *Developmental Psychology* 28 (1992): 126–36.

Zametkin, A. J., and J. L. Rapoport. "Neurobiology of Attention Deficit Disorder with Hyperactivity: Where Have We Come in 50 Years?" *Journal of American Academic Child and Adolescent Psychiatry* 26 (1987): 676–86.

Zunshine, Lisa. *Why We Read Fiction.* Columbus: Ohio State University Press, 2006.

PHOTOGRAPH AND FIGURE CREDITS

P. 4: Artist unknown, courtesy of McGill Rare Books and Special Collections Division

P. 84: Photo by Frances Benjamin Johnston, courtesy of the Library of Congress, Prints and Photographs Division (LC-USZ62-100291)

P. 100: Photo by N. Tsinonis, reprinted with the permission of UNHCR

P. 103: Empathy Quotient (EQ). From: Baron-Cohen, Simon. *The Essential Difference: The Truth About the Male and Female Brain.* New York: Basic Books, 2003, 57. Reprinted with the permission of the author.

P. 153: Reprinted with the permission of Georges Huard

P. 160: Photo by Stephanie Mitchell, reprinted with the permission of Harvard University

P. 205: Photo by Marty Katz. From J. Craig Venter, "An Ointment for the Fly," *Science,* vol. 313, September 29, 2006, p. 1892.

P. 246: Reprinted with the permission of the Orfalea Foundation Archive

TABLE SOURCES

P. 11: "That Was Then, This Is Now: Education": Veterinary medicine (Canada)— Canadian Veterinary Medical Association; veterinary medicine (U.S.) for 1973— National Center for Education Statistics, *U.S. Digest of Educational Stats,* 1975; pharmacy for 1973—National Center for Education Statistics, *Chartbook of Degrees Conferred, 1969–70 to 1993–94;* veterinary medicine (U.S.) and pharmacy for 2003, business, law (U.S.), medicine (U.S.), architecture, engineering—National Center for Education Statistics, *U.S. Digest of Educational Stats,* 2004; law (U.K.)—The Law Society, *Trends in the Solicitors Profession: Annual Statistical Report 200;* medicine (Canada)—Association of Faculties of Medicine of Canada, *Canadian Medical Education Statistics,* 2006; physics—American Institute of Physics, *Women in Physics and Astronomy,* 2005

P. 12: "That Was Then, This Is Now: Occupation": Orchestra musicians—Daniel J. Wakin, "In Violin Sections Women Make their Presence Heard," *New York Times,* July 23, 2005, and Claudia Goldin and Cecilia Rouse, "Orchestrating Impartiality: The Effect of 'Blind' Auditions on Female Musicians," in *American Economic Review* (September 2000); physicians (Canada)—Canadian Medical Association; physicians (U.S.)—American Medical Association, *Physician Characteristics and Distribution in* *the U.S.,* 1973 and 2006 eds.; lawyers, foresters and conservationists, aerospace engineers, telephone and computer line installers and repairers, electricians, plumbers and pipe-fitters—Bureau of Labor Statistics, *Current Population Survey: A Datebook,* September, 1982, Bulletin 2096, and *Current Population Survey: Unpublished Occupation and Industry Table 1,* 2003; federal judges (Canada)—Office of the Commissioner for Federal Judicial Affairs; federal judges (U.S.)—Federal Judicial Center; employed in science and engineering—National Science Foundation, *Minorities in Science and Engineering,* 1986, and *Science and Engineering Indicators,* 2006; legislators (Canada)—Library of Parliament; legislators (U.N.)—U.N. Economic and Social Council, *Commission on the Status of Women, 50th Session,* WOM/1541; U.S. House of Representatives and Senate—womenincongress.house.gov/data/wic-by-congress.html and www.senate.gov/artandhistory/history/common/briefing/women_senators.htm; firefighters—Women in the Fire Service, Inc.; manufacturers' agents—Estimate from the Manufacturers' Agents National Association. *Figures for Canadian lawyers are from the 1971 and 2001 census, as no figures were available for 1973 and 2003. Statistics Canada, "Economic Characteristics, Labour Force: Occupations," *1971 Census of Canada, Volume III, Part 2,* and "Occupation—2001 National Occupational Classification for Statistics (523), Class of Worker (6) and Sex (3) for Labour Force 15 Years and Over, for Canada, Provinces, Territories, Census Metropolitan Areas and Census Agglomerations," 2001 Census

P. 15: Ian Deary, Graham Thorpe, Valerie Wilson, John M. Starr, and Lawrence J. Whalley. "Population Sex Differences in IQ at Age 11: The Scottish Mental Survey 1932." *Intelligence* 31 (2003), 533–542. Graphs by Martin Lysy.

INDEX

Page numbers in *italics* refer to illustrations.

68123